A HISTORY OF THE FOREIGN POLICY
OF THE UNITED STATES

THE MACMILLAN COMPANY
NEW YORK · BOSTON · CHICAGO · DALLAS
ATLANTA · SAN FRANCISCO

MACMILLAN & CO., Limited
LONDON · BOMBAY · CALCUTTA
MELBOURNE

THE MACMILLAN CO. OF CANADA, Ltd.
TORONTO

BEAUMARCHAIS

A HISTORY OF
THE FOREIGN POLICY OF
THE UNITED STATES

BY

RANDOLPH GREENFIELD ADAMS, Ph.D.

*Custodian of the William L. Clements Library of American History,
University of Michigan*

New York
THE MACMILLAN COMPANY
1924

TO
JAMES COLLINS JONES
of the Philadelphia Bar

To the Reader:

I have undertaken a Subject that I am very sensible requires one of more sufficiency than I am Master of to treat it, as, in Truth, it deserves, and the groaning State of Europe calls for; but since Bunglers may Stumble upon the Game, as well as Masters, though it belongs to the Skilful to hunt and catch it, I hope this Essay will not be charged upon me for a Fault, if it appear to be neither Chimerical nor Injurious, and may provoke abler Pens to improve and perform the Design with better Judgment and Success.

—*William Penn*

PREFACE

"The madness of the European powers, and the calamitous situation into which all of them are thrown by the present ruinous war, ought to be a serious warning to us to avoid a similar catastrophe, so long as we can with honor and justice to our national character." That is not President Woodrow Wilson writing in 1915 but President George Washington writing to Edmund Pendleton in 1795. The problem of 1795 was in many respects the problem of 1915 and unless Americans can be induced to take a greater interest in their foreign policy, it is likely to be the problem of the next hundred years.

There is increasing evidence of the need for brief surveys of the history of our foreign relations which will, in a measure, popularize our knowledge of the subject. By this I do not mean that we need popular writers on the subject. We need them, too, but the supply of these is at least equal to the demand. Many of us who have lived through the last ten years have felt the need of books on our foreign policy which will epitomize the results of research in the field, and especially books written in a language which is intelligible to the reader, who, without being in any sense a specialist, yet desires to read on the subject. There are few matters in which history is quoted quite so glibly to prove a point as in the formation of our foreign policy, and yet there are few matters on which the best of us are so ill-informed as to what took place.

In a book which draws from all periods of American History, it is frequently more important to know what to leave out than to know what to put in. A great deal of inherited historical material has been deliberately omitted, because much of it appears less significant to-day than once it seemed to be. The last three chapters, of course, ought to be judged on an entirely different basis from the others. What has happened since 1914 is yet too full of matters of controversy for anyone to make a final judgment. To supplement the treatment given here the reader may turn to the many articles, monographs and books in every library, dealing with our recent diplomatic history.

Without in any way involving anyone but myself in the errors, which undoubtedly will be found in this volume, I want to thank Prof. C. H. Van Tyne of the University of Michigan for having read and commented on the early chapters; Prof. W. E. Lingelbach of the University of Pennsylvania, for having criticized the chapters on the wars of the French Revolution and Napoleon; Prof. A. S. Aiton of the University of Michigan, for his examination of the chapters on Hispanic-American relations; Prof. W. T. Laprade of Trinity College, N. C., and Prof. A. L. Cross of the University of Michigan for their helpful suggestions on the chapters involving Anglo-American relations; Prof. W. E. Dodd of Chicago University and Dr. Herbert Adams Gibbons for their criticism of the chapter on the Versailles Conference. Helpful suggestions and corrections have come from Dr. George P. Winship of Harvard, Dr. Clarence Carter of Miami University, and Dr. Gilbert Chinard of Johns Hopkins. For permission to use their maps I am grateful to Prof. Edward Channing of Harvard, Prof. T. M. Marshall of Washington University and Dr. Isaiah Bowman of the American Geographical Society. For the illustrations I am indebted to Mr. Worthington C. Ford of the Massachusetts Historical Society, Dr. Leo S. Rowe of the Pan-American Union, Mr. Roger Burlingame, Dr. Sidney E. Mezes of the College of the City of New York, Dr. Mario Cosenza of the College of the City of New York, and Mr. A. Page Cooper of Doubleday, Page and Company. I also desire to thank the editors of the *University of Pennsylvania Law Review* and the *South Atlantic Quarterly* for permission to use material which appeared in those periodicals.

R. G. A.

Ann Arbor, Michigan, October, 1924.

CONTENTS

CONTENTS

CONTENTS

LIST OF MAPS

LIST OF ILLUSTRATIONS

A HISTORY OF THE FOREIGN POLICY
OF THE UNITED STATES

HISTORY OF THE FOREIGN POLICY OF THE UNITED STATES

CHAPTER I

INTERNATIONAL RELATIONS

"Since our discussion of law is undertaken in vain if there is no law, it will serve both to command and to fortify our work if we refute briefly this very grave error."—*Grotius*.

Apathy, rather than ignorance, is the chief enemy of an intelligent foreign policy. "What all the nations now need is a public opinion which shall in every nation give more constant thought and keener attention to international policy, and lift it to a higher plane." Such was the last message of James Bryce to the people of the United States. The nations of the world have much to learn about the business of living together. The problems of diplomacy and foreign policy will not be solved until mankind is willing to devote more conscious intellectual effort to the history and principles of human association.

The diplomatic history of the United States is the story of her relations with the other nations of the world. Perhaps no country has risen to greatness in the family of nations with so little conscious attention to her foreign policy. Unlike many of the great imperialistic nations of the past, Great Britain and the United States seem to have built up empires in a fit of absence of mind, and the United States sometimes appears to have been a little more absent-minded about it than even Great Britain, because she has not depended upon her neighbors for her daily bread.[1] The day is past, however, when the people of the United States can afford to disregard their foreign policy. European nations, huddled together on the smallest of the five continents, cannot

[1] Sir J. Seeley, *The Expansion of England* (Boston, 1901), p. 8.

move without jostling their neighbors. Hence they have fought. The commercial nations of Europe could not trade, so they thought, without active competition, which, in the past, has frequently led to wars. The virile nations could not expand without trespassing on their neighbor's territory, and hence, still more wars. But the United States has been peculiarly fortunate, because in the past, when she wanted to sell her wheat, she found a hungry Europe in which the demand exceeded the supply. The market for beef and cotton was large enough, so why quarrel about it? Moreover the United States has been exceedingly fortunate in being able to expand at the expense of neighbors who would not fight back effectively. The frontier in American history has been nowhere more significant than in American diplomatic history.[2]

It is just because the United States has been able to extend her frontiers into relatively uninhabited areas, between the Appalachian Mountains and the Pacific Ocean, that she has not seemed to find it necessary to fight those expensive wars which for centuries have devastated and impoverished Asia and Europe. So Americans have not had to bother very much with the story of their relations with other countries. There is as much geography as there is pharisaism in the doctrine of isolation.[3]

Yet all this is past now. The United States has long since reached her continental limits, and the end of the World War found her warehouses glutted with unsalable goods. The war itself demonstrated to the people of the United States that a petty squabble in a petty corner of a petty Balkan state could expand until it forced the great Republic of North America to raise an army of four millions and spend twenty billions in fighting a war from which she received absolutely nothing of material value. Her sole triumphs at the end of that war were spiritual, and these she failed adequately to safeguard, partly because she had what some critics are bold enough to call an irresponsible government in which the legislative and the executive may be of

---

[2] F. J. Turner, "Frontier in American History," *Am. Hist. Assoc. Rept.*, 1893, p. 199.
[3] E. C. Semple, *The Influence of Geography in American History* (Boston, 1904).

opposite political parties, and partly because her people were not yet sufficiently enlightened in matters international to realize that they had positive ethical obligations toward the rest of the world.[4]

The aim of this volume is to introduce the reader to the elements of American foreign policy. Just as a man cannot construct a great railway bridge without a highly developed knowledge of civil engineering, neither can a political engineer construct an international commonwealth without the aid of scientific knowledge. But, although we insist that none save the trained engineer shall build the bridge, yet we permit every kind of ignorant amateur to trifle with our political edifices. This may be democratic, but it is neither scientific nor efficient. Since it is contrary to our democratic ideals to deprive a man of his right to vote, even though he cannot possibly have an intelligent opinion on the matter about which he is voting, is it not permissible to try to popularize a little of the simple arithmetic of the subject?

International relations, as the words imply, are simply the connections which one nation has with the other nations of the world. But usage has confined the term pretty definitely to the political relations of one state with another. Here a few words require definition. Take for example the term "nation." In diplomatic history a "nation" is a "state," and both are considered to be a community of people, inhabiting an ascertainable territory, having a government to which they habitually render obedience, and who are free from external control. Americans will at once observe that the sense in which they use the word "state" is not correct. Massachusetts may be a political community with definite boundaries, but it is not free from external control. So Massachusetts is not a "state" in the sense in which it will be used here. States, or nations, in this sense are supposed to be "independent" or "sovereign," that is, free from any limitation on their power by any outside state.[5] When this independence is "recognized" by other members of the family of nations,

[4] Wm. MacDonald, *A New Constitution for a New America* (N. Y., 1921). pp. 25-33 H. L. Stimson," The Principle of Responsibility in Government," *Proc. of Acad. of Pol. Sci.*, V, 20.

[5] W. E. Hall, *Treatise on International Law*, 7th ed., pp. 17-18.

the nation so recognized is truly "independent" and may engage in diplomatic intercourse with its neighbors.[6]

Now it must be at once apparent that in fact there is no such thing as either a sovereign state or an independent nation. "No state can claim absolute independence, but only such independence as is compatible with that of others, with the exigencies of international society, and with the conditions, indispensable to the maintenance of the legal organization of that society."[7] Hence the best we can say of independence is that it is present when a state has been recognized to be independent by the other nations of the world, and when it exchanges diplomatic envoys with them. In fact, such a state may be tied fast to the chariot wheel of some imperialistic neighbor, who collects its customs-duties, and supervises the administration of its internal government. Even so, in the language of diplomacy it is still an independent nation and a sovereign state. This is one of the weaknesses of international relations, and the whole of the social sciences of which it is a branch, that the effort is made to make the facts fit the terms, instead of making the terms fit the facts, which would be the scientific method. But this only shows how little progress has been made in this subject, and how much it needs to be studied. However, there are terms which correspond, though ever so roughly, to certain entities. There is a family or society of nations, or states, and there is a term called independence, however vague and uncertain its significance. All the members of the family are supposed to be of equal importance, whatever their size, and to be equal before the law. Of course, they are not. Indeed, the great nations seldom observe the rule of equality save when it is to their interest to do so. But at the same time, they all profess it, and lay it down as a fundamental rule of diplomatic intercourse. It is strictly observed in ceremonies and in external things, and courts which administer international law, always try to make the rule effective.[8]

[6] Yrisarri v. Clement, (2 Carr. & Payne, 233; 1825).

[7] P. Fiore, International Law Codified (tr. E. M. Borchard), pp. 170–1.

[8] H. Wheaton, The Elements of International Law, 5th Eng. ed., p. 261; John Marshall in The Antelope (10 Wheat. 66, 122; 1825).

Another frequently misunderstood term is international law. It is a body of rules, accepted by the nations of the world, and binding on them, for the determination and regulation of their conduct in their mutual dealings. But it rests on each nation to enforce its own right, to be its own judge, jury, and policeman, as in the past, there has been no international government, with courts to adjudge cases and enforce its decisions. One might say, and indeed, many have said, that since there exists no power to enforce this law, no "sanction," as it is called, international law really is not law at all.[9] This is a species of academic argument characteristic of the social sciences, wherein undefined terms permit the clever rhetorician to spin out an endless argument, which is logical and convincing, but not always true or useful. The fact is that all law was once in the state in which we now find international law. Law precedes courts or policemen. The customs of men whereby they regulate their mutual relationships, are as old as man, for man is a political and social animal, and as early as we find him, he is working out rules for the regulation of social intercourse. As man progressed, he was able to construct tribunals for the enforcement of laws which had existed as customs for generations. The custom crystallized into law and its enforcement marks a high degree of the development of mankind. All law has had to pass through the stage of incapacity for enforcement, from which international law now suffers. But that does not invalidate its right to be called law.[10]

In dealing with one another, states act through their governments. But the state and the government are not the same thing and must never be confused. A state may survive a dozen changes in government. In the United States there have been since independence, two different governments, one from 1776 to 1789 and another and totally different government from 1789 to the present day. France has had no less than five different governments in the last hundred years. The government is merely

---

[9] John Austin, *The Province of Jurisprudence Determined*, pp. 147, 207 (2nd ed).
[10] R. G. Gray, "International Tribunals in the Light of the History of Law," *Harvard Law Review*, XXXII, 825. J. B. Moore, *International Law and Some Current Illusions*, (N. Y., 1924) pp. 35–7.

the agent through which the state acts, and the state may change its government whenever and as often as it sees fit, through revolution or through a more constitutional means. But the acts, are the acts of the state, and not of the government. A state cannot evade the responsibility for what its government did, by a mere change in government. If a state borrows money, and then changes its government, it is obviously bound to pay the debts contracted under the first government, because the debts are really contracted by the state and not by the government.

Our ancestors in trying to account for the origin of government, imagined a theory that all men had in their savage state lived without any government, Living in this "state of nature," every man possessed all liberty, and the right to do anything he saw fit, irrespective of his neighbors' rights. Living in a state of nature, men had found it excessively inconvenient, because it simply meant the rule of the ruthless, without regard to right or justice. Every man's hand was raised against every other man. So these men who were possessed of all rights and liberties, decided to give up some of their rights in order that they might the more effectively enjoy the remainder. So they came together and made an agreement, by which they mutually surrendered some of the liberties they had enjoyed under the "state of nature," and entered into a state of society. This society formed a government which all contracted or agreed to obey and by losing some of their liberties they found they could really enjoy the remainder. To live in a state of nature had been found intolerable, because every man was at the mercy of the brute force of the strongest.

Now, of course, this fanciful theory has no basis in fact as far as the origin of any individual government is concerned. History gives scant record of any society which came into existence that way. But the idea does give a fairly accurate picture of the international society to-day, for nations certainly have lived in a "state of nature" toward one another, and every nation has relied solely upon its own armed force to secure and maintain its rights. There has been no international government and nations have been a long time getting out of the "state of nature." So we must remember that in studying the international relations of any country, we are studying primitive international society, as international society is still in the cave man stage, still in the stone age of politics.

It was under the frightful stimulus of one of the bloodiest wars of history, the Thirty Years War in Germany, that the Dutchman, Hugo Grotius, first seriously directed the attention of men to the study of international relations. His great work "De Jure Belli ac Pacis" gives the two sets of relationships which must be observed in diplomatic history. It is humiliating to have to admit that all international dealings must be classed under "Peace" or "War," but such is the fact. For centuries war was the natural and normal relationship of nations, and peace was the exception, the breathing space before another war. Men have only gradually come to understand that it would be a good deal more desirable to have peace the normal relationship and war the exception, until wars become more and more rare and finally disappear altogether, as the tournament and wager of battle have vanished among private citizens.

Another frightful war seems to have stimulated anew the interest of men in the subject of international relations, and among the thinkers can be distinguished several groups which ought to be clearly differentiated. In the first place one discovers somewhat to his dismay that there has grown up a school of thought which professes to believe that war is a good thing, that it is a tonic which mankind requires to rescue it from the debilitating and degenerating effects of a lazy and materialistic life of peace. The chief argument of this school is that war is the universal rule of nature, that animals and plants are in a continuous struggle for existence, in which an overwhelming majority are killed off or choked out of existence, securing thereby the survival of the fittest and the improvement of the human race. Against this it is urged that in fact war kills off the most fit, and leaves only the unfit to survive and propagate the next generation, that it kills off the flower of the young manhood of a nation and leaves only the physically defective to survive. But we need not tarry long with this group who have taken a biological condition and erected it into an ethical principle.[11]

Of those who are working for the elimination of war, there are several distinct types of thought. In the first place there are the idealists, sincere men and women who put their faith solely in Christianity and other great philosophical systems, in the sense that they try by preaching and teaching Christian doctrine to make men better and hence make them see the evil in war. In a second group, there are the more scientifically minded people, who have as great faith in the efficacy of Christianity yet are interested in the scientific demonstration of the fact that war is a wrong because it is a mistake. This second class is trying to make people understand that they ought to apply to the problem of international relations the same canons of criticism they are accustomed to employ in other branches of human knowledge. Among these men are the practical political engineers, more enlightened statesmen, political scientists, and the scientific students of diplomacy and foreign relations who are interested, not only in pointing out the wrong, but in devising some machinery to correct it. A third group are found now for, and now against war, as their interests dictate. An example of this is the German pastors who prayed to the Prince of Peace before 1914 and to the God of War after 1914. They are, unfortunately, not unique in history, nor confined to Germany. Some of the bloodiest wars of history have been fought in the name of organized religion, as, indeed, in some respects, was that Thirty Years War, which occasioned Grotius' book. When Grotius after many years of patient toil produced the first scientifically constructive work on international relations, a work which has inspired many thousands since his day, it was condemned by organized religion. He could only sadly remark that he thought at least those who professed Christianity ought to be interested in avoiding war.[12]

Lastly among the opponents of war we find that group who are

---

[11] James Bryce, "War and Human Progress," *Atlantic Monthly*, CXVIII, 301–15.
[12] A. D. White, *Seven Great Statesmen* (N. Y., 1910), pp. 73, 101n.

present in every reform movement, "the fringe of lunatics," whose ill-considered and too radical suggestions such as philosophical anarchy, take no account of man as he is, and whose activities hurt more than they help the cause of international coöperation.[13] Such a work as the present volume is designed primarily for the second group, the scientific thinkers in international affairs.

When the tide in the affairs of men brought to the United States a peculiar opportunity for moral leadership, her first impulse was to refuse it, because she was unaccustomed to think in international terms. Busy with the building up of a new civilization which in a single century turned the Mississippi Valley from a barren prairie or pathless woodland into a hive of agriculture and industry, intent upon exploiting the resources of a great country to the uttermost gain, bent on the acquisition of greater wealth than the world has known, how could Americans have any time left for a study of their international relations, a thing so remote and so far beyond their borders? But there seems to be a growing sentiment in the United States which finds expression for all types of thought. At one time all government was regarded as a necessary evil, and it existed solely for the negative purpose of preventing wrong. This idea is dying out. The growing social and political ideal is that all government exists, not only to prevent wrong, but for the more positive purpose of advancing good. If the man from Jericho was robbed, it was, according to the old idea, the job of the policemen to protect him. Since there had been no policeman around, that was all there was to it, and the Priest and Levite could pass by on the other side and leave him to his fate. But the newer idea is that nations would do better if their actions were extended toward helping out those who need help; that acting the part of the Good Samaritan is also the function and purpose of government. The first thing, then, for governments to do, is obviously to bind up their neighbor's wounds. The next thing is to try to enlighten themselves and their neighbors so that next time neither they nor

[13] C. E. Merriam, *American Political Ideas, 1865–1917* (N. Y., 1920), pp. 250–68.

their neighbors will get wounded. This last is one of the functions of books.

But, unfortunately, up to the present time only too few books have been written from the point of view of making enlightenment as attractive as war. It is most discouraging to have a reflective man tell us that history is a bath of blood or that war is the romance of history. Yet, sad to say, there is some truth in it. William James, who made those remarks, tried to point out that until we made peace as attractive as war, we need not expect to eliminate war from the world.[14] Wrongdoing has been made too interesting for spiritual values to become apparent. Simon Patten remarked that he attended a religious service where a large congregation, after listening to a convincing peace sermon, sang energetically and without a qualm of conscience "The Son of God goes forth to War." [15] The whole trouble is that the world is not yet sufficiently accustomed to thinking in terms of social values as dramatically desirable things. International relations are so remote from the ken of the busy man in a busy world that it needs some extraordinary presentation to attract him. War is such a presentation. But if we think of international relations only in terms of wars, we certainly are not helping to make those relations more amicable. This book is not written to prove anything. But it is hoped that it may serve to change the focus of attention from the prologues and epilogues of war to those great principles of international association which are the foundations of diplomatic history. Those principles are the basis of such international associations as there are, for they supply the machinery for such relationships as now exist. It is necessary, therefore, to begin with an examination of them.

[14] William James, *The Moral Equivalent of War* (International Conciliation Pamphlet No. 27).
[15] Simon Patten, *Advent Songs* (N. Y., 1916).

CHAPTER II

AMERICA AS A PAWN OF EUROPEAN DIPLOMACY

> "And two great nations can scarce be at war in *Europe*, but some other prince or state thinks it a convenient opportunity to revive some ancient claim, seize some advantage, obtain some territory, or enlarge some power, at the expense of a neighbor. The flames of war once kindled, often spread far and wide, and the mischief is infinite."—*Benjamin Franklin.*

1. EARLY IMPERIALISTS

The history of American diplomacy begins with that bull of demarcation whereby the Pope tried to divide the western hemisphere between his two friends, the King of Spain and the King of Portugal. This act on the part of the Pope was not really so arrogant nor so presumptuous as it may seem to a twentieth-century reader. Back in the fifteenth century the monarchs of Portugal and Spain were accustomed to ask the papal blessing on their commercial and marauding expeditions and whenever possible they got his sanction for what they had done when the members of the expedition returned with whatever plunder they had gathered. Several Popes had confirmed to successive Kings of Portugal the possession of the lands the adventurous Portuguese mariners discovered when first they ventured out on to the Atlantic, and crawled cautiously and slowly down the west coast of Africa in their effort to find their way through to the east. Other Popes had blessed the banners of the King of Spain in his various North African and Mediterranean expeditions and had confirmed his filibusters in whatever they gained. Indeed it had not been so very long since Duke William of Normandy had demanded and received the papal authorization to undertake that Conquest which had ousted Harold from the throne of England and replaced him with the Norman-Frenchman. What could be more natural then, than that the Pope should prescribe the limits of Portuguese and Spanish expansion and exploration? [1]

It was with no intent to affront England, France, or the Netherlands that Pope Alexander VI gave away all the New World to the Kings of Spain and Portugal. It was simply because at the time he found himself already committed to doing such things for the King of Portugal, and because he was himself a Spaniard and was under some obligations to the King of Spain.[2] England, France, and the Netherlands had not as yet figured very largely as maritime or exploring nations; why, then, should they be considered any more than half a dozen other nations or cities such as the Scandinavian nations or the cities of the Hanseatic League? Papal foreign policy was a very real thing in those days, and for the moment it was entangled with the Iberian peninsula. Nevertheless, the exclusive rights granted to the peoples of the Iberian peninsula by the papal Bull of Demarcation of 1493 carried with it a money-making privilege which was bound to make trouble. It practically gave to Portuguese and Spaniards the monopoly on trading with the Indies, East as well as West, and this interfered with the interests of other nations in Europe who wanted to make money, too.

For this was the age in which the peoples of Western Europe were all getting tired of paying tribute to the Italian cities. England, France, and the Netherlands were not going to remain unimportant and insignificant in the realm of colonial expansion. They also had a taste for spices which for too many centuries had been brought to them by the merchant fleets of Venice and Genoa. Too long had they paid toll to these Italians, and the routes of medieval commerce over which the spices had to come involved so many transshipments that when the profits of the middlemen were added to the cost of the goods, the ultimate consumer paid more than he thought necessary. The Spanish trips to the west

[1] C. DeLannoy and H. Van der Linden, *Histoire de l'Expansion Colonials des Peuples Européens: Portugal et Espagne*, (Paris, 1907), pp. 1–5.   H. Harrisse, *The Diplomatic History of America, Its first Chapter* (London, 1897) pp. 40 ff. The text of the various bulls will be found in F. G. Davenport, *European Treaties bearing on the History of the United States and its Dependencies to 1648* (Washington, 1917), pp. 9–79).

[2] R. B. Merriman, *Rise of the Spanish Empire*, II, 199–201.

and the Portuguese trips to the east broke the monopoly of the Italian cities. The cheaper freight rates on the all-water route to India caused the other western nations to send out exploring and trading expeditions, for they had no desire to see the Italian monopoly transferred from Genoa to Portugal. The profit of the middleman explains the discovery of America. The possibilities of trade and commerce begin her diplomatic history. Moreover, the Englishman had something to sell. Was the wool from Spain any better than the wool from England? Why was merino superior to tweeds, cheviots or jerseys? England also produced those shining edge-tools for which all the Indians, east and west, were willing to barter. Could not Sheffield knives be traded as well as Toledo cutlery? It is the duty of a cousul to keep his home government informed as to what the people of a country will buy, and the early consular reports will be found in the pages of Richard Hakluyt's collections, wherein are preserved the lists of things the explorers say the Indians will purchase.[3]

But it was France which first challenged the Iberian monopoly of the East and West Indies, and the Breton mariners braved the wrath of the Spaniard in the waters of the New World. Protests and counter-protests came and went between the courts of France and Spain, but nothing definite or satisfactory to both parties was ever decided before England came on the scene as a rival to them both for the riches of the Indies. Englishmen who desired to share in the wealth of the Americas went thither as pirates, as privateers and as traders, and there is no real way of telling them apart. Diplomatic protests came from the Court of Spain to the Court of Elizabeth, but the English based their claim to an equal share in the trade with the Indies on an ancient treaty between Charles V and Henry VIII, providing for reciprocal free trade in their respective dominions. In vain did the Spaniards insist that this treaty did not apply to the Indies, and in vain did

[3] For the fact that it was freight rates and not the rise of the Ottoman Turks that caused the discovery of America, see A. H. Lybyer, "The Ottoman Turks and the Routes of Oriental Trade," *Eng. Hist. Rev.*, XXX, 577 and "Influence of the Rise of the Ottoman Turks upon the Routes of Oriental Trade," *Rept. of Amer. Hist. Assoc.*, 1914, I, 127-33. For articles of export from western Europe, see R. Hakluyt, *Principal Navigations of the English Nation* (Everyman ed.), VIII, 17-18.

the Spaniards try to drive the English from the seas. The destruction of the great Spanish Armada in 1588 broke the sea power of Spain and thereafter England had might on her side in the diplomatic arguments. Various agreements were patched up, but the clause over the vital point as to whether English traders might trespass on the preserves which the Pope had granted to the Spaniards was always couched in ambiguous terms, which each party might and did interpret to suit itself. Meanwhile the whole question of European diplomacy had been further complicated by the fact that the Netherlands had revolted from Spain and insisted on their right to continue to trade in both Indies. Spain refused to recognize this right and in 1607 would have been willing to recognize the independence of the Netherlands, if only the Dutchmen would give up their claim to make money in America. It was not until the Treaty of Munster at the Congress of Westphalia in 1648 that Spain finally consented to allow any nations to trade in the Indies by name.[4]

But, after all, American diplomacy was but the side issue of a side issue, it was only the subdivision of a subdivision, only the small part of a small part of the great game of European diplomacy. Francis I of France, Henry VIII of England, and Charles V of Spain had many other issues among them besides the interests of their respective merchants trading in the Indies. When they did think of these merchants they were likely to think of the East Indies which produced the spices as of more importance than the West Indies, and when they thought of the West Indies it was the region of South America and the islands of the Caribbean which first occurred to them. So the diplomatic history of North America begins in a very small way. Frenchmen disregarded the Spaniard and settled in Canada as the Englishman had ignored him and taken up land in Virginia and Massachusetts Bay. One of the first steps in the diplomatic history of the United States was taken when these Frenchmen and these Englishmen made a treaty of commerce. The agents of Massachu-

[4] F. G. Davenport, "American and European Diplomacy to 1648" in the *Rept. of the Amer. Hist. Assoc.*, 1915, p. 155.

setts Bay and the French Governor of Acadia (Nova Scotia) agreed to reciprocal free trade by a treaty in 1644 and this treaty was not to be ratified by an English parliament sitting three thousand miles away but by the "Commissioners of the United Colonies of New England." Here begins United States', as contrasted with American, diplomacy, in an agreement to trade.[5]

2. DEVELOPMENT OF THE LAWS OF WAR AND NEUTRALITY

The wars of England and Spain in the Elizabethan period are full of stories which explain the problems of American diplomacy, and without which much of our diplomatic history must be meaningless and incomplete. This was the period of the beginnings of that international law which, as we have seen, constitutes the foundation of diplomatic intercourse. In the latter years of the 16th century English sea power was adopting rules and establishing practices which later have been written into the rules of the law of nations. As has been pointed out, international law is simply the practice of nations. International law on the sea would naturally be very vitally affected by the rules adopted by the principal sea power and the means habitually employed by that sea power in the enforcement of its rights under the law of nations. Spain's objection to England's trespassing on the Indies brought about naval fights between the two powers, and seizures by the Spanish navy of English merchant vessels. When vessels engaged in the forbidden trade were seized by Spain, the English owner had the following redress: he could apply to his own government which would take the matter up with the Spanish ambassador, who would refuse to do anything about it. Then the English government would issue to the injured Englishman the "Letters of marque and reprisal" which gave the Englishman the commission and right to go out and prey on Spanish commerce until his debt was satisfied, and he had gained enough to repay him for his original loss. From this system it was an easy step to granting private shipowners in time of war the right and commission to prey on the enemy's commerce. The shipowner so

[5] *Records of the Colony of New Plymouth*, IX, 59–60.

authorized was known as a "privateer" and privateering became a legitimate practice for the next three centuries. If the privateer exceeded his instructions, or if he went on seizing vessels after the conclusion of peace, he became a pirate, and could be captured and hanged by the vessels of any nation.[6]

Another rule of the Laws of War which was established in the Law of Nations in this period was that which had to do with contraband. When the nations of Europe were actually at war with one another it was important to each that no food or munitions of war should reach his enemy. When England was at war with Spain she resented the fact that Dutch merchants were shipping military stores to Spain. The energetic Dutch shipmasters were carrying timber and ship stores from Russia to the Spanish navy, and cheeses and grain from Holland to feed the Spanish army and these right by England's front door. So England set out to capture neutral vessels laden with these *contraband* articles bound to help her enemy. The right to seize this contraband was of course vigorously opposed by the neutral governments, whose merchants were suffering. But the assertion of this right by all nations was a practice of long standing. In his book on international law in 1625 Grotius had laid the foundations for the rules governing this subject. He had classed the goods of commerce into three groups. In the first class were articles of commerce which were used exclusively for the purpose of war, and they could be seized by a belligerent when being carried to his enemy by anyone on the seas. This was called *absolute contraband*. The second class included all articles of commerce which might be used for warlike purposes, but might also be of use for peaceful pursuits. These goods could be seized by the belligerent when being carried to his enemy only if it could be proven in a prize court that they were destined for warlike purposes. This class of goods was called *conditional contraband*. The third group comprised goods and commodities which could not be used for warlike purposes and which therefore could never be seized as contra-

[6] E. P. Cheyney, *History of England from the Defeat of the Armada to the Death of Elizabeth*, I, 463.

band. This group was designated as *non-contraband*. The exact rules governing these seizures were disputed from the earliest times and they are still disputed. How could a nation know what was and what was not conditional contraband? How could a neutral merchant know what a prize court would say about a proposed shipment whose ultimate destination was unknown? In 1589 we find the English Privy Council publishing a contraband list, and on that list England gives notice that she will seize not only guns and ammunition going to her enemy, Spain, but also ship stores and food. After this the practice became general of publishing at the outbreak of a war just what specific articles would be regarded as contraband. That is to say, each nation published what it would regard as contraband. Naturally England, being mistress of the seas, put a greater number and variety of articles on the contraband lists than France or Spain thought was right. The question of whether food was contraband was endlessly disputed in the wars of Europe, and the exact status remains to-day in a very unsatisfactory condition. In this quarrel the United States has had a very important part, but that part cannot be understood, nor can justice be done to either side unless it be realized that the practice of England has been at least consistent from very early times.[7]

In this quarrel over contraband we see emerging the first assertion of the rights of neutrals in time of war. The rules of international law as to neutrals are of great importance in United States history, as the United States has tried so hard to remain neutral in certain great European contests. But we cannot be fair to either side in the struggle for the rights of neutrals without a frank recognition of the fact that just as the United States has contended manfully for the rights of the neutral and the right to remain neutral, so has England been consistent in her contention from the earliest times that sea power gave her the right to limit the trading privileges of the neutrals to carry aid to her enemy, either directly or indirectly. Twice the United

---

[7] Grotius, *De Jure Belli ac Pacis*, Bk. II, Chap. 2; E. P. Cheyney, *History of England*, etc., I, 477.

States has entered a great European War in the defense of her neutral rights; twice she has spent millions in money and thousands of lives to establish some rules of international law on this question of neutral trading privileges in time of war. She has failed signally and why she has failed and still continues to fail, finds its explanation in the past which goes much further back than the European War, or even the War of 1812.

In the last years of Elizabeth's reign the history of international relations in Europe determined the fact that North America should not be Spanish. Weaker and weaker grew the power of Spain and fainter and fainter her influence in the councils of nations until she fades out of sight, to reappear only as a creature of imperial France. As a result North America is peopled with Englishmen, Frenchmen and Dutchmen as well as Spaniards. Englishmen had surplus capital after Elizabeth's day. But the reaction to that prosperity had also produced a period of unemployment, and there were many laborers out of work. What more natural than that English capital should seek investment by the planting of colonies in the New World, which could be peopled by other Englishmen whom economic pressure and distress drove from their Mother country? The Dutchman, too, had some money, made in carrying goods from the East Indies to Germany. Again the middleman got rich, for the Dutch were making money out of Europe's taste for spices just as the Italian cities had waxed rich and strong in the middle ages from the same trade. The Dutch now sailed the cheap all-water route whereby the Italian cities with their part land, part water route sank into unimportance. The ever present demand for fish led the adventurous Breton fisherman to the Grand Banks of Newfoundland and the Paris market for fine furs put French settlers along the St. Lawrence river. Then follows a century and a half of European diplomacy in which America is a pawn in the game, and at that, but one of a number of pawns.[8]

Yet despite their size, apparently neither America nor India

---

[8] A. P. Newton, *Puritan Colonization* (New Haven, 1914), pp. 1–39; *Cal. of State Papers, Dom. 1629–31*, pp. 8, 403, 419.

was big enough for all, and the consequence of a hundred and fifty years of international relations was that most of North America was English speaking. Central Europe, Germany, Austria and their neighbors, shared not at all in this growth and prosperity, for Central Europe was busy trying to commit suicide in that Thirty Years War, which as we have seen, produced the first great work on international law. But the Thirty Years War had yet another influence on American diplomacy. Because of this war, Germany entered the family of nations a hundred years too late to share in the scramble for colonies. She was too exhausted to recover in time to snatch her portion while the world was being carved up by the maritime powers. Yet the time was rapidly coming when a colony was desirable not only for the raw materials and luxuries it sent home to the Mother country, but because it furnished a market into which the Mother country could dump her surplus manufactured goods and make more money than ever from her colonial customers. Nearly three hundred years later Germany found herself, as she thought, handicapped in the commerce of the world because of the setback of the Thirty Years War, and that thought had far-reaching consequences for the United States.

English diplomacy under James I was a weak maneuvering on his part to help out his relatives on the continent to whom the Thirty Years War brought trouble. Under Charles I, English diplomacy became confused and paralyzed by a series of ineffective moves. Confused, because Charles had not the support of his people, and paralyzed because his obstinacy led him into that great Civil War which ends English diplomacy until Cromwell's days. Meanwhile the Dutch stepped in and extended their possessions while England wasted her substance in Civil War. As the English had settled the valley of the Connecticut River, so the Dutch now put colonists in the neighboring valley of the Hudson, for Holland gin would buy as many furs from the Indians as would French brandy.

When about the year 1650, Oliver Cromwell took hold of the reins in England his foreign policy aimed at recovering for England what she had lost in the Civil War, namely, that commercial supremacy which the Elizabethan seaman had fought so long and valiantly to secure. Now it was no longer a contest between English and Spanish seamen, but a struggle between English and Dutch mariners. Now, too, America came into the game in her own interest. The English settlers in the Connecticut Valley had long resented the Dutch possession of the next-door valley of the Hudson. Here was a chance to get rid of them. A quarrel which began as a commercial competition between the merchants of Amsterdam and the merchants of London became the pretext whereby the English and the English colonists seized the Dutch possessions in America, and the Delaware and Hudson valleys passed into the hands of England, thus linking up her northern and southern colonies on the continent of North America. Once gained, New York was almost lost again when Charles II became the tool of Louis XIV of France and his foreign policy, but it was finally regained for the Anglo-Americans in 1674.[9]

In that same period when Charles' trifling with power gave the Dutchman his chance in North America, France was taken in the iron hand of Richelieu. The prosperity which he gave to her resulted in her having surplus capital to invest abroad, and the end of the religious wars provided the usual crop of energetic filibusters who were eager for adventures in the New World. Richelieu himself was never greatly interested in colonial expansion, for the Thirty Years War claimed some of his attention. But in the following reign the great minister Colbert galvanized the French colonial policy into life. But Colbert's effort explains both the rise and fall of the French American Empire. To stimulate commerce and manufactures he granted monopolies in America which gave individual Frenchmen a chance to get under control vast areas of territory, but he never attracted a large population of Frenchmen and there was not the internal strength necessary to win the coming struggle with England. Colbert and his master Louis XIV tried hard to found a French colony in the New World, that would supply the Mother country with raw

[9] G. L. Beer, *Old Colonial System* (N. Y., 1912), I, 5ff.

materials and food stuffs such as English colonies sent back home. But France was then as now more self-supporting than England from the point of view of food and agriculture, and Louis and Colbert were too intent on transferring the highly centralized bureaucracy of Old France to a wilderness where it was decidedly inappropriate. And so it came about that in the great struggle which decided the mastery of North America, the English flag floated at all points on the Atlantic seaboard from Florida to Labrador.[10]

3. THE SECOND HUNDRED YEARS WAR

The "Second Hundred Years War" between France and England began with William of Orange and ended with Napoleon. It was a series of wars, each of which was a general European War, the preliminary diplomacy of which and the diplomatic interludes of which were conducted in Europe. These were European-made wars. But in every case from 1689 to 1815, there was not a single great European War (and there were seven of them) in which American lives were not lost, American property was not destroyed and in which American soldiers and sailors were not involved. George Washington's farewell address may have been a pious hope that America could steer clear of European quarrels, but it certainly was not a statement of that as a fact. The fact is that never once in the "Second Hundred Years War" was there a general European conflict in which the English-speaking inhabitants of North America were not directly involved as combatants and belligerents. This old world diplomacy had far-reaching consequences and the idea that America can stay out of European affairs has no basis in fact, for America never has done so from the time of the Spanish Armada to the Treaty of Versailles in 1919.[11]

---

[10] S. L. Mims, *Colbert's West India Policy* (New Haven, 1912), p. 68 et seq.

[11] Such an interpretation as this may be challenged, yet if one will ponder on Chapters III–V of J. T. Adams' *Revolutionary New England, 1691-1776* (Boston, 1923), he will see the force of these remarks. One might bolster up this point with even more foot-notes, but perhaps more eloquent than foot-note citations are the names which any traveler can still seen engraved on the walls of the cells and dungeons of the Chateau at Nantes. Even in those days the American soldier and sailor could not refrain from scratching his name and date on the monuments of Europe. Here we have the names of the Americans who were taken prisoners during the colonial wars, Nantucket and Gloucester sailors who are at pains to engrave after their names their American origin.

William of Orange consented to become King of England in
1688, among other reasons, in order that he might have England's
navy in fighting a Dutch war against France. British foreign
policy as far as overseas expansion is concerned began with Elizabeth, but it suffered a serious setback from neglect under James I
and Charles I. Cromwell carried on for Elizabeth and began a
real colonial policy, but his work was in turn neglected by another
Charles and another James. William III carried on for Cromwell. In the last decade of the seventeenth century he organized
Europe against the ambition of Louis XIV, who was the apostle
of "weltmacht" in his day. England and English policy were
but one part of William's scheme of things, and America was but
a smaller part of this. Yet in this war Americans, English colonists from Massachusetts, began that series of efforts to capture
Louisbourg and Quebec which they accomplished so often,
only to have the fruits of their victory bartered back to France
in a European Peace Conference in which they were not allowed
to sit. Quebec was first captured by the English colonists from
the French in 1627, but the English never retained it until the
Peace Conference of 1763. This fact suggests the whole story of
American diplomacy in the colonial period. Victories in America
were traded off for land in India, or balanced against defeats elsewhere. That Americans might have something to say in the
matter was not frequently considered. The Peace of Ryswick in
1697 left the belligerents and their boundary disputes just exactly
where they had started in 1687, as far as America was concerned.

But the machine which William III had built for the purpose
of combating the aggressive imperialism of Louis XIV did not lie
idle very long. More European diplomacy embroiled America
in another war. It did not make any difference to any one in
America who sat upon the throne of Spain, for such was the
ostensible cause of the war beginning in 1701. What did make
a difference was that these Americans were looked upon as
mere appendages of the European powers then at war. When
such failures of European diplomacy resulted in the Indians
bursting in on unprotected frontier villages and scalping the

inhabitants, the colonists felt one consequence of the manipulations of diplomacy by gentlemen sitting three thousand miles away. In this so-called "War of the Spanish Succession" while Marlborough was winning at Blenheim and Malplaquet, fifteen hundred colonial troops joined fifty-five hundred British regulars in the usual Quebec expedition, which marks every colonial war. This conflict ended in the Peace of Utrecht in 1713 by which England was awarded Nova Scotia. But this did not relieve the colonials from the terror on their frontier which they felt as long as France held Canada. The Treaty of Utrecht also provided that a boundary commission should be appointed to decide the line of the frontier between the French possessions in Canada and those of England in North America. It is possible that the boundary commission fixed upon the 49th parallel of north latitude, but it was never accepted by the two parties. This was of no consequence at the time but became of considerable importance later on when England succeeded to the French claims in the north and the United States succeeded to the English claims in the South. The 49th parallel eventually became the boundary between Canada and the United States. But in any case the colonials had the doubtful satisfaction of knowing that the efforts of British diplomacy had been crowned with success in the breaking of the Spanish colonial monopoly to the extent that England could import negro slaves into South America and could send one ship a year of English manufactured goods to the fair at Porto-Bello.[12]

Another general European war broke out in 1740. Again European diplomacy broke down and again disinterested parties in the ends of the earth had to fight in wars which concerned them very little. This was the "War of the Austrian Succession" and was begun because Frederick the Great of Prussia decided that since the Austrian succession had brought a woman, Maria Theresa, to the throne of Austria, he might legitimately plunder Austria of its province of Silesia. This was not the first time Silesia had been stolen, for Austria had taken it from Poland,

[12] J. R. Seeley, *The Growth of British Policy* (Cambridge, 1895), II, 309-384.

but it was the first time Silesia figured in American diplomacy and it was destined not to be the last. Nowhere is the result of this kind of thing better or more eloquently described than by Macaulay who says of Frederick in this war, "In order that he might rob a neighbor whom he had promised to defend, black men fought on the coast of Coromandel [in India] and red men scalped each other by the Great Lakes of North America." Again the citizens of the British dominions in North America raised their quota of troops to attack Louisbourg and Quebec, and this time they captured the former. Again the fruits of an American victory were thrown away at a European Peace Conference, for Louisbourg was restored to France at the Peace of Aix-la-Chappelle in 1748.

The American side of European diplomacy was now finally narrowed down to a struggle between France, Spain and England for the possession of the northern continent. It ended when Spain and England ousted France and when the United States partly displaced both the former. At the outset, England possessed but the proverbial narrow ribbon of territory along the Atlantic seaboard, while France and Spain held all the hinterland and the Gulf Coast. The boundaries of the three were never distinctly marked. Englishmen and Frenchmen had explored all the region east of the Mississippi. Frenchmen and Spaniards had explored the region west of the Mississippi. If mere discovery and exploration gave any rights, the stage was set for a fight because the discoveries overlapped. Many parts of North America were claimed by two nations and some by three. What rights, then, does mere discovery give to the nation of the discoverer? Did France own all the lands drained by the Mississippi because of the work of her Jesuit missionaries and her fur traders whose indefatigable energy led them to explore the innermost recesses of the continent? On this point the early works on international law were not very explicit. Grotius had written in 1625 before the struggle entered that acute stage of colonial rivalry which the next century produced. For that reason we must discover what some later writers on international law had to say, particularly those who wrote after the colonial wars were well under way.

Chief among these authorities is Jean de Vattel. Said he, "The limits of territories ought to be marked out with clearness and precision. If those who drew up the Treaty of Utrecht had applied on so important a subject all the attention it deserved, we should not now see France and England in arms in order to decide by a bloody war what are the bounds of their possessions in America." Vattel denied that mere exploration, discovery or the formal taking possession gave good title to land. He suggested that the better and later practice required an actual occupation and settlement before a nation could declare itself entitled to newly discovered territory. Mere discovery gave but a partial title to newly discovered lands. This partial or *inchoate* title had to be made good by actual occupation, otherwise any other nation might step in and secure the land.[13]

But unfortunately the rules on international law are not established save after years, and sometimes centuries of practice. The rule that discovery gives an inchoate title and must be followed by actual occupation did not receive the consent of the nations till another century had rolled around. Consequently Vattel represented only the enlightened principle of his day, and was merely the interpreter of what was best in the chaotic practice of his time. The claims of French and Spaniards are particularly significant in later United States history, and it is to them that we turn in an effort to find out where Vattel got his rules of practice. Spain claimed all North America west of the Mississippi River. France claimed all the valleys of the St. Lawrence and the Mississippi. These claims obviously conflicted because they overlapped. Where then was actual occupation? The Spanish actually had settlements which in the eighteenth century would have entitled them to claim the Vice-Royalty of New Spain, by virtue of actual occupation, which included what is now Mexico, Texas, California, New Mexico, Arizona and Florida. The French had

13 W. B. Scaife, "The Development of International Law as to Newly Discovered Territory" in the *Papers of the Amer. Hist. Assoc.*, IV, 269; Vattel, *Droit de Gens*, Bk. II, sec. 95; see also J. B. Moore, *Digest of International Law*, I, 258.

actual trading posts or towns which would have entitled them to claim the province of Canada, which included the St. Lawrence Valley and the Great Lakes country, and the Province of Louisiana, which was a great V-shaped section of the Mississippi Valley with its apex at New Orleans. French forts were scattered up and down the rivers flowing into the Mississippi, along the Ohio, the Illinois, the Wabash, the Missouri, the Arkansas and others. The Spanish had pushed north and founded the town of Santa Fé in New Mexico about the same time the first English settlers were landing at Jamestown. The French forts on the Mississippi were so placed, because Louis XIV wanted to offset the rising power of England in America. The King of England had granted charters to his colonists which gave them territory from "sea-to-sea," that is from the Atlantic to the Pacific. In 1697 Louis XIV granted territory to his subject Antoine Crozat, which indicated that Louisiana extended from the present Carolinas to New Mexico, and from Canada to the Gulf of Mexico.[14]

The reasons for the French advance are not far to seek. French buccaneers in the West Indies were now harrying the Spanish trade as Drake and Hawkins had done a century earlier. France needed a naval base on the Gulf of Mexico, somewhere near the mouth of the Mississippi, and in 1685 La Salle set out to secure it. His expedition landed at Lavaca Bay, about halfway down the present coast of Texas, and laid thereby the foundations for a century and half of diplomatic wrangling. A settlement thus made on the shores of Texas gave color to the claim that Louisiana extended on to the southwest as far as the Rio Grande. Moreover Frenchmen from the settlements and forts of Louisiana pushed overland, led by the hopes of illicit trade and the silver mines in New Mexico. Stirred by La Salle's exploit, the Spanish undertook to resist the French encroachments on their preserves, and to make good their claim that no Frenchman was entitled to come west of the Mississippi River at all. By actual occupation the Spanish made Texas secure by 1716, but this did not prevent the unsuccessful La Salle Colony from plaguing the

[14] I. J. Cox, The Louisiana-Texas Frontier," Pt. I, *Texas Hist. Assoc. Quar.*, X, 1.

diplomats for another century. For at least fifty years after Spain's occupation of Texas, the French and Spanish bickered continually over the question of where lay the boundary between Louisiana and New Spain. Even the presence of a Frenchman on the throne of Spain did not serve to allay the dispute. The War of the Spanish Succession, which is another name for the Marlborough Wars on the Continent, was the occasion of one of the numerous attacks on Quebec, as we have seen above. It was in European diplomacy an effort to put the grandson of Louis XIV on the throne of Spain, and it succeeded in doing that. But for the next fifty years the French settlement at Natchitoches in Louisiana lay within a few miles of the Spanish settlement at Los Adaes in Texas and a kind of armed peace was maintained when it was not actually punctuated with open warfare. After 1721 Spain recognized the fact but not the right of French occupation. In 1754 the King of Spain admitted that the boundary between Louisiana and New Spain had never been fixed, and within a year a war broke out which ended with the establishment of the Spanish boundary on the Mississippi.[15]

For the last great colonial war broke out in 1754 as the American edition of the so-called "Seven Years War" in Europe. Again Americans flocked to the banner of Britain and again they fought against the Frenchman and this time against the Spaniard as well, since the Family Compact between the Kings of France and Spain drew the latter to the side of the former. This is one of the most striking examples of wars in which American lives and American property were sacrificed because of the whim and mistakes of European politicians. The blunders early in the war were appalling. The desire of a pair of English politicians, William Pitt (Chatham) and Henry Fox to oust the incompetent Duke of Newcastle from the head of the ministry led to that hasty and ill-prepared Braddock expedition in which Virginian as well as English blood was shed on account of the blunders of an English general selected by family influence. Pitt finally succeeded in

[15] W. E. Dunn, "The Spanish Reaction against the French Advance toward New Mexico, 1717–27," in the *Miss. Valley Hist. Rev.*, II, 348; H. E. Bolton, "The Location of La Salle's Colony on the Gulf of Mexico," in the *Miss. Valley Hist. Rev.*, II, 165.

getting rid of Newcastle and did his best to redeem the war situation by a policy which succeeded admirably in rallying to his support both the colonies and the merchant class in England.   The
existence of the numerous Chatham Counties in the states of the
United States are the tribute the colonials paid to this minister
who after getting them into a war at least saw it through and
repaid them at last by holding on to the territory they had
gained.

By 1763 both France and Spain were beaten to their knees,
and Frederick of Prussia had triumphed over the combined forces
of Russia, France and Austria.   Throughout the war Americans
had fought up and down Lake Champlain and their troops were
in at the finish when the final capture of Quebec ended forever the
French dreams of dominating America.   Defeated France was
compelled to surrender Canada to England and defeated Spain
was forced to yield Florida.   Louisiana was divided down the
middle by the Mississippi River.   The half which lay to the east
of the river was surrendered to England, and the half to the west
was yielded by France to Spain to compensate her for having
been dragged into a war in which she lost Florida.[16]

It is of the greatest importance to notice that Louisiana was
not all given to Spain; it was divided in half.   But unfortunately
no one knew just what Louisiana was.   The negotiators at the
peace conferences were not always men who knew anything
about the localities with which they dealt.   Indeed sometimes
they were men who were conspicuously stupid about things in
which they ought to have been expert.   The classic example is
that of the Duke of Newcastle who talked about Cape Breton for
a decade without knowing that it was an island.   This vagueness
of ideas on the subjects which were really of vital importance to
the Americans, can be imputed in part (but only in part) to the
fact that although Americans were vitally interested in this diplomacy they were allowed no direct share in it.   It is a long way
from Paris in 1763 to Paris in 1919.   One of the most interesting

---

[16] H. Hall, "Chatham's Colonial Policy" in the *Amer. Hist. Rev.*, V, 659; T. W. Riker,
"The Politics behind the Braddock Expedition," in the *Amer. Hist. Rev.*, XIII, 742.

developments of the last hundred and fifty years has been the fact that at peace conferences the Britannic Dominions are no longer merged in the delegation of commissioners who come from London. In the Conference at Paris in 1763, the English represented not only England but also Massachusetts, Pennsylvania, and all the other colonies. In the Conference of Paris in 1919, the Prime Minister of Great Britain represented Great Britain, but the Dominion of Canada was represented by her Premier, Sir Robert Borden, and the Commonwealth of Australia by her Premier, Mr. William Hughes, and the Union of South Africa, by her Premier, Gen. Louis Botha.

Despite the absence of colonial representatives from the peace conference in 1763, the potential worth of the Mississippi Valley had captivated the imagination of British statesmen, notably Earl Shelburne. But in the administration of the newly won territory, a line to divide the settlements of the pioneers from lands reserved for the Indians under British control, was drawn far too close to the eastern seaboard. The royal proclamation line which discouraged settlement beyond the Alleghenies raised the question in the minds of Americans as to whether their destinies could safely be trusted to conferences and colonial offices in which they had no voice.[17]

So the treaty of 1763 became a trouble maker for the future. That part of Louisiana which was east of the Mississippi was ceded to England, and so was Florida. Now the old boundary between Spanish Florida and French Louisiana had generally been reckoned to be at the Perdido River. England now proceeded to prescribe boundaries for the provinces of her newly won territories and thereby to lay the foundation for endless trouble for the future diplomats of the United States. By the royal Proclamation of 1763 the British dominions on the continent of North America were divided into seventeen provinces, and boundaries for them were indicated. Old French Canada became the Province of Quebec, and south of it were Massachusetts, New Hampshire, Rhode Island, Connecticut, New York, New Jersey, Pennsyl-

[17] C. W. Alvord, *Mississippi Valley in British Politics* (Cleveland, 1917), II, 250.

vania, the Three Lower Counties on the Delaware, Maryland, Virginia, North Carolina, South Carolina, Georgia, East Florida and West Florida. By this proclamation the boundary between the Province of Quebec and the Province of New York was fixed at the 45th parallel, where it has since remained. The boundary between the Province of Quebec and that part of the Province of Massachusetts which is now the state of Maine was indicated by the ambiguous statement that it should run along the highlands which divided the waters flowing into the St. Lawrence

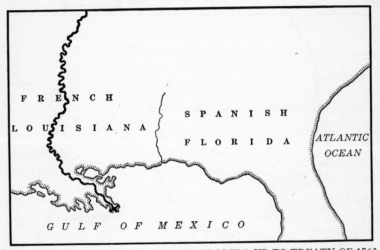

FRENCH LOUISIANA AND SPANISH FLORIDA UP TO TREATY OF 1763
River Perdido was boundary between French and Spanish territories

from those which flowed into the sea. This, as we shall see later, made a great deal of trouble for nearly another century.

However the question of the Floridas was destined to make trouble for many years to come. Incidentally it is impossible for the reader to understand it without looking at the map. (See maps, pp. 30, 31, 50.) The boundary between French Louisiana and Spanish Florida was, as we have said, the Perdido River. That meant that the gulf coast of what is now Alabama and Mississippi was part of Louisiana. Now the new boundary of the British dominions as fixed by the treaty of 1763 ran, as we have remarked, down the middle of the Mississippi River. But it did not go all the way to the mouth of the Mississippi. Just above the city of New Orleans a shallow stream called the Iberville River cut away from the Mississippi to the east and passed out through Lakes Pontchartrain, Maurepas and Borgne to the Gulf of Mexico. Thus the boundary between the Spanish and British dominions ran down the Mississippi and just above New Orleans turned abruptly to the east, thus depriving England of the mouth of the Mississippi but giving her a part of the present Gulf coast of Lou-

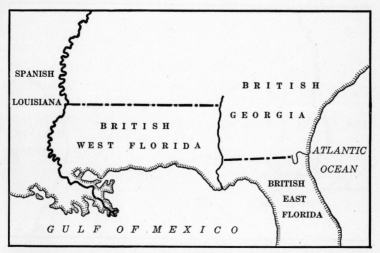

SPANISH LOUISIANA AND THE BRITISH FLORIDAS, 1763 TO 1783

The British created the Province of "West" Florida making the River Appalachicola the boundary between East and West Floridas.

isiana, all the gulf coast of the present states of Mississippi and Alabama and Florida. For the better administration of this area, the royal proclamation of 1763 erected a new province, called West Florida, divided from the older Florida (now called East Florida) not by the line of the Perdido River, but by the line of the Appalachicola River. The northern boundary of West Florida was to be the parallel of 31 degrees. (See map above and p. 50.)

But this is not the end of the story. About a year later it was found that it was difficult to administer the Yazoo region of the present state of Mississsippi from the Province of Georgia to which it was claimed to belong.   So by another royal pronouncement in 1764, the northern boundary of West Florida was fixed at 32 degrees 28 minutes.   This process effectively destroyed the identity of Louisiana east of the Mississippi, and created in its place West Florida.   There was no objection to this, but at least it must be apparent that Louisiana as France had held it in 1756 and Louisiana as Spain had received it in 1765 were by no means the same thing, and this it was that was to make so much trouble in the future.[18]

4. THE RULE OF 1756

One more story of the last colonial war remains to be told before our foundations are complete, and in some respects it is the very corner stone of American diplomatic history.   Certainly it is a milestone in the chronicle of the foreign relations of the United States, which casts its shadow down to the present day and stands as an unsettled controversy between the two great English-speaking nations.   In 1756 France possessed certain small West Indian colonies.   Small in extent they were, but by no means small in importance.[19]   For from these colonies came the Frenchman's breakfast, his chocolate, coffee and sugar.   As usual in the war, Great Britain mastered the seas and deprived the Frenchman of his breakfast.   Now according to the monopolistic principles of the various colonial systems, no one could trade with a colony but the Mother Country.   We have already seen how no one but a Spaniard could trade with the Spanish colonies, and so it was with French and British colonies.   Hence when Britain swept the French navy and merchant marine from the seas, no one could carry on this French colonial trade.   The French thus found that the monopolistic theories of the Mercan-

[18] I. J. Cox, *The West Florida Controversy, 1798–1813* (Baltimore, 1918), 1–3 and map; H. E. Chambers, "West Florida in its Relation to the Historical Cartography of the United States," in the *Johns Hopkins Univ. Studies*, Ser. XVI , 203.   C. E. Carter, "Some Aspects of British Administration in West Florida," *Miss. Valley Hist. Rev.*, I, 364, has pointed out that 1764 was the date of this change of boundary, and *not* 1767 as older historians have it.

[19] This is seen in the undue space given the Island of San Domingo in Eighteenth Century Atlases.

tilist System were a double-edged weapon. Consequently they decided to scrap the theory and open up their colonial trade to the neutral Dutch. The Dutch, being a mercantile nation with a large merchant marine were at peace with England and they gladly entered the field to carry French colonial produce to France in ships which because they were neutral the British might not molest. So Britain saw her naval superiority brought to nothing by the simple device of allowing a neutral to engage in a trade in time of war which was forbidden to it in time of peace. Should Britain stand by helplessly and allow this to go on? By no means; the British asserted that it had long been the practice of nations that a trade forbidden in time of peace by the monopolistic Mercantilist system, should *not* be opened in time of war. As early as 1604 during a war between Spain and Holland, two Venetian vessels (neutrals) were engaged under license from Spain in a certain trade ordinarily reserved for Spanish vessels exclusively. The Dutch promptly seized the Venetians on the ground that by entering this trade which Spain forbade Venice in time of peace, the Venetians had lost their neutral character and became Spanish. Similar incidents had taken place in some of the wars of the period of the Thirty Years War. So the British applied this same rule, which became known in history as the "Rule of the War of 1756," and they seized the Dutch vessels just as if they had been French, thus securing British naval superiority, so necessary for the final victory which drove the French from North America in 1763.[20]

[20] R. G. Marsden, "British Prize Law," in the *Eng. Hist. Rev.*, XXV, 244; *Cal. of State Papers (Venetian)*, 1603–7, No. 148.

CHAPTER III

AMERICAN DIPLOMACY DURING THE REVOLUTION

"Let them know that while every colony honors the mother city
so long as it is well treated, yet that if wronged, it becomes alienated; for colonists are not sent out to be slaves of those who are
left behind, but to be their equals."—*Thucydides*.

1. BEAUMARCHAIS' NEW PLAY

We are now in a position to read intelligently a few sentences
from that document which ushered the new member into the family of nations. Strictly speaking, of course, we should call this a
"Family of States," but usage dictates that when the national
states of the world are considered collectively they are called the
"family of nations." According to the Declaration of Independence, the new nation assumed among the nations of the earth a
separate and equal station, so that the states of which it was
composed were now free and independent, having full power to
levy war, to conclude peace, to contract alliances, to establish
commerce and "To do all other Acts and Things which Independent States may of right do." In international law, this document marks the beginning of the United States, but such a pronouncement is only taken to mark the beginning of a new nation
when in fact that nation subsequently proves that it can assert
and maintain that independence, when the nation from which it
revolts is demonstrably unable to suppress the rebellion, and
when other members of the family of nations recognize that independence by making treaties with the new member or exchang-
ing diplomatic agents with it. The United States had now to
gain this "recognition." What machinery was there by which
the United States might secure recognition? What agencies of
diplomatic intercourse did it possess?

Now the first government of the United States was a very

34

primitive thing. Indeed, it was hardly a government at all. It was rather a conference of ambassadors. It was composed solely of the Continental Congress, which was the legislative department, but it had neither executive nor judicial branches. Consequently as it was at first formed we look in vain for any department or Minister of Foreign Affairs. This is usually a subdivision of the Executive Department and there was no Executive. Hence as it was at the outset, the United States could not communicate with any foreign government or state. But it was very soon apparent that it would be advisable to speak with foreigners, and some agency or device had to be invented whereby the door might be opened to the knockings of a very insistent stranger, who was loitering around the taverns of Philadelphia trying to get in touch with some responsible official of the new government. Morever, since the British Colonial Policy, under the influence of the Mercantilist System had denied the colonies the right to manufacture certain very essential goods, it was of great military importance so get in touch with some foreigners who would sell to the new government what the Americans were not yet ready to manufacture for themselves. In addition to this Americans, still primarily farmers, had not reached the stage of industrial development by which they could supply their own needs. So Congress appointed a "Committee on Secret Correspondence" to find out what the stranger wanted and whether any of America's friends in Europe could be induced to take action in her behalf.[1]

It did not take a very clever person to guess what the stranger wanted from the Committee of the Continental Congress. He represented a nation that wanted "revanche." Now "revanche" does not necessarily mean revenge. It simply means that the defeated player in the game of European diplomacy wanted a chance to play again with a hope of winning. France wanted an opportunity to sit in again at the European game at which she had been so badly beaten in 1763.[2] The Committee on Secret

[1] G. Hunt, *The Department of State* (Yale Pr., 1914), pp. 3–7.
[2] E. S. Corwin, "The French Objective in the American Revolution" in *Amer. Hist. Rev.*, XXI, 33.

Correspondence at once set to work to get in touch with residents in Europe, but more important than this it dispatched the first agent from the United States when Silas Deane went to France in 1776 to facilitate shipments from the French. This was the day of Louis XVI in France. He had employed as his minister of finance, the great Turgot, whose function it was to extricate France from that administrative chaos into which the extravagant wars of more than one Louis had plunged her. In a word, Turgot's job was to avert the impending deluge of the French Revolution by introducing economy and efficiency. But as his minister of foreign affairs, Louis had selected the Count de Vergennes, who was equally intent upon recovering for France that position of prestige in world politics, of which the fatal war of 1756–63 had deprived her. Obviously both these ministers could not have what they wanted, as wars cost money. While Turgot preached reform and saving, Vergennes began a systematic process of trying to embroil his country in a war to aid the revolting British colonies against their Mother Country.

There were many reasons why France wanted to see the United States win its independence, and there was a variety of motives which led Louis XVI first to grant secret aid and then openly to espouse the cause of the colonists. In the first place it ought to be remembered that when we say France we do not mean the French people. As to public opinion, there could be no such thing in the modern sense when the vast majority of the public in France were as illiterate and ignorant as was the rule under the Ancien Régime. When the monarch of France could call himself the state, whether in fact he ever did so or not, the opinion of the public, whatever that might be, could not count for much. True it is that some French follow the lead of an American historian who insists that public opinion drove the French government to aid the United States, but none define public opinion although there is some interesting evidence for their conclusion.[3] But it can be stated with a reasonable degree of certainty

---

[3] J. B. Perkins, *France in the American Revolution* (Boston, 1911), introduction and pp. 205–18.

that France had been the dominant power on the continent of Europe for more than a century. It is likewise clear that she lost this position, as was observed in the last chapter, because of British sea-power which captured her colonies and lowered her prestige. Finally, on the continent of Europe, France's protégée, Poland, was calmly carved up by her neighbors, Russia, Prussia and Austria in 1772, and this was a serious blow to French diplomatic influence.

Moreover we do know that America had become something more than a mere source of raw material for Great Britain and her factories. The old Mercantilist System of Colonial Policy was based on the idea that colonies existed to supplement the riches of their Mother Country. The American colonies were now enriching Britain not only by shipping her timber and tobacco and other raw material, but through buying England's manufactured goods in return for the raw material, the colonies had become her best customers. England had become a vast workshop and her manufactured goods could not possibly all be consumed at home. It was necessary for her to sell her surplus in the colonies, making great profits and waxing ever richer and richer on the traffic. French policy dictated that something be done to enfeeble England and to injure her commercially, to sap her economic strength. For if political greatness is based on a wealth in money and resources, English commercial supremacy must be destroyed before France could hope to regain her former glory. So argued the French Minister of Foreign Affairs, Vergennes, and he had little difficulty in persuading his master to grant secret aid to the revolted colonies in America.[4]

Consequently when Silas Deane reached Paris he got in touch very quickly with a Frenchman who would advance money and supplies. The French agent Beaumarchais, a poet-politician, was apparently empowered to dispense the aid to the Americans. If, in the case of a rebellion, a foreign government grants aid or recognition to the rebels the Mother Country is perfectly entitled

[4] E. S. Corwin, *French Policy and the American Alliance* (Princeton, 1916), pp. 120–48; G. L. Beer, *Old Colonial System*, Pt. I, 50–1.

to regard that as a hostile act.   If Louis XVI were caught openly
sending arms and ammunition to America, or if he recognized the
newly formed nation by receiving its ambassadors, or by dispatching a representative of his own government to it, England
would have a perfect right to declare war on France, on the theory
that this was an unwarranted interference with the domestic affairs of the British Empire.   But although a neutral government,
such as France, might not sell nor send arms to either belligerent
in time of war, nevertheless private merchants of the neutral may
do so, if they are not caught and their goods confiscated as contraband.   Hence between 1776 and 1778 Louis advanced some
millions in money to Beaumarchais, who organized a sham corporation called "Hortalez and Company," which shipped arms
and ammunition to America in the capacity of a private firm,
despite the fact that most of the supplies were drawn from the
royal French arsenals.   The importance of this aid to the badly
armed and badly equipped army of General Washington can
scarcely be exaggerated.   But the ominous thing for the future was
the fact that the French King committed himself to a policy
which now gave Vergennes an opportunity for hurrying France
into open war with England.[5]

Vergennes, prompted by Beaumarchais, now began to argue
with his royal master that if France did not make common cause
with the colonists, the Americans were in a fair way to be defeated.   In the gloomy year of 1777, this seemed possible.   If
they were defeated, claimed Beaumarchais, they would feel
very bitterly toward France and when the next war came along,
they would again join England and sweep the French from their
remaining island possessions in America.   Moreover, argued Vergennes, if both England and America were exhausted, they would
compromise on something less than independence and then in the
next war the coalition of England and the American states would
under Chatham's leadership end forever the French dreams of
recovering their former position in world politics.   There was no

[5] J. de Vattel, *Law of Nations*, Bk. II, sec. 57; B. E. Hazard, *Beaumarchais and the American Revolution* (Boston, 1910); C. J. Stillé, "Beaumarchais and the Lost Million," in
Penna. Mag. of Hist. & Biog., XI, 1-36.

question that this had great weight with the king. But there is a very serious question as to whether in fact Vergennes believed this argument, or whether in fact there was any reason for thinking that any such thing would be likely to occur. Certainly the men who ought to have been thinking about it were strangely silent, and the idea of George III summoning back the much hated Chatham in any capacity whatever was an unlikely one.[6] It is, however, evident that the belief was of as much weight as though it had been a fact.

Meanwhile the Americans were waking up to the possibilities of the situation. Franklin went as envoy to the court of Louis XVI and the "Committee on Secret Correspondence" of the Continental Congress had given way to a "Committee on Foreign Affairs." (1777). At the same time Arthur Lee was commissioned to try to get Spain interested in American independence, because it was felt that if both France and Spain would declare for the colonies, their success was assured. This was not an impossible vision, for it will be remembered that early in the century France and Spain had been tied together by a family relationship between their sovereigns. This relationship had been cemented into the "Family Compact," which had been revived by the French foreign Minister Choiseul in 1761 for the purpose of getting Spain to aid France in the fatal war of 1756-63. We have already noticed how in that war Spain was quickly worsted by British sea power and how in consequence she lost the Floridas to Great Britain at the Treaty of Paris in 1763. Now the substance of this "Family Compact" was that whoever made war on France, would have to make war on Spain, and vice versa; each would aid the other in war. If France was going to get into a war with England in behalf of the United States, Spain must be considered. Spain was at this time, as so often in her history, confronted by a wealth of policies; there were the best of reasons for going to war and for staying out. For half a century Spain and England had been intensely hostile to one another. Four times between 1700

---

[6] C. H. Van Tyne, "Influences which determined the French Government to make the Treaty with the United States in 1776," in *Amer. Hist. Rev.*, XXI, 528, and Corwin's *French Policy and the American Alliance*, 142-8.

and 1750 had there been open war between them, and the causes of those wars were by no means set at rest. England was, as we have noted, building up a great commercial empire, and the ambitions of her merchants knew not the limits of her own colonial markets, for they insisted on breaking into the Spanish monopoly and selling their cloth and their hardware in South America as well. This the Spanish resented, and particularly so, as the English smuggler made profits which would otherwise have gone to Spanish merchants. In addition, the British insisted on colonizing the coast of Honduras for the sake of the valuable woods to be gained there. This was trespassing on what Spain claimed was her property. Moreover, England and Spain were disputing the ownership of the Falkland Islands, and the English had acknowledged Spanish rights in 1748 only to violate them flagrantly in 1771, by practically denying the Spanish title which they had formerly admitted. Spain was quite ready to make war on England in 1775, but Vergennes was not ready to move, as he had not yet won over his own king. This gave the Spaniards a chance to take a second thought in the matter and it dampened their ardor for the war so that when Arthur Lee reached the Spanish border he was practically turned back.[7]

The Spanish were perfectly willing to help defeat England in a war, whereby they too might recoup their losses of the war of 1756–63, but did they want to help America? They paused at the thought. Bad news from America telling of the defeats of the Continental Army at Long Island and at Ticonderoga gave ample excuse for the delay which was now emphasized by the possible danger that the liberation of English North America would provoke a similar revolt in Spanish South America. If the English colonies could break loose from their mother, why could not the Spanish? Spain certainly did desire the overthrow of the British Empire but she had little enthusiasm for the independence of the United States as such. Furthermore, if the Americans gained their independence, the Province of New Spain

---

[7] C. E. Chapman, *History of Spain* (N. Y., 1918), 385–95; for the Family Compact see G. F. de Martens, *Recueil de Traites, etc.*, I, 16ff.

(Mexico) might have these radical revolutionists as a next door neighbor. Still more important, if the United States were to succeed to all the British rights in North America, they would want the right to navigate the Mississippi River and menace the Spanish trade in the Gulf of Mexico. For no sooner had the Revolution released the Americans from all obligation to remain east of the Appalachian Mountains, than a flood of emigrants crossed the watershed and began to fill up the New West. Mr. Roosevelt's story of the "Winning of the West" begins with the story of the pioneers who began to seep through the forbidden barrier between 1763 and 1775. As soon as the treaty of 1763 had made good the English claim to this back country, numerous speculative individuals and land companies got busy in an effort to get new homes beyond the mountains for the malcontents of the eastern seaboard. The same motives which led to the settlement of America led to her expansion.[8]

Salt licks were discovered beyond the mountains and the settlers were no longer held to the eastern seaboard by the need for this essential article of human life. Adventurers and ne'er-do-wells, hunters and farmers, in search of something new, refuge, furs or farms, all set out for the free lands beyond the mountains, and began to settle in the country between the mountains and the Mississippi long before the issue of independence was settled between England and the United States. Now these western folk had to live by their work. They raised corn and hogs and they trapped furs. Since there were no factories on the frontier they had to exchange what they raised for manufactured goods which they needed. But how could they get at the manufactured goods, the knives, and firearms and luxuries of life? Could they carry their corn and hogs back over the mountains and trade with the cities of the eastern seaboard? Obviously not. What then was their outlet to the sea and its commerce? The answer was the Mississippi River. That great artery of commerce was fed by the Ohio and its tributaries, where the new settlements were

<hr>

[8] T. Roosevelt, *The Winning of the West* (N. Y., 1896), I, ch. iii; C. E. Carter, *Great Britain and the Illinois Country* (Wash., 1910), pp. 27–45. P. C. Phillips, *The West in the Diplomacy of the American Revolution* (Urbana, Ill., 1913), 64–68.

being made.   Western produce could be put on flatboats and
floated down the rivers to New Orleans much more cheaply than
it could be dragged back up over the mountains to Philadelphia
or Baltimore.[9]   Hence the United States must secure the right to
navigate the Mississippi to the sea, and the right to use New Orleans as a port of deposit, or the west simply could not live at all.
But Spain owned the mouth of the Mississippi and would control
all this.   Hence Spanish diplomacy aimed at keeping the Americans back, while American diplomacy aimed at getting the Mississippi opened up to American traffic.   The prospect of this energetic neighbor assailing her back door alarmed the Spaniards,
and is it any wonder they hesitated to recognize American Independence?   Self-interest and self-preservation made the Spaniards
hesitate.   They were willing to grant and did give some secret aid
to the colonies by grants of money which were spent in Europe
for supplies, but we can well understand their reluctance to embroil themselves in another colonial war against England.

2. THE FRENCH ALLIANCE

Meanwhile his Most Christian Majesty of France had been
rushed into the conflict.   The defeat of Burgoyne at Saratoga
shocked the British ministry into offering the colonies *home rule
without independence*.   The French intelligence officers got wind
of the matter before it was made public and wrongly reported to
Vergennes that Britain was going to offer *independence* to the colonies, on condition that the United States then make common
cause with Britain in despoiling the French and Spanish of their
possessions in the West Indies.   Beaumarchais was now in a position to recall his warning, and he reminded Vergennes of the fact.
It was a case of now or never; France must act.[10]   Vergennes'
arguments were now seconded by a certain amount of pressure
from the fashionable society in the French court.   Franklin had
captivated the upper class of French society and the intellectuals,

---

[9] F. J. Turner, "Diplomatic Contest for the Mississippi Valley," in *Atlantic Monthly*,
XCIII, 676; F. Wharton, *Revolutionary Diplomatic Correspondence*, III, 344,
[10] C. H. Van Tyne, "Influences which determined the French Government, etc.," supra,
pp. 532ff.

or as we should say to-day, the *intelligentzia*. He made the most
of his personal popularity and did not hesitate to interpret the
American Revolution as a fulfillment of the prophecies of the
French Encyclopædists.[11] What diplomat would not have taken
advantage of such a situation? The time had come, the Americans would win, the French could recover their lost position and
prestige, and so two treaties were drawn up between the United
States and France, the first to be made by the new republic.

A Treaty of Amity and Commerce contained the provision
that each nation would grant to the other the privileges of the
most favored nation. Both agreed not "to grant any particular
favor to other nations in respect to commerce and navigation,
which shall not immediately become common to the other party,
*who shall enjoy this privilege freely, if the concession were freely
made, or on allowing the same compensation, if the concession was
conditional.*" Now this principle of granting a nation the same
privileges of trade that are granted the most favored nation, had
been practiced in European diplomacy for a long time. But this
first treaty of the United States introduced a new interpretation
of the principle. This new interpretation has been engrafted on
to the American diplomatic system, so that to-day there are two
separate, distinct and conflicting usages of the term, "the most
favored nation clause." For this clause seems to give a nation
special commercial privileges. At the same time there is another
sort of treaty, known as the "reciprocity treaty" which nations
may make with one another, whereby each party reduces or re-
moves certain customs duties on condition that the other party
reciprocates by removing certain duties in return. Now the
United States made this treaty in 1778 with the distinct understanding that even if she did grant France the privileges of the
most favored nation, that did not prevent the United States from
granting other special privileges by reciprocity treaty with some
other power, the benefits of which would not extend to France,
unless France was willing to compensate the United States by further concessions based on the reciprocity treaty. In other words,

[11] E. E. Hale, *Franklin in France* (Boston, 1887), I, 77.

there are two forms of the "most favored nation" clause, the conditional and the unconditional. The United States began thus early to adopt the conditional form, whereas most European nations then and now follow the unconditional form.[12]

The treaty went on to make certain provisions for mutual aid in case of war, which were sure to make trouble in the future. The ships of war of either nation and the privateers of either party were allowed to take their prizes into the port of the other in time of war, yet this privilege was not accorded to the enemies of the other. This would have been a clear violation of neutrality in a war in which either party chose to remain neutral. Moreover since in time of war the war vessels of either party might stay as long as they pleased in the ports of the other nation, even if it were neutral, this made the neutral a base of operations against a friendly power. This was all very well in view of the fact that both nations expected soon to be at war as allies against Great Britain. But this was not a part of the treaty of Alliance, but of the more permanent treaty of Commerce, and hence did not expire with the war, but lived to plague the United States when it wished to remain neutral in a later war. The United States then found itself committed to an outrageously unneutral course.

Other sections of the treaty had to do with the rights of neutrals in time of war, and the treaty took a very advanced and enlightened position in the matter. It practically provided that nothing but actual munitions of war should be regarded as contraband. Further it provided that, "free ships should make free goods," that is, that a neutral ship should be allowed to carry the goods of a belligerent unmolested, so long as these goods were not contraband. Heretofore the barbarous practices of the sea powers had frequently allowed the seizure of the private property of non-combatant persons sailing on a neutral vessel, merely because the person happened to be a citizen of the hostile country. All this put France and the United States among the more enlightened nations who were trying to soften the harsh sea law

[12] *Reciprocity and Commercial Treaties*, Rept. of the U. S. Tariff Commission (Wash., 1919), pp. 389ff.

which England had practiced since Elizabethan times, as we have observed. This was a distinct bid for the sympathy and aid of those other European nations, who for a century had suffered under the ruthless English interpretation of the laws of the sea. All the maritime nations of the continent had suffered from English privateers in many a war, and the English had not hesitated to seize the goods of an enemy citizen, even if non-contraband, and even if found on the vessel of a neutral power. This, the neutrals contended, was a violation of their national rights, as the deck of their vessel was considered as the soil of their neutral country.

The European neutrals did not at once join enthusiastically in this move to assert neutral rights in 1778. But two years later the Empress Catherine of Russia got into a high state of indignation because some of the belligerents began to violate the neutral rights of Russia, and treat Russian vessels according to the harsh English interpretation of sea law. So without directly accepting the Franco-American bid, she nevertheless proclaimed that Russia would establish an armed neutrality which included the provisions of the Franco-American agreement of 1778. Russia, she said, would defend its neutral rights by force of arms if necessary. That was exactly what Vergennes wanted. He persuaded the Spanish to join him in an enthusiastic welcome of Catherine's pronouncement, and other neutrals such as Prussia joined in the general clamor and protest against the harsh and ruthless English practices.

The "Armed Neutrality of 1780" practically forced England to observe for a short time the liberal and advanced position taken by France and the United States in their treaty, for Catherine's proclamation laid down the following principles of international law, (1) Free ships make free goods, i. e., an enemy's goods may be safely carried on a neutral ship without fear of capture if not contraband. (2) A blockade cannot be proclaimed on paper unless it is actually enforced by a navy. This was aimed at the British practice of proclaiming an enemy coast blockaded, and then not enforcing the blockade but occasionally capturing a neutral vessel which assumed that the blockade was at an end because so badly enforced. (3) The rights of the privateers were to be strictly regulated and limited. Privateers, as we have seen, were simply private persons, who, in time of war got letters of marque from their government and took any kind of a crew on to any kind of armed vessel of their own purchase and preyed on neutral and enemy commerce alike, unrestrained by the ordinary decency of international dealings which govern the official and regular navy.

When considered as an epoch in the diplomatic history of the world the "Armed Neutrality" was a brilliant phenomenon which soon vanished because the world was not ready for it. As soon as the war was over the nations sank back to the old practices and the next war found them as badly off as ever. Nevertheless, the "Armed Neutrality" had this merit, that it threw a strong flood of light on the dark corner in which the innocent bystander is robbed and beaten in a fight between two nations in which he is not interested. It could not be enforced unless the sea powers wanted it enforced, and in time of war the real positive source of sea law is the belligerent state itself. That is, England could practically make the law of the sea, because it was interpreted in her courts, where English judges sat as the judges in cases where English rights were involved. Hence the "Armed Neutrality" is not very significant from the legal point of view. But historically it is vastly important, because if someone had not started it as an educational process in 1780, it would not have been realized in fact in 1856, when the principles of the armed neutrality found partial expression and acceptance by the actions of the European nations generally. It is necessary to "state the case" before any reform can be effected and the "Armed Neutrality" of 1780 stated the case of the neutral and the rights of private property at sea.[13]

But to get back to treaties between France and the United States in 1778, we observe that there was another treaty. This

[13] J. B. Scott (ed.), *The Armed Neutralities of 1780 and 1800* (N. Y., 1918), 5, 7, 22–29, 116–25, etc.

was a treaty of Alliance, whereby the United States obligated
itself to fight in common with another nation, against a common
foe. The purpose of this alliance was on the face of it to gain independence for the United States, for which France agreed to
fight in case war broke out between France and England. Since
the very act of making a treaty with the rebellious Americans
gave England a right to make war on France, this event was assured. But the treaty went on in such a way that not only did the
King of France guarantee the independence of the United States,
but the United States promised to defend the American possessions of the King of France, i. e., the French islands in the West
Indies and elsewhere. This agreement was designated a "defensive alliance," in so many words. Now the American diplomats had gained both recognition and military aid from an open
ally.[14]

3. RELUCTANT SPAIN

The next work of the diplomats was to get Spain committed
to join in the war on the side of France and the United States.
This was now a good deal more difficult than it might have been
a little earlier. In the first place the Spanish Minister of foreign
affairs, Florida Blanca, seemed to feel that although such a war
obligated him to come in on the French side because of the operation of the "family compact," still France ought to have consulted him before taking final action. This involves a characteristic of Spanish diplomacy of the period. The Spanish court was
notoriously negligent in attending to business and the officials
were equally notorious for their leisurely way of answering their
correspondence. Then, if the correspondents were in desperation forced to act without Spain the Spanish diplomats were
highly offended and explained haughtily that their *amour propre*
had been hurt. The best translation for *amour propre* seems to
be "vanity," and the Spanish monarch and his entourage had
plenty of that to spare. But the others could not always wait
forever for Spain to act. Moreover, as we have pointed out,

[1] W. M. Malloy, *Treaties, Conventions, International Acts, Protocols, and Agreements
between the United States of America and other Powers, 1776–1909* (Wash., 1910), I, 480.

Spain was not at all anxious to have a democratic neighbor tempting her Latin American colonies to revolt, and interfering with Spanish ambitions to control the entire coast line of the Gulf of Mexico. So Spain tried first pompously to mediate between France and England, and being rudely rebuffed by England, she concluded a treaty with France to get into the American war.[15]

This treaty of Aranjuez between France and Spain in 1779 did not betray any desire on Spain's part to play the game in coöperation with her allies. Indeed, the United States can hardly be called her ally, for the United States was not a party to the treaty and Spain did not promise to recognize the independence of the United States, except in her own way and when she saw fit. Moreover Spain was not at all willing to admit that the United States extended west to the Mississippi River, or that the Floridas could be a part of the United States. His Most Catholic Majesty of Spain came in as a limited partner on conditions. He insisted that he had a right to regard the Floridas as still a part of the British dominions, which he might and in fact did capture during the war, through the unusual skill and daring of a young Spanish officer, Bernardo de Galvez, then governor at New Orleans. Now it really was a debatable question as to how far west the revolting colonies actually extended, and this forms the basis for the negotiations between the United States and Spain during the balance of the Revolution.

Arthur Lee had been the first United States envoy to Spain but he had been turned back at the frontier. He was succeeded by a brilliant and very persistent New York lawyer, John Jay, who went to Madrid in 1779 to secure Spanish aid if he could, but in any case to get Spain to admit the right of the United States to navigate the Mississippi River to its mouth, and other rivers flowing into the Gulf of Mexico. The Spanish contended that it was well known the colonies all had western boundaries along the Proclamation Line of 1763, that is, the watershed of the Appalachian Mountains. Moreover the Spanish contended

---

[15] F. Rousseau, "Participation de l'Espagne à la Guerre d'Amerique," in *Revue de Questiones Historique*, LXXII, 444.

that in no case could one of the American colonies be said to extend beyond those mountains. Before committing themselves the Spanish wanted this boundary question settled. Even if it were settled as the Americans contended, giving the Americans the Mississippi as their western boundary, they indignantly denied Jay's contention that just because the Americans bordered on the Mississippi in its upper waters, they were therefore entitled to navigate it to its mouth through territories which were Spanish because both banks of the river at its mouth belonged to Spain. It will be remembered that Spain had held the so-called "Island of New Orleans" since 1763. Hence Jay made but little progress at the Spanish court in his effort to secure a recognition of his arguments. Incidentally, Jay was probably wrong, even by the international law of that day, in his contention that because the United States had land in the upper reaches of the Mississippi that the Almighty had made the river a highway by which the people of the upper country had a right to get to the sea. They only had that right if Spain conceded it to them.[16]

Meanwhile the French were playing a difficult and double game. They had to keep the Spanish in line by promising that the United States should not be allowed to occupy the intervening territory between the mountains and the Mississippi, and at the same time they had to keep smiling at the Americans who were not only insisting on that territory but actually making good their claims. For General George Rogers Clark of Virginia was busy capturing the British posts along the Ohio River and clinching the American claims by force of arms, and Daniel Boone with his fellows was tying up Kentucky to the United States. Similarly, the Spanish captured the British forts in West Florida and sent expeditions up the Mississippi to capture other British posts. Spain and the United States worked independently; indeed, they almost came to blows over the division of the British spoil. True to her policy, Spain was not an ally of the United States, but was

---

[16] J. de Vattel, *Law of Nations*, Bk. I, secs. 245 & 278; John Jay, *Correspondence and Public Papers* (Johnston ed., N. Y., 1890–3), I, 248–461, II, 1, 296.

merely another enemy of America's foe, and she was playing her own game all by herself. Jay was finally instructed to waive the United States' claims to the right to navigate the Mississippi to its mouth, but Yorktown fortunately supervened and Jay did not give up his point.[17]

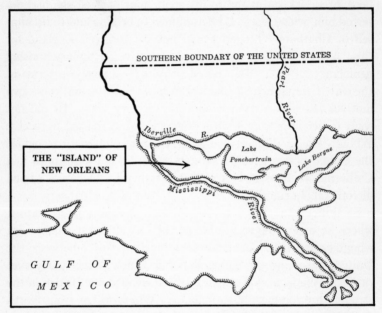

THE "ISLAND OF NEW ORLEANS" WHICH THE U. S. WANTED.

This map illustrates how the Spanish by holding the "Island of New Orleans" were able to shut the United States from the access to the sea by way of the Mississippi River. It was this "Island" which Monroe and Livingston were instructed to purchase when they succeeded in buying the whole of Louisiana. The "Independent State of West Florida" is that region between the Mississippi and the Pearl River which first revolted from Spain in 1810 and was annexed to the United States under the claim of its being part of the Louisiana Purchase, in 1812.

But even less successful than Jay had been William Lee, who was selected by the Continental Congress as its representative to Prussia and Austria. He was never commissioned for the latter place, and in any case it was hardly to be expected that he would meet with anything but a cold rejection at the court of Vienna,

[17] *Journals of the Continental Congress* (Ford ed., Wash.), XIX. 152–4; Wharton, *Revolutionary Diplomatic Correspondence*, IV, 267–9.

where for centuries the Hapsburgs had been breeding conservatism and a belief in the divine rights of royalty. More was to be hoped from Frederick the Great at Berlin, because he still nursed a deep-seated dislike of England for her shabby treatment of him in the Seven Years War of 1756–63. In that war, England had been Frederick's ally and in his great hour of need she had deserted him when George III determined to be king and to rid himself of Chatham. Frederick had not yet forgiven England for this. Yet at the same time, he had little love for the newly rising democracy as such. He viewed the situation solely in terms of the way it would benefit him in European politics, and these two motives led him to somewhat contradictory acts. He did not want to get into trouble with England and so refused to receive William Lee, and consequently he thereby refused to recognize the United States. At the same time he did not hesitate to join Catherine of Russia's "Armed Neutrality" which was aimed directly at England.[18]

So William Lee had returned through Germany to Frankfort, where he met a representative of the city of Amsterdam, with whom he drew up an utterly unauthorized treaty between the United States and the Dutch Republic which neither party ever ratified. We have seen how the Dutch rivalled the British in the struggle for commercial supremacy. When ousted from North America, the Dutch, like the French, had retained certain islands in the West Indies. Chief among these was the tiny island of St. Eustatius, which now jumped into importance as the market in which the revolted colonies could exchange their tobacco for Dutch gunpowder, with which to fight the British. The Dutch had been among the first to abandon the restrictive and monopolistic Mercantilist System, which dictated that a colony's trade should be confined to the Mother Country. The ships of all nations could freely come and freely go in the harbor at St. Eustatius. Now when the clouds of war began to gather in North America, the colonies passed certain non-importation agreements,

---

[18] P. L. Haworth, "Frederick the Great and the American Revolution," in *Amer. Hist. Rev.*, IX, 460.

which did to a certain extent hurt British trade, but to as great
an extent did they injure the Americans by cutting them off
from that flow of manufactured goods which ordinarily came
from England. For the Navigation Acts of the Old British Empire had not only restricted and regulated the commerce of the
British colonies in America. They had practically forbidden
the manufacture of such goods in the colonies as could be made in
England. In the effort to construct an economically self-sufficient
empire, the colonies were ordered to keep the English factories
supplied with raw material, which the English were forbidden to
raise, and the colonies were forbidden to manufacture articles
which it was presumed the English would manufacture for sale
in the colonies. The scheme worked both ways, for if the Americans were forbidden to make machinery, so were the English and
Irish forbidden to raise tobacco. But the sudden cutting off of
the stream of goods from England made a scarcity of manufactured goods in America.[19] Of course the Yankee felt sure he
could ultimately supply all his own needs, but in the meantime
he had to buy from some other European nations. The canny
Dutch merchant saw his chance to supplant the English manufacturer, and manufactured goods without number were shipped
to the little island of St. Eustatius. Here they were picked up
by North American vessels which carried the goods on to New
York or Philadelphia. As the revolution went on, the trade
doubled and trebled. Guns and ammunition were required in
greater numbers than the French "Hortalez et Cie" could supply,
and so tons of Dutch powder were shipped to St. Eustatius.
There it was exchanged for indigo and tobacco which found their
way to Amsterdam while the gunpowder was transshipped and
delivered to Washington's armies in North America. This trade
was extremely lucrative and the Dutch "profiteers" thought it
a bad deal in which they did not get a return of at least one hundred per cent on their investment. The neutral who has supplies
to sell can command his own price from the belligerent who must
get the munitions of war wherever he can at whatever price the

[19] G. L. Beer, *British Colonial Policy* (N. Y., 1907), 192–204, 226.

neutral will charge. Again we have the spectacle of a European war, in which the neutral Dutchman gathers in the proceeds while the English merchant sits in silent wrath and sees his trade disappear. Millions accrued to the profit of the. Dutch merchants, and the little island of St. Eustatius became one of the greatest ports in the western hemisphere, where thousands of vessels came and went every year. The British have never sat silent very long in such a situation and it was not long before they found an excuse for numbering the Dutch among their open enemies.[20]

Naturally the Americans wanted to get in touch with this wealthy neutral, who might be induced to grant recognition and more substantial financial aid in the shape of a loan. Henry Laurens was dispatched as the envoy carrying with him the unratified and therefore illegal draft of the treaty made by William Lee with the pensionary of Amsterdam. Both Laurens and the treaty fell into the hands of an English war vessel. The mere existence of the draft of a treaty, although unratified and made by an unauthorized party, was seized by the British as a pretext for declaring war on the Netherlands, and for wrecking St. Eustatius and breaking up the trade in munitions and American staples. The matter did not justify war but Great Britain was convinced that she had to smash St. Eustatius. John Adams was then selected by Congress to do its work which Laurens had been sent to do, and he succeeded admirably in getting a treaty of Amity and Commerce, and, what was more important, he floated a loan for the United States among the Dutch bankers who had waxed fat on war profits which the activity of St. Eustatius had given them.[21]

Meanwhile the British Admiral Rodney had made haste to get at the obnoxious and now hostile port at St. Eustatius, and he captured the port with all its contents, confiscating private property in a manner totally at variance with international law. But the very violence of his actions is evidence of the intense anger

[20] J. F. Jameson, "St. Eustatius in the American Revolution" in *Amer. Hist. Rev.*, VIII, 683.

[21] F. Edler, *Dutch Republic and the American Revolution* (Balt., 1911), p. 88ff.

aroused in the British heart by the fact that a Dutch port had taken in all the money which might otherwise have gone to Englishmen.   Indeed the prize was so rich that Rodney dallied too long on his plundering expedition and the French Admiral De Grasse slipped away from the English fleet in response to a summons from Rochambeau and Washington.   Sea power, Admiral Mahan tells us, is the dominant and decisive factor in warfare. The war of the revolution had dragged on discouragingly for years. Now for a moment the British lost control of the seas, which she had asserted in so many wars.   For a moment the French fleet controlled the most important bit of sea in the western hemisphere, and that was the stretch of water between General Cornwallis and the British base in New York.   Washington and Rochambeau closed in on the land side and while the British fleet glutted itself on the loot of St. Eustatius the French Admiral De Grasse settled the war of the American Revolution by cutting off Cornwallis' retreat.   Sea power won and for the moment sea power was in the hands of the French.   The war was over and now the task of the diplomats lay not in gaining allies and aid for the United States but in drawing up the terms by which Great Britain was to recognize the independence of the United States.[22]

[22] A. T. Mahan, *The Influence of Sea Power upon History, 1660–1783* (Boston, 1890), 382–400; F. E. Chadwick, "Sea Power, The Decisive Factor in Our Struggle for Independence," in *Repts. of the American Hist. Assoc.*, 1915, p. 173.

CHAPTER IV

DIPLOMATIC PROBLEMS UNDER THE ARTICLES OF CONFEDERATION

> "The speculative trader will at once perceive the force of these observations; and will acknowledge that the aggregate balance of the commerce of the United States would bid fair to be much more favorable than that of the thirteen states, without union, or with partial union."—*The Federalist.*

1. THE TREATY OF PEACE

The war for American Independence was conducted under a government which consisted of the old Second Continental Congress, and very little else. Since this body was but a shadowy legislative, there was practically no executive body, so necessary for the conduct of foreign relations. The old Secret Committee on Foreign Correspondence of 1775 gave way in 1777 to a Committee on Foreign Affairs, which in turn lasted until about the time the adoption of the "Articles of Confederation" gave the United States a central government. Before the ratification of these Articles some of the States, notably South Carolina and Virginia, tried to engage in independent diplomatic intercourse with European nations. But the ratified Articles of Confederation provided that the "United States in Congress assembled" was to have the sole right of conducting the international relations of the new nation and conversing with foreign powers.[1]

The right to be independent members of the family of nations was at the outset denied to the several states. This fact ought never to be lost sight of, because it makes the United States a state in international law and in fact denies that right to each of the late colonies which now wrongly began to call themselves

[1] The Articles of Confederation, arts. II and VI in W. MacDonald's *Select Documents in U. S. History*, 1776–1861, pp. 7–8; C. H. Van Tyne, "Sovereignty in the American Revolution" *American Historical Review*, XII, 540.

states. It is this fact which renders the second article of the Articles of Confederation a contradiction in terms as far as international law is concerned. Article II insists that each "state retains its sovereignty and independence" and then Article VI proceeds to take away from the states the most characteristic mark of external sovereignty and independence. So in the sense of international law, the so-called states, i. e., Massachusetts, New York, etc., are never thereafter either sovereign or independent, because they have not the capacity for sending envoys to foreign powers. Whatever degree of internal sovereignty or independence the states may have retained at this time is far beyond our intention and our province to discuss. Historians have differed endlessly on the subject and a great war was fought over it, yet there still seems to be some difference of opinion. Let us confine our attention to the undisputed fact that the United States, not individual states, had the right to send and to receive ambassadors. This fixed the status of the United States as a "state" in international society. Pursuant of this idea, and indeed before the last belated ratifications of the Articles of Confederation were at hand, a "Department of Foreign Affairs" was now created. Robert Livingston of New York served as the first Secretary of this department from 1781 to 1784, when he was succeeded by John Jay, who served until the New Government was formed under the Constitution in 1790.[2]

Of course the new secretary had no such independent powers as are ordinarily possessed by a secretary or minister of foreign affairs, for he was strictly the creature of that Congress in which all powers were vested, yet whose powers were both few and futile. The practice of European nations had usually regarded the conduct of foreign affairs as an executive function, and had vested it in the king in that capacity. The Americans, in their haste to get rid of all semblance of royalty, and to substitute therefor government by the people, had made the mistake of reducing their administrative officials to a pathetic

---

[2] R. T. Crane, *The State in Constitutional and International Law*, pp. 7-11, 73-74, in *Johns Hopkins Univ. Studies*, Ser. XXV; G. Hunt, *The Department of State*, pp. 14-38.

helplessness so characteristic of the first American government. Indeed the Articles of Confederation still further weakened its diplomatic function by permitting the states to retain jurisdiction over their foreign commerce. Despite the fact that it now possessed a Secretary of Foreign Affairs, Congress had to labor at many things which it ought to have handed over to that secretary, such as the appointing and instructing of diplomats. Indeed it sometimes had additional committees at work on matters of detail, which should have come under the jurisdiction of the Secretary of Foreign Affairs. This only emphasized the incompetence of government under the Articles of Confederation.[3]

But helpless as were the Americans, the British in the year 1782 felt themselves a good deal more helpless. The defeat of Cornwallis at Yorktown had demoralized the administration, and Germain and North both resigned, leaving poor George III to the mercy of the Whigs. England faced a hostile Europe, for she was at war with France, Spain, the Netherlands, and the United States, and the Irish were bestirring themselves as usual when they saw Britain in distress. The new ministry sent word to its commander in America not to risk another man in any cause. In the winter and spring of 1781–2 English representatives appeared at both The Hague and in Paris trying to get in touch with the Americans, for only at those two capitals had the independence of the United States been recognized. In the new ministry, Shelburne was the colonial secretary, and Charles James Fox the foreign secretary. The former sent Richard Oswald to Paris to get into communication with Franklin against the protests of Fox who insisted that since the colonies were now independent the matter came under his jurisdiction. The Americans did not care very much with whom they negotiated, but they wanted it distinctly understood that their independence was to be admitted before they began to talk at all. Vergennes

---

[3] J. M. Mathews, *The Conduct of American Foreign Relations* (N. Y., 1922), p. 28; Q. Wright, *The Control of American Foreign Relations* (N. Y., 1922), p. 138; J. W. Foster, *A Century of American Diplomacy* (Boston, 1900), pp. 103–4; *Journals of the Continental Congress* (Ford ed., Wash., 1914), XX, 615.

wanted them to be satisfied with Oswald's credentials, which did not include the admission of independence, but they refused to heed Vergennes' advice and won their point.[4]

For Congress had authorized its commissioners to treat only in case independence was admitted to start with. John Adams was selected as the American envoy to negotiate peace, he being then the representative at The Hague. Subsequently Franklin was also appointed to share in the negotiations and John Jay was bidden to leave his fruitless mission at Madrid and join the others at Paris. It was Jay who insisted on the correction of Oswald's credentials. Congress, at the solicitation of the French representative in Philadelphia, further instructed its commissioners to consult with their allies, the French, at every move, and to take no action without the consent of the French. These instructions were certainly explicit enough, "to make most candid and confidential communications with our generous ally" and "to undertake nothing in the negotiations for peace without their knowledge and concurrence." But in the meantime the "generous ally" was playing his own game. Vergennes, it will be remembered, did not enter the war from purely altruistic motives and a desire to free America from her oppressors. He had been actuated by a desire to bar the further advance of England, and he was simply using the United States as a lever to serve the interests of France. It seems very clear now that Vergennes was looking forward to the time when France would once more become an American power, through the recovery of Louisiana from Spain. To secure this, he had not the slightest intention of permitting the Americans to gain any territory west of the Allegheny Mountains. Indeed, one of his emissaries, Rayneval, had disclosed the desire of France to divide the territory west of the mountains and east of the Mississippi between England and Spain. Spain had no more desire than she had ever had to have the United States adjoin her air-tight empire in the southwest. Vergennes was not disloyal to the Americans. Indeed, there is

[4] E. Channing, *History of the U. S.*, III, 346–56 has told this story; see also A. C. McLaughlin, *Confederation and Constitution* (N. Y., 1905), pp. 3–16; and F. Wharton, *Revolutionary Diplomatic Correspondence of the U. S.*, V, 845–6, VI, 17.

Portrait by J. L. Mosnier in the William L. Clements Library

WILLIAM, EARL OF SHELBURNE

reason to believe that he had been misinformed by his agents in America and that he really believed the United States would not press its claim to the Mississippi Valley. He thought, in fact, that the United States were getting all they had any right to and all they wanted, if they were shut into the Atlantic seaboard. If he was mistaken, at least he was probably sincere, and certainly he was bound first of all to look after the interests of France.[5]

However, John Jay came to Paris fresh from negotiations with Spain which had convinced him at least of the utter insincerity of both Spain and France. He was alert to the fact that France would willingly sacrifice the United States in a peace which would profit herself and Spain, her fellow member in the "Family Compact." Why should such an old diplomatic combination as that of the French and Spanish foreign offices be expected to break in the face of the new upstart nation like the United States? Acting on his own initiative, Jay got into consultation with Shelburne, who had now become prime minister in England. Since he could not arouse Franklin's suspicions of his beloved French, and since the commissioner's instructions forbade the very step Jay was taking, the New York lawyer took the responsibility of acting without the knowledge of his colleagues. He had no intention of letting Franklin's perfectly natural friendship for the French, or any mistaken idea of gratitude, interfere in any way with what were apparently the interests of America. Shelburne thereby suddenly found himself confronted by a French envoy, Rayneval, working against the American interests, and an American envoy, Jay, acting against the French interests. Of course he was not at all displeased with the prospect of dividing his numerous enemies at the peace table and he encouraged Jay to further communications. The upshot of the whole matter was that Adams, who also distrusted the French, as well he might with his Puritan conscience and his New England training, supported Jay in deal-

[5] F. J. Turner, "Policy of France toward the Mississippi Valley" in the *American Historical Review*, X, 250–3; Lord Fitzmaurice, *Life of Shelburne* (London, 1912, 2 ed.), II, 186; *Journals of the Continental Congress* (Ford ed.), XX, 617; P. C. Phillips, *The West in the Diplomacy of the American Revolution* (Urbana, Ill., 1913), 118–30, 185.

ing separately with the English. The Americans negotiated with England alone, contrary to the instruction of Congress.[6]

The terms they made were really astonishingly successful, although at the time, they did not seem to think so themselves. But when we consider that the Americans represented the youngest member of the family of nations, that they were bargaining for terms with their one-time masters, that they actually occupied by settlement very little of the land west of the Alleghenies, that they had a government that was a pure farce from the standpoint of being a responsible agent for the conduct of international relations, we are bound to admit that they did pretty well. There is no denying the fact that the way was made easy by Earl Shelburne's favorable attitude toward them, for Shelburne wrote to the king's commanders in America that England's object was not merely peace, "but reconciliation with America, on the noblest terms and by the noblest means." [7]

Yet at this very beginning of American diplomacy we see a partial explanation of some of the rather striking successes of American diplomats. The British were represented by a solemn and not at all brilliant Scotchman, who met with three of the very keenest minds in American history. It is characteristic of American diplomacy to select diplomats for their general success and ability in life rather than for their expertness or proficiency in the science of diplomacy. European diplomats were usually trained by long experience at the various courts of Europe. American diplomats have frequently been any clever lawyer or successful business man who seemed able to conduct the negotiations. So at this time the astute Franklin, the learned Adams and the brilliant Jay were more than a match for any trained diplomats the British or French might have selected.[8]

---

[6] P. C. Phillips, *The West in the Diplomacy of the American Revolution*, 216–27; Wharton, *Revolutionary Diplomatic Correspondence*, V, 811; John Adams, *Works*, III, 300ff.; John Jay, *Correspondence and Public Papers*, II, 366ff.

[7] Fitzmaurice, *Shelburne* (2d ed., 1912), II, 136.

[8] W. H. Lecky, *History of England in the XVIIIth Century*, I, 284; E. Channing, *History of the U. S.*, III, 369; F. C. Lowell, "American Diplomacy" in the *Atlantic Monthly*, XCVII, 1; D. J. Hill, "Shall we Standardize our Diplomatic Service?" in *Harpers Magazine*, CXXVIII, 690.

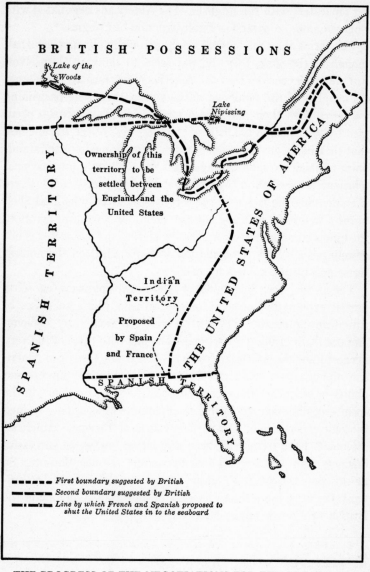

THE PROGRESS OF THE NEGOTIATIONS FOR THE TREATY OF
PARIS IN 1783

The first question to be settled was obviously that of the extent of the new nation. On this point the Americans gained all that they could possibly have desired. They insisted that their boundaries as colonies had extended to the Mississippi River and they would take no less. They frankly disregarded the Quebec Act of 1774 which had assigned a large part of the territory northwest of the Ohio River to the loyal colony of Quebec.[9] Such an act would have deprived them of half their title to the Mississippi Valley. They equally disregarded the schemes and machinations of the French and Spaniards, which aimed at the establishment of an Indian, or Spanish, state in the Southwest, between the mountains and the great river. Such understandings as the Latin allies had among themselves would have deprived the Americans of the other half of their frontage on the Mississippi. The principle of utilizing the old colonial limits formed the basis for negotiations and by that determination the western boundary on the Mississippi was made secure beyond dispute. The northern boundary, i. e., the boundary between the United States and Canada, called forth some discussion. But after considering a proposition to separate the two countries along the 45th parallel, and another to run a line from Lake Nipissing to the source of the Mississippi, it was finally agreed that the line should run thus: —up the St. Croix River and from its source, north to the mountains that separated the Atlantic watershed from the St. Lawrence watershed, to the head of the Connecticut River, thence to the 45th parallel, then due west to the St. Lawrence, and then by running down the middle of the lakes and their connecting rivers to the northwest corner of the Lake of the Woods. From that point the line was to run due west to the Mississippi River and then by way of the River to the 31st parallel, i. e., to the northern boundary of West Florida as it had been in 1763. This left Canada and the two Floridas in the hands of the English and it left the mouth and west bank of the Mississippi in the hands of the Spanish. In fact, however, Spain actually held West Florida, having captured it in the war. So in a secret arti-

[9] Royal Proclamation of that year in *The Annual Register* (1763), 208-13.

cle it was provided that in case England recovered West Florida from Spain in the treaty about to be made at Paris, the northern boundary should be at 32 degrees and 28 minutes. This simply meant that if England got West Florida she got that eighty thousand square miles more than Spain could get if West Florida was assigned to her.[10]

In view of the weakness of the United States at the time, her negotiators certainly did as well as could have been expected of them. Other questions in dispute interested the British a great deal more than the disposition of a few thousand square miles of American wilderness, even if later on those lands were to turn out to contain the most valuable copper deposits in the world. There were the questions of the loyalists, the fisheries, and the debts owed by Americans to British merchants. These concerned the British a good deal more than territorial dispositions. Now these "Loyalists," that is, "Tories" who had remained faithful to the King of England and thereby lost their estates through confiscation by the state legislature, were very much on the conscience of his Majesty and certainly a drain on his pocketbook. Their lands in America had been forfeited by the acts of the various states as a penalty for their failure to adhere to the patriot cause. Thousands of them were now living on the charity of the king and naturally he was anxious to get them paid off in some other way, But there was little chance of getting the state legislatures to restore the estates to people whom they regarded as traitors for not joining the patriot cause during the Revolution. It is characteristic of persons engaged in a war to have a peculiarly vitriolic kind of anger toward any neighbor who sympathizes with the opposite cause. The "copperheads" during the Civil War and the "pro-Germans" during the World War furnish more recent examples of the kind of indignation which the loyalists aroused in America during the Revolution. Now these people were homeless and subsisted on a pittance doled out by the King. The British felt that something should be done to secure for

[10] Wharton, *Rev. Dipl. Corr.*, V, 811, 853, VI, 96-9; W. M. Malloy, *Treaties and Conventions between the United States and Other Powers*, I, 580, 584, 586.

them a restitution of the property which had been taken away from them merely because they had been faithful to their king.[11]

In addition to this the British Commissioners insisted that something ought to be done to make the colonial merchants pay the debts which they had owed the British merchants since 1775. These debts had been contracted before 1775, but during the war, of course, it had been impossible to collect them. Now that America was independent, the only recourse of the British lay through bringing a suit in an American court. Although the debts were just and should have been paid, it would have been rather difficult to collect them through an American court where the jury would probably be men who had suffered from British depredations during the war. The Americans could not very well deny the validity of the claims, yet they could not be sure what difficulties the state legislatures would make about obstructing payment.

To offset these British claims the Americans sought to secure their fishing rights and indemnity for the damage wrought by the British Army during the war. This latter included all the unwarranted spoliation and plundering done by the British which seemed to the Americans quite in excess of what the ordinary exigencies of war required. A certain amount of destruction and depredation is admitted as necessary in war according to the international law of war. But the British were thought to have committed so many unjustifiable acts which in the language of to-day we would probably call "atrocities," that Franklin and his colleagues decided to use them as counterweights against the British claims. Moreover, the Americans had somehow to secure the rights to continue fishing off the Grand Banks of Newfoundland and to keep the inshore fishing privileges, such as the right to land and get water and bait, to dry their fish and to fish in the various creeks and bays of British America. It was impossible in those days for New England fishermen to make a profit in their business, unless they had the same privileges which they had

---

[11] C. H. Van Tyne, *The Loyalists in the American Revolution* (N. Y., 1902), 57, 125, 149; Wharton, *Rev. Dipl. Corr.*, V, 848, 850, 852ff.

enjoyed as members of the British Empire. These, as outsiders, they now attempted to gain, and one can be sure that the shrewd New England envoy, John Adams, was well posted on the needs of his fellow Yankees.[12]

To settle all these conflicting claims required a certain amount of give-and-take, and Franklin with his colleagues could be trusted to make the best of such proceedings. When Oswald began to talk about the claims of the loyalists, the Americans began to stress the amount the British would have to pay for all their alleged wrongdoing and violation of international law. Oswald suggested a set-off, but it was explained that the United States had no power to return the estates confiscated by the individual states. Failing to understand the utter helplessness of the government under the Confederation, Oswald allowed himself to be talked into consenting to the provision that "Congress would earnestly recommend to the legislatures of the respective states" the restitution of the property of the loyalists. On the point of the debts the British were adamant. They knew that no treaty would be accepted by the merchant class who ran the government of England in those days, which failed to provide for them. So article IV provided that no impediment should be thrown in the way of the recovery of debts lawfully contracted at any previous time, but did not stipulate that the debts should be paid.[13]

The question of whether the citizens of the new republic should be entitled to resume those old privileges of fishing off the Canadian coast which they had previously enjoyed as members of the British Empire, ushers in a dispute which required a century for its settlement. It is part of the whole controversy of the subject of the "mare clausum," or the right of a nation to shut off for its own particular use certain portions of the open sea. This controversy had raged in European diplomacy since the celebrated controversy between Grotius and Selden, in which the latter upheld Britain's right to shut off the North Sea and make it an English lake, while the former attacked that right. This question under-

[12] J. Adams, *Works*, III, 303, passim; Wharton, *Rev. Dipl. Corr.*, V, 852, 856, VI, 8, 77–80.
[13] Malloy, *Treaties and Conventions*, I, 588–9.

lay the fisheries controversy. The sinuosities and indentations of the coast of Canada made the determination of the extent of British jurisdiction difficult. Of course the right of a nation to control the sea three miles beyond the low-water mark had long been established in international law. But it made a great deal of difference whether the boundary line marking the three-mile limit followed all the indentations of the coast, or whether passing from headland to headland, it should include great stretches of the open sea. The Americans argued that they had the "right" to all things they used to do as subjects of the British Empire. The British argued that this could not be so, since they were no longer subjects of his Britannic Majesty. Unable to establish a right, the canny New England lawyer finally got written into the treaty that while the Americans should have the right to do as they would beyond the three-mile limit (the Grand Banks are beyond the three-mile limit), they should also have the "liberty" to the inshore privileges previously enjoyed, such as getting bait and water, and drying their fish. This distinction of fishing privileges which the Americans enjoyed as "rights" and those which they had acquired merely as a liberty granted by his Britannic Majesty, came to be of vast significance later on.[14]

The treaty also provided for the speedy withdrawal of the British troops from America, but they were to take away no plunder nor any property belonging to American inhabitants. As to the right to navigate the Mississippi to its mouth, it was not in the power of the British to grant this. But nevertheless, since Britain had acquired from France and Spain in 1763 the right to navigate the river to its mouth, she now presumed to pass on to America that right, and the Americans seemed to feel that this vicarious act on the part of England would be binding on Spain. Of course, as we shall see, Spain did not see the matter in this light. But this was as near as Jay could come to securing that right for which he had striven during four futile years at Madrid.[15]

Although the treaty was now agreed upon, there still remained

[14] J. B. Moore, *Principles of American Diplomacy* (N. Y., 1918), pp. 136–8; Wharton, *Rev. Dipl. Corr.*, V, 238–9, 240, 809, 821, 868–9, VI, 86–7.
[15] For Treaty of 1763 see *Annual Register* (1762), 233–47, art. iv.

the question of smoothing out the susceptibilities of the French, who had been justly ruffled at being totally disregarded, and also there remained the work of securing the approval and ratification of the British and of Congress. There was less trouble with the latter than with the former. Shelburne was mercilessly attacked in Parliament when the extent of Oswald's concessions were made known. It was in vain that he pointed out how he had taken care of the loyalists and the British merchants with their precious debts. He was forced to resign, and in the new ministry Charles James Fox returned as foreign minister. He had no hesitation about granting independence, and his envoy, David Hartley, who went to Paris to take Oswald's place, converted the preliminary treaty into a definitive treaty with hardly a verbal change. Vergennes was handled by the smooth-tongued Franklin, who shrewdly pointed out to the Frenchmen that he had better not let the English know there was any division of opinion between France and America, lest it go hard with the French when they came to settle with England. Rodney's victory over the French Admiral De Grasse gave strength to this argument, for France was put in a worse position by that event, which, however, did not injure the position of the United States. So Vergennes approved of what the Americans had done with the best grace he could muster.[16]

One more treaty had to be effected, and that was the agreement between England and our reluctant ally, Spain. In the War of Independence, the Spanish had captured West Florida from the British, and they now insisted upon the restitution of both East and West Florida to them, if England were to be permitted to retain Gibraltar, which she had defended with heroic courage during the war. So it was arranged with the result that the new republic was surrounded on the west and the south by the dominions of the Spanish king. According to Spain's understanding, West Florida meant West Florida as it had been when she captured it. But according to England's treaty with America it could only have meant West Florida according to the King's

---

[16] Wharton, *Rev. Dipl. Corr.*, VI, 140-4.

proclamation of 1763. The second royal pronouncement, that of 1764, had set the boundary of West Florida at 32 degrees and 28 minutes, and to this line the Spanish claimed. But the Americans would not allow it and from this came a ten years' dispute.[17]

2. IRRESPONSIBLE DIPLOMACY

The making of a treaty involved the assumption of international obligations, and the United States Government under the Articles of Confederation was in no position to assume any international responsibilities. Secretary Livingston of the Department of Foreign Affairs was the head of an office in which he was continually hampered by the vacillation and inefficiency of the Congress to which he was responsible. So he resigned in 1783 upon the conclusion of the preliminary articles of peace and after some delay his place was taken by John Jay. Few American secretaries have had to deal with more difficult problems under more maddening circumstances than those which confronted Jay between 1783 and 1790. In the first place there was France to be placated and paid off for the moneys she had advanced during the Revolution. But Congress had no money nor means of raising it, and it fell to Jay to do the explaining and to stave off the creditors. In the second place there was the treaty with England, the enforcement of which was to take more than ten years of bickering, due to the inability of Congress to comply with its provisions. In the third place there were the boundaries. In both the northeast and the northwest, the gentlemen at Paris had written on paper some adjustments which bore no relations whatever to the facts of geography, and it was fifty years before these difficulties were all straightened out. In the fourth place there was Spain and the ever present question of the Mississippi, complicated now by the secret article whereby West Florida was to have one boundary if it went to Spain and quite another if England kept it. As

---

[17] The Treaty between Spain and England is in the *Annual Register* (1783), 322–38; the Proclamation of 1763 is in the *Annual Register* (1763), pp. 208–13; the commissions to the governors of East and West Florida changing the boundary of West Florida is in Duane's *Laws of the United State of America*, I, 450–52; I. J. Cox, *West Florida Controversy*, pp. 14–20.

this involved some 80,000 square miles of the best lands of what are now the states of Mississippi and Alabama, the Spaniards could hardly be expected to give it up without a struggle and they did not. In the fifth place there was the problem of getting commercial treaties with Prussia and Russia and other European states. All these things had to be done by American diplomats instructed by a powerless secretary, who was responsible to a legislative body which could hardly function and had no power to enforce obligations made by diplomats in its behalf.[18]

In the midst of all this there appeared on the horizon the specter of church diplomacy which had so often stirred up Europe. The Papal Nuncio, as an ambassador from the pope is called, approached Franklin in Paris and asked that he communicate with his government and secure the consent of Congress to the establishment of a Roman Catholic ecclesiastical authority in the new republic. The United States probably saved itself an enormous amount of trouble by telling the pope that since his authority was "purely spiritual, it is without the jurisdiction of and power of Congress" to do anything about it. But getting an Anglican or Episcopal Bishop was a more serious matter for this was an important church in America and yet its bishops had to swear allegiance to the King of England. After some unofficial scurrying around by John Adams, during which he even thought of using a Danish Protestant Bishop, the matter was finally arranged and the Apostolic succession was carried on by the consecration of American Bishops by the Scottish primus and the Archbishops of Canterbury and York.[19]

But "government by supplication" was almost uniformly a failure. The Dutch bankers begged to be relieved of the embarrassment of having to refuse new loans, and their government pointed out the fact that some of the states were passing laws which violated the treaty which the United States had made

---

[18] *The Diplomatic Correspondence of the United States, 1783-1789* (3 vol. ed.) (Wash., D. C., 1837), II, 258, 562, 683.

[19] *Secret Journals of Congress*, III, 493; C. R. Fish, *Documents* in *Amer. Hist. Rev.*, XV, 800; *Dipl. Corr., 1783-89*, I, 453. A. L. Cross, *Anglican Episcopal and the American Colonies* (Harvard, 1902), p. 267.

with Holland.[20] Vergennes hinted that it was not safe to trade with a country whose credit was so dead as that of the United States under its pathetically helpless government. Since both England and Spain were looking for the speedy break-up of the United States, both nations dealt cautiously and slowly with her.

Spain continued to dodge the question of the Mississippi, but she laid claim to the disputed area in West Florida in no uncertain terms. In 1784, Spain distinctly told Congress that England had no right to pass on to the United States her right to navigate the great river, secured under the treaty of 1763. In the following year, Don Diego Gardoqui came to Philadelphia as the first Spanish envoy to the United States and in him Jay found an old-world diplomat as clever as Jay himself, and a good deal more crafty. Gardoqui was empowered to settle the outstanding difficulties, but this did not prevent the Spaniards from carrying on under cover some negotiations which might have had serious consequences. For the Spaniards were not above intriguing with the Indians in an effort to make life as unpleasant as possible for the Americans in the southwest. Indeed there was good precedent in European diplomacy for using savages and stirring them up against a supposedly friendly civilized nation and the Spaniards did not hesitate to use the Indians for that purpose.[21] The negotiations at Philadelphia likewise did not prevent the Spaniards from plotting to detach the southwest from the United States and to make it a new nation, which they might swallow up at their leisure. They found that thousands of Americans were leaving the debt-ridden east and hurrying across the mountains into Kentucky and Tennessee. These were an independent lot of pioneers, who might readily refuse to stand on ceremony. If the diplomats at Philadelphia did not speedily get them their right to navigate the Mississippi, why should they not think seriously of forming another nation in the southwest and negotiating with Spain on their own account for the privilege of sending their

[20] F. Edler, *Dutch and American Relations during the Revolution* (Johns Hopkins Studies, ser. XXIX, No. 2); *Dipl. Corr., 1783–89*, I, 467, 470, 478, III, 437.
[21] *Secret Journals of Congress* (Dec., 1784); Gayarré, *Hist. of Louisiana*, III, 185–92.

corn and hogs down the river? [22] A renegade ex-American army officer, James Wilkinson by name, actually offered his services to Spain and swore allegiance to her king in this nefarious enterprise. Even the more respected names of George Rogers Clark, Sevier and others are found mixed up in this business.[23] Meantime Gardoqui was a good deal more interested in calling the attention of Congress to its inability to prevent depredations on the Spanish territory in the southwest than he was in settling anything, and nothing was settled. The United States was in a sad plight as regards its foreign relations in this direction.[24]

But no less important was the foreign policy in regard to Great Britain. It was imperative for the commercial recovery of the nation that the Americans be able once more to enter the West Indian trade, to sell their lumber for the manufacture of sugar boxes and barrels in the Sugar Islands, and to sell their secondrate fish for the slaves on the sugar plantations. But this was forbidden by those same British Navigation Acts of which we have heard so much as well as by similar provisions of the Mercantilist System in other nations. Illicit trade went on, of course, but the redoubtable Horatio Nelson was now the second in command in the British Navy, West Indian station, and he was ever hot on the trail of the American smugglers. What was lost in the islands might have been made up in the fur trade in the northwest.

However, the British still clung tenaciously to those western trading posts along lakes Ontario, Erie and Huron which they had promised to surrender but had never in fact given up. The motives for British refusal to do as they had promised are now manifest. In the first place these posts were held in pawn by the British until the United States should pay the much talked of debts and compensate the loyalists, as the British assumed had been promised under the treaty. In the second place the British had promised the Indians not to abandon them to the Americans,

---

[22] A. C. McLaughlin, *Confederation and Constitution*, p. 95.
[23] W. R. Shepherd "Wilkinson and the Beginning of the Spanish Conspiracy," *Amer. Hist. Rev.* IX, 490ff.
[24] *Dipl. Corr., 1783–89*, III, 202–4.

and yet had done just that thing, and were now put to it to explain why. They therefore compromised by keeping the posts, and the Canadians, who had most at stake, went on supplying the Indians with arms with which to harry the American frontier settlements. In the third place, the Canadian fur traders drew most of their furs from the American side of the border, and they had not the slightest intention of surrendering this lucrative trade without a protest, merely because some gentlemen sitting in Paris had decreed a boundary line which would ruin their business. In the fourth place, when Sir Guy Carleton had withdrawn the British troops from the soil of the United States, he had taken away with him a great number of negroes who had sought refuge with him from their American masters. This was taking property away from the Americans, in clear violation of the treaty which provided that all such plunder should be left behind by the departing troops.[25]

When our first Minister to England, John Adams, tried to smooth out these difficulties he was bluntly told that the posts would not be surrendered till the debts were paid, although this was not in accordance with the treaty. England's position is of course readily comprehensible. She had no intention of opening up the West Indian trade so as to share the profits with America and take the money from the pockets of her own merchants. Moreover her debts were still unpaid and her loyalists uncompensated. Yet it was in this very field of commercial privilege that the Americans desired the most from Great Britain. Up to 1787, American commerce diminished, and the application of still more stringent navigation acts still further injured American trade. These were years of a serious commercial depression in the United States, due to the usual after-the-war reactions, the inflation of the currency and necessary economic readjustment. But the helplessness of a country that had thirteen separate governments all trying to regulate foreign trade at the same time, and

[25] E. Channing, *Hist. of the U. S.*, III, 392–427; A. C. McLaughlin, "Western Posts and British Debts," *Amer. Hist. Assoc. Rep.*, 1894, pp. 413–45; *Dipl. Corr.*, *1783–89*, 478–81; *Secret Journals*, IV, 186ff.; W. E. Stephens, "Fur Trading Companies in The Northwest," *1760–1816*, *Proc. Miss. Vall. Hist. Assoc.*, IX, 283.

all trying to retaliate in different ways against the British made both their regulations and their retaliations equally futile. Great Britain had naturally no desire to make a commercial treaty with a nation in which thirteen subsidiary governments all had the right to violate the treaty. No treaty of commerce with the United States was worth the paper it was written on. The truth was, of course, that the British knew they would get American rice and tobacco no matter what happened, because the Americans had to sell it. But the Americans were not at all sure to get the English manufactured goods they wanted, as Britain had plenty of other markets and could afford to name her own terms in dealing with the feeble Americans. England had the whip hand and naturally used it.[26]

3. The Barbary Pirates

One other aspect of our diplomacy during the period of the Confederation deserves attention and that is our relationship with the Barbary Powers. The Mohammedan states of Tunis, Tripoli, Algiers, and Morocco occupied the north coast of Africa from Egypt to the Atlantic. They considered themselves perpetually at war with all Christian nations and in view of the fact that the Christians had themselves been preaching that doctrine toward the so-called Infidel for many centuries, it is no wonder that the heathen finally learned it. Acting on this assumption, the so-called Barbary Powers were accustomed to raid all European commerce in the Mediterranean and beyond, and as often as they captured European vessels, they took them into port as prizes and enslaved the crews. The only way to recover Christian sailors thus enslaved was to ransom them at a heavy price, which was regularly done by the Christian nations.

That civilized Europe tolerated this practice so long as it did is really astonishing. A feeling of dread seems to have survived in the European foreign offices, based on what the really formidable Barbary States of the sixteenth century had been. Likewise

---

[26] W. C. Fisher, "American Trade Regulations before 1789" in the *Papers of the Amer. Hist. Assoc.*, III, 223; *Dipl. Corr.*, *1783–89*, I, 728, II, 406, 467–71.

the European diplomats had so many irons in the fire in the eighteenth century, that one can understand how they might overlook changing circumstances in Africa.[27]   At any rate the first-rate powers of Europe meekly paid this international blackmail to the pirates. Of course England was the only first-rate power strong enough to break up the practice, but even she preferred to pay tribute, amounting to hundreds of thousands of dollars a year. There is not lacking the suspicion that England preferred to keep the Barbary pirates in existence as it hurt her trade rivals and saved her the cost of harrying them herself.[28] The fact that the so-called civilized nations of Europe have allowed the murderous Turk to remain in Europe so many centuries, is some evidence of the fact that nations who ought to know better are not above using savage peoples to injure their civilized brethren if it can be done to profit.

However all this may be, the Americans were exempt from such seizure before the Revolution, because they were English and England paid their blackmail and their tribute for them. But when the colonies broke away from the Mother Country, they broke away from her protection likewise. All sections of the United States were interested in trading in the Mediterranean ports. The fish from the New England states, the wheat from the middle states and the rice from the southern states all found some of their best markets in the French and Italian cities on the European coast just across the way from the Barbary States.[29]

The corsairs soon discovered that the Americans were now good prey and booty for them. The United States tried unsuccessfully to get France to assume the job of protecting our commerce, but France politely told Congress to deal with the pirates themselves.[30]   However Congress did nothing, not so much because it liked to endure such insults, as because of its

---

[27] S. Lane-Poole, *Story of the Barbary Corsairs*, p. 256; C. O. Paullin, *Diplomatic Negotiations of American Naval Officers, 1778–1883* (Balt., 1912), p. 47.

[28] E. Schuyler, *American Diplomacy* (N. Y., 1886), pp. 194–5; Letter of Theo. Sedgwick to Caleb Strong, 6 Aug. 1786 in *Amer. Hist. Rev.*, IV, 329.

[29] *American State Papers (Commerce and Navigation)* X, 41-7; *American State Papers, Foreign Relations*, I, 104; *Secret Journals of Congress*, II, 10, 28.

[30] Wharton, *Rev. Dipl. Corr.*, II, 698, 731, 743, 752, III, 192.

inability to act. The loss of the Mediterranean fish market was due to a lack of ability of Congress to make the necessary treaties. Meantime American ships were seized and American sailors enslaved. John Adams, our minister at London, had to go and call on the Tripolitan Ambassador, who was a grade above him in diplomatic rank, due to the American practice of not sending out Ambassadors. The lordly representative of the corsairs admitted that America was a very great country, but of course Tripoli was at war with it, and would be so until the United States made a treaty and paid its tribute to the masters of the Mediterranean. According to his notion, all nations not paying blackmail were *ipso facto* at war with Tripoli. But Congress could not pay and this was another of the many matters in which the United States drifted in helplessness under the Confederation.[31]

One other department of the government under the Confederation deserves our attention, and that is the court provided for cases involving the maritime law of war. In every war the international law of the sea entitles a belligerent to prey on the enemy's commerce. But an admiralty court must be established to which all cases must be brought and in its capacity as a prize court, it determines the validity of the capture, and divides the prize money accordingly. This court administers not the law of its own nation alone, but international law, and it deals with international relations. Hence it frequently becomes interesting to neutral nations as well as to belligerents and its conduct may be a source of infinite diplomatic trouble.

The Revolution did away with the English Admiralty Courts in America and the states began to establish their own prize courts. Seeing that conflicting practices might arise if each state were a law unto itself, the Continental Congress adopted a series of resolutions in 1775 trying to secure uniform usages in the trial of prize cases, and allowing appeals to Congress from the state admiralty court. A special committee took care of these appeals

[31] J. Adams, *Works*, III, 373; *Dipl. Corr.*, *1783–87*, I, 791; Jefferson's *Works*, I, 428; Letter of Stephen Higginson to John Adams, 8 Aug., 1785, in the *Amer. Hist. Assoc. Rep.*, 1896, 723.

until in 1780 a "Court of Appeals in Cases of Capture" was established by Congress. This was consistent with the provisions of the Articles of Confederation that "The United States shall have power of establishing rules in all cases of capture and shall establish courts for determining final appeals in such matters." This court continued to function until the formation of the Supreme Court of the United States which took over this jurisdiction after the formation of the government under the Constitution and the entire reorganization of the government which the inefficient conduct of foreign affairs had proven to be so abundantly necessary.[32]

[32] J. F. Jameson, "The Old Federal Court of Appeals," *Papers of the Amer. Hist. Assoc.*, III, 383; *Journals of the Continental Congress* (Ford ed.), XIV, 885.

CHAPTER V

A FRESH START AND THE EXAMPLE OF NEUTRALITY

"But, if the achievements of Washington and his contemporaries were remarkable in the national sphere, hardly less so were they in the international. . . . I will only say that the foundations were then well and surely laid of the foreign policy which the United States has in the main since pursued."—*John Bassett Moore.*

1. THE MACHINERY OF DIPLOMACY

At last the desperate plea made by those who were trying to run the old government was heeded. A new national constitution was drawn up in 1787 and it went into operation in 1789. The year 1788 was spent in trying to secure the approval of the people of the United States of the new instrument. The strongest and most eloquent appeal for ratification by the states was made in a series of articles known to history as "The Federalist," written by Hamilton, Jay, and Madison in their effort to win the people of New York to adopt the new frame of government. "No nation" argued the *Federalist*, "No nation acquainted with the nature of our political association under the Articles of Confederation would be unwise enough" to enter into any international arrangements with the United States. We were a discredited nation, said the authors, and not the least eloquent of their papers were devoted to a consideration of the proper method of conducting international relations in contrast with the pitiful weakness, in that respect, of the Confederation. Indeed the authors were well qualified to draw a gloomy picture of the conduct of foreign affairs under the old government which they were striving to replace.[1]

Their efforts were crowned with success and in the next year a full-fledged national government with a real executive, a real legislative and a real judicial department came into being. It

[1] *The Federalist*, Nos. XXII and esp. LXIII; see also XI, LXIV and LXX.

was in these particulars that the old government had been so sadly deficient.[2] As the Constitution has been since 1789 the instrument through which the United States has been governed, it is well to look a moment at the provisions it made for the conduct and control of foreign relations. Coincidentally with international law, the constitutional law of the United States is the supreme law under which she talks to and negotiates with other nations.[3] Treaties which are made with foreign nations are part of the supreme law of the land, and they override prior laws made by Congress or by any state legislature, although of course subsequent laws made by Congress may override treaties.[4] Other nations must remember that in their dealing with the United States, the United States is bound by its constitution as well as by international law, and it is the function of the United States government to conduct its foreign relations so as to obey international law and constitutional law at the same time. This is no easy task. It is also the work of the United States government to maintain the good faith and credit of the United States and hence not to pass laws which conflict with the treaty rights previously given foreign nations. This likewise presents some serious problems.

The control and conduct of foreign relations is not under the constitution given to any one of the three departments of government. To the President is given the right to send and to receive ambassadors. To the President and the Senate is given the power to make treaties and other international obligations and bargains. The carrying out of such treaties and other international obligations is partly the work of Congress and partly the work of the executive. To Congress is given the power to declare war, but the position of being commander-in-chief of the army and navy is given to the President. The enforcement of treaties as law and the interpretation of treaties within the United States is given to the new Supreme Court of the United States which now takes over the admiralty jurisdiction and international law func-

[2] Q. Wright, *The Control of American Foreign Relations* (N. Y., 1922), p. 145.
[3] J. M. Mathews, *The Conduct of American Foreign Relations* (N. Y., 1922), pp. 190-2.
[4] Q. Wright, ibid., pp. 1-9.

tions of the old "Court of Appeals" of the Confederation. Thus it is seen that the idea of separation of powers, so dear to the Fathers of the constitution, failed them here, as they could not give the conduct of international relations to any one department. But they did follow out their theory of "checks and balances" by dividing the function up among all three departments.

The fact probably is that those celebrated political philosophers, Montesquieu and Locke, who gave us the idea that there are three departments of government, have been pretty generally misunderstood. Both of them put the conduct of foreign affairs in a separate department, all by itself, and if the United States really wanted to follow their ideas, she ought to have a "fourth department," and a kind of political fourth dimension, to function in this regard.[5] However, the Fathers did not see fit to make this fourth department and divided its functions among the other three.

By practice, the Executive department at once became the organ of international communication. Obviously one department had to conduct the correspondence and talk to the foreign countries, and naturally that would be the department which sent and received the ambassadors. Equally obviously the necessity for dispatch and secrecy in communications indicated the Executive as being the department through which action was best secured. The President then became the sole mouthpiece of the nation in talking to other nations.[6] An Executive Department had at once to be organized to meet this need, as obviously the President had several other things to do besides conduct diplomatic negotiations. So just as a "Department of Foreign Affairs" had been found necessary under the Confederation so a new "Department of Foreign Affairs" was created by act of Congress in 1789, this time responsible to the President instead of to Congress. There were certain tasks of keeping and preserving the records and the seal of the new government, which did not properly fall to the duty of the newly organized departments of

[5] Q. Wright, *Control of American Foreign Relations*, pp. 142-3; John Locke, *Treatise on Civil Government*, secs. 144-48; Montesquieu, *Spirit of the Laws*, XI, c. 6.
[6] Q. Wright, ibid., pp. 21-7.

War and Treasury, and so Congress, apparently deciding that the Department of Foreign Affairs would not have enough to keep it busy, gave those tasks to it.   The duties of being a public office were then loaded on to the Department of Foreign Affairs and Congress decided to change its name and call it the "Department of State." So it was that our Department of Foreign Affairs has a queer title, quite inappropriate to it, and different from that of similar departments elsewhere in the world.[7]

The power of making international contracts, or bargains, which are called treaties, was given to the Executive Department jointly with the Senate. The President could act only "by and with the advice and consent of the Senate." The President may negotiate a treaty, but unless the Senate approves, the treaty is not binding on the United States. This veto by the Senate will become very important, as we shall see, in the course of American diplomatic history.[8]

In the matter of framing foreign policy and dictating what line of conduct the nation shall pursue toward any given nations or situations, the constitution is silent. But by interpretation and construction the President practically has the principal power. This is because he can really guide the course of events by reason of the fact that he alone can talk to foreign nations and hence commit the nation to certain courses of action from which it might be embarrassing to turn back. Of course, there is a limit on this as Congress need not back him up, and Congress has control over war and peace. But, as will appear later, it is quite possible for the United States to be put in such a position by the President that it must declare war, whether Congress likes it or not.[9] Congress by its power to regulate trade may, however, seriously interfere with policies which the President has initiated. The Judicial Department has expressly disclaimed any share in the framing of policies.[10]

[7] G. Hunt, *The Department of State*, pp. 65-74.

[8] Q. Wright, *Control of American Foreign Relations*, pp. 261-2; J. M. Mathews, *Conduct of American Foreign Relations*, 130-68.

[9] W. Lippmann, *Stakes of Diplomacy*, pp. 15-25.

[10] Jones *v.* U. S., 137 U. S. 202 (1890).

It will be seen that very little power is left to the individual states, or component members of the United States. They are, in fact, denied any personality in the international sense. They are not and can never in international law claim to be "sovereign and independent states" because they are in the technical sense no longer states at all, but merely subdivisions of a larger state into which in the international sense they all merged. The only power of affecting foreign relations which is left to them is that of passing laws which might and in certain cases has embarrassed the United States by making it impossible to protect foreigners in the United States whom the state law did not adequately protect.[11]

When Washington was chosen the first chief executive of the United States, he in turn selected Thomas Jefferson as his first Secretary of State. Jay held on to the papers of the old "Department of Foreign Affairs," until Jefferson returned from his station at Paris where he was then the United States minister. A new set of American ministers were then duly selected by the President and confirmed by the Senate and sent abroad as American diplomats to represent the United States at foreign courts. It is to be noticed that although the constitution permitted the United States to send out "ambassadors," none were sent out. Instead, we deliberately chose to send out only those of the second rank in the diplomatic classes, namely, "ministers." This was done on the theory that an "ambassador" represented the sovereign of a country and that we had done away with sovereigns, and thereby it would be more dignified and appropriate to have all American envoys ranked as "ministers." The result was anything but dignified, as the American minister had often to kick his heels in an anteroom while the Ambassador of Turkey took precedence over him merely because he was an ambassador and the American was but a minister.[12] One other appointment of

[11] Q. Wright, *Control of American Foreign Relations*, pp. 129–30; J. P. Hall & C. C. Hyde, "State Interference with the Enforcement of Treaties," *Proc. of Acad. of Pol. Sci.*, VII, 548–64.

[12] E. Schuyler, *American Diplomacy* (N. Y., 1886), 109–13; J. W. Foster, *The Practice of Diplomacy* (Boston, 1906), pp. 21–23.

Washington's should be noticed and that is the elevation of Hamilton to the place of Secretary of the Treasury. The almost bankrupt condition of the United States made his position of importance in foreign relations in which he was a factor as long as he remained in the cabinet.

2. The Policy of Neutrality

No sooner had the new government made its fresh start in the family of nations than it found itself confronted by one of those European quarrels, which had so often before resulted in war and which always before had involved American lives and American property. It came about in this way. The fur trade on the northwest coast of North America was becoming every year more important. A small inlet on the western shore of Vancouver Island, known as Nootka Sound, was the center of the British, Spanish and Russian fur trade, and all three were anxious to secure it. The Spanish held to the old theory that all the lands washed by the Pacific Ocean were theirs by right of discovery and the papal demarcation grant. The British held to the newer theory that actual occupation gives better title than mere discovery. A conflict ensued between the two foreign offices, which was complicated by the violent seizure of some British vessels by the Spaniards.

Thus there was prospect of war in Europe and such a war was going to be a war between two neighbors of the new republic, as British and Spanish territory adjoined ours on three sides. This would inevitably put the United States in the embarrassing position of being a highway across which the two neighbors would like to attack one another. Spain bristled because she thought France would be bound by the "Family Compact" to support her in a war against England. England was indignant that anyone should challenge her sea power. Both wanted the northwestern fur trade, because of the enormous fortunes which could be made from it. Both claimed the west coast of North America. Both now prepared for war. Pitt sounded out his allies in Europe and then decided that the best way to get at Spain would be to send troops from Canada across the United States and capture Spanish Louisiana.[13]

The British minister accordingly sounded out the Washington administration in the matter. This put squarely up to the government the question of whether the United States was to continue to be a football of European politics. Washington's cabinet was divided. Jefferson, always distrustful of England, advised against letting the British through as a matter of policy. He argued that England would inevitably win such a war and if England got the Spanish territory in North America, we would be surrounded on three sides by British territory and would never get the much needed right to navigate the Mississippi.[14] Hamilton took the exactly opposite view and insisted that since England would certainly win such a war, we would be at England's mercy anyway and it would be better to have England under obligations to us and to be on her side, so that we might share in the fruits of victory, and get New Orleans for ourselves.[15]

John Adams presented the sanest view of the matter, for he pointed out that by following the law on the subject we would find the best way out of the difficulty. Any act by which the United States permitted her soil to be used as an avenue of attack by one belligerent on another would be a violation of neutrality. It was clearly to our interest to remain neutral in a fight in which we had no concern, and the law gave us the right to remain neutral and to conduct ourselves accordingly. If we showed any favoritism to either side we gave the other side the right to charge us with unneutral conduct, for which we would have to pay certain penalties.[16] From this mass of conflicting advice Washington formulated a policy of neutrality which was to be our ideal for a century. So in this capacity as secretary of state Jefferson notified England and Spain that we would not be indifferent to their acts and moreover that we were very

---

[13] W. R. Manning, "The Nootka Sound Controversy," *Am. Hist. Assoc. Rept.*, 1904, pp. 412–19; E. D. Adams, *Influence of Grenville on Pitt's Foreign Policy* (Carnegie Inst. Publication No. 13).

[14] Jefferson's *Writings*, II, 100; VII, 568; IX, 412 (Washington ed.).

[15] Hamilton's *Works*, IV, 48.

[16] John Adams, *Works*, VIII, 497.

much interested in any territorial readjustments on our frontiers, but that it was our desire and intention to remain neutral. To stress our interest in the matter he even suggested that in case war broke out, Spain had better cede Florida and New Orleans to the United States, thereby launching not only the doctrine of neutrality but another and more far-reaching idea. The notification to Europe that the United States was not going to join either side was important enough in itself. But the second part of the message gave notice that if any American territory changed hands, the United States was going to see to it that it came to her.[17]

The Nootka Sound episode did not result in war because France could not support Spain. The Spanish were quite unable to handle the British by themselves and trusted to the "Family Compact" to bring France to her support. But about that time the "Family" part of the compact was beginning to go to pieces. The French Revolution was gathering strength and the new French government began to raise questions about the desirability of going into such a war. The war power was taken from the king and Spain was left in the lurch. She soon came to terms with Britain and the affair was closed.[18] It had, however, two interesting aspects. In the first place it was a forecast of the neutral tradition of the United States. In the second place there now appears in international relations that curiously passionate professional revolutionist, Francisco Miranda, who flitted from foreign office to foreign office in an effort to enlist the support of England and of other countries on the side of the Spanish American Colonies in a possible war of independence against their Mother country. This time he laid a definite plan for the emancipation of South America before Pitt, but as the affair simmered down, nothing came of it.[19]

[17] W. R. Manning, "Nootka Sound Controversy" in *Am. Hist. Assoc. Repts.*, 1904, pp. 420-23; Jefferson's *Writings*, V, 216-25.

[18] F. M. Fling, *Mirabeau and the French Revolution* (N. Y., 1908); W. R. Manning, "The Nootka Sound Controversy," *Am. Hist. Assoc. Rept.*, 1904, 388-94.

[19] W. S. Robertson, "Francisco de Miranda and the Revolutionizing of Spanish America," *Am. Hist. Assoc. Rept.*, 1907, I, 498-9; also his *Rise of the Spanish American Republics*, pp. 32-6.

However the spreading conflagration of the French Revolution now drew Europe into that European War which Washington had been afraid the Nootka Sound affair would provoke. This time the question of neutrality was put up to the United States by the French demand that we were bound to come to their aid. Under the Treaty of Alliance in 1778, the French assumed that whenever war broke out between England and France we were bound by the treaty of alliance to go to their help. It will be remembered that the treaty did stipulate that the United States should guarantee "from the present time and forever" the possessions of his Most Christian Majesty in the West Indies. Now England and France were once more at war in Europe and France asked us to assume our obligations under the treaty. True it was that the treaty had been framed to help America win her independence and true it was that that independence had been won. But it was equally true according to the French point of view that such an alliance was a continuing affair and now they in turn needed the help of the United States and asked for it.

In the first burst of enthusiasm for the Revolution in France, there were thousands who felt that the time had now come for the United States to live up to its part of the bargain. But as the Revolution passed into the hands of the radicals, American ardor began to dampen. The bloody excesses which culminated in the execution of King Louis XVI began to divide American sentiment on the subject of the war in Europe. More and more of the Federalists came out as pro-English, and the more the New England shipowners began to think soberly on what was going to happen to them in case the United States acceded to the French demand, the less enthusiastic they were about it. It would mean war with England, and war with England would mean the ruin of the New England merchant marine. Moreover the French Revolution had reached a stage of idolatry or fetish worship on certain abstract political ideas, which was more interesting to the Virginia planter than it was to the calculating Bostonian. So a sectional difference began to appear, in which the canny Yankee favored England while the more emotional southerner supported France.[20]

In the midst of all this uncertainty as to what to do under the treaty of 1778, the new minister from the French Republic landed at Charleston, S. C., and began his triumphal progress to Philadelphia. Now Charleston was probably the very worst place where he could have landed, for there were all his friends and sympathizers, the Jeffersonian faction, who did not by any means represent the dominant interests in the United States. Hence the new minister, Citizen Genet, as he was styled, was decidedly misled on what America proposed to do in the war. Thus misinformed, he utilized the hysterical enthusiasm of the moment to organize hostilities against England when in fact he was on neutral American soil. He began to act as though the United States was at war with England, when of course the reverse was true. He undertook to fit out privateers, i. e., units of the French Navy from the American port of Charleston. These vessels, bought, armed, equipped and manned in an American port then sailed out to prey on British commerce and instead of taking their prizes to the admiralty court of France, Genet organized French prize courts at the headquarters of the French consuls in America. This amounted to establishing a French court on soil where only American courts were supposed to have jurisdiction, a clear violation of the most elementary rights of sovereignty of the United States. Then Genet gathered together in South Carolina certain malcontents of the old American army, and organized them into an armed expedition which was to go overland and attack the Spanish in Louisiana.

The new French Minister found George Rogers Clark much discontented with the United States because of its failure to requite his services during the Revolution, and he found the sinister James Wilkinson ever ready to make trouble in the southwest. Both of these were in communication with Genet, who actually gave out commissions to land forces as he had to naval forces. In international law, this amounted not only to an act of using

[20] J. B. McMaster, *Hist. of the People of the U. S.*, II, 105ff.

a neutral nation as a base of operation against a third party, but it was a frank violation of the territorial rights of that nation. In constitutional law it was an open insult to the United States which was supposed to have jurisdiction over this territory from which the expeditions were set on foot.[21]

However Genet was soon disillusioned. Before his arrival in Philadelphia, President Washington laid before his cabinet the same questions of war or neutrality which he had put before them in the Nootka Sound crisis. He received the same contradictory advice. Jefferson believed that we were bound by the treaty and ought to do what we had promised. Hamilton took the position that that treaty had been made in 1778 with the King of France and that now there was no King of France and hence we were not bound. Washington apparently felt that they were both wrong. The treaty of 1778, like all treaties, was made with the *state* and not with any special king or government. The state of France survived whatever changes in government might occur, so that if the treaty were binding at all, the change in government made no difference. But this treaty had specifically stated that it was a *defensive* alliance, and Washington had about made up his mind that France was waging an *offensive* war.[22]

So the Attorney General Edmund Randolph was directed to draft a proclamation of Neutrality, which Washington then published on his authority as President, stating that it was to our interest and our duty to remain neutral and that we proposed to do so. Further it stated that no Americans getting themselves in trouble by joining or aiding either of the belligerents need look to the United States for help.[23] The proclamation at once raised a storm of protest from the Jeffersonian faction who were pro-French. Hamilton jumped into print to defend his chief under the nom-de-plume of "Pacificus." He was attacked on all sides, but nowhere more bitterly than by Madison, who under the guise

---

[21] F. J. Turner, "Correspondence of Clark and Genet" and Mangourit Correspondence in *Am. Hist. Assoc. Rept.*, 1897, I, 569–679; "Original of Genet's Projected Attack on Louisiana and the Floridas," *Am. Hist Rev.*, III, 650–71; *Amer. State Paper, For. Rel.*, I, 309.

[22] Jefferson's *Works*, IX, 142–3, IV, 17–20, 29–31; Washington's *Works* (Ford ed.), XIII, 280–290.

[23] *Amer. State Papers*, For. Rel., I, 140.

of "Helvidius" had been instigated by Jefferson to "cut Hamilton to pieces in the face of the public." The pro-French argued that the President's act was unconstitutional, since the constitution gave him no such power. But Washington had started on the path of loose-construction of the constitution which gave pain to so many of the Jeffersonian party. The real fact was that the assailants of the President did not really want him to refer the question of neutrality to Congress, but they wanted him to go into the war on the French side, and this the United States was not prepared to do.[24]

Genet arrived in Philadelphia flushed with the gratification of his triumphant progress through the south. He was met with the neutrality proclamation and with Washington's characteristic aloofness and dignity. He felt angered by a rebuff, when he expected fulsome praise. He was further enraged because Jefferson refused to make a treaty while the Senate was not in session. He then flew to Hamilton to get the payments on the debt due France advanced, on the ground that the new French Republic was in dire straits and needed the money. Hamilton refused on the ground that such an act would be construed by England as a wanton violation of the neutrality which the United States had just announced. Despite these hints as to the proper conduct for him to pursue, Genet went on violating the neutrality of the United States, fitting out vessels and condemning prizes. The British minister Hammond very promptly and very properly complained that this was all wrong, and the President directed that the sailing of the privateers be stopped and ordered the restitution of prizes which Genet's boats had taken in open violation of international law. One, indeed, was a British vessel captured by the French within the American three-mile limit. In a rage Genet, unable to get what he wanted from Washington, determined to go over Washington's head and address himself to Congress. This was in clear violation of the principle that a foreign envoy must ad-

[24] Hamilton's *Works* (ed. 1851), VII, 76–117; Madison's *Writings* (ed. 1865), I, 611–654; McMaster, *Hist. of People of U.S.*, II, 114–21; J.B.Moore, *Principles of American Diplomacy*, 213–25; *Digest of International Law* I, 164; E. S. Corwin, *President's Control of Foreign Relations* (Princeton, 1921), 7–28.

dress a nation only through its foreign office, and Jefferson promptly rebuked Genet for his efforts to ignore both the Secretary of State and the President.[25]

But the very proper acts of the administration in enforcing neutrality provoked roars of protest from the pro-French mob. Washington was subjected to vilification and abuse for his foreign policy which has seldom been equalled in our history. Indeed for meanness, violence and scurrility the things that were said of Washington in criticism of his foreign policy exceed anything that was ever said by the bitter enemies of Roosevelt and Wilson in criticism of what they did. Moreover, Washington was harboring in his own official family the cause of much of this abuse. For Jefferson did not scruple to attack his chief, sometimes through dignified agents like Madison and sometimes through such low characters as Philip Freneau. This kind of disloyalty to one's superior is to-day regarded as extremely dishonorable, but in those days it was tolerated as fair play.[26]

The problem of Genet was finally solved by the simple expedient of asking for his recall. Unquestionably that gentleman had overplayed his hand, and the more respectable elements in the community rallied behind Washington. The French government was told that their representative in America was *persona non grata* and they took the hint and called him home in disgrace. The wheel of the French Revolution had taken another turn, so Genet retired from his office but did not return to France. Thus early in American diplomacy was established the precedent that if an envoy is not agreeable to the nation to which he is accredited, he need not be tolerated. A request for recall is practically always granted, for an envoy in Genet's position had simply no further usefulness in the United States.[27]

[25] E. S. Corwin, *President's Control of Foreign Relations*, p. 47; J. B. Moore, *Digest of International Law*, IV, 680.

[26] J. W. Foster, *Century of American Diplomacy*, p. 148; J. B. McMaster, *Hist. of the People of the U. S.*, II, 111.

[27] *Am. State Papers, Foreign Relations*, I, 314; J. B. Moore, *Digest of International Law*, IV, 485; V, 591.

3. TREATIES, PIRATES AND SPAIN

Meantime the fresh start that the United States was making in the troubled sea of international relations was bringing up another question which established some precedents in American diplomacy. The Constitution had given the treaty-making power to the President "by and with the advice and consent of the Senate." As soon as it met, the first Senate had laid before it a treaty which had been held over by Jay from the period of the Confederation. This was the French consular convention of 1788, which Jefferson had negotiated as minister to France under instructions from the Continental Congress. The Senate asked Jay's advice in the matter and he seems to have convinced them that the treaty ought to be ratified because a principle ought to stand behind the acts of its agents, when those agents are acting under instructions. Thus in the first treaty ever ratified by the Senate they tried to commit themselves to the practice of ratifying any treaty properly negotiated under proper instructions.[28] However it soon became apparent that such a practice could not be followed, because it became evident that the President could not always consult with the Senate before he made a treaty. President Washington did try to do that very thing but it was not practical. On one occasion, as the story has often been told, he wanted to make a treaty with an Indian tribe and so he went down to the Senate chamber with his Secretary of War to get their advice and consent. He interrupted them in the middle of other work, presented his plan and introduced Knox to give the Senate any additional information they might require. But the Senate could not act that way. They delayed, and suggested alterations which were not acceptable to Washington; they prolonged the discussion until Washington's patience was quite at an end and he is said to have remarked that he would be damned if he ever brought another treaty to the Senate in advance of his action on it.[29]

[28] R. Hayden, *The Senate and Treaties, 1789–1817* (N. Y., 1920), p. 9; *Senate Exec. Jour.*, I, 7–9; J. B. Moore, *Digest of International Law*, V, 184–202.

[29] R. Hayden, *The Senate and Treaties, 1789–1817*, pp. 23–4; *Journal of William Maclay*, pp. 128–33; J. Q. Adams, *Memoirs*, VI, 427; *Am. State Papers, Indian Affairs*, I, 65–8.

Nevertheless he did try to make the treaty-making power work as the constitution directed. He was confronted with the ever-present question of the Barbary powers with whom an effort was now made to adjust the long standing wrongs. Yet under Washington's administration the United States pursued the shameful old policy of paying blackmail to these freebooters of the Mediterranean. Indeed in the conduct of these negotiations and in the making of treaties with the Barbary states, the President and the Senate kept close touch with one another and with the House of Representatives which had to appropriate the money to pay the tribute to the Corsairs which the treaties called upon us to pay. In a lengthy review of the situation, Secretary Jefferson pointed out that submission, tribute or war were the only alternatives, and the United States seems to have decided on tribute. Consequently millions of dollars of American money was poured out when a much smaller sum spent on the navy would have put the pirates out of existence. However these negotiations were conducted by the administration in such a way that we can fairly say that blame for the continuance of the humiliating practice rests on the Senate and the House quite as much as on the President, for he kept them appraised of the course of events as he went along.[30]

In a sincere effort to do what the constitution directed in the matter of making treaties, the President then took up the long standing disagreement with Spain over the question of commerce, the West Florida boundary and the navigation of the Mississippi. He advised and consulted with the Senate in this matter as he proceeded. He got the Senate to approve the appointment of the American commissioners and then got their advice and consent on an extension of the commissioners' instruction as to the making of a commercial treaty.[31] But by this time the whole process of consulting with the Senate at every step of the way seems to have become too tedious. It involved too much delay and too much talk by senators who really did not have the infor-

[30] E. Schuyler, *American Diplomacy*, 208–22; Hayden, supra, 40–53; *Amer. State Papers*, X, 43.
[31] R. Hayden, *The Senate and Treaties, 1789–1817*, pp. 53–57.

mation necessary for intelligent discussion. In this case Washington did not even consult them about the two most important aspects of the treaty, the boundary and the Mississippi.   The treaty was finally negotiated at San Lorenzo by Thomas Pinckney and the United States certainly gained as much as she could reasonably have expected. The disputed area in West Florida, between 31° and 32° 28′ was handed over to the United States.

The right to navigate the Mississippi to its mouth was also accorded to the United States, thereby giving her citizens in the

THE FLORIDAS UNDER SPAIN FROM 1783 TO THE CESSION
OF LOUISIANA IN 1803

This map makes clear how completely Spanish dominions shut the United States
away from the Gulf ports by their control of the mouth of the Mississippi

southwest the outlet for which they had struggled so long. But equally important to the United States was the necessity of having some port at the mouth of the Mississippi, where goods coming down the river on flatboats or rafts could be stored before being reloaded or transshipped on to ocean-going vessels. The ocean vessels could not sail up the Mississippi, and indeed it was not until the invention of the steamboat that commerce on the great river could go both ways. In 1795 passage down the river with the current was the only kind of traffic that was possible, and the type of vessels which came down the river could neither ascend the river again nor put out to sea. Hence the necessity for a "port of deposit" at New Orleans which the treaty now granted the citizens of the United States. A further provision was made that this right of deposit should endure for three years and be extended at the end of that time, or else Spain would designate some other point at the mouth of the river where the transshipment could be made. The title to the southwest was at last secure and the movement for westward expansion was well under way.[32]

The great outstanding difficulties with Great Britain because of the non-execution of the treaty of peace of 1783 were still hanging fire, but by this time all these were confused with questions of attacks on our neutral rights by England and France, which properly belong in the next chapter. However this much progress could be registered. The United States had made a fresh start. She had a new government which was responsible for what it undertook. The new government frankly assumed the financial obligations of the old government under the Confederation, thus confirming that rule of international law which prescribes that *states* are liable for whatever debts the *government* contracts, no matter how many changes in government there may be. Hamilton secured the restoration of the public credit by paying the debts contracted under the previous government. Treaties could be made with the new government, which the government was competent to enforce on its constituent members. The new national government had taken away from the states their right to regulate commerce, and therefore any foreign nation could make a treaty with us and expect us to live up to what we promised. The great question of the Mississippi had been settled to our satisfaction, but settled in such a way as to usher in an important chapter of American foreign policy, that is, the westward expansion. The now habitable southwest filled up with those who looked longingly across the Mississippi at Louisiana which Spain

[32] R. Hayden, *The Senate and Treaties, 1789–1817*, pp. 55-7; W. Malloy, *Treaties and Conventions of the United States*, II, 1640, arts. ii, iv and xxii.

was not effectively using and which the Americans believed they could use. Our first territorial dispute, West Florida, had been settled in an ominous way, for the United States gained the contested territory at the expense of Spanish America, nor was this to be the last territory so gained. The story is opened which is not yet ended but finds as its latest chapter the managing of a Central American Republic by the American minister and a fruit company. In the midst of all this the new nation was asserting and maintaining its right to remain neutral in the first great European War which it had been able to stay out of for more than a century.

CHAPTER VI

THE FRUSTRATION OF NEUTRALITY

"On the other hand, whenever I am at war with a nation, both my safety and welfare prompt me to deprive it, as far as possible, of everything which may enable it to resist or hurt me. Here the law of necessity shews its force. If this law warrants me on occasion to seize what belongs to another, shall it not likewise warrant me to stop everything relative to war, which neutral nations are carrying to my enemy? Even if I should, by taking such measures, render all these neutral nations my enemies, I had better run the hazard, than suffer him who is actually at war with me, to be thus freely supplied, to the great increase of his power."—*Vattel*.

1. THE PLIGHT OF THE NEUTRAL

England and France were now engaged in that great war which engulfed all Europe for the next twenty years. It was one of those life and death struggles for the "balance of power" on the continent of Europe, which periodically spread death and destruction not only over all Europe, but over all the world. The policy of European nations seems to have been to keep the continent divided into hostile camps. Both groups, armed to the teeth, would watch until one or the other seemed to be getting a little more powerful, either by land-grabbing or other means. This was considered to "upset the balance," and war would ensue until the balance was restored. The "balance of power" frequently resulted in wars, and this was one of the wars. The specific causes of this particular war are found in the French seizure of Antwerp and threat of injuring English commerce by way of the Scheldt River and the fear of French Revolutionary propaganda among the official classes in England. The English could not tolerate a great power in Belgium in 1793 any more than they could in 1914.

When so engaged, each side deemed eternal righteousness to be on its side, and consequently believed it right to use every possible means to exterminate its foe. In this particular case autocratic Europe had ordered Revolutionary France to turn back the hands of the clock and cease her spreading of democratic principle. France had replied by carrying the war into the enemies' own country and had found in Napoleon Bonaparte a consummate leader who soon joined issue with Britain in a desperate struggle to see which side could last the longest. In this contest America essayed the rôle of the innocent bystander, the neutral, who wanted to continue her commerce unconcerned in a world cataclysm.

In all such struggles in history the element of sea power has been of immense importance. There is a great deal in the theory advanced by the American historian, Admiral A. T. Mahan, that in its last analysis every great war is won by the power that controls the seas.[1] For that power which can dominate the waterways of commerce not only has the power to draw on her own resources to fight the war, but she can call upon the resources of other nations, who have munitions and food to sell and will always sell to the needy belligerent if ships can take the goods to the nation at war. This is where the neutral comes in and this is where America comes upon the stage. A war usually tests the staying power of the two sides and it usually happens that he who controls the sea can outlast his opponent. For not only can he capture the ships of his enemy, but he can stop neutrals in their efforts to carry goods which will succor his opponent in time of war.

In the great struggles from 1793 to 1815, practically every important nation was engaged fairly early in the war. The United States alone stood out as the great neutral. That meant that all Europe was consuming food and munitions faster than they produced them and that they would have to buy what they lacked in America, or trust America to carry it for them. So the shippers of the United States made their fortunes by selling to Europe what Europe was too busy fighting to manufacture or to grow. But we have said that a belligerent has a right to stop this neutral trade when supplying its enemy. That is the theme of this chapter.

[1] A. T. Mahan, *The Influence of Sea Power in History, 1660–1783*(Boston, 1883), and also his *Influence of Sea Power upon the French Revolution and Empire* (Boston, 1898).

When the war broke out between France and England in 1793, Washington proclaimed the neutrality of the United States and thereby opened a chapter of world politics which is not yet ended. We have seen how a war divides the world into belligerents and neutrals, and how it has been the practice of belligerent nations to keep the sinews of wars, supplies, ammunition, and the like from getting to their enemies. We have seen that according to international law one belligerent has the right to seize contraband which is going to its enemy. According to international law as enunciated by Grotius, all articles of commerce were (a) Absolute Contraband or (b) they were Conditional Contraband, or (c) they were Non-contraband. The name of each class explains itself. Absolute Contraband was any article of commerce useful for war purposes only, such as arms and munitions. Conditional Contraband was any article of commerce used in both war and peace, peace, such as harness which might be used for innocent farm horses or warlike artillery. Non-contraband was any article which was useless for warlike purposes, such as a ship-load of cosmetics or toys. A belligerent could always seize absolute contraband when being carried to her enemy, in a ship of any nation. Conditional contraband could only be seized if it could be proven it was going to the armed forces of the enemy, i. e., if the harness was really going for artillery horses. Non-contraband could not be seized.[2]

Now of course all the trouble as far as the United States was concerned arose over exactly what articles should go into those various classes. England began the war with the customary instructions to the captains of her fleet to seize contraband and to seize all French vessels. There could be no possible objection to this. But objection did come when Great Britain through an Order in Council (which is merely the British way of making declarations which every belligerent is entitled to make) put grain and flour on the list of absolute contraband and ordered her captains to seize food stuffs going to France.[3] In those days when

[2] Grotius, *De Jure Belli ac Pacis*, III, i, 5; J. B. Moore, *Digest of International Law*, VII, 660.

[3] *American State Papers, Foreign Relations*, III, 264.

there were no adequate means of refrigeration, grain was one of the few perishable food stuffs that could be transported to feed a hungry nation and this British Order was a serious blow to France. It was, however, an equally serious blow to the United States. American farmers and shippers saw that the war in Europe gave them their golden opportunity. All kinds of fancy prices would be paid for food stuffs if the Americans could only get them to France, where the manhood of the nation was fighting instead of tilling the soil. Jefferson promptly protested to Britain that food was not contraband.[4] But the English minister Hammond replied that Jefferson's reading of international law was incorrect, that the authorities on international law did permit a nation to subdue its enemy by starvation and that was what England was trying to do. Moreover, he insisted that it was impossible to distinguish between grain intended for the French armies and that intended for their civilian population, because all French trade was in the hands of the government and therefore Britain had a right to presume that all trade was to help the armed force of France. Indeed the American minister at Paris, Monroe, admitted as much.[5]

But the second step taken by the British to keep the neutral United States from supplying the French with contraband was much less justifiable. It will be remembered that during the Seven Years War (i. e., the French and Indian War, 1756–63) the French were in a similar predicament and they tried to get out of it by licensing the neutral Dutch to bring food stuffs from the French colonies to France, a practice so contrary to all the old colonial and navigation systems that it would never have been allowed by France in time of peace. Further, we remember that the British would not tolerate this evasion of their belligerent rights, and they treated all such Dutch vessels as though they had been French, on the theory that a trade which was forbidden by France in time of peace could not be opened in time of war just to avoid the rights of the British navy. This "Rule of 1756"

[4] *American State Papers, Foreign Relations* I, 239.

[5] Vattel, *Law of Nations*, Bk. III, secs. 72–3; *American State Papers, Foreign Relations*, I, 240, 679.

announced that "a neutral has no right to deliver a belligerent from the pressure of his enemy's hostilities, by trading with his colonies in time of war in a way that was forbidden in time of peace." The British enforced this rule to the cost of the neutral Dutch, and captured neutrals carrying goods from the French West Indies to France.

When the war of the American Revolution broke out, the French attempted to get around the Rule of 1756 by opening up the colonial commerce to other nations in time of peace. At the outset and at the close of that war the French relaxed their colonial monopoly so that the Rule of 1756 might not apply, i. e., so that they might be able to say in cases of capture that the trade had already been opened in time of peace. Whether this was any very conscious act on the part of the French or not, the fact remains that in that war the Rule of 1756 slumbered in disuse.[6] The outbreak of war again in 1793 with the spreading conflagration of the French Revolution again brought up the question of feeding France and getting food from the French colonies to their Mother Country. The colonial monopoly was practically abolished [7] and the French could and did say that this trade via neutral bottoms could no longer be interdicted under the Rule of 1756 because the trade had been opened in time of peace. As a consequence, numbers of neutral vessels, i. e., Americans, took on cargoes at San Domingo or Martinique, French colonies, and carried the goods to France. The English scrutinized this traffic closely. They admitted that certain trade had been opened in time of peace and that therefore the neutrals might continue it in time of war. But the taking of goods from the French colonies to France in time of war in neutral vessels was forbidden by an Order in Council of November 6, 1793, and the Rule of 1756 was reapplied.[8]

A wail of protest went up from the neutral shippers. The Rule

[6] F. Piggott, "Belligerents and Neutrals, 1756–1915" in *Ninteenth Century*, LXXX, 476–8; *Annals of Congress*, 1793–5; pp. 174–95; J. Stephens, *War in Disguise, or the Frauds of a Neutral Flag* (Lond., 1809), p. 18.

[7] Stephens, *War in Disguise*, pp. 30–1; W. E. Lingelbach, "England and Neutral Trade" in *Military Econ. & Hist.*, II, 155n.

[8] *American State Papers, Foreign Relations*, III, 264.

of 1756, said they, should no longer apply, because the French
had opened up the trade in time of peace. Baffled by this fact,
or from whatever other cause, the British relaxed their Order of
November 6, 1793, and on January 8, 1794, issued a new Order in
Council, which allowed the neutrals to trade with the French
colonies, but forbade them to carry the goods of the French colonies directly to France. In this the British were quite within
their rights in trying to shut off supplies from France, while at
the same time endeavoring to be considerate of neutral trade.
Be it noted that this is no yielding in principle of the point the
British had maintained all along, i. e., that a neutral might not
help out a belligerent by evading the other belligerent's sea power.
Americans might now trade with the French West Indies but
they might not carry those goods to France.[9] Vessels which were
trying to carry on the forbidden contraband trade were still liable
under the laws of contraband, and vessels trying to carry goods
from the French West Indies to France were still seized under the
Rule of 1756.[10] The British did not relax that rule, and the policy
of the American state department was from now on to protest
against its application.

But in addition to this other troubles with Great Britain were
now clamoring for attention by the American state department
and demanding that the United States formulate some definite
foreign policy. The Orders in Council had authorized the British
navy to seize French private property as well as contraband, even
on neutral vesssels, and made naval stores contraband.[11] This
meant the British navy was stopping and overhauling every American vessel it sighted. In the state of international law at that
time, private property was more or less at the mercy of the captor.

At just this stage of the game, a terrible tragedy was being
enacted in the French colony of San Domingo. There the principles of the French Revolution, liberty, equality, fraternity and
democracy had suddenly been imposed on a population of planters
and slaves where the blacks outnumbered the whites, ten to

[9] *American State Papers, Foreign Relations*, I, 431.
[10] The "Immanuel," 2 Robinson, 186, (1799) (Sir William Scott).
[11] *American State Papers, Foreign Relations*, I, 431.

one. The result was one of the most fearful servile insurrections in all history, which resulted in the extermination of the whites and the rise of Toussaint L'Ouverture, "the Napoleon of the Blacks." Thousands of Frenchmen, then, were trying to escape from San Domingo in whatever way possible and most of these poor refugees were finding their way to the United States with such meager treasures as they could save from the wreckage of their plantations. But although bound for neutral America in American vessels, they were then all too frequently held up and robbed of their last remaining possessions by the British navy acting under the Order in Council which enabled them to seize French property.[12]

All this outraged the Americans more and more, particularly as the British exercised their right of visit and search with unaccustomed brutality and violence. Of course the British had a perfect right to stop and examine any American vessel on the high seas, but they did not have any right to plunder and insult the passengers and crew and to "impress" the American sailors for service in the British navy. Americans began at this time their assertion of the more humane doctrine that private property and non-combatants should be free from the violence of war.

But the great scarcity of food in Europe, and particularly the great demand for naval stores enticed more and more American shippers into the dangerous trade in the hopes of greater profits. The gain of several hundred per cent was too much to resist.[13] Yet every additional vessel on the ocean merely meant more ships to be searched, plundered, and stripped of their crew by the British. Since the protests of the American minister in London were of so little avail, Congress finally decided to take a hand. The proposal was made that the old pre-revolutionary debts (which we had as yet not paid to the English) should be sequestered and the proceeds used to compensate Americans who had suffered from British depredations. Fortunately this project was

---

[12] T. L. Stoddard, *The French Revolution in San Domingo* (Boston, 1914); The Philadelphia *Daily Advertiser*, July 2, 6, 10, 11, Aug. 7, 8, 13 ,22, 24, 26–9, Sept. 4, 9, 1793; The Philadelphia *Aurora*, Sept. 17, 1793.

[13] "The Letters of Phineas Bond," *Am. Hist. Assoc. Rept.*, Vol. 1, 1895, 523, 564.

not adopted as it was certainly as contrary to international law for the United States to seize private property as it was for them to suffer from the English seizures. Finally the proposal was made and adopted that the United States stop all its commerce and hold all vessels at their docks for two months, in the hope of forcing England to act more reasonably. But such an expedient was suicidal to our commerce and hurt the United States as much as it hurt England, so the scheme was abandoned as there appeared to be some prospect of a treaty now with England.[14]

2. THE JAY TREATY

To settle all these outstanding disagreements without war was a difficult thing, for they had been piling up since 1783 and included debts, western posts, loyalists as yet uncompensated, as well as neutral rights, the Rule of 1756, and the desire to trade with the British West Indies. Any apparent yielding to Great Britain outraged the Jeffersonian party, the Democratic-Republicans, for they were all for France and for helping France, even at the cost of a war with England. But a small group of Federalist senators, representing the New England shipping interests, were equally determined that there should be no war. They suggested to the President that he send a special envoy to England, they told him whom they wanted sent and how he should be instructed.[15] So in 1794 John Jay was dispatched to get whatever concessions from England he could, and as much as was possible.[16] In return for all the demands he made on the British he had very little to offer, save the trade and the good will of the United States. The former, England knew she would get any way and the latter she did not care about.

Jay's task was an almost impossible one, because England ruled the waves, but he certainly made the best of a very bad job. Britain agreed to evacuate the western posts and to leave the

---

[14] *Annals of Congress, 1793–5*, 115, 174, 538, 1303; *U. S. Statutes at Large*, I, 372–6; J. B. McMaster, *Hist. of People of U. S.*, II, 173ff.

[15] R. Hayden, *The Senate and Treaties, 1789–1817*, p. 92; S. F. Bemis, *The Jay Treaty, a Study in Commerce and Diplomacy* (N. Y., 1923), pp. 210–12.

[16] *American State Papers, Foreign Relations*, I, 470–3.

Indians and Canadian fur traders in the lurch. She agreed to a scientific finding of the disputed boundaries in the northeast and the north-west. The United States promised to pay England the much discussed debts, and England promised to compensate the United States merchants for the illegal seizures. England even went so far as to let the United States share in her precious West Indian trade. But she absolutely refused to give up her rights to seize, block or otherwise obstruct neutral commerce, she would not give up the Rule of 1756 and nothing was said as to impressment. Moreover Jay brought back an enlarged rather than a diminished contraband list.[17]

The principles of American foreign policy which Jay tried to assert were these, that the United States would rather negotiate and arbitrate differences than fight about them; that when a fight was going on in Europe the United States had the right to remain an innocent bystander if she wanted to and to use the sea for peaceful commerce even if European nations were using it as a battleground; that international law should be interpreted so as to do as little harm as possible to private persons and property. With the first Great Britain agreed, with the second and third she would have nothing to do. The United States failed signally in this attempt to assert her traditional foreign policy. Jay was abused and reviled for not getting what he set out to get, in spite of the fact that he probably got all that was humanly possible. The Federalists were indignant that the shipping interests had not been better cared for, and the Jeffersonians were enraged that Jay had sacrificed their slaves (i. e., those carried off by the British in 1783) and the cotton interests.[18] The debtor southern states did not want to pay Britain anything and this promise of Jay's only made matters worse. But despite all this opposition the treaty was ratified, because of the same small group of Federalists in the Senate who had engineered the deal in the first place. The Jay treaty is an excellent illustration of the fact that it is not the diplomats, but the business men who frequently determine our

---

[17] W. Malloy, *Treaties and Conventions*, I, 590, 601. S. F. Bemis, *The Jay Treaty*, p. 261.
[18] F. A. Ogg, "Jay Treaty and the Slavery Interests," *Am. Hist. Assoc. Rep.*, 1901, I, 275.

foreign policy, even though there be a great popular outcry against it. This small group of New Englanders would not have their shipping interests ruined for any popular outcry in the north or south.[19] Moreover, it must be admitted that Jay did resist the English attempts to have the northwestern frontier rectified in their favor.[20]

But the stormy career of the Jay treaty was not yet over. It called for an appropriation of money and that was the concern of the House of Representatives. Then arose one of those interesting problems of the control of American Foreign Relations. The House asserted that it had the right to deliberate on the expediency or inexpediency of carrying the treaty into effect, for without the House the treaty obligations could not be met. The situation was and remains an embarrassing one. Fortunately on this occasion, after long debate, the House furnished the money, but the matter is not yet settled, although again in 1871 it followed this precedent and provided funds after reasserting its authority. The best that can be hoped is that the House will in the future as in the past, content itself by stating without trying to enforce its privileges, otherwise all treaty making will be impossible.[21] But the debate brought out another principle of the conduct of foreign policy when the House called upon the President to furnish it with papers such as were consistent with public interest. This recognized the fact which has since been admitted that the President must for reasons of public policy keep many matters of diplomacy secret.[22]

So it came about that if neutral America could not carry French colonial coffee, sugar, and chocolate from the French West Indies to France directly, she now tried to do it by a roundabout route. Goods were taken by Americans from San Domingo or Martinique (French colonies) and carried to United States ports. There the goods were unloaded, duties paid, the goods mixed with the

[19] C. A. Beard, *Economic Interpretation of Jeffersonian Democracy*, 270–4, 295-6; J. B. McMaster, *Hist. People of the U. S.*, II, 264–82.

[20] S. F. Bemis, *The Jay Treaty*, p. 268.

[21] Q. Wright, *Control of American Foreign Relations*, p. 6; *Annals of Congress, 1795–6*, p. 80; G. Hunt, *Life of Madison*, p. 231.

[22] *Annals of Congress, 1795–6*, 463-74.

goods of the United States, becoming thereby, it was claimed, American goods, and then they were re-shipped to France as American goods thereby evading the British Orders in Council and the British navy. Apparently the British were deceived by this device of the "Broken Voyage," and the law officers of the crown admitted that landing in a neutral country broke the continuity of the voyage.[23] The vice-admiralty court so decided in the case of the "Polly." But what the British did not allow was a mere touching at an American port and indeed in the case of the "Polly," the King's advocate expostulated that it was the "most nugatory thing in the world to say that a trade which was not allowed to be carried on directly could be legalized by a mere transshipment in America." [24] But the vice-admiralty judge, Sir William Scott, overruled him and allowed the practice, in this case, which, be it noted, was that of a lower court and might readily be overthrown in a higher court.[25] The higher court distinctly held that the mere touching at a United States port did not break the continuity of the voyage, and seized Americans trying thus to evade the law.[26]

Nevertheless American shippers seemed to feel that the British had yielded a point by allowing them to do by loading and unloading what they could not do by merely touching at the port. Tremendous profits in prospect stimulated the trade and soon the seas were filled with American vessels going by the circuitous route, and actually carrying French colonial produce to France, under the guise of its being American, simply because it had been handled in an American port. The entrance of Spain and Holland into the war only increased the demand for American and colonial food stuffs, and increased the number of vessels in the roundabout trade. Whenever England could capture a vessel which she could prove was frankly doing this in a manner to evade the British navy, she seized the boat and continued to make

---

[23] W. E. Lingelbach, "England and Neutral Trade," *Mil. Econ. & Hist.*, II, 157; *Amer. State Papers, Foreign Relations*, II, 491.

[24] The "Polly," 2 Robinson, 361, 364 (1800).

[25] R. G. Adams, "Growth of Belligerents Rights," *U. of Penna. Law Rev.*, LXVIII, 34–5.

[26] The "Mercury," 5 Robinson, 400 (1802).

good her right to prevent goods from reaching her enemies to help them in the war.[27] She extended her Orders in Council against Spain and Holland, and, as we shall see, she did not long remain quiet while neutrals flaunted her belligerent rights and under cover of a colorable neutral port actually engaged in the very trade forbidden by the Rule of 1756.[28]

Meantime the neutral rights of the United States were being assailed from another quarter. No sooner had Genet been suppressed than France too began to issue Decrees which were as bad as the English Orders in Council. On May 9, 1793, such a Decree authorized the French navy to seize food stuffs and private property of the English, even on neutral ships.[29] Our minister at Paris, Gouverneur Morris, protested vigorously and the Decree was withdrawn. But in the meantime great damage was done and American ships were held up in French ports, while the rapidly changing governments of France were too busy with revolutions to attend to much else.[30] This was nothing compared to the outrages of our neutral rights committed by Genet and his privateers. French warships, equipped in American ports, used those ports as places in which to sell their prizes, in flagrant violation of ordinary international practice. The excuse given by France was of course her expectation that the United States would fulfill its promise under the treaty of Alliance of 1778 and join hands against England. This violation of American soil was due to the fact that the United States did not join in the war as expected and simply piled up more troubles with France to be settled in the future.[31]

3. WAR WITH FRANCE

Therefore at the same time that Washington sent Jay to England he sent Monroe to France to get what he could. Gouverneur Morris had to be withdrawn because he was not in the good

---

[27] Vid. "Immanuel" and "Mercury," *supra*.

[28] 35 Geo. III, c. 80; Lingelbach, *supra*, p. 156, *American State Papers, Foreign Relations*, III, 265.

[29] *American State Papers, Foreign Relations*, I, 364–6.

[30] Ibid., I, 373–4.

[31] Ibid, I, 147–87.

graces of the rulers of France, due to his having been too pro-
nouncedly sorry for Louis XVI.[32] Washington then selected the
pro-French, pro-Revolutionist, Jeffersonian, James Monroe,
who admittedly felt that if the United States was going to get
into the European war, it ought to get in on the French side.[33]
It is good diplomatic practice to be represented by a minister
who is *persona grata* to the rulers of the country to which he is
accredited. But Monroe overdid it. He was sent to care for
America's interests, which meant one thing to the Federalists
who were running the American government and quite another
thing to Monroe.[34]

Monroe did secure the remission of the French Decree of May,
1793, but he failed to press the American claims for indemnity
because he frankly thought that the United States should make
common cause with France.[35] On his own admission, he misled
the French into thinking that Jay would fail, that the United
States would repudiate Washington at the polls in 1796 and elect
Jefferson, who would soon take up the French side against England.[36] Then he woke up to the fact that Jay had done something.
Much to his chagrin he found that far from going to war with
England the United States was going to settle with her. Monroe now proceeded to act as the representative of the American
people and not as the representative of the government. This
was a dangerous thing to do, especially as the election returns in
1796 showed that Monroe had misjudged the wishes of the American people who were electing John Adams rather than Jefferson
as President. Monroe found himself helplessly trying to apologize to France for the conduct of Washington while at the same
time he berated the administration for its betrayal of France.
Indeed his correspondence with the enemies of Washington at
home was more frequent and confidential than that with the
President himself. Washington then decided, and thereby estab-

[32] B. W. Bond, *Monroe Mission to France, 1794–6 (J. H. U., ser. xxv, 1907)*, p. 10.
[33] James Monroe, *View of the Conduct of the Executive* (Phila., 1797), p. iv.
[34] Bond, supra, p. 22.
[35] Monroe, supra, p. xiv.
[36] Bond, supra, pp. 78, 85; Monroe, supra, xxxiii.

lished another precedent in American foreign policy, that although it was very desirable to have the American minister acceptable to the nation to which he was sent, it was more important to have him loyal to the admininstration which sent him. So he recalled Monroe.[37]

The worst of it was, however, that the American claims remained unsettled. C. C. Pinckney then went to Paris to do this work, but the French were thoroughly indignant at the Americans for not doing what Monroe had led them to expect. They snubbed Pinckney, refused to receive him and even threatened him with arrest if he stayed.[38] This insult incensed President Adams, who promptly sent Pinckney back to France supported by Elbridge Gerry and John Marshall. A turn in the political wheel in France had by this time made the French more willing to talk, but they were not willing to do anything about America's grievances until America did something to assuage the French wrath, which had been provoked by the alleged violation of the treaty of 1778 and the making of any treaty with England at all. The American commissioners were blandly told that if they expected to settle anything they must bribe the French foreign office. At this fresh insult, they left, but not so speedily as they might have, considering the indignity to which they had been subjected.[39]

All America backed up President Adams in his feeling that no further diplomatic negotiations could be had with France until she showed some signs of treating American envoys decently, and that if France wanted war she could have it. To the delight of the Federalists, hostilities between the French and American navies soon broke out and it seemed as if a full-fledged war would soon land the United States on the side of England. At this juncture occurred a rather characteristically American diplomatic comic interlude. A well meaning old Philadelphia Quaker, George Logan by name, decided, as laymen frequently

---

[37] B. W. Bond, *Monroe Mission to France*, p. 75; *American State Papers, Foreign Relations*, I, 747.

[38] J. B. McMaster, *Hist. of People of U. S.*, II, 319–21.

[39] *The X. Y. Z. Letters* (Univ. of Penna. Trans. & Reprints, Vol. VI, 1899), pp. 11, 18–19, 30–32.

do, that the diplomats were making a mess of things, so he went to France as a private citizen to bring Napoleon to his senses. He really accomplished nothing save to make himself the laughing-stock of the Federalists and to ensure the passage by Congress of an Act which threatened to imprison anyone in the future who attempted to meddle in diplomatic affairs. Logan thought that he had brought back an olive branch, but, as Washington remarked, if the French wanted to negotiate they had better do it through the proper channels and not through every busybody who wanted to rush to Europe to prevent war.[40]

In fact, however, the French were quite ready to cry quits. The United States navy was playing havoc with what little of their commerce remained in the West Indies and the French armies were faring badly with Napoleon far off on his futile Egyptian campaign. Through the American minister at The Hague, they indicated that they were ready to treat and President Adams promptly accepted their offer. Adams dug his own political grave by that act, for the Federalists were enthusiastic at the prospect of war, but he saved America useless bloodshed. A new mission composed of Chief Justice Ellsworth, William Vans Murray and William Richardson Davie went to Europe, where the now chastened French agreed to the long delayed treaty.[41]

The treaty of 1800 with France settled forever the question of the French Alliance. The Americans practically admitted that they should have come to France's help under the obligations of the treaty of 1778, and they offered to pay for release from that troublesome alliance. But they demanded indemnification by France for all that American neutral commerce had unjustly suffered at the hands of the French navy. After some hesitation on both sides the matter was settled by Napoleon, now a power in France, in a characteristically brusque manner. He simply traded off the two sets of claims. France would say no more about America's failure to live up to the treaty of Alliance, and the United States must say no more about the injuries done

<hr />

[40] J. B. McMaster, *Hist. of People of U. S.*, II, 409-10, 414-16; *U. S. Statutes at Large*, I, 613; *Revised Statutes*, sec. 5335.

[41] J. S. Bassett, *Federalist System*, 247-51; John Adams, *Works*, X, 113.

her commerce. The United States thereby forfeited the claims
of its citizens against France. The treaty made further efforts to
lighten the burden of war on the neutral and non-combatant by
providing that France and the United States would observe the
more humane interpretations of international law. Without
the assent of England, however, this was rather a meaningless
gesture.[42]

When a nation gives up the valid claims of its citizens against
another nation, it is usually bound to assume those claims itself.
Therefore, when the final ratification of the treaty of 1800 relieved France of the obligation of paying those spoliation claims,
the United States government made itself liable to compensate its
own citizens. The victims of the French depredations then tried
to collect from their own government, but by that time the Jeffersonians had come into power with no enthusiasm to pay the bills
of their hated Federalist rivals. For decades Congress remained
under the control of the Jeffersonians and their successors, and
for decades the claims remained unpaid. It was not until after the
Civil War that provision was made for payment.[43] Similar to
this was the fate of certain claims by American merchants against
the French which the treaty of 1800 had allowed as valid. They
were made the object of another treaty in 1803, but were never
paid until under the threat of war in Jackson's administration.[44]

Thus there were two sets of the "French Spoliation Claims."
The one set of claims was that of citizens of the United States
against their own government for rights surrendered under the
treaty of 1800. The other set of claims was for outrages committed later by France which she agreed to pay for under a
treaty in 1803. As observed above, the former claims were not
paid until ninety years and more had elapsed. The latter claims
were not pressed because of France's misfortunes, until another treaty in 1831 provided for their payment. The twentieth
century saw the matter still being discussed in Congress and the

[42] W. Malloy, *Treaties and Conventions*, I, 505.

[43] G. A. King, *French Spoliation Claims* (S. D. 451, 64 Cong., I Sess.) 11–17; The "Concord," 35 *Ct. Cl. Rep.* 432–3, 444.

[44] Richardson's *Messages*, III, 101ff.; Malloy, *Treaties*, I, 513, 524.

Court of Claims, and in 1913 many of the claims were either paid or dismissed for non-prosecution.[45] With France, as with England, the United States had tried vigorously to assert its neutral rights, but it would be difficult to say that we had accomplished any more than to voice a feeble and ineffective protest. However, the United States was certainly no worse off than other neutrals, for Russia and the Scandinavian nations were likewise suffering from England's commercial warfare. They tried to revive the old principle of the "Armed Neutrality," but Nelson's fleet gave the Danish fleet such a drubbing in the Copenhagen roadway, that the second armed neutrality was no better than the first, and was, indeed, not as effective. But to this the United States was not a party. Neutrality seems to have been at best but a weak and unenforceable thing, and neutral rights were as yet in their infancy.[46]

[45] G. A. King. *The French Spoliation Claims*, 50–41; *Claims of U. S. Citizens on the Government of the U. S. for French Spoliations*, pp. 134–45 (Baltimore, 1826).
[46] *The Armed Neutralities of 1780 and 1800* (J. B. Scott ed.), pp. 16–19ff.

CHAPTER VII

DRIFTING INTO A USELESS WAR

"Moreover, the insular and independent position of this state
causes them to be arbitrary judges of the injuries they do to
others, instead of being judges appointed by mutual agreement."
— *Thucydides.*

1. DECREES AND ORDERS

The second part of the great drama of the Napoleonic wars
opened in 1803, when England and France broke the Peace of
Amiens and flew to arms in that great struggle which ended on
the field of Waterloo and at the Congress of Vienna. One of the
fruits of that war was the maladjustment of Europe, politically,
racially, and economically, which was a contributory cause of the
fearful struggle of 1914–1918 in which the United States became
so intimately involved. The spectacle of American foreign policy
in those two world wars, 1803–1815 and 1914–1918, presents an
interesting parallel. In both wars the United States attempted
to assert her principle of neutrality and she ended by being involved in the war in each case. In the first one she distinctly
got in on the wrong side in a desperate effort to stay out. We
shall in this chapter consider American foreign policy up to 1815,
a story in which we see the United States caught between the
upper millstone of England and the nether millstone of Napoleon.

With the recurrence of hostilities, the American merchant
marine began once more its lucrative trade of supplying the belligerents. American vessels filled the ocean, carrying goods,
both contraband and non-contraband, and entering the colonial
trade of the belligerents by the circuitous route of the broken
voyage in their effort to evade the Rule of 1756. We have observed how the case of the "Polly" lulled the Americans into a
false sense of security as to the legality of the trade. England
never meant by that insignificant case to give up the Rule of

1756, as there are abundant cases to prove.[1] But the Americans apparently thought that they could deceive the British prize court judges, and carry the French colonial produce to America, land it there by fiction, reship it in American vessels and thus get it to France as so-called American produce. By this method they thought to violate Britain's belligerent right to stop this traffic when going directly.

The British merchants protested vehemently that these commercial activities on the part of the American shippers constituted a disguised war against Great Britain, and that the frauds of the neutral flag were covering a vast and forbidden trade between the French colonies and France which international law plainly forbade by the Rule of 1756.[2] When a particularly flagrant case finally got to the higher court (we have seen that the "Polly" was a decision in a lower court by Sir William Scott) the Court decided that international law, like all true law, would look at the fact and not at the fiction; further, that the fact was that this so-called "broken voyage" was really a "continuous voyage"; and finally, that a continuous voyage was forbidden. In the celebrated case of the "Essex" and again in the case of the "William," the Lords Commissioners on Appeal, through Sir William Grant, decided that the correct law had been applied in the case of the "Immanuel," in which had expressly been laid down the proposition that a neutral may not help a defeated belligerent to evade the victor's superior sea power by carrying on the defeated one's trade with its colonies, from which the neutral would ordinarily be excluded.[3] Grant ruled in the cases of the "Essex" and the "William" just as the King's advocate had asked Scott to rule in the case of the "Polly," namely, that the interposition of a neutral port and the mere performance of the paper work of landing the goods did not change the character of the voyage, which was in fact just exactly that forbidden con-

---

[1] W. E. Lingelbach, "England and Neutral Trade" in *Milit. Econ. & Hist.*, II, 157–63.
[2] James Stephen, *War in Disguise, or the Frauds of a Neutral Flag* (Lond., 1805).
[3] The "Immanuel," 2 C. Robinson 186, (1799); The "Essex" not reported, but cited in the "William," 5 C. Robinson, 385 (1806); C. B. Elliott, "Doctrine of Continuous Voyage," *Amer. Jour. of International Law*, I, 60.

tinuous voyage between the colonies and the Mother Country. A neutral certainly was not to be allowed to do indirectly what he could not do directly. Even in the early cases the controlling element was the actual intention of the shipper, no matter how he tried to cover it up.[4]

The indignant protests of the American shippers filled the American press. Scott was blamed for reversing his decision in the case of the "Polly." He was assailed for misleading the American merchants into filling the seas with ships and then changing the law in time to give the British privateers a chance to seize every American engaged in the now forbidden traffic. Incidentally, it was not Scott, but another judge, Grant, who delivered the decision, and as a fact the statement made in the latest case was the correct one.[5] It mattered little to the Americans that in law they were wrong, for it was the lost millions that hurt. But England stuck to her guns and from this time on enforced her seizures, breaking up the American efforts to avoid international law and looking clearly at the intention of the American shippers and not at what their ship papers were made to read. From this time on, American policy was simply one of futile protest.[6]

This reopened all the questions that had apparently been slumbering since the Peace of Amiens. The battle of Trafalgar late in 1805 had made England supreme on the seas, but those of Austerlitz and Jena in 1805 and 1806 had made France supreme on land. Most of Europe lay prostrate at the feet of Napoleon, but England ruled the waves. A glance at the map will show how Napoleon now controlled most of the ports of western Europe. This simply meant that the British goods could not be sold in many places as readily as in former years. The British tradesmen felt the loss and so the new foreign minister, Charles James Fox, decided to adopt a frank and open policy of blockade. Now a

[4] L. H. Woolsey, "Early Cases on the Doctrine of Continuous Voyage" in *Amer. Jour. of International Law*, IV, 832ff.; The "Twen Gebrodre," 4 C. Robinson, 33 (1801).

[5] Henry Adams, *Hist of the U. S.*, III, 34–45, gives the classic American protest, which Lingelbach corrects, supra, 162–5.

[6] Henry Adams, III, 124, Lingelbach, supra, 165, *Ann. of Cong.*, 1806, p. 6.

blockade is a simpler process than those previously adopted by Britain for shutting off the neutral trade. A blockade prevents any vessel from coming to or from going the blockaded ports, no matter what the nationality of the vessel or the character of its cargo. The penalty for any vessel attempting to run the blockade is confiscation, if caught. This was a perfectly well-known device in war and was allowed by international law. On April 6, 1806, Fox announced the intention of the British to extend the blockade in such fashion as to exclude all commerce from most of the important sea-ports of the North Sea and English Channel. If the British could thus cut off supplies going to Napoleon by way of the Dutch and German ports, they would have delivered a body blow at their enemy. This, of course, stopped American commerce more effectively than Britain's previous measures ever had.[7]

Although Fox's blockade was badly enforced, yet it opened the type of commercial warfare between France and England in which both were soon way beyond the bounds of international law in their desperate efforts to ruin one another's commerce. If Americans and other neutrals were to be prevented from carrying goods to the French, Napoleon was going to try to keep them from carrying goods to Great Britain. From the capital of defeated Prussia, Napoleon began his policy of trying to throttle British commerce. In his "Berlin Decree" (November 21, 1806) he declared England blockaded. If Americans tried to trade with the ports of Northern Europe, they could be seized by the English; if they tried to trade with England they could be seized by the French.[8]

The British counterattacked with another Order in Council (November 11, 1807) which practically blockaded every European port under Napoleon's domination. Another glance at the map will show that this meant the Americans were excluded from practically every port of continental Europe, save those of Russia and Turkey. This was an effort to drive all American trade into

---

[7] *American State Papers, Foreign Relations*, III, 262–84.
[8] Ibid., 284–92.

English ports, where they must of course pay duties fixed by the British. It was an excellent scheme, not only for keeping trade away from Napoleon, but for making that same trade pay tribute to England.[9] Of course this last order meant that any vessel caught on the high seas going in the general direction of Europe was going to be examined to be sure it was not going to any forbidden port.

Such a practice enraged Napoleon into taking a further step against the British, and by his "Milan Decree" (December 17, 1807) he announced that he would seize all vessels that had either stopped at a British port, or allowed a British warship to search them. Since many vessels forced to go to England, had subsequently to go on to continental ports, seizure was easy. The Americans were now in an impossible position, for they were damned if they did and damned if they didn't. If they observed the British Blockade Orders, the French might seize them, whereas, if they obeyed Napoleon's commands, they must violate the British orders and hence would be seized by the British. Trade with either set of belligerents meant seizure and confiscation by the other. But the story was not all a tale of the efforts of two desperate fighters trying to best one another. The British have tried to show that their Orders were aimed solely at the destruction of Napoleon's empire, but the fact probably is that an equally strong motive for these Orders was the destruction of American competition. For when England was engaged in such a life and death struggle naturally her commerce suffered, and naturally the neutral United States began to come in for a share of the neglected carrying trade. In fact the Americans got more than their share, so the British thought, and the Orders in Council were a double-edged sword which might injure Napoleon and the American competitors at the same time.[10]

The effect of all this on American commerce was disastrous.

[9] E. Channing, *Hist. of U. S.*, IV, 358–78 had worked this out in detail.
[10] W. E. Lingelbach, supra, p. 167, based on the Board of Trade Minutes, and the expressed opinions of the authors of the Orders in Council, *Hansard*, X, 341, 465, XIII, 1160, seem to correct the older opinions of J. H. Rose and others, as, for example, in *Cambridge Modern History*, IX, p. 367.

The period from 1790 to 1807 was unique in the economic history of the United States, because foreign trade absorbed the attention of a greater proportion of people than ever before or since. Manufacturing in the United States did not really begin until these attacks on our commerce drove capital from the merchant marine into factory building. The United States was a great granary for Europe, because the European wars were accompanied by crop failures, due alike to the weather, the destruction incident to war, and the withdrawal of able-bodied men from the fields.[11]

The curve of American foreign trade rises sharply up to 1807, then suddenly it drops to one-fifth of what it had been. This is to be explained not only by the enforcement of the doctrine of continuous voyage, the British and French blockades, but also by the measures which the Americans themselves took for the protection of their trade and commerce. Jefferson was now president and he was faced with a situation in which the United States had either to fight to assert its neutral rights, or weakly to submit. American foreign policy was in the hands of the Virginia dynasty, and the leader of those Virginian agrarians occupied the presidential chair. He had not the slightest intention of fighting to protect the trade of the Federalist capitalists. For this it is not fair to use hard words against Jefferson. One must get down underneath the situation and understand why he pursued the supine policy which characterized American diplomacy for the next six years. His policy went to the very roots of the Jeffersonian principles. He has told us in language that cannot be misunderstood that he did not want the United States to become a predominately industrial and commercial nation. He was not scornful of the shopkeeper, but he believed as a religion that the only solid foundations of national progress and prosperity rested with the farmer and not with the manufacturer or trader.[12] What more natural then, than that such an administration should

---

[11] G. G. Huebner and E. R. Johnson, *History of Domestic and Foreign Commerce of the United States* (Wash., 1915), II, 14–20; W. F. Galpin, "The American Grain Trade to the Spanish Peninsula, 1810–1814," *Amer. Hist. Rev.*, XXVIII, 24n; see also Dr. Galpin's forth coming volume on England's grain trade.

[12] Jefferson's *Notes on Virginia, Works* (Washington ed.), VIII, 405.

simply have agreed that it was better for America to abandon
the seas, since after all the farmer, not the merchant, was the
mainspring of American life and the farmer was not so directly
concerned with these matters of neutral rights.[13]

As early as 1806 Jefferson found a majority in Congress willing
to agree that the best way to reply to England was by a dignified
(or undignified) withdrawal of American commerce from the seas.
Even before the struggle of Orders and Decrees got the French
and English beyond the bounds of international law, Congress
had agreed to furnish the President with a kind of club to hold
over the lawless belligerents, in the shape of a non-importation
act (April 18, 1806). The aim of this act was to prevent the importation of certain British manufactured goods into the United
States, thereby to hurt the British mercantile classes which dominated parliament and thereby to bring Great Britain to terms.[14]
There was some hope that a threat of this kind would be of service to the American commissioners, Monroe and Pinkney, who
were now in London, trying vainly to make some kind of a treaty
by which all these misunderstandings and difficulties could be
straightened out.

But matters got worse instead of better. We have remarked
how the English, desperate for lack of seamen to man their fleets,
had resorted to the impressment of American sailors. This practice began as far back as the Nootka Sound affair in 1790, when
in the face of a possible war with Spain, the British "press-gang"
had visited the rum-shops and saloons at the British ports and
rounded up and kidnapped any sailors they could locate. These
sailors usually woke up several hours later from the effects of
liquor or clubbing to find themselves several miles at sea on one
of his Britannic Majesty's men-of-war. The only trouble was
that with such a process it was quite impossible to distinguish
between American and English sailors and many Americans were
thus "pressed" into the British service. With the opening of the
war in 1793 and again in 1803 there was a tremendous demand for

[13] C. A. Beard, *Economic Origins of Jeffersonian Democracy*, 422–28.

[14] E. Channing, *Hist. of U. S.*, IV, 357–8, 375; *Annals of Congress*, 9 Cong., 1 sess., p. 1259;
2 sess., p. 1249; *Stat. at Large*, II, 379, 411.

sailors from two sources. The British wanted seamen to man their fleet of war vessels. The Americans wanted hands to man their merchant marine. As between these two possible jobs, there could be no doubt as to which was the more attractive. Like all labor, sailors will go to the employer who offers the best wages and living conditions. Since the Americans were making their millions out of feeding Europe, they could afford to offer much higher wages and entice sailors away from the British fleet with its notoriously bad and brutal treatment of its men. But the British were desperate. They were fighting for their very existence against Napoleon and so they began to kidnap sailors not only from the seaport towns but from the deck of any neutral they happened to overhaul. Here again to distinguish between Englishmen and Americans was difficult at best and the British naturally took advantage of this confusion to take any able-bodied seamen who might be needed on his Britannic Majesty's warships.[15]

The grounds on which the British kidnapped or "impressed" these sailors were several. In the first place they wanted to get back numerous deserters from their own navy.[16] In the second place, many naturalized American citizens had previously been British, but English municipal law (i. e., British law as opposed to international law) did not admit that a British citizen could ever change his allegiance. This was the general rule of that day.[17] Hence the British seized American sailors on the ground that they were English, whether naturalized Americans or not. The English insisted that allegiance was indelible, that a man could not "expatriate" himself and that once an Englishman, always an Englishman.

The American strenuously objected, not so much to the doctrine of indelible allegiance, but to the way in which it was asserted. It was, claimed the Americans, a rule of English municipal law. Yet it was applied by British vessels in the exercise of their right of visit and search, and the right of visit and search

---

[15] A. T. Mahan, *War of 1812*, I, 114, 127; E. Channing, *Hist. of U. S.*, IV, 366–7.
[16] Gallatin's *Works*, I, 335.
[17] J. B. Moore, *Principles of American Diplomacy*, 272–4; Kent's *Commentaries on American Law* (1873 ed.), II, 45; "The Charming Betsy," 2 Cranch, 64 (1804).

did not allow Englishmen to enforce English municipal law on the deck of an American vessel any more than in the streets of New York.[18] It is a fundamental principle of international law that the deck of a vessel is part of the soil of the nation to which it belongs. For the British then to enforce their peculiar municipal law on American vessels was an insult and an offense against the sovereign rights of the United States and quite as inexcusable as if the British tried to assert the rights of primogeniture in the state of New York.[19] The American did thereafter also develop a doctrine of expatriation, for by the nature of the case many Americans must once have been something else. Naturalization laws were for the purpose of making them into Americans. But our objection to impressment was not fundamentally on the ground that the British law was wrong, but that they had no right to assert it on American soil.[20]

The British, however, asserted their right with varying degrees of severity throughout the whole period from 1793 to 1815. Toward the end of the first period of war, the British refrained from their practice to some extent, but with the outbreak of the commercial struggle with Napoleon the fire broke out again with renewed fury, and the practice was resumed in a way which could only provoke the United States to war. The most flagrant case on record was that which occurred when the British war vessel *Leopard* wantonly attacked the United States frigate *Chesapeake* and reduced her to helplessness by gunfire, killing several American sailors. The British vessel then took from the American warship several alleged deserters from the British navy and left the much battered *Chesapeake* to find her way back to port as best she could. This outrageous attack on a war vessel of the United States government by a nation with whom we were supposed to be at peace inflamed the whole country. Up to this time, Britain had confined her impressment to helpless merchantmen. She now coolly smashed up an American war vessel and helped herself to the crew. This act was so inexcusable that even the British

[18] J. B. Moore, *Digest of International Law*, II, 987ff.
[19] H. Wheaton, *Elements of International Law* (5th Eng. ed.), 173-80.
[20] *American State Papers, Foreign Relations*, III, 405-6.

foreign office had to admit its navy had gone too far, but it made this admission with such ill grace and with so many delays as only further to exasperate the American government.[21]

"The fundamental cause of the War of 1812 was the irreconcilable conflict of the British Navigation Acts with the commercial development of the United States." [22] If this be true, the next move on the part of the United States certainly played right into the hands of the British. The *Chesapeake-Leopard* affair combined with the other violations of our neutral rights determined Jefferson to take stern measures. But as we have seen, he was firmly convinced of the relative unimportance of trade and commerce as against agriculture, so instead of forcing the British to give up their practices, he forced American shippers to give up their business. Moreover, he controlled a sufficient majority in Congress to effect this very thing.

2. Embargo

The administration had not yet the news of the British Orders in Council of November 11th, 1807, but the *Chesapeake-Leopard* affair seemed enough cause to take drastic measures which resulted in practically calling in all American vessels, and stopping American commerce with all the world. This policy was known as the "Embargo" and was put into force in a series of laws passed by Congress in 1807 and 1808 the aim of which was practically to forbid any one to trade with America and to forbid Americans to trade with anyone else. Into the details of these bills we need not enter. Suffice it to say that the policy certainly had the effect of dealing a staggering blow at American foreign trade and hence at American prosperity, which in every nation is so intimately connected with foreign trade. But Jefferson did not know this elementary principle of economics and if anyone had told him, he would not have believed it.[23] The aim of the embargo system was to bring England and France to terms. It hurt England it

---

[21] Henry Adams, *Hist. of the U. S.*, IV, Chs. 1 and 2; *Amer. State Papers, Foreign Relations*, III, 183ff.

[22] F. A. Updyke, *Diplomacy of the War of 1812*, p. 1.

[23] W. W. Jennings, *The American Embargo* (U. of Ia., 1921), 40-7, 59.

is true, but it certainly did not hurt her as much as it hurt the United States, and above all it failed completely to bring England to terms and to get her to recall her Orders and give up the practice of impressment.[24] As for the United States, in the long run the policy hurt the south more than it hurt any other section. That part of the country which gave Jefferson his principal support was ultimately the worst hurt, simply because the canny New Englander took his capital out of shipping and put it into industry, and the building of great factories, but the southerners were never able to industrialize their section. The south could not recuperate by taking its capital out of plantations and putting it into factories.[25]

The outcry inside the United States against the embargo as a principle of foreign policy was loud in its lamentation at ruined commerce and its abuse of President Jefferson. But the economic group which then dominated the government of the United States was held in line by the Jeffersonian political machine and the policy was maintained a good deal longer than pleased the New Englanders. As a means of forcing England and France to respect American neutral rights, it was a failure. But if it is viewed as a possible alternative to war, the embargo appears in a different light. Thomas Jefferson was something of a pacifist and his humanitarian attitude on foreign affairs fitted in well with the economic interests he represented. Hence he was anxious to avoid war and used the embargo as a substitute for war. Viewed as a laboratory experiment, it had this demerit, that in enforcing it, Jefferson had to rely on the votes of the middle states who held the balance of power between the south and New England. After two years of experimentation, this group broke under the strain. Loyalty to principle was too much to be expected of those who were both losing money and were also convinced that the embargo would not work. The middle states withdrew their support and the system collapsed.[26] It had stimulated manufactures, but it had injured agriculture and prostrated com-

---

[24] W. W. Jennings, *American Embargo* (U. of. Ia., 1921), p. 70.
[25] L. M. Sears, "The South and the Embargo," *So. Atl. Quar.*, XX, 254.
[26] L. M. Sears, "The Middle States and the Embargo of 1808 "; *So. Atl. Quar.*, XXI, 152.

merce.[27] As an experiment in foreign policy it demonstrated that its success must depend on a greater degree of economic solidarity than most nations can command.

When it became apparent that it would not work, the embargo was repealed and a Non-intercourse Act substituted for it. Next year even the Non-intercourse Act was withdrawn and England was able once more to sell her goods in the United States. Now this act was not only an open confession of the failure of American foreign policy, but it came just at the wrong time as far as our relations with the other belligerent, France, was concerned, and it further enraged Napoleon against the United States.[28]

Napoleon, we must always remember, was in the act of trying to put into operation a Navigation System, similar to that which Great Britain had employed for centuries. As he conquered Europe he tried to extend that monopolistic navigation system to all other nations of the continent, particularly with the aim of demolishing the great English commercial edifice which for centuries had enriched the island kingdom. This "Continental System" of Napoleon finds expression, as we have seen, in the "Berlin Decree" which pretended to blockade England and thereby to make it impossible for British manufacturers to sell any goods on the continent.[29] When, a year later, it became apparent that this was not enough, because England had retaliated with her Orders in Council of November, 1807, whereby all goods going to Europe must pass through England in one way or another, Napoleon proclaimed his "Milan Decree." The British tried to force all trade with Europe through the neck of the English bottle, and Napoleon's new decree simply ordered the seizure of any vessel going toward the English bottle.[30] American protests were unavailing, and Napoleon insisted that as long as the Americans recognized the British blockade or allowed the British to search them, they need expect no mercy from him.[31]

[27] W. W. Jennings, *The American Embargo*, p. 231.
[28] H. Adams, *Hist. of U. S.*, V, 33-7.
[29] F. Melvin, *Napoleon's Navigation System* (U. of Pa., 1919), pp. 6-47. F. L. Nussbaum, *Commercial Policy of the French Revolution,*(U. of Penna., 1923) pp. 300 ff.
[30] Ibid., pp. 40-41.
[31]*American State Papers, Foreign Relations*, III, 247-8.

To this, as to the British Orders, all that America had in reply, was the futile embargo, which really played right into Napoleon's hands. For in the next year he seized and sequestered all vessels bearing the American flag coming into French ports, on the ground that since the embargo forbade their sailing at all, they must be British vessels in disguise. By this "Bayonne Decree" (April 17, 1808), the British Orders and the Embargo itself, the Americans were reduced to a state of abject humiliation which it is hard to match in our history.[32]

The ineffectiveness of trying to rely on Napoleon was only further illustrated by the Rambouillet Decree (March 23, 1810) whereby the vessels being seized under the Bayonne Decree were to be sold and the money paid into a "caise d'amortissement," thus providing Napoleon with millions of dollars worth of American property as a pledge of our good behavior toward him.

James Madison had now become President of the United States, and he undertook to get both France and England to repeal their obnoxious decrees and orders. Monroe and Pinkney had been some time in London trying to get a treaty made which would eliminate the difficulties, but the British would not accept the treaty. Negotiations were transferred to Washington, where Erskine, the British minister, appeared to be a very decent sort of an envoy and got as far as making an agreement. This arrangement was promptly disavowed by George Canning, who had now become British foreign secretary.[33] Erskine was replaced by an individual named Francis James Jackson, who is principally renowned in history for his brutal bullying of the Danes before the bombardment of Copenhagen and his general inability to get along with anyone. Indeed George III himself frankly admitted Jackson deserved to be kicked downstairs.[34] Jackson was sent home flying after having grossly insulted the President and the situation was worse than ever.[35]

[32] F. Melvin, *Napoleon's Navigation System*, p. 72; E. F. Heckscher, *The Continental System* (N. Y., 1922), p. 140.
[33] H. Adams, *Hist. of U. S.*, V, 97 ff.; *American State Papers, Foreign Relations*, III, 301.
[34] Campbell, *Lives of the Lord Chancellors* (Phila., 1848); *Life of Lord Eldon*, VII, 192.
[35] H. Adams, *Hist. of U. S.*, V, 115ff.; *Am. State Papers, Foreign Relations*, III, 308-19; *Annals of Congress*, 1808-9, I, Dec. 5.

By 1811 matters at home began to force both Britain and France to take a more reasonable view of the American protests. How far this may have been the result of the American commercial restrictions, it is difficult to say. The protracted war, the rumblings of labor discontent and warehouses filled with unsalable goods resulted in numerous failures in England which in turn began to sober the British ministry.[36] At the same time, the Bordeaux merchants began to prod Napoleon with protests against that navigation system which was so fatal to their business.[37] Napoleon made some gestures which implied that he might relent, and his foreign minister Cadore in a letter of August 5, 1810, announced the revocation of the Berlin and Milan Decrees, it being understood that the English would revoke their Orders in Council. Madison was quick to jump at the offer contained in the Cadore letter. In fact, he was too quick. He tried to induce the British to agree to withdraw their obnoxious orders and blockades on the ground that Napoleon was going to withdraw his decrees. But in fact Napoleon was merely acting one of his characteristic bits of diplomatic treachery, for what he offered with one hand he withdrew with the other. The net result was that the British rather sarcastically intimated that they wanted some better evidence than Madison's word, that the French had actually withdrawn their decrees.[38]

This illustrates the essentially humiliating position of American diplomacy throughout this period. Britain and France, each fighting desperately for their lives in the face of a weakening morale at home, behaved like a pair of spoiled children, each promising to be good if the other would do so. Madison allowed himself to play the rôle of the distracted nurse who permits herself to get caught in such an argument instead of letting each belligerent distinctly understand that he would discuss French relations with France and English relations with England, and

---

[36] W. Cunningham, *Growth of English Industry and Commerce* (Camb., 1917), II, 686; Bland, Brown and Tawney, *English Economic History, Select Documents*, pp. 501-2.
[37] F. E. Melvin, *Napoleon's Navigation System*, 292, 314-17.
[38] H. Adams, *Hist. of the U. S.*, V, 245-8, VI, 189-90; *Amer. State Papers, Foreign Relations*, III, 421.

would allow neither discussion to be in any way dependent on the other.[39]

By 1812 both France and Britain were capturing and burning American vessels in reckless disregard of any laws. Many Americans were angry enough to suggest that war should be declared against both powers at once. It was evident that only one could be fought with any hope of success and so war was declared on that one which the political party then in power would most naturally hold most to blame. Madison was probably not driven to war so much by the threats of Calhoun, Clay and the "War-Hawks" with their threat to refuse him the renomination for the presidency, as he was simply consistent with his own party politics.[40] He and his secretary of state, Monroe, blandly and blindly assumed that the French decrees had in fact been withdrawn and that therefore the British should repeal their Orders. Foster, the British minister at Washington, was tied with impossible instructions and seemed only able to talk about the still unsettled and five-year old *Leopard-Chesapeake* affair. At the last minute England did withdraw the Orders in Council, not so much because the Americans demanded it as because of their disastrous effects on British commerce.[41] Napoleon, apparently at the height of his power, was just starting out on his ambitious Russian campaign and affairs inside of England had seldom been worse. This, however, did not stay the war, as the notice of the withdrawal of the obnoxious orders did not reach the United States in time to prevent Madison from laying his war message before Congress. Six years of accumulated wrath and the apparently un-negotiable question of impressment could not be appeased by Britain's yielding on the question of the Orders in council.[42]

Thus began the second war between the United States and Great Britain in 1812. Probably the less said about the conduct

[39] C. K. Webster, in *The Cambridge History of British Foreign Policy*, I, 526.
[40] H. Adams, *Hist. of U. S.*, VI, 196–7; F. A. Updyke, *Diplomacy of the War of 1812*, 125–6.
[41] Updyke, p. 139, *American State Papers, Foreign Relations*, III, 433.
[42] Henry Adams, *History of the U. S.*, VI, 286; *Amer. State Papers, Foreign Relations*, III, 665.

of this war the better. It was once the custom for both sides to claim victory. But as more dispassionate historians view the contest there seems to be a general tendency for both nations to admit they made a sorry mess of the war. Certain it is that the United States was worsted in the land fighting, her capital city occupied and her capitol building burnt. The important thing is that this war was very much of a side issue with the British, and that despite the acknowledged American naval victories, after the thing was all over the British could still boast that Britannia rules the waves.

3. TREATY OF GHENT

So it was that when the commissioners met to consider the peace negotiations, the British assumed the attitude of victors and undertook to dictate terms to the Americans. Some color was lent to this idea from the undue haste with which Madison snatched the first opportunity to make peace. In 1813, the Czar of Russia offered mediation and without waiting to hear whether the British would also accept, Madison dispatched his envoys to St. Petersburg to meet the British. On their arrival at the Russian capital, the Americans discovered for the first time that the British were by no means ready to stop the war.[43] In order to save the situation, Albert Gallatin, who had been forced to resign from the Treasury Department in order to become one of the American Commissioners, got in touch with his friend the English banker, Alexander Baring. Through Baring the Americans kept the door open and kept in touch with the situation. Meanwhile internal conditions in England led the ministers to listen to its bankers and merchants who were beginning to feel the pressure of nearly twenty years of war. So in 1814 the British undertook to make advances to Madison of which the latter promptly took advantage and notified his envoys.[44]

John Quincy Adams, James Bayard and Henry Clay joined Gallatin at the little Belgian town of Ghent. Their instructions

---

[43] F. A. Updyke, *Diplomacy of the War of 1812*, pp. 142ff.
[44] Ibid., pp. 142, 148, 157, 168, 187.

were drawn up by Monroe and the Senate confined itself to discussing whether a member of the cabinet could also act as commissioner. This signalizes the development of the conduct of the United States foreign relations wherein the Senate waits until the President has negotiated a treaty before giving their "advice and consent." The American envoys were of course instructed to get what they had fought the war to secure, namely, their maritime rights. They were further instructed to try to gain Canada and if possible the definition of a blockade, as Britain's loose interpretation of the law of blockade had been one of the chief causes of the war.[45]

The British dispatched to Ghent an amazingly mediocre group of diplomats. Whatever victories they gained during the war they certainly threw away at the peace table. Of course Lord Castlereagh, the British foreign minister, was at the time busy with very much bigger game at the Congress of Vienna. Indeed the brains of British diplomacy would naturally be where the map of the world was being revised after the fall of Napoleon. But even this does not explain the extreme dull-wittedness of the ministry in imagining that such men as they selected would be any match for the American delegates. The United States was unquestionably saved by superior brain work. Adams could be trusted to take care of the New England commercial interests and Clay was most solicitous about his precious new west and the Mississippi. But the greatest service was rendered by Albert Gallatin who spent a good part of his time smoothing out difficulties which inevitably arose between the strait-laced Puritan Adams and the poker-playing Kentuckian Clay.[46]

But if the British thought that they would gain anything from treating the American war as a relatively insignificant part of their great victory over Napoleon, they played a very mistaken game of diplomacy. They opened up with a series of impossible propositions, which involved the creation of an independent Indian barrier state between the United States and Canada, at

[45] C. K. Webster in *Cambridge Hist. of British Foreign Policy*, I, 534.
[46] *A Great Peace Maker, Diary of James Gallatin* (1914).

the expense of the United States. Moreover, the United States as the defeated party was summoned to surrender territory in both the northeast and the northwest, at the source of the Mississippi and in Maine. As the Americans intimated that such talk would speedily break up the conference the British were forced to soften their demands. About this time Castlereagh passed through Ghent en route to Vienna and he directed the British envoys to be more reasonable in their demands.[49]

The British then attempted to adjust the territorial differences on the basis of *uti possedetis*, i. e., let each belligerent retain what he had captured during the war. The Americans insisted on the *status quo ante bellum*, i. e., let each belligerent hold that which he had had at the outset of the war. The British delayed the negotiations in an apparent effort to see whether some news of British victories might not help their case. Moreover the stupidity of the British commissioners certainly did change the ideas of the British foreign office and couch them in language a good deal more insulting than Castlereagh had any desire to employ. But when the news of British victories, such as the capture of Washington, did come, it only served to strengthen the American case by solidifying the United States as nothing else had done. Moreover on top of the news of British victories came the news of the British defeats at Plattsburg and on the lakes, and the English found the delay had netted them nothing. On the contrary, the very obnoxious property tax, on which the British had helped finance the wars, was about to expire and the British ministry was in no position to get Parliament to reimpose it to fight a purely aggressive war in America. One after another the British surrendered their demands. They could no longer insist on the formation of the Indian buffer state, they had to give up their pretensions to an exclusive control of the Great Lakes, and now they had to consent to the *status quo ante bellum*.[48]

The Americans certainly helped their case by a bit of Madison's "shirt-sleeve" diplomacy, for when the President of the United

---

[47] F. A. Updyke, *Diplomacy of the War of 1812*, 201–23.
[48] Ibid., 231, 255–64, 288–94, 302, 313.

States saw the extent of the British demands, he simply published the correspondence to date and revealed Britain's imperialistic designs. This enraged the Americans into getting together, and caused an uproar in Parliament where the mercantile classes showed they had no desire to support their own commissioners in keeping up a useless war.[49]

On the other hand, the Americans certainly failed to get the principal things they had set out to attain. The British did not surrender the right of impressment; they did not define a blockade; they did not give up the Rule of 1756 or any of their other claims to hold up neutral trade in time of war. In addition to this, they claimed that the United States had lost their inshore fishing privileges secured under the treaty of 1783, on the ground that a war voids such a treaty and that they were not bound to renew these rights. Clay was willing to trade the fishing rights in order to exclude the British from the Mississippi Valley, but Adams was intent on protecting his Gloucester men. The result was that both questions, the fisheries and the Mississippi, were omitted from the treaty along with the other controverted points. The best that can be said of the treaty is that it secured a badly needed peace.[50]

Indeed, when as the practice now was, the treaty came to the Senate for ratification, there was no objection. The Senate Committee on Foreign Affairs had just emerged from a confusion of special committees to which foreign affairs had been entrusted during the past twenty years. Instead of appointing a new committee every time a new aspect of foreign affairs arose, the Senate was now developing the practice of giving the matter over to a standing committee on foreign relations, which was destined to play such a large part in the later conduct of American diplomacy.[51] Indeed the general tendency throughout the period was for the Senate to take a less and less active part in the initiation of foreign affairs. In 1805–6 when the grievances against Britain began to assume their more serious form, the Senate actu-

[49] F. A. Updyke, pp. 313–14.
[50] Ibid., pp. 363ff.
[51] R. Hayden, *The Senate and Treaties*, 1789–1817, pp. 169–96.

ally went on record as asking the President please to handle these affairs. After he had made a treaty, the Senate would ask for the papers "not inconsistent with public interest" and would then consider the advisability of ratifying the agreement. The origin and conduct of diplomatic negotiations became more and more an executive, rather than a legislative function, but the ultimate disposal of the negotiations still rested with the Senate, and, as we shall see in years to come, this ultimate disposition of the treaties could give the Senate a very effective veto on whatever foreign policy the executive department chose to initiate.[52]

The War of 1812 had two consequences, unforeseen, yet of tremendous significance. In the first place the war gave the United States a navy, and that navy was immediately turned loose on the Barbary states. We have noticed that at the outset of its diplomatic career, the United States followed the cowardly practice of European nations in attempting to buy off the Barbary states by the payment of tribute. Under Jefferson's administration a naval force was dispatched to deal with the pirates and in 1805 Captain John Rodgers, in command of the Mediterranean station, made a show of force which surprised the Barbary powers. At the time American interests were handled a good deal more creditably by Rodgers than had ever been done before. But unfortunately the matter was not followed up and as Jefferson began to be economical about the navy at that time, little came of it in the matter of the principle involved. From 1807 to 1815 the Americans continued the disgraceful system of giving "presents" to local potentates along the north coast of Africa.[53]

After 1815, however, a real fleet went to the Mediterranean under Decatur and Bainbridge. The Barbary powers had been so anxious to please the British that during the War of 1812, they had actually allowed the British to seize American vessels inside the north African harbors, in flagrant violations of their obligations as neutrals. The British assured them that the American

[52] R. Hayden, *The Senate and Treaties; 1789–1817*, pp. 199–208.
[53] E. Schuyler, *American Diplomacy*, pp. 216–22; C. O. Paullin, *Diplomatic Negotiations of American Naval Officers, 1778–1883* (Balt., 1912), pp. 71–107.

navy would be swept from the seas speedily and so there seemed
no objection to the practice on the part of the Barbary powers.
But, as we know, the American navy was far from being swept
off the sea in 1812–14. Moreover in 1815 those same warships
were turned loose on the corsairs, who were speedily brought to
their knees, much to their chagrin. Decatur captured the principal Algerine vessels and then went from one Barbary port to
another dictating the terms on which the United States would
refrain from chasing the pirates off the ocean altogether. This,
at least, was a language the Moslems could understand, and
the upshot of the whole matter was a series of treaties, by
which the United States, first among the nations of the world,
refused to pay the tribute which Europeans had been willing
to pay, and which was the price of not maintaining a decent
navy.[54]

But this masterful dealing with the Barbary States was only
further evidence that the War of 1812 had had a profound effect
on America, internally. The consolidation of the nation and the
growth of the national spirit were both apparent results of the
war, despite the unpatriotic conduct of New England. During
the period from 1793 to 1815, the United States seems gradually
to have learned the lesson that in dealing with outsiders she must
subordinate her family quarrels. The pro-French attitude of the
Jeffersonians and the pro-English attitude of the Federalists had
all but torn the new republic asunder. By 1815 a new group of
younger statesmen were coming to the front, who had been
brought up under the idea that there was such a thing as the
United States, and that it was a good deal more important than
the state of Massachusetts, or the state of Virginia. These men
were turning their faces not toward the Atlantic, on the other
side of which the quarrelsome nations of Europe were periodically cutting one another to pieces, but they were turning their
faces westward. Beyond the Appalachian Mountains thousands
upon thousands of emigrants were making their way, driving

[54] E. Schuyler, *American Diplomacy*, pp. 222–32; C. O. Paullin, *Diplomatic Negotiations of American Naval Officers*, pp. 107–21.

back the Indian, cutting down the forest and looking with greedy eyes at the possessions and claims of England and Spain to the western country. The story of American diplomacy and foreign relations now becomes one of the efforts of the United States to get that land.[55]

[55] N. M. Butler, *Effect of the War of 1812 upon the Consolidation of the Union.*

CHAPTER VIII

MANIFESTLY DESTINED DIPLOMACY

"An organized society which limits its ideas of civilization to the accumulation of material abundance, and of justice to their equitable distribution among its members, will never make its great cities anything that differs essentially from the heaping up of anthills."—*José Enrique Rodó.*

1. LOUISIANA

"Up to our own day American History has been in a large degree the history of the colonization of the Great West" says the distinguished historian of the frontier.[1] Long before the epochal year of 1815 had come the realization that "the west, rather than the ocean, was the real theater for the creative energy of America." [2] In 1790 barely a quarter of a million people lived on the other side of the Appalachian Mountains. In 1920 sixty-two million lived west of those mountains. In 1790, five per cent of the population of the United States was transappalachian; in 1920 nearly sixty per cent made their homes somewhere in the "west." In 1790 the United States extended westward only as far as the Mississippi and only as far south as the northern boundary of the Floridas. How did the United States gain the other land in North America that is hers to-day? Probably in no division of American history does the story of the rise of the west belong more logically than in the history of foreign policy.[3]

"By this peaceful process of colonization a whole continent has been filled with free and orderly commonwealths, so quietly, so naturally, that we can only appreciate the profound significance of the process by contrasting it with the spread of European

[1] F. J. Turner, *The Frontier in American History* (N. Y., 1920), p. 1.
[2] F. J. Turner, "Significance of the Mississippi Valley in American History" in his *Frontier*, p. 182.
[3] E. Channing, *Hist. of U. S.*, V, 48, passim; *Statistical Abstract of the U. S.*, 1921, pp. 38-9.

nations through conquest and oppression."[4]   The breezy and optimistic westerner may think that this statement is true, but the
people at whose expense the United States has acquired the land
for its sixty-two million are likely to have serious doubts on the
subject.

The heralds of this story we have already encountered in the
mighty conflict for the Mississippi Valley between France and
England. We met it again in John Jay's efforts to open the
mouth of the Mississippi during the period of the Revolution and
the Confederation. From the administration of Washington to
that of Monroe the United States was intensely interested in her
foreign policy, because she was the football of France and England. Every time the Europeans gave the ball a kick, they dis-
located American trade and industry in some way and every time
they did so a new group of people were thrown out of work who
picked up their beds and moved across the mountains into the
west. So the rise of the west is intimately associated with foreign
policy for it had its initial impulses so largely in the vicissitudes
of foreign affairs. The surge of westward migration soon began
to break down the barriers which the Peace of Paris at 1783 had
set for the new nation, and right there began a new set of negotiations and a new set of foreign relations which did not end
until the vanguard of the sixty-two million had reached the
Pacific and made good their claims from Vancouver to Lower
California.[5]

Before 1815 the tide of emigration had set in strongly toward
the southwest, for there lay the dominions of the King of Spain
which effectually shut off the Mississippi Valley from its necessary contact with the ocean. History is full of diplomatic negotiations, wars and conquests incident to the desires of a growing
nation for a seaport through which it could sell its surplus produce. Russia's century old search for her ice-free port or Jugo-
Slavia's desire for a window on the Adriatic at Fiume or elsewhere
are but other illustrations of the same kind of historic events as

[4] F. J. Turner, "The Ohio Valley in American History" in his *Frontier*, p. 169.
[5] J. B. McMaster, *Hist. of the People of the U. S.*, IV, 319, 331–46, 348–50.

interested the fathers of the republic in their insistence that any foreigner who held the mouth of the Mississippi must be a foe of the United States.[6] From 1795 to 1800 the diplomacy of the United States was concerned principally with one thing and that thing was the acquisition of the delta of the Mississippi.[7]

The explanation of the desire for Louisiana is simple enough. The astonishing fertility of the Mississippi Valley provided the newly arrived emigrant with a superabundance of corn and hogs, and that grain and pork had to find a market somewhere. Obviously it could not go back across the mountains to the eastern sea-board cities. Equally as obviously the only logical outlet was down the Mississippi River to the market at New Orleans or to transship at that point to feed hungry Europeans or the slaves of the West Indian plantations where the raising of a single crop, sugar, made the importation of food imperative. Prior to the Treaty of San Lorenzo in 1795, the Spaniards practically prohibited this passage through the mouth of the Mississippi. But the treaty of that year served to increase the grip of the United States on the whole valley because it settled the northern boundary of West Florida, thereby giving more secure land titles so attractive to the emigrants, and it gave the United States the much desired right of deposit at New Orleans. Hundreds of flatboats then began to float down the river carrying an ever increasing quantity of goods from whiskey to onions.[8]

But the Spaniard retained his right to close the river and in fact American expansion was at the mercy of a far-away-king living at Madrid. The situation was all the more intolerable because that king controlled all the other Gulf ports east of the Mississippi. Nowhere could the pioneer float his produce down a river to the Gulf of Mexico without crossing the dominions of the King of Spain. Consequently the Committee reported to the House of Representatives:

[6] T. Jefferson's *Works* (Washington ed.), IV, 431.

[7] J. A. James, "Louisiana as a Factor in American Diplomacy, 1795–1800" in *Miss. Valley Hist. Rev.*, I, 44–56.

[8] L. Pelzer, "Economic Factors in the Acquisition of Louisiana" in *Proc. of Miss. Valley Hist. Assoc.*, VI, 114–21; A. B. Hulbert, "Western Ship-Building" in *Amer. Hist. Rev.*, XXI, 720.

" . . . . the possession of New Orleans and the Floridas will not only be required for the convenience of the United States but will be demanded by their most imperious necessities. The Mississippi and its branches drain . . . one half of our whole territory. The Floridas and New Orleans command the only outlets to the sea, and our best interests require that we should get possession of them." [9]

Then the committee did not hesitate to go on and say "War may be the result."

All this was well known to the Spaniard and he worried about it a good deal. The eagerness, the enterprise and the remorselessly increasing number of settlers from the United States who burst through the mountains and flowed like waters through a broken dyke, engulfing the Mississippi Valley and threatening the whole Spanish Empire to the south, all these were enough to fill the Spaniard with alarm, even if he could not understand what it was all about.[10] After the treaty of San Lorenzo in 1795, the Spaniards pinned their hopes on being able to persuade the western United States to secede from the east and thus to force them into the Spanish Empire whose grip on the jugular vein at New Orleans was Spain's only hope of checking American expansion.[11] Numerous pretexts for delay in the enforcement of the treaty were indications of the fact that the Spaniards hoped something would turn up to make it possible for them to retain that grip which was obviously weakening from successive blows from the north.[12]

But a greater power than either Spain or the United States now took a hand in the matter. After all, France had given Louisiana to Spain with the secret hope that since it was all in the same family she might some day regain that great empire of which her explorer La Salle had been the first to catch the vision. We have seen how at the Peace of Paris in 1783, Vergennes had secretly plotted with Spain and England to keep the United States

[9] *Annals of Congress, 1802–3*, 7th Cong., 2 sess., p. 373.

[10] I. J. Cox, "The New Invasion of the Goths and Vandals," *Proc. of Miss. Valley Hist. Assoc.*, VIII, 181–2.

[11] W. R. Shepherd, "Wilkinson and the Beginning of the Spanish Conspiracy," *Amer. Hist. Rev.*, IX, 490, 533, 748.

[12] F. L. Riley, "Spanish Policy in Mississippi after the Treaty of San Lorenzo," *Amer. Hist. Assoc. Rept.*, 1897, pp. 175–83.

walled in by the Appalachians, so that France might the more
easily regain her title to the whole of the Ohio and Mississippi
Valleys.[13] The reconquest of Louisiana was probably a fundamental purpose in Genet's mission to the United States.[14] The
same policy now became the peculiar pet of Talleyrand, recently
returned from a first hand acquaintance with the United States
and now minister of foreign affairs for the French Directory.

In a paper before the Institute in 1797 Talleyrand launched
his idea of a new Colonial System built on the recovery of Louisiana from Spain. That nation, he rightly insisted, was in no condition to shut the Americans in to the seaboard. He did not
realize that such a thing was already past hope, for by that time
Whitney had invented the cotton gin and the march of the cotton
plantations to the west was already pushing before it thousands
of emigrants whom this new adjustment in economic life was
bound to drive from the Old South into the New Southwest.
But Talleyrand saw in Louisiana a great granary for the West
Indies and an outlet for malcontents at home.[15] Talleyrand's
ideas became the model for Napoleon's policy of a new overseas
empire, for no man of Napoleon's imagination could possibly
overlook the importance of the Mississippi Valley. Something
must be done and right quickly to keep the English-speaking
peoples from overrunning the whole of North America. Spain
had been given that responsibility and had failed miserably, so the
French decided to try it themselves.

But first the French must get Louisiana back from Spain. In
1795 at the Peace of Basle, the French had acquired from Spain
the Spanish end of the troublous island of Santo Domingo, of
which France already occupied the western end with her inflammable colony of St. Domingue. When Napoleon returned from
his Marengo campaign he felt strong enough to dictate further to
Spain and this time he demanded Louisiana. Talleyrand and

[13] F. J. Turner, "Policy of France toward the Mississippi Valley in the Period of Washington and Adams," *Amer. Hist. Rev.*, X, 250ff.

[14] F. J. Turner, "Origin of Genet's Projected Attack on Louisiana and the Floridas,"
Amer. Hist. Rev., III, 650.

[15] H. Adams, *Hist. of U. S.*, I, 355ff.

Berthier went to Madrid to win over the Queen Mother, who, in turn, agreed to convince King Charles IV that he ought to give the Mississippi Valley to Napoleon. The affair was entirely successful from the French standpoint and from it came the celebrated Treaty of San Ildefonso between France and Spain, in 1800. By this contract Spain agreed to retrocede Louisiana to France on the condition that France elevate the son-in-law of the Spanish king to the throne of a certain "Kingdom of Etruria" which was to be created for the purpose out of the old Duchy of Parma, Tuscany and a few papal states. Delivery of Louisiana to France was made conditional on Napoleon's being able to metamorphose this petty prince into a king, and Louisiana was to go to France, "with the same extent that it now has in the hands of Spain, and had while in the possession of France, and such as it ought to be in conformity with the treaties subsequently concluded between Spain and other states," whatever that might mean. For obviously since half of Louisiana had gone to England in 1763 and was now a part of the United States, Louisiana could not possibly be given to France "with the same extent that it had while in the possession of France." [16]

The Peace of Amiens in 1802 gave France a breathing spell during which she might take possession of Louisiana. Napoleon did create the shadowy title for the "King of Etruria" but it was no more than a shadow. Yet on the strength of it Bonaparte dispatched General Leclerc with an army of French veterans to reconquer Santo Domingo and then move on and reoccupy Louisiana. Leclerc defeated the blacks in Santo Domingo but was in turn defeated by yellow fever which practically annihilated his army. The grandiose scheme for the reoccupation of Louisiana had to go by the board. Just about this time (1802) the Spanish Intendant at New Orleans, scenting the fact that Spain would soon lose Louisiana, and conscious that the right of deposit guaranteed the United States under the treaty of 1795 was depriving him of valuable revenues, decided to suspend that right of deposit and choke off the flood of American goods coming down the

[16] H. Adams, *Hist. of U. S.*, I, pp. 353ff.

Mississippi. Immediately the growing empire of the west was given a taste of just what it meant to have some foreign power controlling the mouth of the river. If this had been serious in 1792 it was much more serious in 1802 when thousands more settlers had been pouring into the west and producing a surplus which had to seek its market by way of New Orleans.[17]

On coming into the presidency in 1801 Jefferson had tried to ascertain the status of Louisiana and had been assured by the smooth Talleyrand that France had not acquired it. At the same time another suave Frenchman was assuring the king of Spain that France would never dispose of the territory which Talleyrand denied she had.[18] Into this Machiavellian diplomacy went the President of the United States in an effort to protect his now loudly indignant westerners. Livingston, the American minister at Paris, was under instructions to protect the interests of the United States in the event that Spain did surrender Louisiana to France and Jefferson wrote his famous letter about the United States being forced to marry herself to the British fleet in case France got New Orleans.[19] Rufus King, American minister at London, finally got hold of a copy of the Treaty of San Ildefonso and sent it to Jefferson as evidence of the fact that France actually had Louisiana.[20]

Meantime the Spaniards had been complicating the situation by protesting that France had not fulfilled her part of the bargain and made the Kingdom of Etruria a fact. With all this going on the prospect of constant interruption of commerce at the mouth of the Mississippi led Jefferson to send James Monroe to Paris to help Livingston try to buy the Island of New Orleans (See Map, p. 50.) But there were wheels within wheels. The building of the great French Empire in the Mississippi Valley might be a dream of Talleyrand's, but the First Consul had a dozen other dreams as well. He wished to get Louisiana back

---

[17] H. Adams, *Hist. of U. S.*, I, 406–18; T. L. Stoddard, *French Revolution in San Domingo* (Boston, 1914).

[18] H. Adams, *Hist. of the U. S.*, I, 400.

[19] T. Jefferson's Works (Washington ed.), IV, 432.

[20] *Amer. State Papers, For. Rel.*, II, 511.

from Spain, but he was even more anxious that it should not fall into the hands of England. Ambitious designs on the Near East, troubles aplenty all over the continent of Europe, and the yellow fever in Santo Domingo combined to decide Napoleon to scrap the whole Louisiana idea. It was no longer a question of whether or not he should give up Louisiana, but to whom should he give it? The fact that he was under obligations to return it to Spain weighed but lightly with him. The important thing was to get rid of it in some way to hurt England. It took but a glance for him to see that the United States was the great commercial nation of the future likely to rival England. Why not give Louisiana to the United States and thereby aggrandize her at the expense of England and gain at the same time several millions in gold for his war chest which was going to be needed in the new campaigns against Austria? To think was to act with Napoleon. Talleyrand had lied about the business so many times that the First Consul intrusted the matter to Barbé-Marbois with orders to sell to the United States. Livingston, who had been trying desperately for weeks to get a small piece of Louisiana at the Island of New Orleans, suddenly found the whole thing thrown at him. He tried to close the deal before Monroe's arrival but more diplomatic fencing was caused by Talleyrand's reëntrance into the game. Whereupon Napoleon took matters into his own hands, fixed the price at $12,000,000 and bade the United States assume $4,000,000 worth of claims due to its citizens from the French Government and then told Livingston and Monroe that they could take it or leave it. They took it.[21]

The terms of the Louisiana Purchase Treaty provided that the United States should acquire it "in the same manner as it had been acquired by the French Republic" in the Treaty of San Ildefonso, which, as we have already seen, made perfectly unintelligible boundary provisions. The boundary of Louisiana on the south was fixed by nature, but every other boundary was

---

[21] W. M. Sloane, "World Aspects of the Louisiana Purchase," *Amer. Hist. Assoc. Rept.*, 1903, I, 89–100; H. Adams, *Hist. of U. S.*, II, 24–50, *Amer. State Papers, For. Rel.*, II, 522ff.; G. Chinard, *Volney et L'Amerique* (J. H. U., 1923) throws some new and exceedingly interesting light on Napoleon's motives.

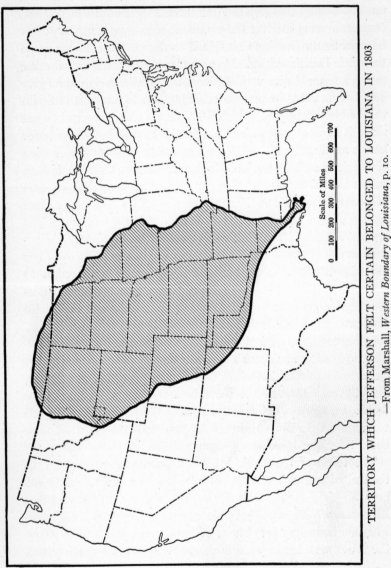

TERRITORY WHICH JEFFERSON FELT CERTAIN BELONGED TO LOUISIANA IN 1803

—From Marshall, *Western Boundary of Louisiana*, p. 10.

vague and meaningless. When the Americans sat down to find
out what they had bought, the French refused to help them.
Napoleon remarked cynically that if some obscurity as to the
boundaries did not exist, it would be good policy to put some
there.[22] Talleyrand blandly told the Americans that they had
made a noble bargain and had better make the most of it.[23]
Jefferson at first seems to have thought that he was only buying
the western watershed of the Mississippi Valley but after he had
studied the history of Louisiana he rather came to the conclusion
that it included Texas and Oregon as well. In buying Louisiana,
the United States purchased two boundary disputes which resulted in nearly half a century of diplomatic wrangling.[24] (See
Maps, pp. 142, 149.)

2. FLORIDA

American diplomacy can claim very little credit to itself for
the acquisition of Louisiana. The flood of western migration
hounded the United States into action and Napoleon fairly threw
the country into the hands of Livingston and Monroe. But the
purchase did quiet forever those timid spirits which talked about
the Mississippi as the "natural boundary of the United States."
The resistless tide of emigration continued to pour pioneers into
the west and American settlers soon began to fill up that portion
of old French Louisiana which was now claimed by the Spanish
under the name of West Florida.

If there is one story in American diplomatic history which cannot possibly be understood without the aid of maps, that is the
story of West Florida. Again it is necessary to go back to the
treaty of 1763. Prior to the French and Indian War, there had
been no "West Florida." There had been a "Florida" and a
"Louisiana," the one owned by Spain and the other by France.
The boundary line between them had been the Perdido River.
(See Map, p. 30.) But, as we have seen, in 1763 France surrendered

---

[22] Barbé-Marbois, *Histoire de la Louisiane* (Paris, 1829), p. 312.
[23] Henry Adams, *Hist. of U. S.*, II, 44; *Amer. State Papers, For. Rel.*, II, 552.
[24] T. M. Marshall, *Western Boundary of Louisiana Purchase, 1819-41* (Berkeley, 1914),
pp. 10-16.

all claim to her lands on the continent of North America, and Louisiana was divided between Spain and England. The British then occupied both Florida and Louisiana east of the Mississippi. They erected part of their share of Louisiana into a new province in 1764, which they called "West Florida" the northern boundary of which was originally fixed at 31° but was later raised to 32° 28'. The new province was separated from "East Florida" by the line of the Chattahochee and Appalchicola Rivers. (See Map, p. 31.) Thus the divisions of land remained till 1783, when the termination of the American Revolution gave the Floridas back to Spain and caused a dispute with the United States as to the ownership of the territory between 31° and 32° 28' which, as has been seen, was finally awarded to the United States by the treaty of San Lorenzo in 1795.[25] (See Map, p. 192.)

If the United States bought Louisiana as it had formerly been in the hands of France, she certainly got a large part of West Florida. This was, of course, not Spain's understanding of the Treaty, but Spain could only protest feebly as the vicissitudes of European politics combined with Napoleon to put her where she was quite incapable of complaining at anything. Louisiana in the hands of France and Louisiana in the hands of Spain were in fact two very different things and the Americans undertook to make the best of their bargain. American settlers poured into West Florida and made it into an English-speaking community of American-born people, no matter what foreign potentate might claim the jurisdiction. "The Spaniards were attempting to control a pioneer population, alien in spirit, custom, and political training, but land hungry and unscrupulous in appeasing their appetite." [26] This is, after all, the typical American way of expanding and the following rather bitter criticism by a Mexican statesman, when the United States was doing the same thing at the expense of his country, does not seem to agree that our process of expansion has been highly moral when contrasted with the European:

[25] H. E. Chambers, *West Florida*, J. H. U. Stud. XVI (Baltimore, 1898), No. 5, pp. 18–35.
[26] I. J. Cox, *West Florida Controversy, 1798–1813* (Baltimore, 1918), p. 63.

"They (the Americans) commence by introducing themselves into the territory which they covet, upon pretence of commercial negotiations, or of the establishment of colonies, with or without the assent of the Government to which it belongs. These colonies grow, multiply, become the predominant party in the population; and as soon as a support is found in this manner, they begin to set up rights which it is impossible to sustain in serious discussion, and to bring forward ridiculous pretensions, founded upon historical facts which are admitted by nobody." [27]

In the matter of West Florida the United States soon reached the stage of making claims on section after section of the country. In 1810 the American inhabitants of the westernmost section called a convention, declared themselves independent of Spain and notified the United States of their existence as a sovereign and constitutional state. President Madison promptly took them over as part of the Louisiana purchase in utter disregard of the now very feeble protests from the Spaniards. The British chargé-d'affaires in Washington protested against this action because his nation had designs on the Floridas, but Madison curtly shut him up with the information that the United States was handling that matter through its minister in London.[28] In justifying this to Congress President Madison laid down the following principle of American foreign policy,

"The United States could not see, without serious inquietude, any part of a neighboring territory in which they have in different respects, so deep and so just a concern, pass from the hands of Spain into those of any other foreign power." [29]

If any territory in which the United States has any vital interests seems to be slipping from the grasp of its real owners, the United States would feel justified in taking it rather than allowing it to fall into the hands of any other foreign power.

All this time Spain had been practically silent, not from any wish on her part, but simply because Napoleon was sitting on her neck. But after 1815 when Napoleon was safely out of the way, Ferdinand came back to his Spanish throne and there appeared

[27] Lucas Alaman in *House Exec. Docs.*, No. 351, 25 Cong., 2 sess., 313.
[28] Cox, *West Florida*, pp. 312–88; *Amer. State Papers, For. Rel.*, III, 395, 398, 400.
[29] Richardson, *Messages*, I, 488 (Jan., 1811).

in Washington a certain Don Luis de Onis, who blandly informed
the Secretary of State that he was the new envoy of His Most
Catholic Majesty of Spain and was prepared to reopen negotiations in regard to the whole question of Louisiana and Florida
as it had been in 1808. But a great deal of water had passed
under the bridge since 1808. The whole period had been one in
which the Spanish colonies had been asserting their independence
from the Mother Country. Not only had West Florida broken
away, but every provincial capital from Mexico to Buenos Ayres

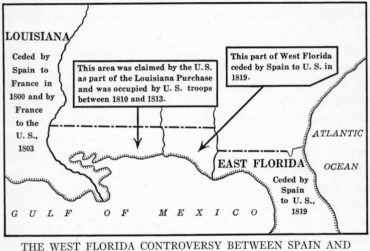

LOUISIANA

Ceded by
Spain to
France in
1800 and by
France
to the
U. S.,
1803

This area was claimed by the U. S.
as part of the Louisiana Purchase
and was occupied by U. S. troops
between 1810 and 1813.

This part of West Florida
ceded by Spain to U. S. in
1819.

ATLANTIC

EAST FLORIDA

OCEAN

Ceded by
Spain
to U. S.,
1819

GULF   OF   MEXICO

THE WEST FLORIDA CONTROVERSY BETWEEN SPAIN AND
THE UNITED STATES, 1803–1819

The question was whether the Louisiana Purchase included West Florida

was seething with the forces of revolution. If Spain had been
incompetent to settle boundary disputes in 1808, she was helpless
in 1815.[30]

Meantime the boundary disputes were being complicated with
diplomatic difficulties of many different kinds. De Onis politely called the attention of Secretary of State Monroe to the fact
that dozens of filibustering expeditions were fitting out from New
York and Baltimore to help free the South American colonies,

[30] *Annals of Congress*, 15th Cong., 2nd Sess., II, 1819, pp. 1630–34.

and that other armed expeditions were being set on foot in New Orleans to deliver Mexico from Spain. Monroe could not deny this, but he replied a little less politely that the United States had hundreds of claims against Spain for the illegal action of Spain in suspending the right of deposit in 1802 and for stoppage of neutral commerce during the Napoleonic wars. He likewise pointed out that those claims were still unpaid and were being daily increased by Spain's inability to police East Florida which had become a nest of pirates and marauding Indian bands, who preyed on American commerce and destroyed American frontier settlements and then took refuge on Spanish territory beyond the reach of the United States army and navy. Bands of thieving and murdering Seminole Indians dashed out of Florida, armed with weapons and whiskey supplied by British traders and made life miserable for the pioneers in southern Georgia. English pirates and filibusters used the excellent harbors of Amelia Island on the east coast of Florida to organize raids on United States commerce and liberating expeditions into Spanish America.[31]

All this was bad enough and delicate enough, but it soon became much worse because of the fact that the United States War Department put General Andrew Jackson in command of the troops on the southern frontier. He was instructed to stop the raids of the Seminoles and such orders were the very breath of life to him. He made war on the Seminoles wherever he could find them, crossed the border into Spanish Florida, captured Spanish forts and strongholds in the process, harried the Seminoles out of their lands, captured the towns of St. Marks and Pensacola, offended Spanish territorial sovereignty and picked up a pair of English traders whom he accused of supplying arms to the Indians, tried them by court-martial, hung one and shot the other and in general enraged both England and Spain against the United States.[32] De Onis was beside himself with indignation and the British minister Castlereagh assured the United States minister

[31] *Amer. State Papers, For. Rel.*, IV, 199–201.
[32] See Jackson's "Exposition" in T. H. Benton's *Thirty Years View*, I, 169–80; Niles, *Register*, XV, 156, 270–81.

Rush that war with England might have resulted by "holding up a finger."[33]

President Monroe and his cabinet were quite perplexed by the way General Jackson had forced their hand. Officially Jackson's action was disapproved by both the Cabinet and the House Committee on Military Affairs, partly on the ground that making war was primarily the business of Congress and not of the Executive and partly because the execution of the British traders was an extreme measure unknown to international law. Nevertheless, a close scrutiny of the documents will convince most readers that Jackson's stern measures were amply justified by the bad faith and duplicity on the part of Spain and by the incendiary activities of the British agents. The whole episode is another illustration of the way the executive department can get the nation to the brink of war, although the constitution gives the war power to Congress. The country in general seems to have secretly, if not openly, admired Jackson's deeds, and he found an unexpected but strong advocate in the Secretary of State, John Quincy Adams.[34]

Secretary Adams notified the Spanish minister in words of one syllable that if Spain was incompetent to take care of her own territory and to keep pirates, bandits, and Indians from annoying the peaceful citizens of the United States, that the United States was perfectly justified in taking matters into her own hands and invading Spanish territory for the protection of her own frontier. Meanwhile the United States kept careful account of the claims due her citizens from Spain for those same border raids, and the claims were now piling up into the millions. Spain was put on notice that she must either police the Floridas, or else cede them to someone who could take care of them, meaning, of course, the United States.[35]

As if there were not enough diplomatic troubles, more appeared

---

[33] R. Rush, *Memoranda of a Residence at the Court of London, 1819–25*, pp. 152–3.

[34] James Monroe's *Writings*, VI, 54ff., 74–5; *House Doc.*, No. 82, 15th Cong., 2d sess.; J. C. Calhoun's *Correspondence*, in *Amer. Hist. Assoc. Rept.*, 1899, II, 285ff.

[35] *Annals of Congress*, 15th Cong., 2d Sess., 1818–9, I, 1738–9, 1776–7; *Amer. State Papers, For. Rel.*, IV, 200–1, 496–9; *Amer. State Papers, Mil. Aff.*, I, 680ff.

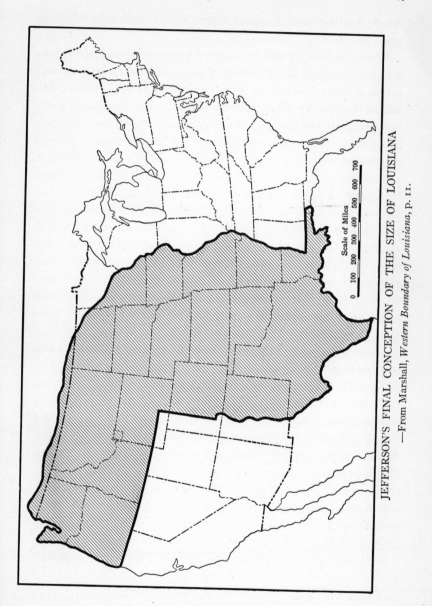

JEFFERSON'S FINAL CONCEPTION OF THE SIZE OF LOUISIANA
—From Marshall, *Western Boundary of Louisiana*, p. 11.

in the far southwest. The pioneers were pushing ever onward and began to cast greedy glances at Texas. The claim was made by the Americans that the Louisiana Purchase included Texas as far as the Rio Grande. In 1803 Jefferson had no idea that Louisiana included Texas, but as we have seen, as he began to read up the subject, his ideas expanded, and he did not hesitate to push our claims that far. The disputed area between the mouth of the Mississippi and the mouth of the Rio Grande was the subject of many wrangles in the administrations of Jefferson and Madison and finally in Monroe's administration it came to a head along with all the other difficulties with Spain. Many suggestions of a neutral strip between the extreme Spanish and the extreme American claims were made by the envoys from the two countries, but the nations could no more decide on the neutral strip than they could decide on the boundary itself. Spain insisted that the Mississippi should be the western boundary of the United States and the American envoys were equally intent on the line of the Rio Grande to its source and thence to the Pacific.[36] (See Map, p. 151.)

Out of this tangled mass appeared the treaty of 1819. By it the United States got all the Floridas and Spain got Texas. Each power owed the other a heavy bill of damages and each consented to give up those claims. But the American claims were different from the Spanish. Spain had claims against the United States government for indemnity due the Spanish government for the violation of United States neutrality during the South American Wars of Independence. These she surrendered. But the American claims were claims of private citizens of the United States against the Spanish government for damages done, and they could not so easily be disposed of. Finally it was agreed that if Spain would surrender her claims against the United States, the United States would assume the obligations due its own citizens by Spain to the amount of $5,000,000. The western boundary of Louisiana was fixed at the Sabine River and thence to the 42d parallel, giving the United States her claim to the Pacific

[36] H. E. Bolton, "Spanish Occupation of Texas" in *Southwestern Hist. Quar,* XVI, 11–15; T. M. Marshall, *Western Boundary of Louisiana,* pp. 11–13, 30–69; T. Jefferson's *Works* (Ford ed.), VIII, 261–3 (Washington ed.), IV, 501–3.

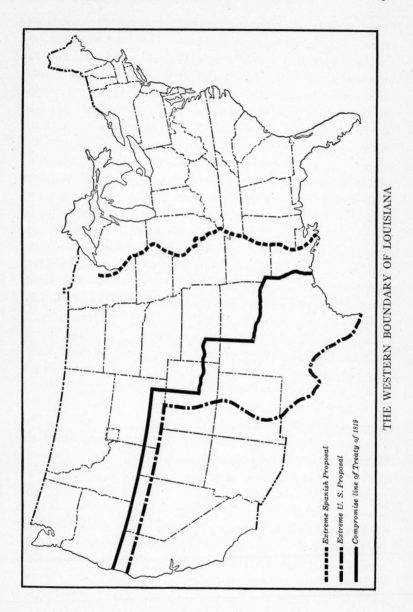

THE WESTERN BOUNDARY OF LOUISIANA

Extreme Spanish Proposal

Extreme U. S. Proposal

Compromise line of Treaty of 1819

coast above that line. Spain kept Texas and California and everything between. (See Map, p. 151.) [37]

But the year 1819 did not by any means end this story. The treaty was not ratified by Spain in that year nor in the next. The Spanish suddenly discovered that they wanted to stipulate that before they gave up Florida, the United States must promise not to recognize the revolting colonies in South America. Delay followed delay while Secretary Adams tried to urge upon Spain that a treaty negotiated within the scope of the instructions given by the King of Spain was binding on him and he must ratify. When arguments from international law were of no avail, he finally took a sterner attitude and informed the Spaniards that unless they ratified quickly the United States would not only refuse to assume the $5,000,000 in claims but would likewise reopen the Texas question, with the implication that the United States would take that province as well as Florida. Finally the Spanish did ratify, but it was already too late for them to save Texas. [38]

3. Taking Texas

The panic of 1819, one of those periodical business depressions in the United States, had only succeeded in stimulating the emigration of the unemployed to the west. Louisiana and Florida being now a part of the United States for colonization purposes, the restless pioneer pushed further west. He did not like a neighbor so near that he could see the smoke from his chimney. The man out of a job, the land hungry pioneer, the fugitive from justice, the drunkard, the malcontent and the ne'er-do-wells of a dozen types began to wonder why the United States had ever surrendered her claims to Texas and began to emigrate into Texas in spite of the fact. [39] The reorganization of the public land system in the United States in 1820 put an end to the credit system and forced the pioneer to pay cash for his land. Many hundreds

[37] Marshall, *Western Boundary of Louisiana*, pp. 63–70.
[38] F. E. Chadwick, *Relations of Spain and the United States, Diplomacy*, pp. 139–46; Marshall, *Western Boundary of Louisiana*, pp. 68–70; *Amer. State Papers, For. Rel.*, IV, 681–5, 691–2.
[39] Anson Jones, *Autobiography*, pp. 8–10.

of settlers promptly left the unhospitable United States and moved across the border into Texas where hundreds of thousands of fertile acres were unoccupied.[40] In that same year one Moses Austin went to Mexico City and got permission from the Spanish authorities to bring several hundred emigrant families from the United States into Texas. Before the deal could be closed Moses Austin died and Mexico revolted from Spain. The work was carried on by his son, Stephen F. Austin, who finally brought into Texas that group of Yankees settlers who were to be a thorn in the flesh of Mexico for many years to come. The newly formed Mexican government granted numerous favors to the colonists to induce them to come to Texas, including a certain freedom from taxation and from the imposition of customs duties for a period of years.   In return for this and for their land, the emigrants promised to become good Mexican citizens and good Roman Catholics.[41]

For a short time, all went well. The periodically recurring revolutions in Mexico left her very little time to bother with what was going on in her far-away northern province of Texas. The rapid succession of emperors, presidents and dictators in the stormy history of Mexico left Texas to herself in a period of salutary neglect, during which more and more land hungry ne'er-do-wells poured into Texas from the great Republic to the north. By 1830 the Mexicans were thoroughly aroused to the fact that they had allowed their fair northern province to be filled with an unassimilated and unassimilable mass of Anglo-Americans, who had not the slightest intention of becoming either good Mexicans or good Catholics. Stephen Austin strove nobly to make the Americans abide by the terms of his agreement but it would have required many regiments of Austins to mediate between the changing, suspicious and ultra sensitive set of rulers in Mexico City and the unruly set of frontiersmen who seemed to think they were sovereign in Texas and had only contempt for their

[40] J. B. Sanborn, "Some Political Aspects of Homestead Legislation," in *American Historical Review*, VI, 19–26.

[41] E. C. Barker, "Government of Austin's Colony, 1821–31," in *Southwestern Historical Quarterly*, XXI, 223ff.

Mexican rulers.[42] There is some ground for saying that the Texan Revolution was not a patriotic outburst of indignation against Mexico, but that it was a scheme engineered by a group of radical Yankees who were aided by the Latin's inherent distrust of the Yankee.[43] Moreover, at the end of the ten-year period the Mexican Government began to collect taxes and to threaten the abolition of slavery and these attacks on the property rights of the Texans helped them to decide that they would no longer remain a part of the Republic of Mexico. But unfortunately in the Mexican mind it was difficult to differentiate between the Yankees in Texas and the Yankees in the United States and from this point the story is merged in the diplomacy of the latter country.

The United States had been among the first to recognize the independence of Mexico by sending thither, as minister, in 1826, Joel Poinsett, an exceptionally able man, who unfortunately became involved in one of the numerous revolutions. This raised some suspicion of the disinterestedness of the country he represented. He went to Mexico in the first place instructed to get Mexican assent to the western boundary provision of the Spanish treaty of 1819. The fact soon came out, however, that the United States still had designs on the Rio Grande boundary and that Mexico still clung to the idea that she should own all the way up to the Mississippi. President Adams authorized his secretary of state, Henry Clay, to offer a million dollars for Texas in 1827, which was promptly, not to say scornfully, turned down by Mexico. When Jackson became President, Poinsett had to be withdrawn from Mexico at the request of the Mexicans, but Jackson replaced him with one Anthony Butler, an ignorant, bullying, swashbuckling, and thoroughly disreputable individual who had a personal financial interest in getting Texas for the United States. Such circumstances as these did not tend to make our relations with Mexico any happier, nor to dispel the idea now rapidly growing in the Mexican imagination that the United States intended to take Texas away from them at the first con-

[42] E. C. Barker, "Stephen F. Austin" in *Southwestern Historical Quarterly*, XXII, 1.
[43] E. C. Barker, "Texan Revolutionary Army" in *Quarterly of the Texas State Hist. Soc.*, IX, 260.

venient opportunity. Butler offered five million for Texas and was turned down as curtly as had been Clay's offer. Emigrants from the United States continued to pour into Texas, and claims against the Mexican government, of the same sort which had gained Florida for the United States, now began to pile up against Mexico.[44]

Under these unhappy circumstances began our century of misunderstanding with Mexico. When, in 1836, Texas revolted against her Mother Country, there is little wonder that the Mexican authorities "felt sure that from the beginning to the end, in the colonization, rebellion and successful defense of the region, the hand of the American government could plainly enough be seen."[45] Yet throughout the period of the Texan Revolution the United States government tried to maintain an attitude of correct and strict neutrality. This does not imply that the citizens of the United States were neutral, any more than they were neutral in the European War between 1914 and 1917. Nor is there lacking considerable proof that armed hostile expeditions were actually set on foot in the United States for service in the Texan War of Independence. Great enthusiasm was manifested for the Texan cause, in the north as well as in the south.[46] As long as this took the form of the activity of private individuals in holding mass meetings, in collecting funds for the Texan cause, or in selling or giving arms to the Texans, there could be no charge against the United States government for breach of neutrality.[47] But when the United States government permitted the actual enrollment of troops inside the United States, and the arming and organization of those troops prior to their departure from New Orleans for service in Texas, it most certainly did allow its neutrality to be violated and gave Mexico just cause for complaint.[48] Unfortunately the Mexicans did not seem to be able to

[44] J. Smith, *War with Mexico* (N. Y., 1919), I, 62, 74ff.
[45] Ibid., I, 63.
[46] J. E. Winston, "Pennsylvania and the Independence of Texas" in *Southwestern Historical Quarterly*, XVII, 266, 274-5, 280-1.
[47] J. Smith, *Annexation of Texas*, pp. 11-33.
[48] E. C. Barker, "Texan Revolutionary Army" in *Texas State Hist. Soc. Quar.*, IX, 227, 242.

differentiate between what was and what was not allowed under international law, and charged the United States government indiscriminately with unneutral conduct, whereas the United States did exercise a good deal of care under the circumstances.[49]

The whole affair was further complicated by the fact that the treaty of 1831 between the United States and Mexico contained a promise on each side to prevent the Indians from raiding across the border. About the time the Texans were asserting their independence in the battle of San Jacinto, the Indian tribes on the Louisiana frontier flamed up in an insurrection and since the Mexicans were entirely helpless to prevent them from raiding the United States side of the border, the American General Gaines in the southwest crossed the border into Texas and put down the Indians in an effort to protect the settlers in Louisiana. Occurring at the same time as the battle of San Jacinto, it started all sorts of ugly talk about the support given the Texans by Gaines. Possibly there is no truth in the story, but in our Mexican relations it is not so much the truth that counts as it is what people believe to be the truth. It has been difficult to convince the Mexicans that Gaines' troops were not there to aid the Texans and the fact that some of Gaines' troopers did desert and join the Texans lent color to the Mexican suspicion.[50]

Jackson certainly wanted Texas but he would not go to the extent of war to get it. He even moved with the utmost caution in the matter of recognizing the independence of Texas. For this there were several motives. In the first place he was just extricating himself from a near-war with France over the non-payment of the long delayed French spoliation claims. These claims arose out of the attacks on our neutral trade during the later stages of the Napoleonic wars and had been acknowledged by France who solemnly promised to pay them, but never did. Jackson determined to collect the bill and rode roughshod over French susceptibilities. The upshot of the affair was that France

---

[49] J. Smith, *War with Mexico*, I, 63.
[50] Ibid., I, 64-5, 420-23.

and the United States broke off diplomatic relations, when Jackson sent a stinging message on the subject and France made an angry gesture indicating that she would not be bullied into paying the debt. Jackson even went so far as to recommend that the United States prepare for war when the fortunate intervention of England with an offer of mediation brought both nations to their senses. But for a while the situation looked decidedly nasty and Jackson had no desire to handle more than one foreign crisis at a time.[51] In addition the presidential election of 1836 was not far off and as Jackson was trying to turn the ship of state over to his faithful Martin Van Buren, he suddenly discovered that the United States was not by any means a unit in its desire for Texas and he trimmed his sails accordingly.

The change in American public opinion on the subject of Texas was largely the result of a bad attack of Puritan conscience on the part of John Quincy Adams. It seems to have happened in this way. Benjamin Lundy, the famous abolitionist, made a trip to Texas in 1832 with the aim of planting free colonies there. In a hasty trip during which he viewed Texas through glasses colored by his own intense hatred of slavery, he came to the conclusion that the whole effort to get Texas was a slaveholders' conspiracy to get more land into which to extend the peculiar institution. His principal informant in the matter was the Mexican Almonte, bosom friend of Santa Anna, who saturated him with Mexican point of view, which Lundy was only too willing to believe. It made such splendid anti-slavery propaganda. This tale of the Texan Revolution as a slaveholders' conspiracy engineered by John C. Calhoun and his ilk was swallowed whole by Lundy's good friend John Quincy Adams, and it passed into history as fact, from which historical research is only just beginning to extricate us.[52] Here again it is not so much the truth which counts as it is what people believe to be the fact. Thousands of Americans were misled by John Quincy

[51] Richardson's *Messages*, III, 157, 188, 213; J. S. Bassett, *Life of Andrew Jackson*, II, 663-73.
[52] E. C. Barker, "Public Opinion in Texas preceding the Revolution" in *Rept. of Amer. Hist. Assoc.*, 1911, I, 219; N. W. Stephenson, *Texas and the Mexican War*, pp. 104-5.

Adams to believe the whole Texan affair a mere invasion of a friendly neighbor by North American brigands to get room for half a dozen more slaveholding states.

With such conditions, Jackson naturally waited until after the election in 1836 and then when Van Buren was safely elected he put the matter up to Congress. Congress promptly passed the responsibility back to him by tacking on to a Civil Service bill provision for the salary for a Texan minister as soon as the President should think fit to dispatch a diplomatic envoy to that new Republic. On the very last day of his administration Jackson sent a minister to Texas and then got out from under the trouble and let Van Buren shoulder the responsibility and take the blame. Naturally this act only intensified Mexican indignation against the United States, as Mexico was not yet willing to admit that her chance of retaking Texas was desperate.[53]

Prior to recognition, the Texans had voted by an overwhelming majority for annexation to the United States. But at this time the United States apparently did not feel justified in going so far, as annexation would certainly have justified Mexico's vehement charges that the whole Texan Revolution was a thing engineered in and by the United States simply as a step toward swallowing Texas in the great Republic of the north. Moreover as soon as Jackson left the White House certain other events distracted the people of the United States for a few years and made the annexation of Texas impossible for the time being. No sooner had Van Buren become President than the panic of 1837 swept the country. Caused by circumstances quite beyond the control of the United States, by economic and meteorological conditions thousands of miles from the United States, this panic nevertheless did postpone American intervention for some time.[54] Americans were too busy salvaging the wreckage of their own business to embark on any more ambitious undertakings in the far southwest. Nevertheless, like all business depressions, this panic produced its crop of unemployed who trekked to Texas

---

[53] E. Z. Rather, "Recognition of the Republic of Texas by the United States," in *Quar. of Texas State Hist. Soc.*, XIII, 155ff.

[54] E. Channing, *Hist. of U. S.*, V, 455–58.

or to Oregon. In addition to this the year 1837 also saw the murder, by an Illinois mob, of the abolitionist Lovejoy, a dastardly crime which stirred up the wrath of the anti-slavery forces in the United States, and renewed John Quincy Adams' bitter denunciations of the whole Texas affair as a slaveholders' conspiracy.

In the interim the British, ever covetous of cotton lands, cast longing eyes at Texas. The great Lancashire mills were dependent so largely by this time on the supply of raw material which came almost entirely from the United States, that it was the care of several successive administrations to look for some independent supply of cotton. Moreover, Texas was a magnificent market for the sale of surplus English-manufactured goods. England had the same interest in the new Republic in the southwest that she had had in America from earliest time. Her vessels could go out to the ends of the earth laden with manufactured goods and could come back freighted with raw materials. As early as 1837 Texas was producing a tremendous quantity of cotton and timber. The British consul's messages to the government in London were full of thoughts of what a remarkable place Texas was for marketing English goods and getting raw material in return. As early as 1840 the same consul reported finding many of the celebrated Bowie knives made in Sheffield, England, and pointed out that these "genuine Arkansas toothpicks" could be made as readily in England as in Arkansas. Failing to get Texas themselves, the British worked for the independence of Texas, but apparently were handicapped by the fact that cotton culture meant slave labor, whereas the Peel Cabinet which came into power in 1841 was largely supported by the English abolitionists.[55]

Once again British policy crossed the American at every turn, but on this occasion the British actions were somewhat confused. The United States wanted Texas: that was both clear and simple. But the British seemed to want both an independ-

---

[55] "Correspondence from the British Archives Concerning Texas" (E. D. Adams ed.), *Southwestern Hist. Quar.*, XV, 294–355. Vid. also vols. XVI–XXI (incl.).

ent Texas for its cotton and the abolition of slavery, which seemed essential to cotton culture. Here again it was not so much the fact of British interests and activities as it was the interpretation put upon them by Americans that makes all the difference because at this period in American history it was always possible to stir up fervid patriotism by dragging in the bugaboo of Great Britain. Moreover at this time the United States and Great Britain were at odds over boundary questions from Maine to Oregon and this did not help matters.[56]

With the coming of the Harrison-Tyler administration the Mexicans re-opened the trouble with numerous border raids which enraged the Texans and sent more adventurous spirits from the States into the Texan army of retaliation. At the same time Santa Anna's minister of foreign relations began a vigorous diplomatic onslaught against the United States by sending out to all the world a circular letter accusing the United States of all sorts of outrageous violations of neutrality with the ulterior motive of stealing Texas. So offensive and so threatening was the language of the Mexican that one might have been justified in thinking that a declaration of war would speedily follow. Exactly this interpretation was put on the affair by Commodore Jones of the United States Pacific fleet, into whose hands a newspaper account fell. Jones jumped to the conclusion that war must be already declared and rushed his small fleet to the Mexican town of Monterey on the coast of California, captured the place, hauled down the Mexican flag and replaced it with the Stars and Stripes with great enthusiasm. Then he listened long enough to the wails of the local Mexican commander to learn that there was no war at all. Somewhat abashed he pulled down his flag and sailed away. Explanations were very much in order, and Mexico was rather justly outraged by this high-handed proceeding on the part of an American naval officer.[57]

All this gave John Quincy Adams a chance to vent his spleen on the Administration, which by this time had become thor-

---

[56] E. D. Adams, *British Interests and Activities in Texas, 1838–1846* (Baltimore, 1910).
[57] J. Smith, *War with Mexico*, I, 67–69.

oughly identified with the slaveholder cause through the death of William Henry Harrison and the succession of the Vice-president John Tyler, of Virginia. The affair was characteristic of the American system of government in the matter of the selection of vice-presidents. Harrison had been elected as Whig, but on his death the Whigs discovered that they had chosen a man as vice-president who was certainly a Democrat if he was anything at all, and they had a president who was very likely to do exactly what they did not want done. The whole cabinet resigned, Secretary of State Webster only remaining long enough to negotiate the Webster-Ashburton treaty which he had under way. When Webster got out, Tyler appointed in his place Able P. Upshur of Virginia, a slaveholder, a strong states-rights man, and a traditional hater of England. Upshur was closely in touch with John C. Calhoun, the real leader of the Democratic party, and between them they proceeded to round out a foreign policy for the United States which was at once nationalistic and anti-English, and involved getting Texas and Oregon for the aggrandizement of the United States.[58]

It cannot be fairly charged against Upshur and Calhoun that they were slaveholders out to get more slave-territory. They were southerners of the old school who still remembered the War of 1812, who still hated England and would leave no stone unturned to hurt England, and they were real Americans of the expansionist school. Upshur negotiated a treaty with the Republic of Texas in 1843 for the annexation of the Lone Star Republic, in which he promised that the United States would protect Texas during the consummation of the treaty. This frankly meant that the United States was prepared to go to war to get Texas and is another interesting illustration of how the war power really rests with the executive department, no matter what the constitution says about it. At this juncture Upshur was killed in an accident and Tyler quite logically called Calhoun to take his place. No one can justly impugn or question Calhoun's motives in the matter today, but in 1844 it was like waving a red flag to a bull to call

[58] J. S. Reeves, *American Diplomacy under Tyler and Polk* (Baltimore, 1907), pp. 114–137.

this prince of the slaveholders to get Texas when the Administration had been elected to do no such thing. Calhoun submitted the annexation treaty to the Senate with a letter which was intended to be patriotically anti-English. But because of the dramatic effect with which he urged that the British be told to keep hands off the abolition business and stop trying to free the slaves in Texas, instead of stirring up anti-English feeling all he really did was to stir up anti-slavery sentiment. Partly for this reason and partly because the Van Buren Democrats were angry at the failure of their candidate for the nomination in 1844 the Senate rejected Calhoun and Upshur's treaty and a second attempt to get Texas into the United States failed.[59]

However other forces were at work to get Texas. Whatever John Quincy Adams might say in the matter the northerners as well as the southerners did manage to get stirred up again with the grandiose expansionist scheme of getting both Oregon and Texas, for messages from both the northwest and northeast began to pour back to Congress indicating that the English menace was a real thing. In the election of 1844 the wily Clay ran for the Whigs on a platform which he thought would capture the abolitionist vote by opposing the annexation of Texas. James K. Polk was the Democratic standard bearer and ran on a platform which called for the "re-annexation of Texas and the re-occupation of Oregon." Too late in the campaign Clay found that he was totally wrong in his interpretation of public opinion. But his effort to change horses in midstream only resulted in the election of Polk.

Rightly or wrongly (for there were many other issues in the campaign) President Tyler interpreted the election of Polk as a mandate from the people of the United States to go ahead and get Texas at once. Before Polk could be inaugurated, Tyler got a now willing Congress to annex Texas by joint resolution of the two houses. The invitation to Texas reached that Republic just as it was considering an offer from England to guarantee Texan

[59] J. S. Reeves, *American Diplomacy under Tyler and Polk*, pp. 138–61; E. J. McCormac, *James K. Polk, A Political Biography* (U. of Cal., 1922).

independence and secure Mexican acknowledgment thereof on condition that Texas remain independent.   Texas decided in favor of the United States against England and by the time Polk was fairly in the presidential chair he found himself with a war staring him in the face.[60]

What was this Texas which the United States had received? The province of Texas, so the Mexicans contended, went only as far as the Nueces River, but under such shadowy and ancient claims as that of the La Salle discovery, the United States claimed as far as the Rio Grande.   Pending the settlement of the boundary with Mexico Polk ordered the United States troops to occupy the disputed area between the two rivers.   This naturally resulted in an attack by the Mexicans on the United States troops and Polk promptly announced to Congress that war existed by the act of Mexico.   So it did in a sense.   Meanwhile Polk made an effort to avoid war by listening to the blandishments of Santa Anna, temporarily in exile in Cuba.   Santa Anna promised to sell out his country to the United States if Polk would let him slip back into Mexico through the United States squadron now blockading Vera Cruz.   Santa Anna thereby got back to Mexico where instead of settling the matter as he promised Polk, he sold out Polk and the United States instead and was soon leading the Mexican armies against the Americans.   The United States now had a real war on its hands.

[60] J. S. Reeves, *American Diplomacy under Tyler and Polk*, pp. 162–189.

CHAPTER IX

"THE AMERICAN HEMISPHERE"

"The great declaration of Monroe, made in the infancy of Latin American liberty, was an assertion to all the world of the competency of Latin Americans to govern themselves."—Elihu Root.

1. INDEPENDENCE OF HISPANIC AMERICA

Although the good fathers of the Republic piously counselled their contemporaries to keep out of European Wars, alliances and entanglements, they evidently did not feel the same way about relations with South America. It is a fact not to be denied that the founders of the foreign policy of the United States felt that Europe was one thing and that the Americas were another thing and they did not care very much if the two never met. Geographical distance meant infinitely more in those days than it means now, and Washington and his colleagues wrote the geographical fact of their day into the foreign policy of the United States with a naïve but perfectly natural disregard for the fact that invention might annihilate space and make London infinitely nearer than any Latin-American port. In fact Buenos Aires has always been more distant than London in space as well as in time. So the matter of American isolation from Europe is not wholly a matter of geography. The true explanation of why the early statesmen of the United States kept insisting on the separation of the European and American continents will not be found so much in Washington's farewell with its warning not to "entangle our peace and prosperity in the toils of European ambition, rivalship, interest, or caprice," nor in Jefferson's inaugural with its solemn admonition against entangling alliances, as, indeed, it will be found in the homely diary of the first of that great American family of diarists, John Adams.[1]

[1] G. Washington, *Writings* (Ford ed.), XIII, 316; T. Jefferson, *Writings* (Ford ed.), VIII, 4, 273.

The first minister of the United States at the Court of St. James records the following conversation with Richard Oswald, the British peace commissioner in 1782:

> "'You are afraid,' says Mr. Oswald today, 'of being made the tools of the powers of Europe.' 'Indeed I am,' says I. 'What powers?' said he. 'All of them,' said I. 'It is obvious that all the powers of Europe will be continually manœuvering with us, to work us into their real or imaginary balances of power. They will all wish to make us a make-weight candle, when they are weighing out their pounds. Indeed it is not surprising; for we shall very often, if not always, be able to turn the scale. But I think it ought to be our rule not to meddle.' " [2]

Yet the American determination to be rid of Europeans, bag and baggage, did not mean that they were not vitally interested in what happened to the remaining colonies of Europe in the New World. We have already seen how the prospective transfer of Louisiana from Spain to France excited Jefferson, and very shortly it was not only Louisiana which seemed likely to change its political status, but all the other provinces of the great Spanish Empire which stretched from Texas and California to Cape Horn. The eighteenth century had seen numerous abortive revolts in this Spanish America, and the example of the revolt of the British colonies in North America had apparently been a great object lesson to them. [3] Then came the French Revolution, and as a nation with which Spanish America had even greater cultural relations, its lesson was taken to heart. The final impetus to revolution came when Napoleon invaded Spain and cut the head off the Spanish Empire, for it was the kingship rather than any imperial organization which held the Spanish Empire together. The cuttlefish of Latin America fell apart and each tentacle became in turn a new nation. It is with those nations that the United States now had to reckon.

The Spanish Empire had tried to retain to the last its old monopolistic mercantilist policy of not allowing anyone to trade with

---

[2] John Adams, *Works* (C. F. Adams ed.), III, 316.

[3] B. Moses, *Spain's Declining Power in South America* (Univ. of Cal., 1919); C. L. Chandler, *Inter-American Acquaintances* (2d ed., Sewanee, 1917), pp. 62, 87, 91; P. S. Reinsch, "Some Notes on the Study of South American History" in the *Essays* in American history, dedicated to Frederick Jackson Turner, p. 272.

its colonies except Spaniards. But by 1801 the Spanish government was reduced to such straits in the matter of revenue that the Viceroy at Buenos Aires received notice to admit Anglo-American vessels to trade in the waters of the River Plate. At last the Spanish learned that foreign trade meant money and their need for money was so great that they had to allow the Yankee skippers to import and export legally the goods which for years they had smuggled in and out of Spanish America. Apparently the Spanish felt that if the trade was going to go on, they might as well be getting some revenue out of it. Soon the River Plate was teeming with American vessels. The background of this trade is simple enough. Coffee, cocoa, sugar and molasses were needed in the United States which did not produce these commodities. Hides for shoes, wool for the Massachusetts mills and horsehair for that dreadful parlor furniture of the nineteenth century were all things which Latin America produced in abundance and for which Anglo-Americans would pay hard cash or food. For Latin America needed then as it needs to-day such things as fish, flour, bacon, butter and the like to feed the workers on the plantations which produced a single crop. Likewise, then as now, Latin American countries were not manufacturing countries, nor was Spain. Therefore from the United States or England had to come their textiles, their shoes, their candles, crockery, furniture and a thousand little luxury articles which were demanded by the beef barons of the Argentine.[4]

Hence, American foreign policy was shaped by the requirements of business, and the fate of the Spanish-American colonies became a matter of intense concern in Washington. Naturally the matter came to an issue first in regard to those parts of the Spanish American colonies which lay nearest the United States. The tradition already established in American politics that Europe was one thing and America another led President Madison to notify Congress in the matter of West Florida in 1811, as we have seen before.

[4] C. L. Chandler, *Inter-American Acquaintances*, pp. 25–6, 56–65.

"The United States could not see, without serious inquietude, any part of a neighboring territory, in which they have, in different respects, so deep and so just a concern, pass from the hands of Spain into those of any other foreign power." [5]

Congress indorsed this stand of the President in words that cannot be misunderstood. If Spain lost Florida, the United States was going to get it. Thus early was the principle established in American foreign policy that American territory was not to be handed from one European power to another, and this many years before the Monroe Doctrine. Moreover this took place when the United States was distracted by the impending war with England. Yet so great was her concern, material and spiritual with Latin America, that even the War of 1812 did not prevent Congress from appropriating money with which to load five ships of food to relieve the suffering victims of the earthquake at Caracas in 1812.[6]

For the next ten years the foreign policy of the United States is constantly concerned with the question of whether or not it should recognize the independence of the newly arrived nations to the south. Popular enthusiasm, if not public opinion, in the United States, was unquestionably on the side of those, who, like ourselves, were struggling to free themselves from the yoke of an old-world mother. It did not occur to most congressmen that the wars for Spanish American independence did not begin as an attempt to get rid of a tyrannical king or parliament, but rather in an effort to retain their king and get rid of a Napoleonic puppet. "Our Old King or None" was Belgrano's watchword for Buenos Aires, and this ought to have made it clear that the Spanish American struggle was rather a fight between two groups of Spaniards in Latin America than any fight between Latin Americans and Spaniards. Perhaps this is why Miranda failed so completely in his efforts to revolutionize South America, for he was bent on separation for its own sake.[7]

However, it was not long before the Spanish Americans made

[5] J. Madison's *Writings* (Hunt ed.), VIII, 131.
[6] C. L. Chandler, *Inter-American Acquaintances*, pp. 72–3.
[7] W. S. Robertson, *Rise of the Spanish American Republics* (N. Y., 1918), p. 145.

up their minds that there was no salvation to be found under the ægis of Spain and they began to set up provisional governments which lost little time in dispatching agents and emissaries to the United States in quest of recognition. The earliest Declaration of Independence in Latin America was that of Venezuela in 1811 and in November of that year she sought recognition in Washington. In the same month came President Madison's message to Congress officially taking cognizance of the state of affairs and expressing a friendly interest.[8]

Now we have seen that this problem of recognition is one of the most serious which faces a nation in its international relations. Premature recognition according to international law very properly involves war with the offended mother country. That is what happened to France in 1778 and the United States was bound to admit that any recognition of the South American nations would give Spain a just grievance and cause of war against her. Bent on being scrupulously correct in the matter, President Madison had in 1809 refused to send an agent to Caracas to help Miranda's filibusters out of jail.[9] President Monroe was careful to follow with the utmost rectitude the straight and narrow path of perfect neutrality prescribed by international law in these cases. The question of where lies the power to recognize a new state was at this time somewhat in dispute. Chief Justice John Marshall attributed it on one occasion to the executive [10] and on another to the legislative and executive.[11] In this case of the Spanish American colonies, it was the executive which became the controlling element in the situation and in general it is the President and his Department of State which have since retained this right.[12] Despite the popular enthusiasm for the Spanish American Republics, the United States government under the guidance of Monroe moved cautiously and with due regard for

---

[8] W. S. Robertson, "Recognition of the Hispanic American Nations by the U. S.," *Hispanic American Hist. Rev.*, I, 241–3.

[9] F. L. Paxon, *Independence of the South American Republics* (2d ed., Phila., 1916), p. 108; *Annals of Congress*, 11th Cong., 1st sess., pp. 306, 315.

[10] U. S. v. Hutchings, 26 Fed. 442.

[11] U. S. v. Palmer, 3 Wheaton, 634, 644 (1818).

[12] Q. Wright, *Control of American Foreign Relations*, p. 270.

the law.[13] There was the usual amount of filibustering in the ports of the United States, which the federal agents made proper efforts to suppress. But these were perfunctory enough to draw from Spain some rather caustic complaints.

At the same time characteristic American political ideals began to show themselves and to shape a distinct recognition policy for the United States. This policy was first enunciated by Jefferson when as Secretary of State he was forced to deal with the question of recognizing the French Republic in 1792. At that time he notified Minister Gouverneur Morris:

"It accords with our principles to acknowledge any government to be rightful which is formed by the will of the nation substantially declared." [14]

This was of course, merely the logical conclusion from the American Revolution and from Jefferson's theories of government by the consent of the governed and its corollary the right of revolution. The United States would and did make the usual distinction between the *de jure* and the *de facto* governments, i. e., the government which might have a technical legal right to rule, e. g., the exiled King Ferdinand VII, and the actual government which was functioning, and was known therefore as the *de facto* government. When Ferdinand came back to rule and the South Americans repudiated him, he might remain the *de jure* ruler, but he could not possibly be *de facto*. Of course it comported with the American ideas to recognize only the fact of the people's will and not the fiction of the divine right of an absent monarch. Naturally then, the only question which concerned Monroe was whether or not, in fact, these revolting provinces had governments which did rule.[14a]

John Quincy Adams counselled delay in recognition and laid down a fundamental principle of recognition which has ever since been of great weight,

"But there is a stage in such contests when the parties struggling for independence have, as I conceive, a right to demand its acknowledgment

[13] F. L. Paxon, *Independence of the South American Republics*, p. 103.
[14] T. Jefferson, *Writings* (Ford ed.), VI, 131.
[14a] J. Goebel, *The Recognition Policy of the United States* (N. Y., 1915), pp. 97–115, 122.

by neutral parties, and when the demand may be granted without departure from the obligations of neutrality. It is the stage when independence is established as a matter of fact so as to leave the chance of the opposite party to recover their dominion utterly desperate . . . . I am satisfied that the cause of the South Americans is just. But the justice of a cause, however it may enlist individual feelings in its favor, is not sufficient to justify third parties in siding with it. The fact and the right combined can alone authorize a neutral to acknowledge a new and disputed sovereignty." [15]

Adams' advice was based on the finding of the commissioners who had been promptly sent to South America to report on conditions. These agents gave such contradictory testimony that the cabinet agreed with the Secretary of State that it was best to defer recognition.[16]

Moreover the Florida negotiations had now reached a stage due to Jackson's attack on Pensacola where Monroe deemed it advisable to move slowly indeed and in strict accord with neutrality. It was the American policy to investigate conditions and to try to discover any development which might enable her to take steps favorable to the rising states.[17] But the cautious moves of the President were constantly being attacked by Congress and particularly by Henry Clay, who took up the cudgels for the South Americans with such enthusiasm that his name is still associated with Pan-Americanism. Clay insisted that this was a parallel case to our own and that it was part of America's pride to recognize a set of nations whose *de facto* governments had scrapped their old *de jure* kings. In his famous speech of the 24 May, 1818, he whipped up his emotions with a lot of flamboyant, old-fashioned southern oratory which was not very sensible and does not read as well to-day as it did a hundred years ago. Nevertheless in the latter part of his oration he did get down to business. He was an advocate of the so-called "American System" which involved the protection of American industry, and the protected industries soon had a surplus which required markets in South America, quite as keenly as did the British. Clay and Canning

[15] *Sen. Doc.*, 56, 54th Cong., 2d sess., pp. 52–3.

[16] F. L. Paxon, *Independence of South American Republics*, pp. 114, 136–7.

[17] W. S. Robertson, *Hispanic-American Relations with the United States* (N. Y., 1923), pp. 29–30.

represented similar interests.. The most important part of Clay's speech was not his frantic gesture toward "eighteen million struggling to be free" but his remark

> "We may safely trust to the daring enterprise of our merchants. The precious metals are in South America, and they will command the articles wanted in South America, which will purchase them. Our navigation will be benefited by transportation, and our country will realize the mercantile profits. Already the item in our exports of American manufactures is respectable. They go chiefly to the West Indies and to Spanish America. This item is constantly augmenting." [18]

Moreover Clay's enthusiasm was partly pique against John Quincy Adams and Monroe, because of the fact that Monroe selected Adams rather than Clay as his Secretary of State, in the days when the secretaryship meant succession to the presidency. But Adams declined to be hurried by the gentleman from Kentucky whose residence in the Mississippi Valley so naturally made him hostile to Spain and everything Spanish. Recognition probably did not come any sooner because of the advocacy of Henry Clay.[19] Meantime the Spanish minister at Washington was making desperate appeals to the government to do this, that and the other thing to avoid the inevitable admission of independence. Monroe's caution was amply justified when Spain refused to ratify the Florida Treaty unless the United States would promise never to recognize the revolted provinces. Adams promptly and properly replied that he would give no such promise at all.[20]

The shadow of England was on this as on every phase of the diplomacy of the United States at the time. Under the guidance of Castlereagh it had become England's policy to approve the movement for independence in South America. When George Canning succeeded Castlereagh in the ministry he carried out the same idea. But the motive for British policy was not the same as that of the United States. The revolutions had at last

[18] *Annals of Congress*, 15th Cong., 1st sess., vol. II, 1485.
[19] F. L. Paxon, *Independence of the South American Republics*, pp. 146, 155.
[20] J. Goebel, *Recognition Policy of the United States*, p. 126; Richardson's *Messages*, II, 70 ff.

opened up the South American ports to British trade, and Canning determined to keep them open. If Spain reconquered her South American possessions, she might want to reimpose the old monopolistic Mercantilist ideas. But the principles of liberty and freedom did not count for as much in his policy as in the policy of America, for Canning would have been perfectly willing to restore Spanish rule in South America, provided he could have maintained a relatively free commercial intercourse between England and the colonies. Monroe was at one time tempted to act with Great Britain, but when he discovered her real attitude, he refused to have anything to do with any scheme that did not ultimately look toward complete South American independence.[21] Castlereagh hastened to assure the United States that although England would participate in the Holy Alliance's Congress at Aix-la-Chapelle which was going to make an effort to mediate between Spain and her revolted provinces, still Britain would not countenance any measures which might seem to assume the character of force.[22] The Holy Alliance, be it remembered, was a combination of European rulers, started by Tsar Alexander with lofty motives for the peace and tranquillity of Europe, but which had degenerated into a tool of the Austrian Chancellor Metternich for foisting on the world again those old ideas of the divine rights of absolute monarchy, which the French Revolution had overthrown.

But events on both sides of the water soon took a hand in forever dispelling any idea of Spain's ever recovering her dominion in South America. In 1820 there was a revolution in Spain itself and the army which Ferdinand VII had assembled at Cadiz to reconquer South America, turned and mutinied. The timorous monarchical powers of Europe, which had overthrown Napoleon and formed the famous Holy Alliance, determined to get together and restore Ferdinand to his throne as they had restored Louis XVIII to his in France. But marching a victorious army into Paris or Madrid was a very different thing from

---

[21] James Monroe's *Writings*, VI, 60, 84-5.

[22] C. K. Webster, "Castlereagh and the Spanish Colonies" in *English Historical Review*, XXVII, 95.

trying to send that army across the Atlantic Ocean. In June of 1821 Simón Bolívar finally defeated the Spanish Royalists under Morillo at Carabobo. In July José de San Martín, after having crossed the Andes in a march which makes Napoleon's crossing the Alps seem like child's play, had liberated Chile at Chacabuco and thence had gone north by sea and entered the very capital of the old Spanish empire at Lima, in Perú. In August the O'Donojú treaty practically established the independence of Mexico. Thus all four of the old vice-royalties, Buenos Aires, Perú, Caracas and New Spain were lost to the mother country. Spain, in the throes of revolution herself was helpless. Surely that time had at last come when "the chances of Spain to recover her dominion were absolutely desperate." So at last Monroe and John Quincy Adams decided. In March of 1822 Congress asked the President to inform them as to the progress of South American independence and the President replied with a message which advised the appropriations necessary for recognition. On the 19th of June, 1822, Señor Manuel Torres was presented to President Monroe as the official representative of the Republic of Colombia and the recognition of other republics followed in quick succession.[23] Spain protested as a matter of course, but Secretary Adams' dignified reply left little room for debate.

Monroe's action was the first recognition accorded the South American states and it was a ringing challenge of the New World to the Old World principle of legitimacy. In sharp contrast with the philosophy of the Congresses of Vienna, Troppau and the like, it announced to the world the principle of American foreign policy that a people should be entitled to chose their own rulers, and that having chosen, they would receive the recognition of the United States, kings and princes to the contrary notwithstanding. Clay's unsuccessful effort to force the hand of the executive showed where the real power of recognition lay in American constitutional practice, and Monroe with his great Secretary were now ready for the next step whereby the United

[23] J. Q. Adams, *Memoirs*, V, 491.

States not only welcomed the new republics into the family of nations, but helped insure them against further vengeance from the elders in the old world family.[24]

2. THE MONROE DOCTRINE

The Europe of that day was under the domination of an Alliance of Emperors variously known as the Quadruple Alliance and the Holy Alliance. It was outwardly the creation of the rather fanatical Tsar Alexander of Russia who wanted all Europe to be well behaved and to be ruled by benevolent despots, monarchs of divine right. It was actually only one of Metternich's tools of oppression, whereby he stifled every outbreak of democratic or constitutional agitation in any part of Europe he could reach. The "Metternich Political System" was a machine for uprooting every sapling of liberty. Naturally he turned his eyes toward South America where democracy was running riot and where the so-called legitimate rights of the divine-right Ferdinand were being scoffed out of existence. The Holy Alliance commissioned Austria to put down a popular revolution in Naples and directed France to suppress a revolt in Spain. Both orders were obeyed with alacrity and the next job was to recover the King of Spain's colonies for him.[25]

But in this business England was increasingly ashamed to play any part at all. Not only would the reconquest of South America break up that lucrative trade she had built up since 1801 but the principles of the Holy Alliance were out of all accord with the principles of English liberty. Canning determined to do two things and he set about them with dispatch. First he was bent on getting the promise of France not to interfere in the South American question, for it was after all the French troops which had reconquered Spain for the Holy Alliance. In February of 1823 he got into touch with Prince Polignac the French minister and threatened him that if France interfered to restore Spanish rule in South America, it would be followed by a war with Great

24 J. Goebel, *Recognition Policy of the United States*, p. 141.
25 W. P. Cresson, *The Holy Alliance* (Oxford, 1922), pp. 97ff.

Britain. Polignac gave way and promised that France "abjured in any case any design of acting against the (Spanish) colonies by force of arms." [26] On her part Great Britain disclaimed any desire to acquire any of the South American territories herself and warned other powers she would fight them if they attempted to do so. Canning next turned to the United States and suggested that Great Britain and the United States agree not to take any Spanish American territory themselves and that the two nations act together against the Holy Alliance.[26a]

President Monroe took this matter on his vacation with him and a vacation always meant a trip back to the Virginia plantations near where Jefferson was living in retirement. On private consultation, both Jefferson and Madison advised him to accept Canning's proposition, although Monroe warned them that it meant a breach of the policy of isolation and would certainly involve the United States in European entanglements. In their days of reflection the two Virginian Presidents who had strongly advocated isolation began to have their doubts about it.[27] But many other factors were shaping the situation. Russia, one of the originators of the Holy Alliance, notified the United States that she would not recognize the Spanish colonies and employed language rather insulting to the ideas of free government. Moreover she notified the world that she was going to claim the Oregon country as well as Alaska, and warned American fishermen to stay a hundred miles off shore on pain of confiscation. It was an open menace to the United States. In August of 1823, *Niles Register* published the text of the treaty of Verona whereby the Holy Alliance had commissioned France to put down the rebellion in Spain. It was nothing if not a distinct slap at the whole American system and all the diplomacy involved in freeing the South American States.

"The system of representative government is as incompatible with the monarchical principle, as the maxim of the sovereignty of the people is

---

[26] H. W. V. Temperley in the *Cambridge History of British Foreign Policy*, II, 66-7.

[26a] W. C. Ford, "J. Q. Adams and the Monroe Doctrine" in *Amer. Hist. Rev.*, VII, 682-3, 685.

[27] T. Jefferson, *Writings* (Ford ed.), X, 278.

opposed to the principle of divine right. (The Holy Alliance) engages in the most solemn manner to employ all their means and unite all their efforts to put an end to the system of representative government wherever it is known to exist in the state of Europe, and to prevent it from being introduced into those states where it is not known." [28]

When Monroe got back from his holidays the Canning proposals, the Russian warning and the threats of the Holy Alliance made action imperative. On top of this came another Russian note rejoicing in the triumphs of the French troops in reëstablishing despotism in Spain. But most important of all there were coming in requests from the South American nations themselves asking the United States to give some more substantial evidence of its good will than mere recognition, which would not preserve them from the fate Spain had just met. It may not be too much to say that the South American States asked the United States to step forward and challenge the Holy Alliance in the name of the Americas. [29]

In the face of all this Monroe laid the matter before his cabinet in November of 1823 and was there met with the counsel of confusion. Calhoun and the President were inexplicably timid. The advice of Jefferson and Madison was to coöperate with England and some cabinet members agreed with them. But the master mind of the situation was John Quincy Adams, who had decided that the time had come to throw down the gauntlet, not only to Russia, but to all Europe, with a notification to England that this was a matter in which the United States would be glad to set the world straight, without any assistance from anyone. Canning's proposition for joint action was definitely rejected. [30]

A reply was drafted to Russia which contained Adams' ringing challenge to the old-world political philosophy. The United States did not care whether Russia recognized the fact of South American independence or not. Even Monroe's effort to soften down the statement did not change the words.

[28] *Niles Register*, XXIV, 347.
[29] W. S. Robertson, *Hispanic American Relations with the United States*, pp. 43ff.; W. C. Ford, "J. Q. Adams and the Monroe Doctrine" in *Amer. Hist. Rev.*, VIII, 30.
[30] W. C. Ford, "J. Q. Adams and the Monroe Doctrine," *Amer. Hist. Rev.*, VII, 696.

"The United States of America could not see with indifference the forcible interposition of any European power other than Spain, either to restore the dominion of Spain, or to establish monarchical governments in those countries, or to transfer any of the possessions heretofore or yet subject to Spain in the American Hemisphere to any other European Power."[31]

Furthermore, Adams specifically warned the Emperor of Russia that the American continents were no longer the subjects for any new European colonial establishments and he would take warning as to his proposed aggressions on the northwest coast. Russia was not going to be allowed to have Oregon.[32]

In November of 1823 Adams sent a dispatch to Canning which is a classic in its exposition of the Doctrine which historians have rather unjustly associated with the name of Monroe. England was warned that she was hopelessly a member of the "European community," and until she recognized explicitly the independence of the Spanish South American colonies, any attempt at coöperation was futile. England had two sets of policies, one European and one American. As long as she put her European interests first, we could not act jointly with her.[33]

All these doctrines of American foreign policy were then at once embodied in the President's famous message of December, 1823, and thereby brought to the attention of every nation in the world. The United States published as the cardinal principles of its foreign policy that (1) the American continents should no longer be available for European colonization, i. e., let Russia get out of Oregon; (2) she viewed the revolutionary movements in Spain and Portugal with the approval which her own past dictates, i. e., the United States disapproved of the actions of the Holy Alliance; (3) she was concerned with any attempt to interfere in South America and any attempt to impose an old world political system on it, i. e., "any attempt to extend that political system to any portion of this hemisphere (is) dangerous to our peace and safety;" Europe had one set of political systems and America represents a totally different one, let us live and

---

[31] W. C. Ford, "J. Q. Adams and the Monroe Doctrine," *Amer Hist. Rev.*, VIII, 43–4.
[32] A. B. Hart, *Monroe Doctrine*, p. 50.
[33] Ibid., VIII, 46.

let live, for there shall be no extension of the Metternich ideas of politics to the New World.

The Monroe Doctrine thus embodies all the principles of American diplomacy which John Quincy Adams had been so carefully building up for five years and it is to him that the real authorship of the Doctrine ought to be attributed.[34] It included a reiteration of the doctrine of isolation and an implied denunciation of European systems of government. As far as the prohibition of colonization was concerned, that involved not a prohibition of emigration from Europe, but only an extension of their jurisdiction. This principle still stands and with it the other principle that European nations cannot shift their possessions in the Western Hemisphere to one another nor can they attempt to gain territory at the expense of Latin America.

It was not so much the actual threat of the Holy Alliance as the fear of irresponsible potentates which led to the pronouncement of the Monroe Doctrine. It is extremely doubtful whether the United States was justified in its belief that the Holy Alliance was conspiring to put back the old régime. Certainly Austria and France disbelieved in the possibility of reconquest, and Russia was a good deal more concerned with England than she was with the United States. On the whole the influence of the United States on the policy of the Holy Alliance was slight, as that group had already passed the zenith of its power. Canning's memorandum to Polignac had probably done more than Monroe's Doctrine to break up any more ideas of suppressing revolution and extending the Metternich system. Many other influences were acting in behalf of the Latin Americans whose destiny as free nations was assured by the facts of international politics and the inexorable progress of events.[35] The non-intervention principle of the Monroe Doctrine was praised in many European

---

[34] See Mr. Ford's article, supra; an effort to enhance Monroe's share is made in W. A. MacCorkle, *James Monroe, Personal Genesis of the Monroe Doctrine* (N. Y., 1923).

[35] D. Perkins, "Europe, Spanish America and the Monroe Doctrine" in *Amer. Hist. Rev.*, XXVII, 207; W. S. Robertson, "Monroe Doctrine Abroad in 1823-4" in *Amer. Pol. Sci. Rev.*, VI, 563.

Journals, even if the noncolonization feature was questioned in both England and France.[36]

Indeed Canning's chagrin at the form of the Monroe Doctrine forever robs him of his right to claim the authorship of it. He went at once to the American Minister Rush to get an explanation of the noncolonization feature which, in his own words, was so decidedly displeasing to him. Canning's subsequent boast in 1826 about "calling into existence the new world to redress the balance of the old" was the merest gesture of a parliamentarian trying to say something clever in a debate. But this cannot deprive Canning of the real credit which is his due in the matter of the Polignac memorandum.[37]

As for Russia, she was really in no position to colonize the northwest coast. Her threat of occupation down to 51st parallel was not so much to get Oregon as it was to exclude the Americans and English from participation in the fisheries. Her claim to exercise jurisdiction over the sea for a hundred miles from the shore was an attempt to make Bering Sea and a large part of the Pacific Ocean a *mare clausum*. This was contrary to international practice since the celebrated controversy of Grotius and Selden which we have noted before. The Englishman Selden had taken the position that England could close the North Sea to all except English vessels, and Grotius has combated the idea on behalf of the Dutch who fronted on that same sea. Practice has finally given the victory to Grotius and the customary three-mile line has been prescribed as the limit of territorial jurisdiction. On this occasion England forgot all about Selden and joined the United States in refusing to permit the Tsar of Russia to interfere with their now rapidly growing whale and seal fisheries. Whale oil was by this time a tremendously important article of commerce, since petroleum had not yet been commercialized and electric illumination was still far off. Moreover from the time of Chaucer to that of the dandy Prince George IV, gentlemen had been accustomed to wear beaver hats. It is a curious coin-

[36] J. Bagot, *George Canning and his Friends* (London, 1909), II, 209, 217; A. B. Hart, *The Monroe Doctrine, An Interpretation* (Boston, 1916), p. 66.

[37] H. W. V. Temperley, in *Cambridge History of British Foreign Policy*, II, 68.

cidence that the treaty of 1824 by which the United States induced Russia to give up her pretensions to make the Pacific
Ocean a *mare clausum* and her pretensions to lands south of the
54th parallel occurred in the same year in which the introduction
of silk hats on the streets of Paris sounded the death knell of the
old fashioned fur-hat. But there were other uses for the beaver
and seal skins and the American traders in the northwest were
soon laying the foundations of an American Empire in the
regions which Russia had so lately claimed.[38]

3. BEGINNING OF PAN-AMERICANISM

The reception accorded the Monroe Doctrine in South America was moderately enthusiastic, in so far as it was noticed at all.
Bolívar and Santander in Colombia, Carvalho e Mello in Brazil
and Rividavia in Argentina all expressed their approbation of the
attitude taken by the United States, and in Chile the Doctrine
was certainly given a warm welcome. But these did not include
all the Latin American states, nor even most of them. Certain
it is that in Mexico the Doctrine was practically ignored by such
men as Alamán who frankly regarded Britain's action in withdrawing from the Holy Alliance as a far more potent factor in
Latin American independence. In many South American states
the opinion pretty generally prevailed that the British fleet was
the real wall between Latin American and the Holy Alliance,
and the mention of the Monroe Doctrine was frequently coupled
with a corresponding reference to and appreciation of Canning
and his firm stand. From the start, Latin America had no desire
that the protective Monroe Doctrine should turn into a mere
cloak for United States' hegemony.[39]

But certain South Americans, notably Simón Bolívar, were not
satisfied with the mere pronouncement by the United States that

[38] G. Heinz, *Die Beziehungen zwischen Russland, England und Nord Amerika im Jahre
1823* (Berlin, 1911); W. Malloy, *Treaties and Conventions*, II, 1512ff.; E. S. Meany, "Towns
of the Pacific Northwest," *Am. Hist. Assoc. Rept.*, 1909, 169; *Amer. State Papers, Foreign
Relations*, IV, 857.

[39] W. S. Robertson, "South America and the Monroe Doctrine, 1824–28" in the *Political Science Quarterly*, XXX, 82ff.; J. B. Lockey, *Pan-Americanism: Its Beginnings* (N.
Y., 1920), pp. 261–2.

Europe must suspend her expansion into the western hemisphere. If the Holy Alliance could gather together the nations of Europe in a confederation, dedicated to perpetual tyranny and despotism, why could not the nations of the New World get together in a more holy alliance dedicated to the principles of freedom and liberty? This idea captivated many Latin American minds and suggested a coöperation between the Americas. The idea was not new; Miranda had thought of it and so had Thomas Jefferson when he sent the famous and infamous General Wilkinson into the southwest. Rozas of Chile wanted a single nation on the American continent and as early as 1822 an agreement between Perú and Colombia under Bolívar's influence was an infant League of Nations to which Central America adhered in 1825.[40]

Simón Bolívar was unquestionably a man of great vision. After he had participated so actively in the liberation of South America, his restless imagination took hold of this idea of a great inter-American Union to act as a counterpoise against the Holy Alliance. He believed it might do a great deal for the political education of those backward South American states which he realized only too well were not yet ready for self-government. The result was the calling in 1826 of the First Pan-American Conference at Panama, where it might be equally free from the influences of North and South America. He was insistent that the United States should be invited and seems only to have been fearful lest she would not accept. England was also invited to be present as an American Power.[41]

The Conference met with representatives of Peru, Colombia, Central America, Mexico and Great Britain present. The question of the participation of the United States occurred during the presidency of John Quincy Adams and under Clay as Secretary of State. Such a combination should have insured favorable action by the United States. But domestic wrangles in Congress ruined it all. Adams and Clay had to deal with a Congress which

[40] I. J. Cox, "Pan-American Policy of Jefferson and Wilkinson" in *Miss. Valley Hist. Rev.* I, 212ff.; J. B. Lockey, *Pan-Americanism: Its Beginnings*, pp. 284–92.

[41] W. R. Shepherd, "Bolivar and the United States," in *Hispanic American Historical Review*, I, 292.

had been chosen in that famous election of 1824 which gave a plurality of votes in Jackson for President. When the House of Representatives selected Adams because no one had a majority and when he in turn appointed Clay as Secretary of State, there were many who insisted that there was collusion and corruption between them, as Clay had certainly delivered his influence in the House to Adams. When the question of appropriating money for the representation at the Panama Conference came up, it was not discussed on its merits, but used as an opportunity to thwart Clay and Adams. The question of slavery and the participation of our delegates in a conference with negro nations was dragged in solely to inflame party feeling. In fact the matter was of no consequence as the negro Republic of Haiti was not even invited to be present at Panama and had never been recognized by any of the American nations. Partisan politics delayed the appointment so long that one of the American delegates never left the United States at all and the other, who was directed to go from Bogota, was taken ill and died at Cartagena before ever getting to Panama.[42]

The Conference failed to meet the high expectations of Bolívar, for since the most advanced nations of our own day find it so difficult to form such an idea as a League of Nations, it was hardly to be expected that the backward states of a hundred years ago could work out such a conception. Moreover the instructions given by Clay to the American delegates were necessarily very cautious. The United States would have no part in any assembly to legislate for the whole continent, would not aid in forming a counterweight against the Holy Alliance and would not join with South America in guaranteeing the independence of the Latin American States. These instructions are interesting because they illustrate the position the United States has usually taken toward proposals of this sort. Any international body which is likely to infringe on national sovereignty is viewed with the utmost suspicion and such a Pan-American Union or alliance, would certainly have done so.[43]

[42] J. B. Lockey, *Pan-Americanism: Its Beginnings*, pp. 314, 398.   [43] Ibid. pp. 426.

The Conference adjourned to meet next in Mexico, which Bolívar regretted, not so much because he feared the influence of the proximity of the United States, but because he also seems to have felt that Mexico might get too influential in Latin American affairs.[44]

The idea was noble in its conception, but utterly impractical in its day, and Pan-Americanism had to slumber many years before it was resurrected again in a much modified form. The Panama Conference made certain international agreements designed to secure greater coöperation between the Americas, but Colombia was the only nation which ratified them. Such a scheme could only have been carried out with the enthusiastic support not only of the United States, but also of those South American nations which were destined to become the leaders on the southern continent. Brazil failed to send any delegates to Panama and Chile was so lukewarm that her delegates arrived too late. The United Provinces of Rio de la Plata declined to take any part in the matter and has always been rather frigid on the subject. The coöperation of the Argentine might have done a good deal at the outset, but shortly after the Panama Conference an event occurred which has proved a most difficult thing for the United States to explain away in its later support of the Pan-American principle.

The Falkland Islands lie off the coast of the Argentine Republic and were used as a port of refuge by American sailors. In 1829 Buenos Aires declared these islands a part of that republic and two years later seized some American sealing schooners there. The result was the coming of a United States war vessel, which took the islands under control pending a settlement and Buenos Aires' promise to give the Americans the right of refuge. There was no intention on the part of the United States to seize the islands themselves, but suddenly the British appeared and claimed that the Falkland Islands had been their territory for sixty years. If Great Britain had any such right, she had certainly rendered herself liable to lose it by her failure to assert

44 W. R. Shepherd, "Bolívar and the U. S." in *Hisp. Amer. Hist. Rev.*, I, 293.

it for such a long period of time. Buenos Aires therefore requested the United States to assert the Monroe Doctrine and warn Great Britain away. Instead of doing so the United States acknowledged British sovereignty and left Buenos Aires without support. This immediately aroused the suspicion that the Monroe Doctrine would be used only when it helped the United States, and was not such an unselfish thing as it appeared on the surface.[45] Technically the United States may have been correct, but it has not made any easier the gaining of Argentinian coöperation in Pan-Americanism.

[45] G. H. Stuart, *Latin America and the United States* (N. Y., 1922), pp. 299–302.

CHAPTER X

A CENTURY OF MISUNDERSTANDING WITH MEXICO

"Therefore if a man should sum up and say that they were born neither to have peace themselves, nor to let other men have it, he would simply speak the truth."—*Thucydides*.

"To save themselves from Yankee Imperialism, the [South] American Democracies would almost accept a German alliance, or the aid of Japanese arms; everywhere the Americans of the North are feared."—*Francisco Garcia Calderon*.

1. THE NATURE OF MEXICO

"The name of Mexico, the synonym of gold and silver, possessed always an invincible charm for the people of the western states," said Senator Benton, who watched the first thirty years of our Mexican American relations in and out of Congress. Add oil and hemp to gold and silver, and there is no reason why the Senator's statement should not be as true to-day as it was seventy-five years ago. No sooner had Mexico achieved her independence from the old Spanish colonial system than a brisk trade sprang up between that country and the United States. How could it be otherwise? Why should not the United States trade extensively with her nearest neighbor? Especially when that neighbor is so blessed with natural resources as is Mexico? The latest commercial traveler's guide to Latin America remarks that Mexico is not a manufacturing country, and therein lies the fundamental fact of our century of misunderstanding with her. Mexico has to sell some things the United States needs for the nourishment of her industrial life, and the United States is in a most favorable position to sell to Mexico those manufactured goods which our Spanish-American neighbor has not yet developed the craft to make for herself. It would be impossible to keep the citizens of Mexico and the United States apart, even if it were desirable to do so. The question is not how they can be separated, but how can they be induced to live together most amicably.

For they are neighbors on the same continent and this chapter is a chronicle of a hundred years of what looks perilously like failure in the business of living together.[1]

It is not the function of the historian to justify the one side or the other, nor is it the task of such a work as this to recount all those facts which constitute such an unhappy chapter in our diplomatic history. But it is necessary to notice those characteristics of Mexican American relations which seem to explain the difficulty. The thing which one must keep constantly in mind is the fact that two totally different civilizations have grown up side by side on the American continent. To the north in the United States and Canada are nations built from the emigrants of northern Europe, and equipped with the laws, institutions, and a language which are essentially English. To the south is a nation which is predominately Indian and half-breed, and which has been successively dominated by Aztec conquerors, Spanish Conquistadores, and is now ruled by a small minority of its more brilliant white and mixed blood landowners. In the Dominion and Republic to the North there has been a century of fairly orderly progress, industrial growth, economic development, increasing wealth, political stability and culture. Below the border for a hundred years there has been alternating revolution and tyranny, sometimes benevolent, sometimes malevolent, but seldom conducive to betterment of social conditions.

The explanation of this is not far to seek. A hundred years ago the population of the United States contained a vast majority of civilized white people, who had exterminated the Indians, and who could build their civilization on a thousand years of European culture. In Mexico, on the other hand, there were a million whites, four million Indians, and two million mestizos or half-breeds.[2] In Mexico "the inheritance from Spain had been unfortunate, but there had been time to recover from it; and instead of improving, the Mexicans had even degenerated." [3] The pres-

---

[1] T. H. Benton, *Thirty Years in the U. S. Senate*, I, 41; E. B. Filsinger, *Commercial Travellers Guide to Latin America* (Wash., 1920), p. 65.

[2] J. H. Smith, *War with Mexico* (N. Y., 1919), I, 3.

[3] Ibid., I, 57.

ent day reveals relatively the same situation that existed a century ago. The United States is a white nation with a hundred million heirs to the European tradition, who have made the most of their inheritance. Mexico is still struggling with her appalling race problem. Her population has increased too, but to-day she has two million whites, six million Indians and eight million mestizos, many of whom are in habits, types of mind, and degree of civilization not far above their Indian brethren.[4]

The United States has built on a foundation of political education laid in Europe. Mexico has been busy laying the very foundations themselves. Americans whose ancestors were killed in Wat Tyler's rebellion, the Jacquerie, or the Peasants' Revolt ought to remember that Mexico is simply having a similar experience four hundred years later. Above all, *Americans* cannot be too critical of this. The world is apt to forget that Mexico was not ready for popular self-government and that the imposition of that form of government on her uneducated and illiterate population has simply produced a hundred years of the same kind of thing that negro-carpet bag rule produced in the South after our own Civil War. One must think of Mexico as enduring a century of political anarchy, interspersed with occasional benevolent tyrannies such as that of Porfirio Diaz.[5]

Side by side on the continent of North America have grown up these two civilizations which in development lie centuries apart. During the last hundred years the United States has made astonishing progress in education and civilization. Even the most optimistic Mexicans admit that their country has experienced pitifully little educational growth. Mexico has every excuse; the United States herself has spent millions on the education of her handful of Indians with painfully small results. Mexico has practically had twelve million Indians to educate and at that has had to spend most of her revenue fighting Civil Wars. Suppose eighty per cent of the inhabitants of the United States were Indians? How much progress would we have made? The causes

[4] F. Starr, "The Mexican People," in *Mexico and The Caribbean* (Clark Univ., 1920), p. 15.
[5] T. Esquivel Obregon, "Are the Mexican People Capable of Governing Themselves?" in *Mexico and The Caribbean*, p. 13.

do not concern us, but the fact is undoubted that Mexico then and now was predominately illiterate. The friends of Mexico admit this and some fairly critical observers even go so far as to contend that she has made practically no progress in four hundred years.[6]

As to the characteristics of this vast majority of Mexican citizenry, it is most difficult to generalize. But the labor system has been a system of peonage, or virtual serfdom, where the peon remained all his life in debt to his landlord. By law he might not leave the estate until the debt was paid, and he never had any money with which to release himself. Naturally such a background tended to produce a race of easy going and somewhat irresponsible people who lacked initiative and who will require a long time to emancipate themselves from the effects of the centuries of subordination which have placed them low in the educational scale. Living with and dominating such a people has naturally produced a ruling class of educated men and women who are proud, sensitive, and domineering. The Mexican gentleman is as much a gentleman as any man in any nation. But a nation is not to be judged by its exceptions.[7]

The conditions of public health in Mexico may account for other characteristics. There are said to be seven times as many sick children in Mexico as in the United States. May not sickly children in some cases tend to produce men who are over-sensitive, backward, and sometimes inclined to be a little bit petty? [8] Social morals in Mexico are certainly on a very different plane from those in the United States. Competent observers sometimes feel that the Church is partly to blame for these conditions because of its apathy toward education in some cases and its opposition to modern scientific education in other cases.[9] It has

[6] J. Vasconselos, "Education in Mexico: Present Day Tendencies," *Bull. of Pan-American Union*, LVI, 230; F. Starr, supra, p. 27.

[7] R. J. MacHugh, *Modern Mexico* (London, 1914), pp. 111-2; E. D. Trowbridge, *Mexico Today and Tomorrow* (N. Y., 1920), 105-30.

[8] E. Huntington, "The Factor of Health in the Mexican Character," in *Mexico and the Caribbean*, p. 13.

[9] M. Barranco, *Mexico—Its Educational Problem* (N. Y., Col. Univ., 1915); *A Study of Educational Conditions in Mexico and an Appeal for an Independent College* (Cin., 1916).

even been alleged that instead of being a great force for civic righteousness, the Church has too often merely followed the lead of the Spaniard and plundered the people. Yet there is probably some truth in the remark of a Roman Catholic critic who denies that either the Spaniard or the Church is the primary cause of Mexico's troubles. In his opinion there is another cause—"His name is Greed, and he is still alive and active." [10]

At any rate the demoralization of Mexico has been the cause of many of the diplomatic difficulties between her and her northern neighbor. All too often only the master class of "Cientificos" have been educated. Mexican statesmen seem to have inherited the Spaniard's love of logic and quibbling, and in negotiations frequently seem more interested in scoring an intellectual victory than in getting something done. The Anglo-Saxon has learned that it is possible to be logically right and actually wrong. Much more might be said to explain the two utterly different civilizations which lie on opposite sides of the Rio Grande, but surely enough has been said to explain the century of misunderstanding. [11]

2. The War With Mexico

Mexico was among the first of the Latin American republics to receive the recognition of the United States after the Spanish Empire broke up. In 1825 in a burst of generous enthusiasm to welcome a new nation in America, the United States sent thither our first minister Joel Poinsett. As we have seen his first work was to secure a confirmation of the treaty of 1819 with Spain, fixing the boundaries between the United States and Mexico. Then followed the usual story of delay, time-wasting, insincerity, and wretched artifice on Mexico's part, with alternate periods of great patience and very offensive bullying on the part of the United States. Despite the kaleidoscopic rapidity with which Mexican chieftains succeeded one another in the capital of Mexico, the treaty was finally confirmed in 1832. However, on ac-

[10] E. A. Ross, *Social Revolution in Mexico*, (N. Y., 1923) and F. C. Kelley's review in the *Catholic World*, CXVII, 489.

[11] W. Thompson, *The Mexican Mind* (N. Y., 1922), pp. 144–5, 157.

count of this constant ferment it was rather difficult for the United States to maintain any consistent policy.

The story of Texas has already been related from the point of view of the Yankee, but from the point of view of the Mexican it were best here to ponder again the words of Lucas Alamán:

> "Their (the American) machinations in the country they wish to acquire are then brought to light by the appearance of explorers, some of whom settle on the soil, alleging that their presence does not affect the question of the right of sovereignty or possession to the land. These pioneers excite, by degrees, movements which disturb the political state of the country in dispute."

and further

> "When things have come to this pass, which is precisely the present state of things in Texas, the diplomatic management commences; the inquietude they have excited in the territory in dispute, the interests of the colonists therein established, the insurrections of adventurers and savages instigated by them, and the pertinacity with which opinion is set up as to their right of possession, become the subject of notes, full of expressions of justice and moderation, until, with the aid of other incidents, which are never wanting in the course of diplomatic relations, the desired end is obtained of concluding an arrangement as onerous for one party as it is advantageous to the other." [12]

"The claim-making stage" of American expansion thus noted by Alamán is certainly as characteristic of Mexican American relations, as it was of Spanish American relations, which culminated in the acquisition of the Floridas. No sooner had Poinsett arrived in Mexico and set to work to negotiate a commercial treaty than he began to be interrupted with constant complaints from United States shipowners, whose vessels and cargoes were being seized by Mexican officials on all sorts of pretexts, good and bad. The Mexican commercial system was extremely rigid in the type of goods it excluded and also in the imposition of the customs duties upon which the constantly changing governments principally relied for their revenue. Weird consular regulations were trumped up to secure additional income, and the American ves-

---

[12] W. S. Robertson, "Recognition of the Hispanic American Nations by the United States," in *Hispanic American Historical Review*, I, 261; *H. Ex. Doc.* No. 351, 25th Cong., 2d sess., p. 322.

sels were charged therewith; the valuation of cargoes was suddenly changed after the unloading of a vessel, for the purpose of increasing the duties payable thereon. Tariff rates were varied whimsically to meet revenue needs, without any regard for the published rates under which shipments had originally been made.

Frequent revolutions and recrudescences of the war of independence necessitated the constant declarations of blockade and this state of affairs made possible a great many seizures of United States vessels on the grounds of contraband, or breach of blockade, which no one knew even existed. These troubles were complicated by the undeniable fact that high-handed practices on the part of Mexico had been partly responsible for an extensive and highly organized smuggling trade between the two countries. This gave the Mexicans some excuse for their conduct. The chronic disorder in Mexico left American travelers and merchants at the mercy of bandits, and the police who were sent out to cope with the bandits, were just as likely as not to plunder their own convoys. All these conditions piled up claim after claim against Mexico on the part of United States' citizens.[13]

As troubles over Texas increased, more and more Americans came into constant contact and conflict with the Mexican authorities, and more and more claims for illegal seizures accumulated. Two separate Claims Conventions were negotiated and duly ratified by both governments, one in 1839 and the other in 1843. Provisions for adjustment and satisfaction were duly made and Mexico finally started in to pay damages. But the first payments apparently bankrupted her, and the great majority of the claims were yet unpaid when the manifold difficulties between the two countries resulted in war.

In addition to this, it was the policy of the United States to keep careful account of the damage done the property of its citizens in Mexico, and periodically to present a bill. In general Mexico would claim at that time, as she has claimed since, that she gave as much protection to the Americans as she gave her

---

[13] W. R. Manning, *Early Diplomatic Relations between the United States and Mexico* (Balt., 1916), pp. 256, 259, 261, 262, 275.

own citizens. But this meant nothing, as she did not protect her own citizens and their property. What the Americans were demanding in fact was a greater degree of protection for their rights than Mexico gave her own citizens or than she was able to give anyone. Whether or not they were entitled to it is a matter which is still in dispute, and in this case at least, the United States collected immense damages by the acquisition of half of what was then Mexico.

After years of failure to suppress the Texan revolt, Mexico seems finally to have pinned her hope on the friendly offices of England and France. Lord Aberdeen, the British Minister of Foreign Affairs in 1844, proposed that if Mexico would acknowledge the independence of Texas, the British would oppose annexation by the United States.[14] The Mexicans were foolish enough to believe that the British had any power to do anything in the matter, and would not take the sage counsel of Aberdeen who warned her of exactly what would happen if she got into a war with the United States. The British peril was exaggerated by both Mexico and the United States. It seems as though Mexico depended too much on English diplomatic aid and the United States feared unduly the possibility of British interference. In fact, although some of the British wished to seize California as "compensation" for the United States' acquisition of Texas, Lord Aberdeen followed the enlightened policy of refusing to establish an artificial colony just for the sake of being able to protect it. Finally, too late, Mexico decided to recognize Texan independence on condition that Texas would not join the United States. But, as we have seen, this offer came at the same time as the last offer of annexation and the Texans chose to join the United States.[15]

The annexation of Texas did not necessarily cause the Mexican War. After annexation, President Polk sent John Slidell to Mexico to reopen negotiations in an effort to secure peace. Slidell was told to try to convince Mexico that inasmuch as she owed

[14] E. D. Adams, *British Interests and Activities in Texas, 1838-46*, p. 168.
[15] G. L. Rives, "Mexican Policy on the Eve of the War with the U. S.," in *Amer. Hist. Rev.*, XVIII, 282, 291-4; J. H. Smith, "Mexican Recognition of Texas," in *Amer. Hist. Rev.*, XVI, 36.

us a hopelessly large amount of money, which she could never pay, the United States would accept a territorial indemnity. A new aspect appeared when Slidell was instructed to get California as well as Texas, for Polk's expansionist dream now envisaged the Pacific as the only limit for manifest destiny. Polk wanted both Oregon and California and Slidell's mission was to secure the latter. Slidell failed utterly to reopen the negotiations and wrote back to Secretary of State Buchanan, "Be assured that nothing is to be done with these people until they have been chastised." Polk held the same opinion, but having the whole Oregon question under way with England at the time, he had made use of Slidell to temporize till he could settle the northwestern question. Slidell could have protracted negotiations indefinitely with people like the Mexicans.[16]

But if Polk wanted war, he also wanted to be able to put all the blame on Mexico. Fortunately the Mexicans played into his hands by attacking General Taylor's troops on the Rio Grande, whither Polk had ordered him. This violence (whether provoked by the United States or not) on the part of Mexico enabled Polk to send Congress his almost savage war message in which he argued quite convincingly that war existed by the act of Mexico. It was quite vain for Calhoun to argue that the war power resided in Congress under the Constitution. Academically, Calhoun was right, but in fact the power of getting the United States into a war lay then, as it lies to-day, with the President. In this case Polk's action in ordering Taylor to occupy the disputed area between the Nueces and the Rio Grande was enough to insure an attack by the Mexican troops, who claimed the same area.[17]

Mexico was invaded at several points by the United States armies, the Mexican troops were defeated in battle after battle, her coasts were blockaded, her ports occupied, and finally her very capital city itself was stormed and captured by the American troops. Mexico lay absolutely prostrate and her government was so disorganized that it was difficult to find anyone with whom

[16] J. S. Reeves, *American Diplomacy under Tyler and Polk*, 274–6, 284, 285.
[17] J. H. Smith, *War with Mexico*, I, 181–2.

to negotiate a treaty of peace. When General Scott was on his final triumphant march to Mexico City, Polk had sent Nicholas Trist, chief clerk of the Department of State, to accompany him and make peace whenever possible. Trist's instructions made him think that he was authorized to suspend hostilities, and naturally he and Scott had various undignified altercations which did no one any good. Finally Trist was recalled, but before he went home the Mexicans did manage to get together enough of a government to negotiate a treaty with him. In this Treaty of Guadalupe Hidalgo, the United States not only got Texas to the Rio Grande, but also the territory contained within the present states of Nevada, Utah, California, New Mexico, Arizona and Colorado. The southern boundary of the United States was to be along the lines of the Gila and the Rio Grande. For this immense empire, the United States agreed to pay Mexico $15,000,000 and to take care of the vexatious claims due her own citizens by Mexico, which Mexico was now in no position to think of paying. At the time Trist had no authority to negotiate a treaty, but he took it upon himself to act without authority.[18]

Meanwhile the United States was intoxicated with victory. All sorts and conditions of men talked about annexing the whole of Mexico on every possible ground from the highly altruistic to the crudely selfish. Mexico was a "poor foundling," unable to educate and care for herself. Let the great United States fulfill that destiny which Providence had so obviously assigned to her and take over Mexico. Crocodile tears in abundance were shed in sympathy toward our erring sister Republic whose manifest and frequent misconduct had resulted in such frightful punishment. But the treaty was not destined to have an easy path through the Senate. Some senators, like Hannegan of Indiana, did not like it because they wanted all of Mexico. Some like Webster of Massachusetts, disliked it because they wanted none of Mexico. Polk soon saw that the extreme friends and extreme

---

[18] J. H. Smith, *War with Mexico*, II, 236–40; E. I. McCormac, *James K. Polk* (U. of Cal., 1922), pp. 488–544.

enemies of annexation might get together and make common cause against the treaty, in which case the United States would probably lose what it had gained. He decided therefore to waive the fact of Trist's lack of authority to act and recommended ratification. There is good reason for saying that the United States could easily have had all Mexico at the time if only she could have agreed that she wanted it or if she could have kept it. Finally the ratified treaty gave the United States clear title to those lands westward to the Pacific for which she had been struggling so long.[19]

But the war left Mexico in a sad plight. The money she received from the United States did not benefit her in her disorganized state. Moreover, the victory of the United States did not prevent the continuance of the boundary disputes. It merely shoved the disputed area a little farther over into the southwest. The line of the Rio Grande was comprehensible enough, but the southern boundary of New Mexico and the line of the Gila were to produce five years of fruitless bickering, surveying, negotiation, and the like. It resulted in the formation in 1853 of another treaty whereby for ten million dollars the United States got another slice of Mexico, this time at last with an intelligible boundary based on the parallels of latitude and not on undiscoverable or nonexistent rivers. Santa Anna, the Mexican dictator, was as usual, hard up for ready cash, and was glad enough to dispose of the land for nearly as much as the United States had paid for half the Mexican national domain five years earlier. The United States was prompted to pay this sum, not only to settle the boundary, but also to acquire a southern route for a Pacific railway. Santa Anna defended this further loss of national territory on the ground that the United States would have taken it anyway. While it is not true that the United States occupied the disputed area prior to the purchase by Gadsden, yet it is a fact that the United States had had enough experience with Mexican diplomacy to make the concentration of troops on the frontier a

[19] E. G. Bourne, "Proposed Absorption of Mexico in 1847-8," in *Amer. Hist. Assoc. Repts.*, 1899, I, 155; J. H. Smith, *War with Mexico*, II, 245-7.

discreet as well as a precautionary measure. This was hardly calculated to secure cordial relations between the two republics, however justifiable it might have been.[20]

3. MAXIMILIAN'S FIASCO

But even more tragic days were in store for the unhappy republic below the Rio Grande. The imposition of a democratic and representative government on a largely illiterate people produced those alternations of tyranny and disorder which are so characteristic of Mexican history. The tyrants usually borrowed money, which could rarely be repaid, from gullible and greedy European bankers. Periods of disorder entailed destruction of the lives and property of Americans in Mexico whereby bills and claims for damages without number piled up against the unfortunate republic. Between 1848 and 1860 more than $10,000,000 worth of damage was done to citizens of the United States by Mexican bandits and border raiders, whom Mexico was unable to control. Now and again the government of the United States, distracted as it was with the approach of its own Civil War, found time to send in its ever-increasing account marked "please remit." In 1857 an experienced diplomat, James Buchanan, became President of the United States and he offered to take over Lower California in lieu of the $10,000,000, an offer which Mexico promptly rejected. Mexico's inability to pay her debts revived the talk of absorption of all that country, and Buchanan even went so far as to recommend that the United States send an expeditionary force for the collection of the debts. Such an act was desirable, not only to satisfy the claims of the American creditors, but also to forestall the apparently imminent intervention by European powers.[21]

But Congress was now too busy with the acute question of slavery to pay any attention to Mexico. The result was just

[20] J. F. Rippy, "Boundary of Mexico and the Gadsden Treaty," *Hispanic American Historical Review*, IV, 71; J. F. Rippy, "Ray of Light on the Gadsden Treaty," *Southwestern Historical Quarterly*, XXIV, 235; P. N. Garber, *The Gadsden Treaty*, (U. of Penna., 1924).
[21] *Mr. Buchanan's Administration* (N. Y., 1866), pp. 274–5; J. Musser, *Foundation of Maximilian's Empire in Mexico* (Univ. of Pa., 1918), 18–31.

what Buchanan had foreseen, for the European powers took matters into their own hands. During the Three Years War in Mexico (1857–60) a full-blooded Indian, Benito Juárez, came to the front, and became president. English, Spanish, and French claims for unpaid interest on bonds, and for damages done, were accumulating against Mexico at a tremendous rate. As early as 1823 Mexico had borrowed money from English bankers, and by 1860 she had gotten into such a state of bankruptcy that in municipal law her business would long since have been taken over by a receiver in bankruptcy. But there was no international authority to appoint a receiver in bankruptcy for her and to make her set her house in order. Consequently, as is always the case, the creditor nations had to take care of their own interests and be their own sheriffs. They moved cautiously and asked the United States to join them in a forcible intervention in Mexican affairs. The United States declined to participate because of the Monroe Doctrine, and because of the doctrine of isolation which would seem to advise her to reject possible European contacts. Moreover, this was a move for the violation of the sovereignty and territorial integrity of an American Republic, such as our traditional policy disapproved, and it would be most embarrassing if we participated. However the real explanation of our position was the Civil War.[22]

Since Mexico now owed over $80,000,000 ($69,000,000 to England and only $9,000,000 to France) a joint military expedition was undertaken by England, France and Spain. The expedition was fruitless, as it is quite impossible to get money where there is no money. France, then under the leadership of Napoleon III, determined to make this the occasion for the establishment of a new French colonial empire, under the guise of a new Empire in Mexico. Under the headship of an Austrian Hapsburg Prince, Maximilian, Mexico was soon officially an Empire again, and occupied by French troops who kept the new puppet in place. England and Spain promptly withdrew from this high-handed

---

[22] J. Musser, *Establishment of Maximilian's Empire*, 29–31; *H. Ex. Doc. No. 100*, 37th Cong., 2 sess.

business, and the United States, now hopelessly enmeshed in her Civil War, could only protest cautiously and cite the Monroe Doctrine.

But the Mexicans, like most people, will unite long enough to expel a foreigner. Juárez simply moved his capital from Mexico City and kept his governmental organization together while the bayonets of Marshal Bazaine supported the Austrian on his unstable throne at Chapultepec. Such a situation could not last. As the Civil War in the United States drew to a close, actual conditions within Mexico made it quite clear that Maximilian could not stay. His friend Napoleon now had enough troubles at home without wasting strength on foreign exploits which failed to pay interest to the French investors. The Second Empire was tottering to its fall, and in 1865 the French Corps Legislatif was clamoring for the return of their soldiers from the useless expedition overseas. Long before Lee's surrender at Appomattox, 8,000 of the French troops were already on their way home, and the French ministry assured the Chambers that the balance would return by the same month which saw the end of the Civil War in the United States.

While the French did not return quite that quickly, because of unavoidable delays, yet Bismarck's sabre rattling in the Schleswig-Holstein affair soon prodded Napoleon into getting the rest of his army back to France as quickly as possible. The result was that by the time the United States was ready to throw down the gauntlet of the Monroe Doctrine to France and summarily order her out of the western hemisphere, France was already getting out as fast as she could. The French intervention failed to secure anything, and Maximilian, bereft of his French soldiers, was soon caught by Juárez' troops and met the usual fate which is meted out to Mexican dictators who do not get away in time. He was shot somewhat as was the first Emperor, Iturbide, yet with more formality than were Madero and Carranza in our own times. The whole affair has frequently been hailed as a triumph of the Monroe Doctrine, but it is now apparent that the French taxpayer and Bismarck had a good deal more to do with the

French withdrawal than Secretary Seward's peremptory dispatch.[23]

4. THE INVITATION TO FOREIGN CAPITAL

But all this was of no avail to get Mexico to pay her debts or to settle the border strife. Unable any longer to borrow money on the outside, and having put United States' citizens very much on their guard about going into Mexico at all, her internal condition was in a sad state. The inhabitants of northern Mexico began systematic pillaging expeditions into the southwestern part of the United States, for the purpose of stealing the now rapidly increasing cattle herds from the Texan and New Mexican ranches. Revolts in the Mexican states of Sinaloa and Chihuahua made protection and protests via Mexico City quite futile. The cattle stealing raids along the border soon grew into regular plundering expeditions which left in their wake a trail of burned ranches, of slaughtered and mutilated corpses of American men and women. The raiders would dash across the border before the United States troops could arrive on the scene, and in the words of Governor Hubbard of Texas

"Our claims for redress are met with indifference, and our demands for fugitive thieves, murderers are laughed to scorn from the other side of a shallow river, almost within sight of the victims." [24]

But relief was in sight in the only way it would ever come. That is by the formation of a strong and self-respecting government in Mexico herself by Mexicans. By 1876 Porfirio Díaz had forged to the front and fought his way to the presidency, that being the normal method of election in Mexico at the time. Díaz was a man who caught the vision of the possibilities of the economic development of Mexico. He saw that all her debts were but trifles if only she would get to work and turn some of her natural resources to good account. Within a very short time a most astonishing change was noticed. He suppressed banditry by turning the bandits into policemen. He straightened out the

---

[23] C. A. Dunniway, "Reasons for the Withdrawal of the French from Mexico," *Amer. Hist. Assoc. Repts.*, 1902, I, 315–27.

[24] *Foreign Relations of the United States*, 1873, 634, 643 and passim.

chaotic financial situation in Mexico and began to pay back some of the borrowed money. He understood that the investment of foreign capital in Mexico for the building of railway lines, the opening up of agricultural fields, and the exploitation of Mexico's wonderful natural resources, would be necessary. By being more careful than his predecessor to honor the obligations of Mexico, he was soon in a position where foreign capital would accept his invitation to come in and help make Mexico rich by developing her lands. He had a good deal of difficulty at first with the border raids, as the border is a long way from the capital and the raiders had influential friends.

In 1877 President Hayes decided that the United States was entitled to protect herself from raids, even if it were necessary to pursue the bandits into Mexico. Troops were ordered to the border and on various occasions they followed the marauders into Mexican territory after a raid which had resulted in the loss of life and property. At once the Mexican newspapers and officials raised howls of protest about "invasions from the United States." Secretary of State W. M. Evarts then directed our Minister John W. Foster to reply to these protests in a language which is a good statement of our policy:

"The first duty of a government is to protect life and property. For this, governments are instituted, and governments neglecting or failing to perform it are worse than useless. Protection *in fact* to American lives and property is the sole point upon which the United States is tenacious. So far, the authorities of Mexico, military and civil, in the vicinity of the border appear not only to take no steps effectively to check the raids or punish the raiders, but demur and object to steps taken by the United States. The pretense that the United States are plotting or executing invasions for conquests in Mexico is fallacious and absurd. No American force ever goes over the Rio Grande except in pursuit of 'invaders' who have already 'invaded' the soil of the United States and are escaping with their booty. The United States have not sought the unpleasant duty forced upon them, of pursuing offenders who, under ordinary usages of municipal and international law ought to be pursued and arrested or punished by Mexico. Whenever Mexico will assume and efficiently exercise that responsibility, the United States will be glad to be relieved from it." [25]

[25] *Foreign Relations of the U. S.*, 1878, pp. 572-4 (abridged).

Apparently this was the kind of language which Mexico could understand. At any rate it was not long before President Díaz had the situation sufficiently well in hand to give American citizens the protection which under international law they were entitled to receive. As order was restored in Mexico the outlying provinces were brought under control and could no longer harbor the criminals whose periodic raids had caused such damage to the United States. The matter was settled in the only possible way by removing the cause of the irritation, which was, after all, the feeble government in Mexico.

Foreign capital was soon transforming Mexico into a hive of industry, exploiting her natural resources, giving employment to her citizens, and producing millions in wealth, part of which went to Mexico in taxes or to Mexicans in wages, but the profits of which accrued to the foreigner who loaned the capital. In this way railroads were built all over Mexico and many industries started which, properly pursued, would soon have ranked Mexico among the leading exporting nations of the world. But Díaz' methods laid the foundations for trouble. In his anxiety to induce foreign, and particularly American, capital to invest in Mexico, he had the laws of mines and mining changed to attract that capital. Under the old rule of the Roman Law, which the Spaniards had introduced into Mexico, the owner of the surface soil does not necessarily own the mineral wealth beneath it, which is supposed to be vested in the state. In operating the old mines of Peru and Mexico in colonial times, the Conquistadores had to pay a "royalty" of one-fifth to the king's treasury in acknowledgment of this. In order to make foreign capital feel more secure in Mexico, Díaz had Congress change the law and adopt the principle of the English Common Law, which gives to the owner of the surface all the mineral wealth he can tap beneath. This was established in the law of 1884, confirmed in the laws of 1892 and 1909.[26]

Under this favorable and attractive law, millions of dollars

---

[26] *Documentos Relacionados con la Legislación Petrolera Mexicana* (Mexico, 1919), p. 21, 40, 42; W. S. Robertson, *History of Latin American Nations* (N. Y., 1922), p. 498.

worth of capital from the United States now flowed into Mexico and paid for the labor and machinery which brought to the surface the valuable gold, silver, lead, and copper which she has in such abundance, and above all, for the development of her vast petroleum fields. Petroleum was becoming tremendously important in human affairs by the opening of the twentieth century and we must pause for a moment to understand its significance in diplomacy. There was an increasingly emphatic demand for a fuel that was cheaper and more economical than coal, which, for a century had dominated the industry of the world. Mexico possessed that new fuel. Petroleum does not have to be mined by expensive labor digging hundreds of feet in the earth. The cost of production is infinitely cheaper than coal. Oil does not have to be hauled in heavy bulk, in immense and expensive steel cars over railroads whose upkeep is increasingly costly. Oil is simply pumped into long pipe lines which carry the fluid for hundreds of miles overland. Oil has infinitely greater explosive force per unit of weight than has coal, and hence is more efficient. The transportation of the future which will be so largely in the air gives us a graphic illustration of the superiority of petroleum to coal. Think of an aëroplane being run by a steam engine and trying to carry enough coal to run a hundred miles! The bulk would be so great that the aëroplane would never leave the ground. The future of transportation is much more involved with petroleum than with coal. Even many of the great ocean liners to-day are oil burners and the tremendous increase in automobiles in the last twenty years is enough by itself to show why diplomacy the world over has been a rush for oil fields.[27]

Now, as we have seen, American capital poured into Mexico during the peaceful and orderly régime of Díaz, building transportation lines, opening up oil fields, and enriching the investors. The first American oil operators bought their lands from private individuals and under the then existing laws of Mexico were entitled to all the oil they could get. In reliance on these laws

<hr/>

[27] J. E. Spurr, *Political and Commercial Geology* (N. Y., 1920), pp. 1–20; *Senate Document No. 285*, 66th Cong. 2 sess. (The Fall Report), p. 255.

a trackless jungle was by American skill and energy transformed into a commercially important country.   Pipe lines ran for hundreds of miles; terminal facilities such as huge oil tanks and refineries were built; lines of "tankers" or specially designed steamboats were constructed to carry the oil from Mexico to New York, and all these called for more and more capital, which was readily forthcoming. The value of the product and the increasing demand for automobiles promised the investor a fair return on his money. But political stability in Mexico was absolutely essential to such a profitable business. Díaz was a little alarmed at the predominance of United States investors and so he encouraged the great English oil interests associated with the name of Lord Cowdray to come to Mexico, too. As Cowdray had contracts for supplying the Royal Navy with petroleum for the oil-burning units of the British fleet, his holdings in Mexico soon became extensive.[28]

But Díaz did not succeed in removing the cause of Mexico's troubles.   Popular education was still struggling for existence; political education still left much to be desired. Elections were a farce conducted under the bayonets of Díaz' troops. The fundamental ills of Mexican civilization as outlined in the earlier part of this chapter were hardly improved under the great benevolent despot, and sooner or later another Revolution was bound to break out. One of the greatest injustices of the Díaz régime was the taking of the Indians' lands and the incorporation thereof into some of the big estates. This stirred up a mighty discontent which was not long in finding expression.

5. The Cycle of Revolutions

After thirty years of peace the crash came. In 1910, the aged President lost his grip on the situation and fled to Europe, and another awful era of Civil War was ushered in. Now it was much more serious than ever before because the "bandits," the "patriots," and the "-istas" of a dozen sorts turned Mexico into a

[28] L. S. Rowe, "The Scope and Limit of Our Obligations Toward Mexico," in *Annals of the Amer. Acad.*, LIV, 222-3.

battle ground, and if foreign property was in the way, so much the worse for the foreigners. Francisco Madero, a political doctrinaire of high ideals, became president, but scarcely was he seated, when General Huerta, a kind of second Santa Anna, usurped the position in a military *coup*, in which Madero was killed. In Mexican history there is nothing abnormal about this, and had the United States followed her usual policy she would have waited till things quieted down and then recognized Huerta as the constitutional president of Mexico until he in turn was overthrown.

But a peculiar thing had just happened in the United States. A presidential campaign had just been waged in which Theodore Roosevelt had gone up and down the country whipping up the people of the nation to a greater appreciation of morals in politics. While the people did not elect Roosevelt, they did elect another political moralist, Woodrow Wilson. Wilson believed that world diplomacy had become not so much the plaything of be-ribboned diplomats as a crudely materialistic struggle for business interests, new markets, and raw materials. Certainly, if our history demonstrates nothing else, it shows that Wilson was not altogether wrong. Wilson let it be known that Principle and not Policy was going to dictate foreign relations. Policy would have dictated that Huerta be recognized as soon as he demonstrated his ability to master Mexico. He was hailed as a second Diaz who would rule with an iron hand and make it possible for the English and Americans to conduct business as usual.

However, the new Revolution had a new aspect. Its leaders claimed it was no longer merely a set of quarrels between petty Indian chiefs, but an agrarian revolt for the liberation of the peasant farmer class from serfdom and for the redistribution of lands. Ruthless suppression by a strong man like Diaz would have been simply sitting on the safety valve, and would have been an attempt to suppress those very political ideals for which America was supposed to stand. The historian pointed out (and Wilson was a historian) that Mexico's unhappy plight was largely due to a century of these strong-arm methods, and Wilson had no intention of encouraging any more of them, although the oil interests begged for the recognition of Huerta which would at least give them a breathing spell from the destructive effects of the revolutions which were ruining their holdings.[29] Yet a high-minded business man admitted "No one believes that the recognition of Huerta would have solved Mexico's problem; it would have only made it worse." [30]

Yet the situation was infinitely complicated. The United States Ambassador to Mexico, Henry Lane Wilson, was a survival of the previous Republican administration and he knew Mexico like a book. He was sincerely convinced that the Diaz policy was the right one. He believed in the "strong man" theory, and had no use for Woodrow Wilson's "New Freedom." [31] The new President felt that by his actions toward Mexico, Latin America was going to judge whether the Monroe Doctrine was a benevolent or a malevolent thing. He announced that governments owing their origin to murder and violence would not receive the sanction of the United States. Of course the obvious criticism which Ambassador H. L. Wilson made of President Wilson's idealism is the fact that a free election in Mexico was impossible and the efforts to impose our democratic forms on our neighbor is just what had produced a century of revolutions there.[32]

Jefferson's principle of recognition had prescribed that we recognize any revolutionary government which represented the people's will. For a century the United States had been interpreting that to mean that any revolutionary government was representative of the people's will. Wilson introduced into American foreign policy the idea that we would scrutinize some of these revolutionary governments and see whether they really represented the people's will. The old Jeffersonian ideal rather

[29] A. B. Hart, "Postulates of the Mexican Situation," in *Annals. of Amer. Acad.*, LIV, 143.

[30] Franklin K. Lane, in J. B. Scott's *Foreign Policy of Woodrow Wilson*, p. 305.

[31] H. L. Wilson, "Errors with Reference to Mexico," *Annals. of Amer. Acad.*, LIV, 148.

[32] L. S. Rowe, "Scope and Limit of Our Obligations toward Mexico," *Ann. Amer. Acad.*, LIV, 219.

presumed that any revolution was a popular thing and that any revolutionary government represented the people against the tyrants. But Wilson saw clearly that a revolutionary government might be merely an exchange of one set of tyrants for another.

The President forged straight ahead with his ideal, despite criticism. As he saw it, the material interests of the country wished him to recognize Huerta and sanction the acts of that dictator for the sake of securing the dividends of the oil and mining companies, but without regard for the rights of millions of Mexicans who had been oppressed for centuries. It was a case of "human rights, national integrity, and opportunity as against material interests." He declined to intervene and he would not recognize Huerta, announcing to Congress that there would be no peace until Huerta got out.[33]

Naturally this bred bad feeling between Huerta and Wilson, when Wilson's hand was suddenly forced by the action of a rather tenacious naval officer, Admiral Mayo, whose fleet lay off Vera Cruz. Some American sailors were mistreated in the streets of Vera Cruz. This was an insult to the United States, and Huerta promptly apologized. But Mayo, instead of being satisfied with the apology, complicated the situation by demanding a salute to the American flag which Huerta very resolutely refused to give. This brought matters to a head and the President seemed obliged for the sake of naval discipline to support his officer. Mexico frankly began to prepare for war with the United States and when a shipment of arms from Germany to Mexico made it evident to Wilson that if he did not act quickly he would be simply allowing the Mexicans to arm themselves, he ordered Vera Cruz occupied by the United States marines. This was done with bloodshed which amounted to war.[34]

Fortunately before things got any worse, the Republics of Argentina, Brazil, and Chile offered to mediate, and Wilson promptly accepted their good offices. But his firm refusal to

[33] J. B. Scott, *President Wilson's Foreign Policy*, pp. 23–29.
[34] J. P. Tumulty, *Woodrow Wilson as I Know Him*, pp. 145–6.

recognize Huerta, even in the face of the fact that the British did so, resulted in the ultimate withdrawal of that General, and the coming into power of the constitutionalist chief, Venustiano Carranza. Wilson had won his first round, but he had certainly not succeeded in reëstablishing order in Mexico nor had he protected American property interests there. He said quite frankly "I have to pause and remind myself that I am President of the United States and not of a small group of Americans with vested interests in Mexico." [35]

But the "small group of Americans" were very active and very noisy, and their complaints became constantly more justifiable. That they received at first scant attention and courtesy from the Department of State is due partly to the fact that the Secretary of State was no other than that William J. Bryan who had spent most of his life traveling up and down the country attacking those same "vested interests" in behalf of the "common man" who would have to pay the bill with his blood. Wilson determined to play the game of "watchful waiting," as he called it, with the firm conviction that Mexico herself must settle her own problems and with the statement that the function of being a policeman in Mexico did not appeal to him.[36]

Despite Wilson's high hopes in General Carranza's régime, there were still a good half dozen revolutionary chieftains roaming around Mexico, defying his authority and destroying American life and property. Chief among these was one Francisco Villa, who revived the old practice of raiding the border, stealing cattle and murdering Americans on their own soil. Wilson negotiated with Carranza and got permission for an American Expeditionary Force to follow Villa into Mexico. But it never caught him, and Carranza soon made things so unpleasant for the expeditionary force that it was withdrawn. This invasion of Mexico and Carranza's ill-natured attitude toward it stirred up bitter feeling on both sides. Mexico was in no position to make war on the United States, but she was in a position to fight a guerilla war-

---

[35] J. B. Scott, *President Wilson's Foreign Policy*, p. 383.
[36] Ibid., 388.

fare which would have wasted thousands of American lives and gotten us no nearer a solution of the Mexican problem than before.

But troubles were ahead. Carranza now secured the adoption of a new Constitution for Mexico wherein the provision of the old Spanish Law as to sub-soil minerals was once more adopted. Oil hereafter was to belong to the Mexican nation and not to the owner of the surface. Article 27 of the Mexican constitution of 1917 became the center of controversy, and the American investors expressed their rage and indignation at having been induced to invest their money in Mexico under one set of laws and then had the laws changed so as to cause them to lose the title to their holdings.[37] But this was not all. The railways in Mexico were owned almost wholly by capital in the United States. The Carranza Government taxed, regulated, confiscated, and manipulated the railways till they were practically ruined and the American investor ceased to get any return on his money. American interests in Mexico were at the mercy of the troops of Carranza, who frequently joined in the general game of plundering the foreigners. Americans in Mexico were not allowed to carry arms in their own defense and soon hundreds of Americans were killed in the riots and revolutions which took place in and around the mines and oil wells.[38]

Since the Carranzistas were incompetent to give the Americans any protection against the bandits, the Americans in desperation often turned to the bandits themselves and bought immunity for themselves and their property. This unfortunately laid them open to the charge of paying money to help the enemies of Mexico. The charge could not well be denied, but the American oil-owners could not do anything else, as the taxes they paid the Mexican government got them no protection. Note after note was exchanged between Washington and Mexico City until 1917, when the entrance of the United States into the European war made it necessary to lay aside these grievances. Mexican oil was needed

[37] H. I. Priestley, *The Mexican Nation, A History* (N. Y. 1923), p. 438.
[38] F. R. Kellogg, "The Mexican Oil Situation," in *Mexico and the Caribbean*, p. 54; A. W. Donly, "The Railroad Situation in Mexico," in ibid., p. 73.

by the torpedo-boat destroyers which kept the lanes of the Atlantic open while America sent her millions to France.[39]

But with the end of the war in Europe there recurred all those questions of Mexican-American relations which have plagued both for a hundred years. The Mexican correspondence of the Wilson administration reads just like that of almost every other administration since 1825. The Americans have charged the Mexicans with failure to protect American citizens in Mexico. The Mexicans replied again that Americans were getting as much protection as the Mexicans themselves. This might be true, but the United States contended it was not sufficient.

"An alien is not bound to accept the treatment accorded nationals, if such treatment is in violation of the ordinary principles of civilized justice." [40]

says a leading authority and in pursuance of this idea the United States has claimed it did not have to accept Mexican standards of justice. But as we have pointed out, Mexico and the United States have two totally different ideas of civilization. The question which confronted Wilson was the same that confronted Andrew Jackson: does the flag follow the investor? Despite the ever increasing volume of criticism for his policy, Wilson kept away from the intervention in Mexican affairs, knowing full well that the one thing which would unite all Mexicans of all classes was the threat of invasion from the Yankees who had dispoiled Mexico of half her national domain in 1848.

In 1920 Carranza went out with another revolution, and was killed as were Maximilian and Madero. He was succeeded by a "strong man," Alvaro Obregón, who announced that he would maintain order, and began by pensioning off Francisco Villa. But the vexed question of American rights under Article 27 is still not altogether adjusted, and American capital which received such crushing blows from successive revolutionary movements that Mexican railway securities, Mexican Oil stock and Mexican

[39] The N. Y. *Nation*, CVIII, 609; *Sen. Doc. No. 285*, 66th Cong. 2d sess. (*The Fall Report*), pp. 285, 297, 996.

[40] E. M. Borchard, *Diplomatic Protection of Citizens Abroad*, p. 107.

government bonds are hardly the most attractive investment possibilities on Wall Street. Mexico can hardly expect further assistance from the United States till she has settled these outstanding troubles. But as far as the rest of Latin America is concerned, Wilson's policy of refusing to war on Mexico has probably won the United States more friends in Latin America than the opposite policy would have done. As far as protecting United States' property was concerned, Wilson's policy failed. As for saving lives of thousands of American soldiers, saving millions of dollars, and keeping the good will of Latin America, it was a success.

As far as the diplomacy of oil is concerned it is the same problem that the whole world is facing to-day, and which confronts every so-called civilized nation in its relations with the so-called backward nations:

> "In Mexico's oil fields to-day is being settled the question of whether enterprise shall have the right to bring the riches of the earth to the aid of humanity, of whether industrial power belongs to the backward people who by accident find that power in their inept hands, or to those who can develop and raise it up to the service of mankind. Upon the issue in Mexico depends not only the usefulness of all the petroleum resources of that country, but the future development of oil in Colombia, Venezuela, all South America, all Asia, all Africa." [41]

What attitude American foreign policy takes on this question will have great weight on international politics the world over.

In 1923 Mexican and American negotiators met and drew up treaties, whereby Mexico promised to indemnify Americans for the damage claims which had been piling up for ten years. The government of Obregón was thus recognized by the United States and the two nations agreed to live peaceably—until the next revolution.

This came early in 1924, and the United States concluded to adopt a more positive attitude toward it. The Department of State was evidently convinced that President Obregón's administration was worthy of support. Placing an embargo on arms going to the rebels was an expedient which had been adopted

[41] W. Thompson, *Trading with Mexico* (N. Y., 1922), p. 198.

before by the United States. This was done at once but this time the United States went a step further and the War Department at Washington actually sold war material to Obregón with which to suppress the revolt. Besides this the War Department wired President Obregón that the Governors of Texas, New Mexico and Arizona had consented to allow Mexican Federal troops to pass over the soil of those states in pursuit of the rebels. Partly as a consequence of this new and vigorous attitude of the United States, the revolt was suppressed and order maintained for the Obregón régime.[42]

[42] C. W. Hackett, in *Current History*, XIX, 963.

CHAPTER XI

ONE HUNDRED YEARS OF SUCCESSFUL DIPLOMACY WITH GREAT BRITAIN

"But then, during these eighty-four years, what tremendous questions we have had, what heated words, what threatening demonstrations on either side, and yet, while those questions were such as would inevitably have brought any other nations into open conflict, they have all been arranged and adjusted between us without ever a resort to arms."—*Joseph Hodges Choate.*

1. THE WEBSTER-ASHBURTON TREATY

Contrasting vividly with our century of misunderstanding with Mexico, is a century of increasing cordiality with Great Britain. Our relations with Britain have been in every way more varied and more important than our relations with Mexico, indeed there have been a dozen occasions when such old world powers as France and Germany, or Italy and Austria would have flown at one another's throats over things which the United States and Great Britain have managed to settle without bloodshed. The history of our foreign policy from 1815 to 1914 is preëminently worth reading as a lesson in international decency. A hundred years ago the feeling between Englishmen and Americans was hardly cordial. Ignorance, provincialism, crudeness and self-righteousness on the part of democratic America were constantly irritating to the arrogance, haughtiness and insolent contempt for the ex-colonials which characterized aristocratic England of that day. The American Revolution had left in its wake many unfortunate, not to say, stupid, prejudices against England, and these had been accentuated and magnified by the offenses of British sea power which led up to the War of 1812.

The Treaty of Ghent in 1815 left the most important disputes between the two nations unsettled and the end of the war discovered both sides feverishly at work building naval armaments for the next war on the Great Lakes. But if the people of the two countries had to spend the next century learning to understand one another, the two governments soon realized that they could not afford to spend too much time glorifying their own questionable military records and trying to belittle the other side. Within six months after the conclusion of hostilities an agreement was patched up to allow the Americans to sell their surplus food in the British West Indies, and, what was just as important, to allow the British islanders to send their sugar products to the United States in exchange for the food they did not raise for themselves. Thus the old mercantilist system had to give way before the interests of Yankee fishermen and Jamaica sugar planters.

In 1817, President Madison decided that the competition of naval armaments on the Great Lakes would impoverish both nations and inevitably lead to war. The obvious alternative of an agreement on both sides not to maintain a navy on the Lakes, was too apparent to escape notice and the American Minister at London, John Quincy Adams, suggested to Lord Castlereagh

"It is evident, if each party augments its forces there with a view to obtaining the ascendancy over the other, vast expense will be incurred and the danger of collision augmented to a like degree." [1]

Just as great wars produce jingoists who want to waste national money in outbuilding the world in armaments, they also produce a revulsion of feeling against wars and a real necessity for economy and retrenchment in national expenses. So in spite of Parliamentary opposition Castlereagh finally accepted the American proposition.[2] Even without the formality of a treaty, Secretary of State Richard Rush arranged with the British Minister Charles Bagot an agreement by which both nations agreed to maintain in the lakes only such vessels as were necessary to police the waterways. President Monroe was careful to submit this agreement to the Senate for its consent [3] and thereby wrote into Amer-

---

[1] *House Document* No. 471, 56th Cong., 1st Sess., p. 5.

[2] Hansard's *Debates*, XXXIII, 376–8, 567–91; J. Q. Adams' *Memoirs*, III, 287, 329.

[3] *Amer. State Papers, Foreign Relations*, IV, 202.

ican foreign policy the principle of disarmament as a means of preventing war. Europe, crossed with illogical frontiers, all bristling with armed men, is a good illustration of what the Canadian border might have been without this sensible arrangement.[4]

In the next year another treaty was negotiated which settled the difficult matter of the Canadian fisheries and the north-western boundary. It will be remembered that in what is now northern Minnesota, the old treaty of 1783 had made a meaningless boundary provision. The purchase of Louisiana necessitated the extension of the boundary between Canada and the United States indefinitely to the westward. The line which was to run "from the North-west corner of the Lake of the Woods due west to the Mississippi" was, as we have seen, geographically impossible. In default of exact geographical knowledge the two countries now agreed to run the line either north or south, as the case might turn out to be, from the northwest corner of the Lake of the Woods to the 49th parallel and thence along that parallel to the Rocky Mountains. The Americans wanted to run the line on to the Pacific Ocean, but the British were not yet ready to settle that country in the far northwest and so as regards what was known as "Oregon" both countries agreed on a "joint occupation" for the next ten years, at the end of which time the boundary was to be fixed.[5] (See maps opposite and p. 227.)

The fisheries question was much more difficult, for it involved competition with the English fishermen in pursuit of the sacred cod of Massachusetts. It will be remembered that the Yankee fishermen had to use the coasts of Newfoundland and Labrador for their "inshore privileges" of drying fish, and taking bait, water and fuel. This practice had been perfectly proper when New England and Newfoundland were both parts of the British Empire, but after 1783 the New Englanders were interlopers on the shores of Labrador. Nevertheless under the treaty of 1783 the British had accorded this privilege to their ex-colonial sub-

[4] J. M. Callahan, "Agreement of 1817," *Am. Hist. Assoc. Rept.*, 1895, p. 369, and his *Neutrality of the American Lakes*, J. H. U. Stud., ser. XVI (Balt., 1898).

[5] J. S. Reeves, *American Diplomacy under Tyler and Polk*, pp. 208–24.

Courtesy of Dr. Edw. Channing.

NORTHWESTERN CORNER OF MITCHELL'S MAP OF 1755

This was the map used at Paris in 1782, when Oswald and Franklin made the impossible boundary provision (see p. 62), for a line drawn due west from the Lake of the Woods will never intersect the Mississippi. A glance at this map shows how the negotiators were misled. The inset of Hudson Bay covers up just the portion of the map they needed.

jects in the United States.   The War of 1812 ended this arrangement because the British contended that wars abrogated treaties
as between the belligerents.   At Ghent John Quincy Adams tried
hard to regain the liberty of the "inshore privileges" which his
New England constituents had always enjoyed, but the British
contended this was not a right, but merely a liberty which the
British had accorded under the treaty of 1783, which they had
quite properly withdrawn in 1812.   The same treaty which settled
the northwestern boundary provided further that the Americans
should surrender their notion that they had any "natural liberty"
to use the Canadian shores (an argument which the Americans
had advanced with more shrewdness than logic) and the British
would again accord them the "liberty" to use certain sections of
the Canadian shore under certain conditions.[6]   This agreement was
found inadequate during the nineteenth century and whenever it
made trouble, American fishermen exercising the inshore privileges were at the mercy of the British revenue cutters, who ruthlessly seized the American vessels for violating Canadian territorial waters.   Such a practice always created discord and the
case had to be argued out all over again.   This rather helpless
handling of the situation was further complicated by the question of maritime territorial jurisdiction.

According to international law, it had long been the practice of
nations to allow a state to control the sea three miles from shore.
But the ragged indentations of the Canadian coast made it
difficult to say where this three-mile limit ran.   Should it follow
the multitudinous sinuosities of the coast, or should it pass from
headland to headland, thus including great stretches of the
open sea within the British jurisdiction?   As a result of nearly a
century of failure to agree on a permanent set of rules, the whole
matter was finally submitted to the Hague Court in 1909.   This,
the first international judicial tribunal, finally settled the matter
by affirming the right of the British or Dominion Government
to make such laws as it saw fit for its own territory, thus denying
that the Americans had any "natural rights" to use other people's

[6] Moore's *Digest*, I, 769; Malloy's *Treaties and Conventions*, I, 631.

territory, and it further allowed Canada to consider bays not more than ten miles wide as wholly within her territorial jurisdiction. Thus the Americans could use such inshore privileges as were accorded them, but must report their presence to the Dominion Government, and a new treaty was drawn up providing for the rules and regulations under which the Americans might take advantage of the inshore privileges, and further providing for an opportunity of revising the treaty every ten years.[7]

But in the years following 1818 Anglo-American relations were seriously affected by not a few psychological and mental troubles which still frequently disturb the good relations between the two countries. A new generation was growing up in America which was being fed on the legend of the victories of their country in the wars of the Revolution and of 1812, and the glorification of these now garbled legends was used to incite to patriotism and to provoke an aversion to England and things English. The new generation was being presented with a somewhat pernicious interpretation of the Declaration of Independence which stamped upon the minds of children in school a wholly wrong idea of Great Britain. The Declaration of Independence is a document in which, as Dr. Samuel Johnson would have said, one must distinguish between Thomas Jefferson when he was talking for victory and when he was talking for enlightment and information. The first part of the declaration contains an excellent statement of eighteenth-century political philosophy. The second part is a statement of grievances couched in a language which to-day we would probably be inclined to call propaganda. It is these "propaganda clauses" which have done the mischief. While true, they are not always the whole truth, and have not always been understood by political orators in America in just the sense in which Jefferson would probably have liked to have them interpreted in later years. They have been used to excite an anti-English sentiment not altogether based on fact. This unfortunate interpretation of American history has done its part in rendering

---

[7] J. B. Moore, *Principles of American Diplomacy*, 135–47; his *Digest of International Law*, I, 785ff.; *Treaties and Conventions*, III, 2632.

difficult the work of the diplomats. It was, in a way, the natural result of that expansive sense of nationalism which has characterized the nineteenth century throughout the world. It is only just beginning to be whispered in scientific and enlightened circles that nationalism may be as great a menace to the human race as it was once thought to be a benefit.[8] In the first part of the nineteenth century, however, English travelers in America and other English literary people were writing somewhat patronizing memoirs of their residence in the young republic or books about it, which expressed open contempt for the queer experiment in democracy being tried out in the New World. Sidney Smith insolently inquired what of intellectual or artistic merit an American had produced. Mrs. Trollope wrote her *Domestic Manners of the Americans* in a general vein of captious criticism which was hardly improved by Dickens' *American Notes*.[9]

In view of this general attitude on both sides of the water, it is a great tribute to the diplomats that they managed to keep the peoples of the respective countries out of constant warfare. Another influence was steadily growing stronger to keep the peace. With the gradual surrender of the old Mercantilist Navigation System, England admitted the United States to trade with her colonies, because among other things, it was evident that the colonial monopoly idea was more disastrous to the British sugar colonies than it was to foreigners. But the advent of free trade in England (1846) and the final surrender of the Navigation System (1849) was an admission of the fact that England could no longer produce enough food to supply the wants of her growing population, and that she could not, within herself or her colonies produce all the raw material required to keep her mills and factories going. England simply could not afford to go to war with the United States, because she derived the bulk of her cotton supply from the southern states, and because her population would starve without the regular shipments of grain, beef and pork from overseas. A war would mean the serious interrup-

[8] H. M. Stephens, "Nationality and History," *American Hist. Rev.*, XXI, 225.
[9] *Edinburgh Review*, XXXIII, 78.

tion of that food supply.[10]   In addition to this, the old landed
aristocracy of England was giving way to a new type of commercial and industrial aristocracy, "profiteers" we should probably
call them, who had made money from the numerous wars, or
"entrepreneurs" who had made the most of the factory system
before the advent of protective legislation, or colonial magnates.
These people often had big investments overseas which would
have been seriously jeopardized by a war with the United States.
There was that rising class of industrial capitalists whose money
was not tied up in big estates in the south of England, but was
invested in factories in the north of England, or plantations overseas.   This new ruling class made itself felt in the Great Reform
Bill of 1832.   The party alignments had changed.   The Tories
who went out with Wellington in 1830 were by no means the same
Tories who came back with the cotton-mill magnate Peel in 1841.
The old Whigs who identified themselves with Charles James
Fox, were not of the same type of mind as Bright and Cobden in
the new era.[11]

It is no wonder then, that diplomatic difficulty after diplomatic
difficulty was irritated into life only to be smoothed out when
sober second thought made it clear that these two nations simply
could not afford to make war on one another.   The old question
of the northeast boundary between Maine and New Brunswick
would have been ample to bring on a war between a Frederick
the Great and a Maria Theresa, but England and the United
States had another method of settlement.   Even though the
Maine lumber-jacks virtually made war on the Canadian lum-
bermen the matter could be and was adjusted by diplomacy.

In 1837 some Canadians staged an abortive insurrection in
which certain New Yorkers tried to aid the rebels.   The Canadian
insurrection was in some respects more popular in the United
States than it was in Canada, for there have never been wanting
politicians in the United States who periodically promised them-

---

[10] W. Cunningham, *Growth of English Industry and Commerce, Laissez Faire* (Lond., 1903),
p. 624; A. P. Newton, *Cambridge Hist. of British Foreign Policy* (N. Y., 1923), II, 233.
[11] M. R. P. Dorman, *History of the British Empire in the 19th Century* (Lond., 1904),
II, 355.

selves and their constituents that some day Canada would fall away from Great Britain and join their brethren who revolted in 1776. When the Canadians demanded home-rule, many short-sighted Americans thought the time had come, and aid was sent across the border to the Canadian rebels. The Canadian loyal militia who put down the revolt, retaliated by capturing in the waters of the United States an American vessel suspected of helping the rebels and let her float to destruction over Niagara Falls. All this intensified the ill feeling between the two countries and when one of the Canadian militia who sent the *Caroline* over the Falls was subsequently caught on the American side of the border and arrested for murder, international complications were threatened. This Canadian, McLeod by name, was a soldier who had acted in accordance with instructions in the *Caroline* affair which had resulted in the death of one American. Hence the charge of murder lodged against him in the New York Courts. But England at once bristled and demanded his surrender on the perfectly proper grounds that a soldier cannot be held liable in a civil court for acts committed by him in his military capacity when under competent orders. But the curious organization of the United States which forbids the interference by the federal government in such state matters made it impossible for the United States government to secure the release of McLeod. The British threatened war if he were executed.[12]

But even this accumulation of grievances did not produce war, for Britain had no real desire for it. The years from 1837 to 1842 were years of great financial difficulty in which the expenses of running a big army and navy were beginning to tell on the English taxpayer.[13] Peel had come into power determined to economize and not to waste money in further ambitious imperialistic schemes. Passing over some of the bigger figures in English diplomacy he chose the banker Alexander Baring, Lord Ashburton, who had proved such a friend of the United States in 1814, and sent him to Washington to straighten out the troubles with

[12] A. P. Newton in *Cambridge History of British Foreign Policy*, II, 241.
[13] J. E. T. Rogers, *Industrial and Commercial History of England*, p. 432.

Webster, who was now Secretary of State. Between them Webster and Ashburton soon agreed that the boundary provision for the northeast border as written into the treaty of 1783 was as unsatisfactory as many other provisions in that famous document, for there were several sets of "the Highlands which divide those rivers which empty themselves into the St. Lawrence from those which fall into the Atlantic Ocean." Some compromise line had to be reached and the people of Maine demanded what the English could not possibly grant.

But Jared Sparks of Harvard University had recently discovered in the French archives a copy of a map of the Maine boundary which was suspected of being the one Franklin had given to Vergennes informing him of the settlement made by Great Britain and the United States in 1783. The red line which indicated the boundary agreed upon was practically the same line for which the British were contending. If the British could get hold of this map, the American case would be lost. Carefully concealing this document from Ashburton, Webster used it to induce the people of Maine to compromise. A line was therefore agreed upon in which each side gave up something and the boundary was fixed as it is to-day. The newspapers on both sides howled their disgust, and in England Ashburton was the more reviled when the story of the red-line map came out. But shortly afterward it became known that at the time a similar map had been resting in the British archives, which was suspected of being the map on which Richard Oswald, the British commissioner in 1783, had drawn his idea of the location of the boundary. This map had been carefully concealed by Palmerston, because it supported the American contention. Thus each side held the trump card most needed by the other! Webster was accused of being a trickster and Ashburton of being an imbecile, but the truth is that both avoided a war by not insisting on the extreme claims of his country.[14]

Further difficulties were ironed out when Great Britain apolo-

[14] J. S. Reeves, *American Diplomacy under Tyler and Polk*, 1–28; E. Channing, *Hist. of U. S.*, V, 536–41.

gized for having invaded American soil to destroy the *Caroline*. The McLeod case was settled when the New York court acquitted him and relieved the United States from its absurd position of

THE MAINE BOUNDARY

being unable to protect foreigners on its own soil. But the principle remained unsettled as we shall see. The Webster-Ashburton Treaty was one of those which was violently attacked at the time, but seems more sensible in the light of later events. Certainly England had every motive for settling, as her American affairs were the least of the many irons she had in the fire of international politics at that time.[15] At the same time the Texas matter was looming larger in American foreign policy than justiciable quarrels with England.

The question of the suppression of the slave trade made trouble at this same time. Britain had freed her slaves and now added economic to moral reasons for getting everyone else to do so. She had insisted on exercising her belligerent right of search to break up the trade during the Napoleonic Wars. But, both the English and American courts had declared that slave-trading was not piracy,[16] and the United States would not tolerate the search of vessels flying the American flag in time of peace by British cruisers, as this smacked of the whole controversy which led up to the War of 1812. The result was that "the American slave trade finally came to be carried on principally by United States capital, in United States ships, officered by United States citizens and under the United States flag."[17] It was not until the Civil War when the United States decided to get rid of the evil institution that she finally consented to play with Great Britain and coöperate with her in breaking it up by permitting a mutual right of search.[18]

2. THE OREGON TREATY

But the boundary between the United States and Canada had yet to be run to the Pacific. The treaty of 1818 had expressly left open for joint occupation the lands between the Rocky Mountains and the Pacific Ocean. Spain had claimed all the west coast of North America by virtue of prior discoveries, and if mere discovery could give any good title the Spanish claims were certainly better than those of the English who could only cite Sir Francis Drake's celebrated voyage in 1579, and much better than the Americans who could cite nothing so early. But in the very next year Spain gave up forever her claims to the northwest coast in

15 S. Walpole, *History of England*, IV, ch. xvi.
16 "Le Louis," 2 *Dodson*, 210; "The Antelope," 10 *Wheaton*, 66, 116 (1825).
17 W. E. B. DuBois, *Suppression of the Slave Trade*, p. 162.
18 C. C. Hyde, *International Law, Chiefly as Interpreted and Applied by the United States* (Boston, 1922), I, 408.

the treaty of 1819 with the United States when the boundary between the United States and Mexico was run out along the 42d parallel to the Pacific. The contest then narrowed down to a conflict between the claims of Russia, England and the United States. By the treaty of 1824 Russia was put out of the running and forced to confine her activities to Alaska, north of 54° 40′.

It was the English Captain Cook whose voyage in 1779 first indicated the commercial importance of Oregon, for his sailors discovered that sea-otter skins could be picked up for a few trifles among the northwest Indians and sold for a hundred dollars a piece in Canton, China. Fur is the explanation of the earliest contest for Oregon, and "Oregon," be it understood, ran from the 42d parallel to the 54th parallel including the present states of Washington, Oregon, Idaho and most of British Columbia as well.[19]

We have seen how the Nootka Sound Affair of 1790 nearly brought England and Spain to war over the northwest coast and how England emerged victorious with a strong hold on the present Vancouver Island. George Vancouver, who had sailed with Cook in 1779, was the next actor on the stage and he appeared in the service of the British trying to find a waterway through the continent. The ever-sought-after "northwest passage," would not only facilitate the fur trade but would strengthen the British hold on all the country where the great Hudson Bay Company and Northwest Company were now rivals for that lucrative commerce. But the discoverer of the great waterway of the northwest and with it a substantial claim to the title of Oregon was destined not to be either an Englishman or a Spaniard but a Boston skipper, Robert Gray, who entered the Columbia River in 1792 and gave it the name of his vessel. Hearing of Gray's exploit, Vancouver promptly sailed up the river, but the discovery and whatever rights go with it belonged to the American. However the rights of the Americans did not rest upon this slender foundation for at the same time that Jefferson was dreaming of

[19] J. Schafer, *History of the Pacific Northwest*, pp. 1–15.

Louisiana, he was also dreaming of the northwest and he dispatched Lewis and Clark on their great overland expedition in 1804 into the valley of the Columbia.

Lewis and Clark made the start and finish of their trip at St. Louis, which even in that early day was a great American fur emporium. The fur traders had long been accustomed to trade up the Missouri River. When Lewis brought back word that a pelt worth several hundred dollars in New York could be secured from the innocent Indians for an old chisel, he stirred the imagination of John Jacob Astor whose capital ever sought new fields of investment. Astor soon gave the United States its strongest claim to Oregon by following up the discoveries of Gray, Lewis and Clark by actual occupation. In 1808 the American Fur Company was organized, and started its vessels out of Boston and New York laden with trinkets and the cheapest knicknacks. These were traded on the northwest coast for valuable furs and the profits were enormous when the furs were sold in China. But when the profits were reinvested in silks and tea which was then brought from China back to the United States, the return on the original investment was tremendous.[20]

In 1811, therefore, the settlement at Astoria on the Columbia River gave America good title by effective occupation, which antedated any British claims in the Columbia Valley. Astoria was sold out to the British in time to prevent its capture in the War of 1812, but Monroe sent a special dispatch to the Commissioners at Ghent to remember the little trading post at the mouth of the Columbia and to recover it.[21] Since the treaty of Ghent provided for the *status quo ante bellum*, Secretary of State Monroe insisted that the British must give up their claims to the Columbia River Valley. This the British disputed, leading to the joint occupation treaty of 1818, which, as we have just seen, was to last for ten years.[22]

Joint occupation meant a race for empire which concerned the pioneers of both nations for the next twenty years. The Astor

[20] J. Schafer, *Conquest of the Pacific Northwest*, pp. 63–69.
[21] *American State Papers, Foreign Relations*, III, 731.
[22] J. S. Reeves, *American Diplomacy under Tyler and Polk*, pp. 224–43.

Company made desperate efforts to interest Congress.[23] Certain congressmen caught the vision, notably Floyd of Virginia and Baylies of Massachusetts, who urged that the United States support the venture, pointing out that the expansion of America to 1822 had been sufficiently remarkable to justify the assumption that the Pacific was the only possible boundary for manifest destiny. But timidity and ignorance hampered their efforts when the so-called hard-headed business men like Tracy of New York and Breckenridge of Kentucky rather shortsightedly insisted that no community of interest would ever be possible between the United States and such far-away lands, or foolishly talked about the limits which nature and Providence had fixed for the United States in the Rocky Mountains. But even their own day had seen man pass the "natural boundaries" which "Providence" had set at both the Appalachian Mountains and then the Mississippi River.[24] For the time being, however, the counsel of timidity prevailed and the English built Fort Vancouver on the Columbia River in the heart of Oregon, where for the next twenty years the great-hearted Dr. John McLoughlin gave aid to English and American settlers alike.

At the end of the ten-year period Albert Gallatin opened up diplomatic negotiations looking toward the acquisition of all of Oregon for the United States based on (1) Gray's prior discovery, (2) Lewis and Clark's exploration, (3) the settlement at Astoria, and (4) the acquisition by the United States of the old Spanish claims. Canning was now guiding British foreign policy and he built his schemes on a claim to the whole thing with a willingness to divide with the United States at the line of the Columbia River. The United States insisted on the whole of the Columbia River Valley and suggested again the line of 49° as a proper boundary between the nations west of the mountains as it already was east of the Rockies. The negotiations failed and the joint occupation was continued for another period of years.[25]

[23] E. G. Bourne, "Aspects of Oregon History previous to 1840," in *Quar. Oregon Hist. Soc.*, IV, 255.

[24] *Annals of Congress*, 1822–3, pp. 680–4, 693–4.

[25] J. S. Reeves, *American Diplomacy under Tyler and Polk*, pp. 239–41.

But in the thirties and early forties, the United States accumulated its greatest and most forceful argument for Oregon when thousands of emigrants began to pour into the west and their advance guard appeared in Oregon. Fur traders were succeeded by missionaries and missionaries by those who learned of the wonderful farm lands of the northwest. By the forties the adjustment with Britain could no longer be delayed because the settlers were clamoring to Congress that their lands and lives were without protection by their own government. Hard times came in the Mississippi Valley when the overproduction of the farms fed the fires in the Mississippi steamboats with bacon fat. The Mississippi Valley farmer felt the pressure of low prices which drove him once more to the covered wagon and impelled him to follow the Oregon Trail in the Great Migration of 1843. As far as the region south of the Columbia River was concerned, certainly occupation by American settlers gave their country the best title, and the American negotiators apparently did not choose to know enough geography to make any distinction between that land and the coveted territory between the Columbia River and the forty-ninth parallel. Again the Americans offered the line of forty-nine and yet the British clung to their claims a little longer and irritated the United States into claiming all of Oregon.[26]

The "Whole of Oregon" up to 54° 40′ now became the popular cry in the United States and, it will be recollected, Polk became president in 1845 on a platform for Texas and the whole northwest. He reiterated in his inaugural that our "title to the whole of Oregon is clear and unquestionable." But while Sir Richard Pakenham, the British minister at Washington, was refusing the compromise at the forty-ninth parallel events were shaping themselves in the northwest for a British retreat.

The part played by the Oregon pioneers has probably been exaggerated as some of our historians have attributed too much to the drivers of the covered wagon. During the negotiations hardly a handful of Americans were in fact north of the Columbia River as the Willamette Valley to the south tempted them with

[26] J. S. Reeves, *American Diplomacy under Tyler and Polk*, pp. 249ff.

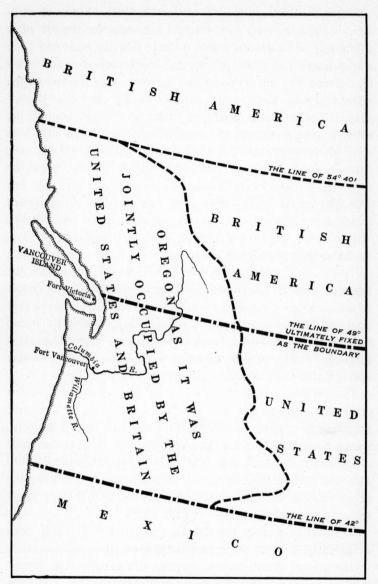

THE OREGON BOUNDARY

its fertile lands. But the proximity of these audacious, not to say lawless, pioneers, raised in the minds of the officials of the Hudson Bay Company a fear for the safety of the stores concentrated at Fort Vancouver. They withdrew these stores and shifted their base from the Columbia River to Fort Victoria on the tip of Vancouver Island. This retreat of their principal economic interest made it simpler for the British negotiators to give up their claims to the whole of the lands between the Columbia River and the forty-ninth parallel.[27]

Moreover, here again one must bear in mind that Peel and Aberdeen had something else to consider when weighing the advisability of committing their fortunes to an armed conflict. In the autumn of 1845 the harvest of much of western Europe was spoiled by an excessive rainfall, which resulted in the loss of the potato crop in many countries. In England and other parts of Europe the failure of one crop simply meant that the people turned to a cheaper crop. But in Belgium, Ireland and Scotland, where the peasantry subsisted almost entirely on potatoes because they were the cheapest of all crops, this meant famine. As a consequence England soon had a fearful domestic problem on her hands, which involved not only trying to save millions of inhabitants of the British Isles from starvation, but also involved the question of importing grain into the Islands to relieve the distress. This involved a reconsideration of the whole question of the Corn Laws and tariff and the consequent readjustment of these definitely turned England from a nation which supplied much of its own food to one which frankly admitted it could not supply its own wants. Such a readjustment was fraught with peril and was no time to go to war with anyone, least of all with a maritime nation like the United States which could seriously cripple English commerce and bring all Britain to the verge of starvation.[28]

Moreover, the British cotton manufacturers in Lancashire were coming more and more to depend on the supply of raw

---

[27] F. Merk, "Oregon Pioneers and the Boundary," *Amer. Hist. Rev.*, XXIX, 681.
[28] J. E. T. Rogers, *Industrial and Commercial History of England*, 449-50.

material from the United States, which a war would have cut off. The cotton magnate Peel was changing his mind even if the British minister at Washington was still worshiping at the shrine of Canning. Peel saw that the Americans would not really fight for 54° 40', but that they would not yield one inch below the 49th parallel. Even so ardent an advocate of expansion as Senator Benton of Missouri attacked the "Fifty-four Forty or Fight" idea, but he insisted that the United States would fight for the line of 49°, including the Columbia Valley. Peel disavowed in effect Pakenham's rejection of the American proposition. When the next proposal came, it came from the British side and offered the very line of 49° which the Americans had so many times suggested and had finally indicated would be their "fighting line." As a matter of fact Polk had long since given up the slogan of "Fifty-four Forty," as he had no desire to have two wars on his hands at the same time. After taking the "advice and consent of the senate" in advance he accepted Peel's offer and the boundary line between the United States and Canada which already ran for more than a thousand miles along the 49th parallel, was continued on out to Puget Sound. The United States thus got the whole valley of the Columbia, with its valuable fish, fur, timber and agricultural possibilities.[29]

3. THE CLAYTON-BULWER TREATY

Our next difficulty with Britain came over the question of the construction of an interoceanic canal somewhere in Central America. The freak of nature which had joined two immense continents with such a narrow neck of land as Central America had long been a standing challenge to the ingenuity of the commercial states, whose vessels were compelled to take the long trip around Cape Horn. Various proposals had been made early in the nineteenth century which came to nothing. The route which first recommended itself on paper lay through the Republic of Nicaragua, via the San Juan River and Lake Nicaragua.

[29] J. S. Reeves, *American Diplomacy under Tyler and Polk*, 261–3; *Cong. Globe*, 29th Cong. 1st sess., pp. 851–62; J. K. Polk's *Diary*, I, 69, 120, 147, 248, 324, 377; E. I. MacCormac, *James K. Polk*, pp. 606ff.

It is necessary to look at the map here and see how from the vantage point of Washington this seemed much the best route when the first Americans made their investigations on the isthmus. But matters rested while the United States busied herself with the acquisition of Texas and California. This gain of territory on the Pacific together with the Gold Rush of 1849 once more turned the attention of the Americans to getting some short route through the continent. Mexico herself possessed one pos-

THE NICARAGUAN CANAL QUESTION.

The Map illustrates the possibility of a canal at Nicaragua over which there has been so much diplomatic negotiation. The San Juan River, which is seen flowing from Lake Nicaragua to the Atlantic Ocean is exaggerated in size to make clear the possibility of a canal. However the navigability of the River and the question of the conflict of Nicaraguan and Costa Rican rights in it at its mouth are only some of the perplexing problems which arise in this connection. On the surface it seems as though merely digging through from Lake Nicaragua to the Pacific would make a canal. The engineering problems involved, however, are by no means so simple as this.

sible route, that across the isthmus of Tehuantepec. As long as he was dispoiling Mexico anyway Polk offered to double the $15,000,000 he was giving for taking half her territory, if Mexico would grant the United States a right of way across the isthmus. Mexico, however, declined since she properly felt that the United States was getting all she was rightfully entitled to.

Then as thoughts turned once more to Nicaragua and her conveniently located waterways, the fact came to light that Great Britain had prior rights and prior interests in Central America, and had had them a century before the United States came into being. For a hundred years the British had been encroaching on the log-wood and hard-wood countries of the eastern coast of Central America and there were British settlements at Belize, the Bay Islands and along that part of the shore then known as the "Mosquito Coast." Another glance at the map will show how the possession of the Mosquito Coast gave Britain the control of a possible canal route through Nicaragua. Dealing with the Nicaraguan government the British gained certain rights in connection with the navigation of the San Juan River, whereupon the Nicaraguan government in cheerful disregard of its obligations to Great Britain proceeded to give Americans the right to construct a canal and to grant the United States a possession on Tigre Island in the Gulf of Fonseca on the opposite side of the isthmus. Tigre Island, as we shall see, was necessary for a naval base to protect the western end of any canal that might be built. Nevertheless if the American diplomats on the spot outwitted the British by getting these concessions, the British navy proceeded to occupy Greytown and the San Juan River region and to put the British flag up on Tigre Island before the Americans could get there.[30]

By this time the situation had grown so acute between England and America that both sides agreed to rebuke their over-enthusiastic envoys and settle the matter by treaty. But the significant thing is the fact that at this time Great Britain had actual occupation of Belize, the Bay Islands and the Mosquito Coast, despite her oft-repeated admission that the real sovereignty in the region still rested with Spain. But Spain's title was the merest courtesy and the American rights were the merest paper. The matter was extremely delicate from every point of view by the time President Taylor directed his Secretary of State, John Clayton, to

[30] M. W. Williams, *Anglo-American Isthmian Diplomacy, 1814–1914* (Wash., 1914), pp. 53–66; W. F. Johnson, *Four Centuries of the Panama Canal* (N. Y., 1906), 39–65.

negotiate. Moreover, both these Whig politicians realized that they had to deal with a Democratic Senate which would be very critical of yielding a single inch to Great Britain. Democrats

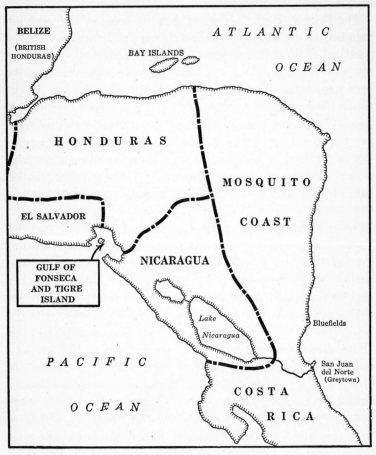

PART OF CENTRAL AMERICA
Showing the British and American Rivalries between 1850 and 1860

had frequently been particularly cantankerous in their suspicion of all things British and by this time the eastern seaboard cities were filling up with the Irish refugees from the potato famine who usually became Democrats in America, but whose Democ-

racy was then and has always been secondary to their hatred of
Great Britain. Moreover Clayton had to deal with Lord Palmerston, a truculent Briton, whose diplomacy the world over was
marked by aggressiveness.[31]

The British claims in Central America were in law very ill-
founded, so our Minister, Abbott Lawrence, informed the Department of State in a series of very able dispatches. But Clayton went serenely ahead and made a treaty which has usually
been regarded as the classic blunder in American foreign policy.
In the Clayton-Bulwer Treaty of 1850 it was agreed that neither
nation "will ever obtain for itself any exclusive control over
any ship canal" or fortify it, "or colonize or assume to exercise
any dominion over Nicaragua, Costa Rica, the Mosquito Coast
or any portion of Central America." This surrender on the
part of both nations involved the mutual promise to protect
any private company which might undertake to build a canal.
In order to get the British out, Clayton had to promise that the
United States would never build the canal herself. In addition
the United States agreed that if any canal ever were built "the
parties owning or constructing the same shall impose no other
charges nor conditions of traffic than the aforesaid governments
shall approve as equitable," and that "the said canals or railways
being open to the citizens and subjects of Great Britain and the
United States on equal terms, shall also be open on like terms to
the citizens and subjects of every other state." In return for
giving up the right to build a canal and promising that Britain
should have equal tolls therein with America if a private company ever built it, Clayton expected the British to withdraw
from the Mosquito Coast, although Bulwer insisted in the ratification that the treaty did not include Belize and its dependencies. Clayton replied admitting that it did not include Belize,
but said nothing about dependencies.[32]

The ratifications had barely been exchanged when it became
evident that the British were going to consider the Bay Islands as

---

[31] M. W. Williams, *Anglo-American Isthmian Diplomacy*, p. 36.
[32] Ibid., p. 156.

part of the "dependencies of Belize" and further that they had no intention of leaving the Mosquito Coast. They now landed more marines and fired on an American vessel for not paying customs duties to the British at Greytown. This act evoked vigorous protests from Webster, who had become President Fillmore's Secretary of State and the two nations were again on the verge of a conflict. However, the Crimean War in Europe distracted England, and in 1856 she offered to arbitrate the matter. The war in the Near East gave the British a taste of the horrors of modern warfare and although the matter was not arbitrated, the British soon acceded to the American demands and in direct negotiations with Nicaragua acknowledged the sovereignty of that Republic both over the Bay Islands and the Mosquito Coast in 1860.[33] But this was by no means the end of the Clayton-Bulwer Treaty.

The Crimean War ended at the Congress of Paris in 1856, where the British were finally induced to admit some of the rights of neutrals for which the United States and the nations of continental Europe had been contending since the days of the armed Neutrality of 1780. The Declaration of Paris declared (1) that privateering was abolished, (2) that a neutral flag would protect the enemy's goods, except contraband, (3) that neutral goods, except contraband, should not be liable to capture under the enemy's flag and (4) that a blockade was not a blockade unless it was made effective. These principles had been insisted upon by the United States many times in its relations with England. Instead of taking advantage of this great step forward in international law, the United States refused to adhere to the Declaration of Paris, because it did not go far enough and protect private property at sea.[34] But Europe, and particularly England, could not move that fast. However, since the United States had long contended for these propositions, the Declaration of Paris could not help but remove some more long standing causes of irritation between the United States and Great Britain and render naval

---

[33] M. W. Williams, *Anglo-American Isthmian Diplomacy*, p. 266, 326ff.
[34] J. B. Moore, *Digest of International Law*, VII, 561; J. D. Richardson's *Messages*, V, 412.

warfare more humane in accordance with the wishes of the United States. The whole episode is curiously illustrative of a tendency sometimes seen in American foreign policy to cry for something and then refuse what it asked for because of the form.[35]

4. The Geneva Arbitration

Hardly had President Buchanan announced the settlement of the Central American difficulties when the Civil War broke out in the United States. This involved England from the start, for it was in the south that England sold annually millions of dollars worth of manufactured goods. From the south came England's supply of raw material. This was all a matter of great moment in England, for there was a growing realization that the working classes must be kept busy if England was to avoid labor troubles, and her surplus manufactures must find a market if her great workshop was to continue running. Consequently England was compelled to make up her mind quickly what attitude she would take in the American conflict.

Although the orators from the southern states had insisted that each state in the union was "sovereign and independent," this position had always been unsound under international law. The test of a nation in international law is whether or not it sends envoys to foreign nations who are there received. The United States had done so for seventy years while the individual states had never done so. Therefore in international law, South Carolina was wasting her breath in announcing that she was a sovereign and independent state. The only other position in which the southerners could be regarded was as traitors or rebels against authority. If any foreign power prematurely recognized their independence, it would furnish a good cause of war on the part of the United States. So England could not and did not recognize the independence of the Confederate States of America, although her Tory upper classes desired to do so, and even though the historian E. A. Freeman did launch upon the market

[35] C. C. Hyde, *International Law, Chiefly as Interpreted and Applied by the United States,* II, 392.

his *History of Federal Government from the Foundation of the Achæan League to the Disruption of the United States.*

But the position of the Confederacy in International Law was not to be fixed by British policy but by the act of President Lincoln himself. It was apparent to the leaders of the Federal government at once that if the south could be economically isolated it could not survive. The south was practically devoid of manufacturing establishments. Her necessities of life had to come from northern or from English factories. So Lincoln proclaimed a blockade of the ports of the Southern Confederacy, warning all neutrals that they and their vessels must not come in nor go out of the ports under blockade. This perfectly legal practice in international law forced England to take some position, for England had hundreds of vessels trading in southern ports. Naturally the only position she could take was the one she was compelled to assume by Lincoln's proclamation. She had to announce her neutrality and warn her merchants to take cognizance of the fact. Thereby she had to recognize the belligerency of the Confederate States of America. It was therefore Lincoln, and not Britain, who accorded to the Confederacy its belligerent status, for after the proclamation of blockade it would have been suicidal to her merchant marine to refuse to recognize the existence of war.[36]

The people of the north, nevertheless, ever on the lookout for affronts from England, could not make this simple distinction in international law between the recognition of belligerency and the recognition of independence. A wave of indignation swept over the United States, particularly in view of the fact that the recognition of belligerency was accorded before the arrival in London of Lincoln's minister, Charles Francis Adams. In fact, England could not have done otherwise than she did, but the United States in the sixties was in no mood to understand anything that England did. Moreover, the ruling classes in England were outspoken in their rejoicing at the long predicted failure of the only hitherto successful example of a Democratic Repub-

[36] "The Amy Warwick," 2 *Sprague*, 123; Gideon Welles' *Diary* (Boston, 1911), I, 165-72.

lic. This evident sympathy of English official classes with the south enraged the people of the north and the fires of their anger were fed by the next action of Great Britain which showed how disagreeable she could be.[37]

The Confederate States at once dispatched John Slidell and James Murray Mason to France and England respectively to gain recognition. An English vessel, the *Trent*, carried them from Havana to Liverpool but was overhauled by a Federal war vessel, the *San Jacinto*, and the two precious envoys were removed and taken to Boston. The north applauded this exploit vigorously and Captain Wilkes of the *San Jacinto* was wined and dined for giving Britain a taste of her own medicine which she had so often given neutrals in the Napoleonic wars. But in England the testy Palmerston burst into a flame of rage which was shared by the Tories everywhere. It mattered not that the law officers of the crown had already told him that under British practice this was a perfectly proper thing for the United States to do. In fact it was just the kind of thing that the United States had in the days of impressment always contended was illegal. Positions were certainly reversed since 1812, and the British dispatched an ultimatum to Washington which practically threatened war for this invasion of the deck of a British vessel, if Mason and Slidell were not released immediately.[38]

Lincoln saw at once that he could not fight Great Britain and the Confederate States at the same time and he wisely surrendered the two Confederates. But Secretary of State Seward accompanied their surrender with a note in which with ill disguised sarcasm he rejoiced that the English had at last come over to the American point of view in the matter of the removal of persons from the deck of a neutral ship and pointed out that America was following out consistently the British policy in regard to the impressment of seamen. Seward contended that the only mistake Captain Wilkes had made was in not seizing the whole vessel for carrying contraband persons and in this, too,

---

[37] J. W. Foster, *Century of American Diplomacy*, p. 373, passim.
[38] J. B. Moore, *Digest of International Law*, VII, 768-779.

the British legal authorities were quite in accord with Seward. The good offices of Albert, the Prince Consort, were a no small factor in smoothing out the ruffled feelings on the English side. England's victory was indeed a hollow one and the danger of war at this critical juncture was avoided by America's being true to her own traditional policy of the freedom of the seas.[39]

But it was not only in this that the traditional rôles were reversed. The Confederate States could not produce enough manufactured goods, guns, artillery harness, clothing, uniforms and munitions to supply their own wants. England could and did make immense profits by sending these commodities in through the blockade. Strictly speaking the United States navy could hold up direct shipments from England to the Confederacy and soon stopped that practice. But the British dealers in contraband and other goods much needed in the Confederacy soon developed another practice. Just off the coast of Florida lie the Bahama Islands, British possessions, with their port of Nassau. Just across the Rio Grande from Texas lies the little Mexican town of Matamoras. Obviously both Nassau and Matamoras were neutral and in them were neutral merchants who were only too glad to take in goods ultimately designed for the Confederate States. They could easily be shipped across the intervening space without too much risk of being overhauled by United States cruisers. Suddenly these sleepy little towns developed an enormous trade, which in theory was entirely neutral, and could not well be stopped unless the United States warships were entitled to overhaul the goods on the first leg of the voyage, i. e., from England to Nassau. This, the English contended the Americans could not do, as during that leg of the voyage the goods were neutral traveling from one neutral port to another neutral port. A glance at the map will show how important it was to catch the goods before they ever reached Nassau or Matamoras.

However, the old Rule of 1756 was now dragged out to work the other way. The fundamental rule, as we remember, is that

[39] C. F. Adams, "The Trent Affair," in *Proc. of Mass. Hist. Soc.*, XLV, p. 35.

the belligerent has a right to intercept the sea-born commerce of his enemy. The United States now proceeded to give England another dose of her own medicine. She had a right to break up the shipments of contraband to the Confederacy and did so. Under the cases and practice of the Napoleonic wars, she also had the right to stop shipments consigned to a neutral port but which were actually destined ultimately to the Confederacy, on the same theory that the courts will look to the fact and not to the fiction under which Sir William Scott had so often ruled in the early part of the century. Could any sane man say that the tons and tons of clothing and shoes piling up in the tiny port of Nassau were going to be used there? Obviously the goods were going on to the Confederate States under the guise of being shipments to a neutral. The "Doctrine of Ultimate Destination" took its place in international law beside that of the "Broken Voyage" and the "Rule of 1756" and the goods were seized en route to Nassau.[40]

These decisions are of the utmost importance in the story of American foreign policy, because they mark the surrender of the traditional American stand on the subject of the commercial rights of neutrals in time of war. Britain had contended during the Napoleonic wars that she might hold up similar shipments going to France under the guise of neutrality and neutral trade. Although the United States had vigorously protested against the development of this doctrine, it remained the English interpretation and was followed by the French practice during the Crimean War against Russia. When in the Civil War the United States proceeded to practice it against England, although the British shippers complained, their own government refused to uphold them, realizing that this was after all the traditional British practice. The decisions of Chief Justice S. P. Chase in these cases mark a great step forward in American international law, and a decided yielding to the English point of view.[41]

But the most far-reaching in its consequences of all Anglo-

[40] The *Bermuda*, 3 *Wall.* 514 (1865); the *Peterhoff*, 5 *Wall.* 28 (1866).

[41] C. B. Elliott, "Doctrine of Continuous Voyage," *Amer. Jour. Internat. Law*, I, 60; R. G. Adams, "Growth of Belligerent Rights," *Univ. of Penna. Law Rev.*, LXVIII, 20.

American relations during the Civil War came over the offenses of the British in allowing their ports to be used as a base of operations against northern commerce. Confederate cruisers were built in British shipyards and allowed to slip out to sea, ultimately destined for commerce raiding. This has always been regarded as a serious violation of a country's neutrality and the country which so allows its neutrality to be infringed must ultimately pay the belligerent whose commerce is thus damaged. Finally when the famous *Alabama* was about to leave Liverpool, Charles Francis Adams expressly warned Foreign Minister Russell that the vessel must be stopped. A chapter of accidents ensued, involving the sudden insanity of a crown law officer and Lord John Russell's evident desire to let the *Alabama* get away. Due to this admittedly wanton negligence [42] on Russell's part, the *Alabama* got out to sea and Captain Semmes began his famous career of burning United States vessels and others carrying contraband.

Ordinarily international law insists that a captured prize must be brought into port and adjudged before a prize court before either it, or its cargo, may be disposed of. But Captain Semmes of the *Alabama* could not bring in his prizes because of the Union blockade. Therefore he calmly instituted a prize court on his own vessel and with the single assistance of a set of Phillimore's "International Law," he acted as advocate and judge in his own cases, condemned his own prizes, and burnt them.[43] The losses occasioned by this vessel were naturally blamed on the English whose unneutral conduct permitted her to escape. When Charles Francis Adams learned that there were more ironclads being outfitted for the Confederate navy in the Scottish shipyards, he called Foreign Minister Russell's attention to the fact and demanded that the British government take steps to prevent these vessels from getting to sea also. Russell again tried to minimize the question and was on the verge of letting another group of commerce raiders get away when Adams in a thoroughly dignified

---

[42] *Diplomatic Correspondence of the U. S.*, 1862, p. 152; *Recollections of Earl Russell*, p. 235.
[43] R. Semmes, *Service Afloat* (N. Y., 1900), p. 483.

CHARLES FRANCIS ADAMS

manner warned him that another such bit of negligence on England's part would be equivalent to war. But Russell had no intention of attaching Britain's fortunes to the sinking ship of the Confederate states. By that time Gettysburg and Vicksburg showed which way the wind was blowing and the British kept the "Laird Rams" from leaving port.[44]

The victory of the north put her in a position to demand redress from Great Britain for these wrongs, and again the two nations were on the verge of war. But the aggressive Palmerston was now out of the way and England was under the guidance of Gladstone who insisted that the internal problems of Britain were the most important things she had to solve. He had no intention of letting England waste her substance in any further riotous foreign policy while her laborers at home were starving because of the maldistribution of wealth and unsanitary working conditions, or when the celebrated Irish regiments could only be filled up with the disgruntled victims of the English maladministration. Therefore when the United States presented her bill for damages for flagrant violations of neutrality committed by Great Britain during the Civil War, the British allowed themselves to be bound by treaty to submit the trouble to an international arbitral tribunal.

Unfortunately the United States Senate Committee on Foreign Relations was then under the charge of Charles Sumner whose policy it was to insist that the British should pay not only for all the direct damage caused by the Confederate cruisers she sent to sea, but also for all the indirect damages caused by the loss of commerce and the prolongation of the war due to British aid to the Confederacy. It was a distinction between damages and war costs. The British were willing to consider the payment of damages, but not of the war costs insisted on by the fire-eaters, the Anglophobes and professional Irishmen in the United States. A new treaty was necessary because of the Senate's actions, and this left the question of war costs to the tribunal.[45]

---

[44] *Diplomatic Correspondence of the U. S., 1863,* pp. 361–3, 418; Brooks Adams, in *Proc. of Mass. Hist. Soc.,* XLV, 243–333.

[45] Chas. Sumner's *Works* (Boston, 1874), XIII, 53–93.

An arbitration treaty was signed in Washington in 1871 and pursuant of this the arbiters met at Geneva in 1871. Five judges sat, one each from Italy, Switzerland, Brazil, Chief Justice Cockburn from England and, appropriately, Charles Francis Adams as the judge representing the United States. The American side of the case was presented by William M. Evarts and an array of counsel who insisted that the British had failed to use due care and diligence on keeping the Confederates from using her ports as a base of operations. They demanded $25,000,000 in direct damages and untold millions in indirect damages, or war costs. The Court decided at once to exclude the whole question of the indirect damages, as being incalculable and because there was no international law on the subject. Charles Francis Adams agreed with his fellow judges that this demand on the part of the United States was unreasonable. The Court then decided that England had in many instances been guilty of negligence in failing to maintain her neutrality and directed her to pay $15,500,000 in damages, with the English judge dissenting on practically every point. The principle of arbitration triumphed and again the two nations adjusted a serious difference without war.[46]

At about the same time the vexed questions of impressment and expatriation were settled by a treaty in which Great Britain gave way completely to the American point of view, and acknowledged that each nation must fully and faithfully recognize naturalization acquired under the laws of the other nation. No longer would the British take American citizens from the decks of American vessels under the pretense that they were English by birth. The Americans had not finally taken the position that naturalization ends a former allegiance until 1845, and not until 1868 had this been embodied in the Statutes of the United States. In the treaty of 1870 England consented to cease questioning the right of a person to so change his allegiance, and another source of irritation was laid at rest.[47]

Moreover, the Treaty of Washington of 1871 resulted in the

[46] J. B. Moore, *International Arbitrations*, I, 495, IV, 4057.
[47] C. C. Hyde, *International Law Chiefly as Interpreted and Applied by the U. S.*, I, 662-5; C. Malloy, *Treaties and Conventions*, I, 691.

settlement of the extreme end of the old Oregon boundary. As arbiter, the German Emperor drew the line of division through Puget Sound and the Straits of Juan de Fuca, so as to give San Juan Island to the United States.

Yet at more than one step in these controversies, the chances for a peaceful settlement were hampered by the Irish-Americans. These expatriates from the Emerald Isle brought their hatred of England to their new country. The so-called "Fenian Movement" of the sixties manifested itself by an attempted armed invasion of Canada by Fenians from the soil of the United States. When this failed utterly, the Fenians kept on making wanton attacks on England, frequently involving assassination, and then when caught red-handed would expect their American citizenship to protect them. The importance of the Irish-American vote forced politicians like Senator Sumner to pay some attention to these folk and thus constantly to imperil the delicate negotiations by which British and American diplomats were trying to avoid war.

5. VENEZUELAN AND ALASKAN ARBITRATION

Finally England and the United States came to a clash which went right to the heart of the Monroe Doctrine itself. In the Clayton-Bulwer Treaty, the United States had admitted that Great Britain was an American power. Did this exclude Great Britain from the operations of the Monroe Doctrine? The question was soon to be decided. In 1815 England became a neighbor of the Republic of Venezuela, by the acquisition of part of Dutch Guiana. The boundary between British Guiana and Venezuela had never been accurately fixed and various attempts at settlement had been broken up because about the time the Venezuelans made up their minds to accept a British offer, the British pushed their claims even farther into the disputed territory. In the eyes of the Venezuelans, this amounted simply to a British seizure of the land of a South American Republic. The question was primarily one of gold mines which the British wanted to include on their side of the frontier. Venezuela kept asking Great

Britain to arbitrate the matter, but the arbitration was always refused or postponed on one pretext or another until Venezuela undertook to complain to the United States and ask the intervention of the Monroe Doctrine. The United States formally extended its good offices, mentioning the Monroe Doctrine as a reason why they were interested in the matter.

The British kept on evading the issue and extending their mining operations farther and farther into Venezuela when finally in 1894 President Cleveland brought them up sharply by a dispatch in which Secretary of State Richard Olney informed them in rather startling language that the United States was practically sovereign on the American continents and that its fiat was law on the subjects to which it confined its attention. This note, with its implication, the British vigorously denied, for it insinuated that Canada was destined to break away from England, and that the United States was entitled to interfere in every boundary dispute in the Americas. The British again refused to arbitrate.[48]

President Cleveland then laid the whole matter before Congress in a message which practically threatened war on England if she persisted in her refusal to arbitrate. Both nations stood aghast at the pass to which their relations had come. Although the Anglophobes in the United States and the Tories in Britain demanded more peremptory action there was an increasing volume of opinion on both sides of the water that this business must be settled without war. England would not admit that the Monroe Doctrine was a part of international law to which she must bow, but just at this time occurred Dr. Jameson's ill-starred raid into the Transvaal in South Africa, which evoked the Kaiser's truculent telegram and warned England that her real foe was not the United States, but Germany. The United States appointed a Commission to discover the Venezuelan boundary and England politely gave them every opportunity to find the facts. After this there was no real reason why Britain should not arbitrate

[48] *Case of Venezuela* (trans. of case submitted by the Venezuelan Ministry of Foreign Affairs), (Atlanta, 1896), The British *Blue Book*, to which it is a reply; *Foreign Relations of the United States, 1895–6*, I, 552ff.

with Venezuela, which she did and the matter was settled.   The award of the arbiters was for the most part in favor of Great Britain.   Great Britain distinctly yielded at the behest of the United States, but she was not yet willing to admit that the Monroe Doctrine was international law, although in this instance it was certainly enforced against her.[49]   To avoid such sudden clashes in the future, a general arbitration treaty between the two countries was then negotiated, but the agreement was amended and talked to death in the United States Senate, where, it seems, there can always be found some members who actually do not want our relations with England to become too cordial. This, however, was no fault of the department of our government which has especial charge over foreign affairs, nor in any way can it be blamed on diplomats or diplomacy.   The Senate rejected the general arbitration treaty in the face of evident popular favor, partly because it was jealous lest it lose some of its power over foreign relations, and partly because of the traditional suspicion of all things European.[50]

Misery makes strange bedfellows, and none stranger than Russia and the United States.   Nevertheless, this century of bickering with Britain did much to provoke sympathy with that other great victim of British imperialism.   Every Russian effort during the last two hundred years to reach an ice-free port, on the Black Sea, the Bosphorus, the Persian Gulf or in the Far East, has met with unvarying British opposition.   A tradition of friendship between the United States and Russia had been established during the Civil War.   At that time when England was giving so many evidences of hostility toward the Federal government, Russia sent fleets to both New York and San Francisco, and allowed the interpretation to be put on that act that if England supported the South, Russia would, in the event of the general war which would follow, be found on the side of the North. War between Russia and England in the Crimea during the fifties gave rise to talk of the sale of Alaska by Russia to the United

[49] *Report of the Special Commission on the True Divisional Line between Venezuela and British Guiana* (Wash., 1898), Sen. Doc. No. 91, 55th Cong., 2d sess.

[50] N. Y. *Nation*, LXIV, 236; *Cong. Rec.*, 54th Cong., 2d sess., Vol. 29., pt. 2, pp. 1046ff.

States to prevent it from falling into the hands of Great Britain. War between Russia and Britain was not a remote possibility in the sixties, nor at any of half a dozen times since. Moreover, the Russian American Company lacked the vision and initiative to make the fur, coal and lumber resources of Alaska pay dividends. So in 1867 Russia offered the Russian territory in North America to the United States for $10,000,000. In a midnight conference between Baron Stoeckel, the Russian minister, Secretary of State Seward and Chairman Sumner of the Foreign Relations Committee of the Senate, Manifest Destiny once more came to life and the next morning the United States practically had Alaska for $7,200,000. Opposition developed on the part of Senators who had a personal spite against Seward, and on the part of Representatives who decided to support a trumped-up claim against Russia by an American citizen in the hopes of getting something personally out of the business. Despite this pettiness on the part of Congress the price was absurdly cheap for the great mineral resources which the United States thus acquired. There is an unaccounted for hundred thousand dollars, which may partly explain Stoeckel's enthusiasm for the sale, while Andrew Johnson records with evident relish that "the uncorruptable Thaddeous Stevens" got a sop of $10,000 for letting the appropriation bill get through the House of Representatives. It is not necessary to accuse any particular Congressman to make clear that some of them had to be bought. The only thing that can be said is that their motives for opposing the purchase were in many instances as unworthy as their willingness to be bribed to change their minds.[51]

The rivalries of England and the United States were again turned to the Pacific Northwest, and where another thousand miles of boundary were now added to the frontier between Canada and the Republic. The last dispute on the Oregon boundary came in 1870 over the misunderstanding as to where ran the international boundary through Puget Sound. Several

[51] J. M. Callahan, *The Alaska Purchase* (Univ. of W. Va. Stud., 1908); W. A. Dunning; "Paying for Alaska," *Pol. Sci. Quar.*, XXVII, 385; F. A. Golder, "The Purchase of Alaska," *Amer. Hist. Rev.*, XXV, 411.

islands were at stake, when the matter was submitted to the
arbitration we have mentioned above, and the islands went to
the United States.   Then came a battle royal for the fur-bearing
animals of Bering Sea.   It is a peculiarity of the Alaska seal
that his breeding season takes him to the Pribiloff Islands, which
are several hundred miles from shore in the midst of Bering Sea.
Killing the seals en route to and from the Islands was an easy
matter, but frightfully wasteful and the American and Canadian
seal hunters were soon busily engaged in exterminating the whole
seal herd.   The United States in a hasty but well-meaning attempt to save these useful animals from the ravages of the
hunters took the untenable position that having bought Alaska
and the Aleutian Islands, we had exclusive jurisdiction to all
the waters of Bering Sea, much as back in the days of
Selden England had claimed jurisdiction to the waters of the
North Sea.   A look at the map will show that Bering Sea is
a kind of triangle with the United States owning two sides
of it.[52]

England could be found on whatever side of the freedom of the
seas question best suited her interests at the moment and at
this time she decided that a strict enforcement of the three-
mile limit on the United States would best advance the interest
of her seal fishermen, so she denied the right of the United States
to protect the seal outside its own territorial jurisdiction.   The
matter was submitted to arbitration in 1892 and while the ar-
bitrators wrangled, the seal herd steadily diminished.   The court
decided against the United States and forced her to pay a large
indemnity to Britain for interfering with the Canadian fishermen.
In 1911 the contentions of the United States for the conservation
of the seal herd were embodied in joint treaties between Great
Britain, Japan and the United States, prohibiting the wasteful
"pelagic killing" and limiting the number of seals each nation
might get in a year.   By this time the British were truly anxious
to preserve the herd, because although they were at first willing to
let the Canadians get their share of the booty, it soon became ap-

[52] *Alaska Fur Seal Arbitration, 1893*, 53d Cong., 2d sess., S. Ex. Doc. No. 177.

parent that the annihilation of the seals would throw out of work in London some ten thousand people who made their living by dressing sealskins.

Next the boundary between Alaska and Canada presented the usual trouble which comes from drawing a line on paper which has little relation to the geographic facts. The original boundary had been fixed in 1825 as between England and Russia, and in the southern tongue it was provided that it should follow the sinuosities of the coast line, ten leagues back from the shore. But the multitudinous islands complicated the situation and Britain claimed that the outer shore of the islands was the coast line, thus giving them the headwaters of numerous sounds and bays which the United States also claimed. The arbitral tribunal of 1903 decided on a compromise line which in the main followed the contentions made by the United States. Another boundary dispute with England was straightened out peacefully with the English Chief Justice Alverstone voting with the United States and against the Canadians. [53] This was in great contrast with the actions of Lord Cockburn in 1871, who could only see the British side and acted rather like a lawyer and advocate than as a judge. Indeed, for this action, Lord Alverstone was severely criticised by the Canadians, but his conduct is a good measure of the increasing Anglo-American understanding which was coming into being in those thirty years. The foundation of Johns Hopkins University with its graduate school of history was beginning its work of rescuing us from the hatred-breeding history books of the past. Scores of historical scholars were turned out from this and other graduate schools who now dominate the historical field in every state in the Union and whose scientific researches have made possible the truthful telling of Anglo-American relations which show so conclusively that there has been much right as well as much wrong on both sides.

It was not until 1906 that a treaty was made for the settlement of our last boundary disputes with England, and that

[53] *Alaska Boundary Tribunal*, 58th Cong., 2d sess., S. D. No. 162.

provided for commissioners to discover and fix the line of the 141st degree west longitude which marked the division between Canada and Alaska up to the Arctic Ocean.

6. THE HAY-PAUNCEFOTE TREATY

But greater triumphs of Anglo-American diplomacy were yet to come. The Spanish War with its spectacular trip of the battleship *Oregon* around Cape Horn and the now congested traffic lines from coast to coast made evident that the time had come for the building of the long delayed interoceanic canal in Central America. The failure of the De Lesseps Company illustrated some of the reasons why private capital could not be trusted with this gigantic enterprise. To imagine that any one of the bankrupt and revolution-ridden Republics of Central America could ever build a canal was fantastic. All signs pointed to the United States government as the one agency capable of putting through such a work. But for fifty years the Clayton-Bulwer Treaty had stood as a prohibition against action by the United States. How was Britain to be induced to release us from our promise never to build a canal?

Secretary of State John Hay and the British Ambassador Sir Julian Pauncefote got to work at this task and in 1900 evolved a treaty which freed the United States from the shackles of the Clayton-Bulwer Treaty. The United States could now at last acquire the necessary territory in Central America, build a canal, manage a canal and do all other things needful thereto, subject to the single condition that equal tolls should be charged to all nations using the canal. The United States pledged herself not to charge the British any greater tolls in the canal than she charged her own vessels, in a language which cannot be misunderstood:

> "The canal shall be free and open to the vessels of commerce and of war of all nations observing these rules, on terms of entire equality, so that there shall be no discrimination against such nation, or its citizens or subjects, in respect to the conditions or charges of traffic or otherwise." [54]

[54] W. Malloy, *Treaties and Conventions*, I, 783.

The treaty got by the Senate on a second attempt because that body insisted that the United States should retain the right to fortify the canal. The United States was free at last from the galling restrictions to which Clayton and Bulwer had subjected her, and the building of the canal was now assured. But a year before the canal was to be opened the Republican party, then in power (1912), passed an act regulating the tolls in the canal and exempted from charges all vessels engaged in the coastwise or coast to coast trade of the United States. Inasmuch as previous legislation restricted this traffic to American vessels, England thought it was a flagrant violation of the Hay-Pauncefote Treaty. Various plausible and specious arguments were adduced to prove that the United States had a right to do whatever she wanted to with her own Panama Canal, and the Republican party went out of power without adjusting the matter in 1913. But just before the ending of that Congress, Senator Elihu Root of New York, a lifelong Republican of the old-guard type, crowned his career in the senate with an eloquent appeal to his own party to withdraw their action in this affair. He made it perfectly clear that from the standpoint of history, international law and international decency, the United States had no right whatever to discriminate in favor of its own vessels, when it had pledged its solemn word to do no such thing.[55]

President Woodrow Wilson came into office shortly thereafter and gave the matter considerable study. He came to the same conclusion as the Republican Senator. The Hay-Pauncefote treaty forbade us to do the very thing we had done. In the words of Mr. Walter Page, whom Wilson had sent as Ambassador to the Court at London,

"Whatever Mr. Hay might or could have done, he made a bargain. The Senate ratified it. We accepted it. Whether it was a good bargain, or a bad one, we ought to keep it." [56]

On March 5th, 1914, President Wilson went in person to Congress and asked them to repeal the Panama Canal Tolls Bill. He

[55] E. Root, *Addresses on International Subjects*, pp. 208, 241.
[56] B. J. Hendrick, *Life and Letters of Walter H. Page* (N. Y., 1922), I, 247.

made the question simply one of national honor. The exemption clearly violated the Hay-Pauncefote treaty. As Page said, "We have made a bargain—a solemn compact—and we have broken it." That to the President's mind was unthinkable. He concluded with the prophetic and ominous words:

> "I ask this of you in support of the foreign policy of the administration. I shall not know how to deal with other matters of even greater delicacy and nearer consequence, if you do not grant it to me in ungrudging measure." [57]

England rang with applause for this speech, which Sir Edward Grey, the British foreign minister, said, "helped to lift public life to a higher plane and to strengthen its morale." In the Senate the debate on the bill waxed violent and the parties split asunder. What Mr. Page has so aptly called the "Anglophobiacs" raised the discordant note in both parties. Republicans like Root, Lodge, and Kenyon upheld the Democratic President whom they thought right. But the hyphenated Germans of Missouri and the hyphenated Irish from New York found their leaders in men like Reed and O'Gorman who joined with the Hearst newspapers in attempting to resurrect the unfortunate and erroneous old tales about our relations with England which they had from old-fashioned history texts, or which had been handed down from the days of the potato famine.[58] The pages of the *Congressional Record* were clogged with denunciations of the President because he was anxious to do the decent and honorable thing. However the "Anglophobiacs" cried to no effect and the Tolls Bill was repealed by a decisive vote in April of 1914, rounding out a century from the signing of the Treaty of Ghent.

This one hundred years of Anglo-American relations marks some startling developments in the foreign policy of the United States. It had shown that two nations can get along together in the world without war. This is not due primarily to the

[57] J. B. Scott, *Pres. Wilson's Foreign Policy, Messages, Addresses and Papers* (Wash., 1918), p. 31.
[58] C. Altschul, *The American Revolution in our School Text Books* (N. Y., 1917).

good will of the two peoples, one for another. Time and time again they have come to the verge of a conflict and have been halted by economic factors, or by the distraction of other and more important aspects of foreign policy. Time and again professional demagogues in the United States have done their best to whip up indignation in America against England, just as the supercilious professional Tory in England has enraged both English and Americans who sought a better basis for understanding between the two nations. But through it all runs the story of common sense in the diplomacy of both sides and a growing understanding in America of the remark made by Walter Page:

"Blood carries with it that particular trick of thought which makes us all English in the last resort. Thus, despite the fusion of races, and all the great contributions of other nations to her hundred millions of people and her incalculable wealth, the United States is yet English led and English ruled." [59]

There is food for thought in a remark made by Roosevelt shortly before his death,

"Moreover, I am prepared to say what five years ago, I would not have said, I think the time has come when the United States and the British Empire can agree to a universal arbitration treaty. In other words, I believe the time has come when we should say that under no circumstances shall there ever be a resort to war between the United States and the British Empire, and that no question can arise between them that cannot be settled in judicial fashion." [60]

The great controversies in international law which seemed to separate the two nations at the beginning of the century are being gradually eliminated. In some cases, like impressment, the British have given way to the point of view of the United States. In others, such as the Rule of 1756 and its implications, the United States has undoubtedly come around to the British point of view. Thus international law had grown and been en-

[59] Hendricks, *Life and Letters of Walter H. Page*, I, 258; many are inclined to doubt this broad statement of Mr. Page, and it is well to read W. S. Rossiter, "What are Americans," *Atlantic Monthly*, CXXVI, 270.
[60] Quoted in J. F. Rhodes, *McKinley and Roosevelt Administrations*, p. 260.

riched by Anglo-American relations, becoming that true rule for the conduct of human affairs which alone can eliminate war.   Moreover, the whole relationship is just another illustration of Justice O. W. Holmes' remark that the life of the law is not logic, but experience.   Neither side has insisted on being strictly logical and as a result their troubles have been adjusted by tribunals of law and not by wager of battle.

CHAPTER XII

ANOTHER WHITE MAN AND HIS BURDEN

"Far from us indeed, is the cheerful optimism which refuses to see that the process of civilization is often a cruel process . . ."
—Frederic William Maitland.

"'I want to call your attention to the remarkable change that has come over the spirit and dream of the Republicans. Your slogans of the past—brotherhood of man and fatherhood of God—have gone glimmering down through the ages. The brotherhood of man exists no longer.' These statements of Mr. Tillman have never been challenged and never can be."—*George Frisbie Hoar.*

"Our only difference is that those who do not agree with us have no confidence in the virtue or capacity or high purpose or good faith of this free people as a civilizing agency, while we believe that a century of free government which the American people have enjoyed has not rendered them irresolute and faithless, but has fitted them for the great task of lifting up and assisting to better conditions and larger liberty those distant peoples who, through the issue of battle, have become our wards."—*William McKinley.*

1. The New Civilization.

We have seen the United States as the plaything of European diplomacy. We have also seen the United States deeply engrossed in foreign affairs, because her relations with other nations were bringing in great increments of territory, Louisiana, Texas, Oregon, and the southwest. But in this brief survey of American foreign policy we shall devote little time to the period between the Civil War and the Spanish War, because in that epoch, the United States was interested in almost everything except her foreign policy. From the establishment of the republic to the proclamation of the Monroe Doctrine, the United States was intensely interested in world politics, because Europe was still threatening our very existence, resenting as she did our experiment in democracy. From the enunciation of the Monroe Doctrine to the Civil War, we turned our back on Europe as such, but kept up our interest in foreign affairs, as our adroit diplomats followed the policy of "manifest destiny," and gathered in slice after slice of land until the Pacific was reached. But by 1865 the foreign menace was forever dead, and the United States secured what was apparently the last available bit of territory on the continent when Seward bought Alaska in 1867. We had no further interest in Europe as we neither feared her nor wanted anything she had. The United States then busied herself with the great work which was to prepare her to take the first place among all the nations of the world.

Between 1865 and 1900 a tremendous transformation took place in the United States. In the histories of the future this change will probably loom much larger than such events as the American Revolution or the Civil War. It is futile in this short space to try to convey any idea of the vastness of the change which took place in American life. Yet somehow the reader must understand that between 1860 and 1920 the population of the United States increased from 30,000,000 to 100,000,000. Secondly, he must ever bear in mind that in 1860 barely 20% of the population of the United States lived in cities and that in 1920 more than half the population were urban dwellers. This increase in population filled the west with farmers who produced infinitely more food than the United States could consume itself. It populated the cities with laborers and factory workers who in their turn produced many more manufactured goods than the United States needed for itself. Agriculture was stimulated by a hungry Europe, and industry by a half century of protective tariff. It is a trite saying, yet very true, that during this period the American subordinated everything to getting rich. If he did, he certainly succeeded. Plenty of work, plenty of labor, a bounteous nature did their part; but the historian cannot overlook that wonderful race of American captains of industry, half heroes, half buccaneers, but wholly the most remarkable race of money-getters the world has ever seen.[1]

[1] C. E. Merriam, *American Political Ideas, 1865-1917* (N. Y., 1920), ch. i; B. J. Hendricks, *The Age of Big Business* (Yale, 1919); *Statistical Abstract of the U. S., 1921*, pp. 38, 54.

These circumstances transformed America from a nation interested in benefiting herself at home, to a nation in which wealthy men had a great deal of money which they were willing to invest in enterprises overseas which promised a return of 15% instead of 6%. These circumstances transformed America from a nation which had to borrow from Europe in order to build factories and railways into a nation which had money to lend and to invest.[2] She changed from an importing to an exporting nation, and not the least of her exports was capital, money, to be used in developing hitherto uncivilized, or partly civilized, portions of the world, that they might be induced to send their increase to the United States.

When a nation changes from an importing to an exporting country, its foreign policy undergoes a change, and that time of change had now come to the United States. We have seen how England extended the tentacles of her empire over all the world, in order that she might acquire new markets in which to sell her goods, and new sources from which she might derive her raw materials. In this way was built up the British Empire. The time was now at hand when the United States was to build a similar empire, in the same way, and for the same reasons which built the British Empire. Whenever the white man goes forth on an errand to sell his goods, he has encountered somewhere the backward peoples of the colored races. He could sell and they would buy. But their ideas of business were not the same as his, and finally, to get his pay, he must needs summon the armies of the white man to assure a regular payment of his bills. Once the white man's troops came, they stayed, and the end of the story was that the white man took the colored man's lands, for the good of the colored man, so *he* said. Thus were the two Americas and Africa divided among the white men, and thus were Asia and the islands of the Pacific being partitioned when the United States came on the scene—another white man looking for markets, and destined to assume his share of dominating the backward peoples who could not understand the white man's

[2] A. M. Schlesinger, *New Viewpoints in American History* (N. Y., 1922), pp. 259–60.

business morality, and who, because they could not understand it, were taken under his wing to be civilized for their own good and exploited for his. Now all this may seem to be very much against the traditional American ideas of freedom and liberty for all men, and so the change in the foreign policy of the United States which came about to meet the needs of her altered economic life, deserves the closest study.[3]

2. HAWAII

One of the chief burdens of the white man is his sweet tooth. Moreover the American is the greatest consumer of sugar in the world. In 1865 the per capita consumption of sugar in the United States was eighteen pounds. In 1921 the per capita consumption was ninety-seven pounds. In other words, the present generation consumes five times as much sugar per head as did the last generation. In some way this appetite had to be satisfied. The trouble with sugar is that it is heavy and must be carried as freight. It cannot be sent over wires like electricity nor pumped through pipe lines like oil. When the settlement of California and the Pacific coast after 1850 developed a civilization in that part of the world the people who ate sugar had to pay for having its transported all the way around Cape Horn. Moreover, when the gold rush was over, California settled down to make a living by canning those wonderful fruits and vegetables for which her fertile valleys were so well suited. The canning industry requires enormous quantities of sugar.[4]

The Hawaiian, or Sandwich, Islands, had long been of interest in American foreign policy because they were the stopping place for vessels en route to China and Japan. It would be very desirable to have a good port at Honolulu, owned by the United States. In addition to this the soil of Hawaii is peculiarly well adapted to the production of vast quantities of sugar. When Hawaii became the sugar bowl of California, its annexation became a matter of considerable importance. As the export of cap-

[3] L. Woolf, *Economic Imperialism* (N. Y., 1920), ch. i.
[4] *Statistical Abstract of the U. S., 1921*, p. 601.

ital had begun, millions of dollars in American capital were invested in Hawaiian sugar plantations. Indeed what more fitting place could be found for the investment of the surplus American capital than the islands whose backward population would furnish cheap labor? But the introduction of American brains and American capital soon created a situation in which the chief prosperity of the island depended on the ability of the sugar growers to sell their crop in the United States. Yet the native Hawaiians showed no capacity for self-government, nor for the maintenance of a stable government. A stable government was absolutely essential to the filling of California's sugar bowl.[5]

As early as 1876 the United States made a treaty with Hawaii by which the Hawaiians promised not to give themselves to any other nation and the United States agreed to allow the importation of Hawaiian raw sugar free of duty. The Hawaiians did not object to the first part of this agreement, which frankly looked toward the absorption of Hawaii into the United States, because they knew they were more or less at the mercy of the United States sugar tariff. A hostile tariff might temporarily have ruined the Hawaiians and they knew it. But if reciprocal free trade satisfied the Hawaiians, it did not satisfy the United States sugar investors, for their business was at the mercy of the Hawaiian government as well.

Other events now hastened the coming of annexation. The native Hawaiians never took to labor, and they soon began dying off with terrific rapidity. Their place on the sugar plantations was taken by Japanese laborers, whom the American planters deliberately imported for the purpose. The Japanese would soon predominate on the islands, in which case Japan would probably seize them if the United States did not. Continued misgovernment on the part of the native kings and queens forced the American planters to revolt for their own protection and in 1893 a revolution abolished the monarchy and set up a republic. Unfortunately in this affair some American marines were landed to

[5] F. R. Clow, "Our Commercial Relations with the Hawaiian Islands," *Jour. of Political Economy*, I, 280.

protect American property. The new government asked the United States for annexation and as it was the only *de facto* organization in sight, President Harrison endeavored to annex the islands by treaty.[6]

But while the treaty was still before the Senate, awaiting ratification, President Cleveland succeeded President Harrison and reversed his policy. Cleveland seems to have been convinced that the revolution was mainly a framed up affair in which the United States marines had overawed the natives. He therefore withdrew the treaty from the Senate and ended annexation ideas. On the surface, President Cleveland was certainly right, for the revolution had all the earmarks of having been trumped up to satisfy the longing for protection of the American sugar investors. But there are other things besides those lying on the surface. The native queen was utterly unable to maintain either her throne or any stable government and the republic struggled along for several years longer. Then came the Spanish-American War.[7]

When in 1899 the United States began to cast her eyes toward prospective possessions in the Philippine Islands, it became absolutely necessary to get a coaling station midway to those islands. The modern steam-vessel was helpless without frequent coaling stations. The desire for annexation was now emphatic on both sides. A Republican administration under President McKinley was back in power and it took the matter up where President Harrison had dropped it. By 1899 the native Hawaiians were less than one-fifth of the population of the islands. The ever-increasing Japanese population aroused Japan to protest against plans for annexation by the United States. It was a case of now or never. Unless the United States took Hawaii, Japan would. Following the precedent in the case of Texas, President McKinley had Congress annex the Islands by a joint-resolution of both Houses of Congress and Hawaii ultimately became a territory of the United States. The invest-

---

[6] The Japanese are an ever increasing and the native Hawaiians an ever decreasing percentage of the inhabitants of the Hawaiian Islands. *U. S. Census for 1920*, III, 1172.

[7] J. W. Foster, *American Diplomacy in the Orient* (Boston, 1903), ch. xi; A. H. Allen's *Report, Sen. Ex. Doc. 45, 52* Cong., 1st sess., 14-22.

ments of American capitalists were now safe from fluctuating tariffs, and the livelihood of the laborers on the plantations was assured as it never could have been with Hawaii as an independent nation.

Thus does the white man assume his burden. His penetration of the lands of uncivilized peoples creates problems which demand a stable government to protect property. Obviously the backward and half-civilized peoples cannot run the kind of a government he needs, so the white man must needs assume the burden of government himself. Meantime in all too many cases the native population, unaccustomed to the white man's diseases and his whiskey, die off as did the North American Indian, leaving the white man the whole burden of administering the newly acquired territory.[8]

3. SAMOA

A coaling station en route to China and Japan was not the only requirement of our Pacific policy, however. Australia was a land of growing commercial importance which necessitated a stopping place somewhere south of the equator as Hawaii was north of that line. Ideally located on the route from San Francisco to Melbourne and Sydney were the Samoan Islands whose splendid harbor at Pango-Pango had tempted the American naval strategists as early as 1872. But Germany was discovered to have a commercial right of way. As the empire of the Kaiser set out on the race for its place in the sun, German merchants interested themselves in the copra business in the Pacific Islands, and particularly at Samoa. Copra is the dried meat of the cocoanut, and from it was extracted an oil which made candles for the German peasants. The residue was pressed into oil cakes which provided food for the German cattle who could not always find enough to eat on the barren sand wastes of northern Europe. When the United States secured from the innocent natives the splendid harbor at Pango-Pango, the inevitable

---

[8] In 1920 sugar was about 84% of the whole agricultural product of the Islands in value. *U. S. Census, 1920*, VI, pt. 2, p. 382.

conflict with Germany was at hand. However in 1878 when this was done, the state department was not as advanced as the navy department in understanding the importance of what it had secured. The official attitude toward Samoa was the same at first as our attitude toward Hawaii, that is, we wanted the Samoans to run their own government giving us only the trading privileges. Thus reluctantly did this particular white man assume his burden. In 1878 the United States had just refused to accept the free gift of Santo Domingo, she had deliberately allowed the Panama Canal to slip into the hands of the French and she was still laughing at Seward's "ice-box" in Alaska.[9] (See Map, p. 422.)

Germany on the other hand was not so indifferent to her interests. She had embarked on a policy of protecting her overseas enterprise, and she was soon treating Samoa as a prospective colony which she might seize when times were ripe. British interests loomed up here, as ever, and the question of Samoa soon became a three-cornered affair. Numerous unfeeling acts on the part of Germany provoked the Samoans to armed resistance and the Samoans asked both the United States and Britain, in turn, to annex them. But both nations declined the honor. The United States still clung to the old policy of not entangling herself in things far away from the American continent.[10] But a change in attitude was already under way, for the American capital which was seeking investment in Hawaii soon appeared in Samoa. British and Americans were accustomed to smoothing out the difficulties which resulted from the conflicts of their commercial interests, but here was a case where a third party appeared. Fortunately for the historian there was on the spot no less a person than Robert Louis Stevenson and his comment on the third party is a classic, "In the Germans alone, no trace of humor is to be observed, and their solemnity is accompanied by a touchiness which is almost beyond belief." [11] In the eighties,

[9] J. Keim *Forty Years of German American Political Relations* (Univ. of Penna., 1919), pp. 126ff.

[10] Ibid., pp. 137, 151.

[11] R. L. Stevenson, *Letters and Miscellanies*, XIX, 396.

therefore, the three powers glared at one another and the consuls of each were busy insulting the consuls of the others with acts which kept the home governments busy disavowing the acts of belligerent representatives and changing consuls to keep out of war.[12]

To settle matters Bismarck called a conference at Berlin in 1889, just after the great hurricane of that year had prevented the German and American war ships in Samoa from opening fire on one another. The hurricane sank both squadrons. The conference agreed that Samoa was to remain independent with a policy similar to that of the "open door," whereby each nation was to have equal commercial opportunities, instead of granting Germany preponderating rights because of her admittedly greater commercial interests. This was a violation of the traditional American policy because it then went on to commit the United States to an active participation with European powers in the actual supervision and administration of territory thousands of miles away. "Independence," acknowledged in treaties of this sort, is usually accompanied by qualifications which make that independence something of a farce.[13]

But the scheme did not work. The Samoans were utterly incapable of self-government and, as in Hawaii, the business interests of the great powers demanded a stable government for the protection of their investments. The only alternative was for the great powers themselves to take over the government and virtually to annex the islands. This they could not do co-operatively, so the islands were divided up. In the division the United States got the prize harbor at Pango-Pango and the Germans got all the rest. The British were compensated by the title to the Gilbert and Solomon Islands elsewhere in the Pacific. But the United States still did not take the affair very seriously and the whole thing seemed to suggest a musical comedy to the officials of the Department of State who persisted in talking about Britain's share of the bargain as the "Gilbert and Sullivan

---

[12] Keim, supra, pp. 155ff.
[13] Ibid., pp. 194–200.

Islands." In fact that was about as seriously as the average American could take his foreign policy in those days.[14]

This time the United States did not refuse to accept what was offered to it, for by now (1899) it was definitely embarked on its imperialistic career under President McKinley and Secretary of State John Hay. McKinley had frankly been elected president by the business and commercial interests of the country in the exciting campaign of 1896 and it was only natural and proper that he would be the kind of a man who could understand that the time had come when the United States, for better or for worse, would have to depart from its traditional policy of insisting on the freedom of all the nations of the world and take into consideration some other things. It had certainly been the policy of the United States to stand for the autonomy of Samoa against German aggression, but when it became evident that a native government was necessarily a farce and that the tripartite government was impracticable, the United States had nothing left to do but to accept its share of the territory and the responsibility. Moreover the question of a canal at Panama was now once more a pole star in our diplomacy and the harbor at Pango-Pango was necessary as a coaling station for the traffic which such a canal would inevitably promote.[15]

4. Cuba and the Spanish War

For a hundred years the statesmen and politicians of the United States had been casting covetous and hungry glances toward the "Pearl of the Antilles." From the moment we acquired Louisiana and the Floridas, Cuba became the next logical step in our expansion to the south. Statesmen who disagreed on almost everything else could be found to agree that Cuba ought ultimately to find her resting place in the American Union, for the protection of the mouth of the Mississippi, for the extension of slave territory or for the satisfaction of the further dictates of "manifest destiny." Jefferson's remark that he

---

[14] Keim, supra, pp. 210, 215; W. R. Thayer, *Life of John Hay*, II, 281–2.
[15] Keim, supra, pp. 175–215.

looked upon Cuba as the most interesting addition which could be made to our system of States,[16] was echoed at the same time by his political opponent John Quincy Adams who did not hesitate to say:

> "These islands (Cuba and Porto Rico) from their local position are natural appendages to the North American continent, and one of them is almost within sight of our shores . . . in looking forward to the probable course of events for the short period of half a century, it is scarcely possible to resist the conviction that the annexation of Cuba to our Federal Republic will be indispensable to the continuance and integrity of the Union itself." [17]

It was largely the fear of England in 1823 which placed two such men as Adams and Jefferson on the same side of a question. Undoubtedly Canning was at that time angling for Cuba. But as we have seen, it was then written into American foreign policy that the United States was going to prevent Europeans from extending their holdings in the western hemisphere. No sooner had the menace of England passed than the Puritan arose in his wrath and attacked the whole movement of expansion to the south and southwest as a slaveholders' conspiracy to get more land into which to extend that despised institution. Yet with Cuba, as with Texas, there could be found hundreds of young Americans who would persist in joining filibustering expeditions, which now set sail from the ports of the United States with the avowed purpose of stirring up trouble in the Caribbean. Of the motives of these filibusters, we shall have more to say later, but suffice it here to remark that the net result of their expeditions sailing from New Orleans and New York and applauded by such slaveholders as General John Quitman of Mississippi, was to increase the suspicion of the Puritan. Rightly or wrongly, it was felt in many quarters that there were those classes in the United States, who held vested interests in slave property and who would back any movement to drag the United States into a war with Spain for the acquisition of Cuba.[18]

---

[16] T. Jefferson's *Works* (Ford ed.), X, 278.

[17] J. B. Moore, *Digest of International Law* (Washington, 1906), VI, 381.

[18] F. E. Chadwick, *Relations of the United States with Spain, Diplomacy* (N. Y., 1909), p. 251; Claiborne, *John A. Quitman*, II, 207.

In 1848 Secretary of State Buchanan tried to buy Cuba from Spain for $100,000,000. Failing in this, the United States soon had her hands full restraining the ardent filibusters who joined in the celebrated Lopez expeditions in the next year. Lopez had an ambition to liberate Cuba from the yoke of Spain and then to invite the annexation to the United States, much as had been done in the case of Texas. But the Cubans seemed most apathetic and the Lopez affairs only served to enrage the Spaniards against the United States for her failure to observe a strict neutrality and keep the filibusters at home. Officially the United States did maintain the correct attitude of an impartial neutrality, but her inability to keep the filibusters from slipping away did not help international relations. In 1853, the United States made matters worse by appointing as minister to Spain a fire-eating southerner, Pierre Soulé, who had openly applauded the Lopez expeditions. Soulé was no sooner at his post than the Spanish authorities in Cuba showed their ill will toward the United States by seizing the *Black Warrior*, a United States merchant vessel, on a flimsy pretext. Her cargo was confiscated and Soulé demanded reparations from the Spaniards in rather insulting language. This did not help matters and Spain in her turn exasperated Soulé with her usual habit of forgetting to answer letters. Soulé brought the United States almost to the point of war before he was checked by Secretary of State Marcy and the affair was patched up.[20]

By this time the slavery controversy was at fever heat in the United States. The Compromise of 1850 was evidently a failure and the bloodshed in Kansas showed to what desperate lengths both sides would go. The slaveholders felt they must have more territory. Besides this, the danger of servile insurrection was always a bugaboo for the slaveholders, and Cuba was showing distinct signs of revolutionary restiveness under Spanish misrule. A conflagration in Cuba with its hundreds of thousands of blacks and mulattoes might easily communicate itself to North

---

[19] *Black Warrior Affair, H. Ex. Doc. 93,* 33d Cong., 2d sess., pp. 30–120. R. G. Caldwell, *Lopez Expedition to Cuba* (Princeton, 1915).

America. The United States, it was felt, must have some sort of a Cuban policy. Unfortunately the administration of President Pierce confirmed the worst suspicions of the abolitionists by letting this same Pierre Soulé formulate our Cuban policy in the famous Ostend Manifesto. The American ministers to Spain, France and England met at Ostend at Secretary Marcy's request, to give him some advice on the subject. James Buchanan of Pennsylvania, John Y. Mason of Virginia and Soulé of Louisiana were a trio whose whole lives show their subserviency to the slaveholding property interests in the United States. They frankly and publicly advised the President in 1854 that if Spain would not sell Cuba, "then by every law, human and divine, we shall be justified in wresting it from Spain, if we possess the power." [20]

This amazing piece of effrontery would have committed the United States to a foreign policy utterly at variance with her many pretensions of right and justice. Fortunately Europe was too busy with the Crimean War to bother with the thing, and the slavery controversy in the United States overshadowed foreign politics. The Civil War in the United States ended this on the part of the slaveholding interests. But the coveting of Cuba was destined to survive the war between the States as another set of economic interests supplanted those of the slaveholders in the domination of American foreign policy.

When Spain ruled her far-flung dominions in the seventeenth century, she believed, in common with all the other colonial powers, that colonies existed for the purpose of enriching the mother country. The trouble with Spain was that she carried those ideas over into the nineteenth century when England was learning to give her colonies home rule and self-government. Oppression, corruption, and misgovernment were the symbols of Spanish rule in Cuba and as a result of all these things there came the Ten Years War in Cuba, from 1868–1878. During this unsuccessful revolt of Cuba against Spain, President Grant was

---

[20] F. E. Chadwick, *Relations of the United States and Spain, Diplomacy*, 262ff., which also reprints text of Manifesto.

on the verge of granting recognition to the insurgents, who in fact were without that *de facto* government which our recognition policy had always dictated should precede any recognition by us. Grant was saved from this blunder by his Secretary of State, Hamilton Fish, who pointed out that no such recognition was possible and quietly suppressed Grant's recognition of belligerency.[21]

The whole business was complicated by further filibustering expeditions from the United States in which Spain finally got tired of temporizing and shot the crew of a vessel called the *Virginius*, which was falsely flying the American colors. Most of the crew were English and Americans, although the vessel was actually owned and controlled by Cuban insurgents carrying supplies to the rebels. The United States protested vigorously when Spain turned the tables by proving that the *Virginius* had no right to fly the American flag. But rights or wrongs in law make little difference in a case like this and relations between the United States and Spain were as a result anything but cordial. The Ten Years War ended with Spain still in control of Cuba, but the nuisance that it created in the Caribbean left a heritage of hatred which was sure to show itself again.[22]

But between 1870 and 1898 the United States laid the foundations for a Cuban policy which brought swift and terrible results in the latter year. As we have seen in the earlier part of this chapter, it was during those years that the United States changed from a nation which imported capital to a nation which exported capital. We have also seen in an earlier chapter how American capital began to pour into Mexico and we shall see presently how the white man assumed his burden in China by investing his surplus capital in that country. Capital and brains are the white man's contribution to the backward states and nations of the world. Judged by her state of misgovernment and civilization, Cuba must be classed among these, during the years up to 1898. If the Californians had to have sugar, much more did the populous east and that sugar had long come from the islands of the

[21] C. F. Adams, *Lee at Appomattox, and Other Papers*, pp. 117–23; 5 J. B. Davis, "Hamilton Fish," *Atlantic Monthly*, LXXIII, pp. 217–218.
[22] F. E. Chadwick, supra, 306–58.

West Indies, notably from Cuba. That ninety-seven pounds of sugar per person must come from somewhere and the Louisiana sugar fields cannot begin to supply our need. The result was that Americans became interested, commercially and financially, in the Cuban sugar fields.

Under reciprocity agreements with Spain sugar had been coming in from Cuba free for many years. Even the McKinley tariff of 1890 did not disturb matters very much as it left sugar on the free list and satisfied the Louisiana growers with a bounty, or subsidy, to encourage production. But in 1894 came the famous Wilson tariff. Two sets of sugar interests were busily at work in the corridors of Congress. The Louisiana sugar growers wanted a protective tariff, on all raw sugar. The American Sugar Refining Co., or "Sugar Trust" wanted a protective tariff on refined sugar. The lobbies of these two sets of interests have now become a classic example of how legislation was secured in the last century. The "Sugar Trust" had contributed liberally to the campaign funds of whichever party was going to help them get a tariff they wanted, and carried the amount thus paid out on their books as part of the expenses of their business! A Committee which investigated their activities subsequently reported that there was no doubt of the existence of

"Importunity and pressure to which Congress and its members are subjected by the representatives of great industrial combinations, whose enormous wealth tends to suggest undue influence, and to create in the public mind a demoralizing belief in the existence of corrupt practices."[23]

Such "practices" easily secured for both sugar producer and sugar refiner just the legislation he wanted. Duties were placed on *both* raw sugar and refined sugar, thereby effectually terminating the reciprocity and free trade in sugar in expectation of which the Cubans had been building up their sugar business and in further expectation of which other Americans had been investing their money in Cuba.

The result of this is best seen in the comparison of consular reports on Cuban sugar exports of 1894 and 1895. 95% of what

[23] C. R. Lingley, *Since the Civil War* (N. Y., 1920), pp. 277–8.

Cuba sent to the United States in 1893 was sugar. This shows the importance of the industry. Comparing 1894 with 1895 we find that the exports of sugar from the principal ports of Cuba fell off between 30% and 50% in 1895. No such dislocation in business can possibly take place without an industrial depression with a consequent period of what the economists call readjustment and unemployment, but which to many laborers simply means they are out of a job. It made no real difference that the setback was temporary, for the United States would ultimately buy all the sugar Cuba would produce. That fact of a temporary commercial depression meant men out of jobs, and men out of work in most Latin American countries mean revolutionists. As we have seen, it was to avoid a situation of this sort that the Hawaiians, whether American or native, wanted annexation to the United States.[24]

In 1895, therefore, we need hardly be surprised to find another revolution breaking out in Cuba. It is not necessary to allege that the sugar interests in the United States deliberately stirred up this revolt to take advantage of it later on. Business men seldom see that far ahead, and most business men are not of the type who would deliberately do any such thing anyway. But what must interest us in connection with our foreign policy is that our acts, however apparently remote from our foreign policy, may ultimately involve it. Indeed few episodes in history can be charged to a single cause and there were other contributing causes of the Cuban Revolt of 1895.[25] There were in addition plenty of obvious reasons why the Cubans should revolt. A new system of colonial administration had been introduced which was more farcical then ever without any hope of Home Rule or dominion self-government. Combined with this there was practically no security of person, or property or freedom of press or speech under the stupid tyranny with which Spain ruled Cuba.[26]

[24] F. W. Taussig, "The Tariff Act of 1894," in *Political Science Quarterly*, IX, 598–600; *Commercial Relations of the United States, 1893*, 265; *1894–5*, pp. 414–17.

[25] One should reflect on E. P. Cheyney's "Law in History," *Amer. Hist. Rev.*, XXIX, 231, in this connection.

[26] H. Taylor, "A Review of the Cuban Question," *North American Review*, CLXV, 610–35.

The revolt of 1895 speedily developed into a serious revolution and to suppress it the Spaniards resorted to methods of refined and atrocious cruelty which seem incredible even to those who have lived through the European War. Guerrilla warfare made it impossible to distinguish between a Cuban rebel at night and peaceful Cuban farmer in the daytime. Therefore, General Weyler, the Spanish commander, herded the men, women and children who were suspected of being rebels, into great barbed wire stockades. In these concentration camps there was terrible overcrowding, little food, and an absolute neglect of any sanitary measures. The victims soon began to die off by the thousands from various infectious diseases, neglected and uncared for. The sufferings of the victims of this brutal policy were disregarded by the cynical Spanish officials with all the indifference to human agony which seems to have been characteristic of that nation from the days of the inquisition.[27]

The Spaniards, however, had reckoned without one of the greatest and most unrestrainable forces of modern times, the American newspaper. It was about the time of the campaign of 1896 that two new forces appeared in the newspaper world, Hearst and Pulitzer, in a stage combat to see which one could produce the more lurid headlines and write the more sensational stories. Sydney Brooks has tried to epitomize the conflict when he said of Hearst that

> "He had sat at the feet of Pulitzer and had studied the methods by which that consummate master of phosphorescent effects had raised the New York 'World' to the unquestioned primacy of the sewer."

This is a very unfair estimate of Pulitzer's career, but it indicates the shock created by the new journalism. For a time Mr. Bryan and his flaming oratory supplied the needs of the "yellow journals." But when the campaign in 1896 was over, Mr. Hearst and Mr. Pulitzer began to look around for more inflammable material out of which they could create a journalistic conflagration. What a splendid opportunity the

[27] *Affairs in Cuba, Senate Reports*, 5, 55th Cong., 2d sess., p. ix.

Cuban mess afforded them! The American appetite for the ghastly and sensational had been whetted and must be appeased. So Hearst and Pulitzer set about to appease it. In this case the simple truth was enough, but instead of putting it under the small and dignified headlines of the Boston *Transcript*, these two modern journalists told their stories heralded by headlines sometimes six or seven inches in height.[28]

On going out of office, President Cleveland in 1897 had warned McKinley that he was bequeathing a war to the incoming administration, and that foreign affairs would require some expert handling. But McKinley and Mark Hanna, who had virtually made him president, went serenely on their way with the idea that the gold standard and the full dinner pail were the chief issues of the day. With an utter disregard for the importance of foreign relations, so characteristic of the period, they considered the office of Secretary of State as being merely a convenient corner into which they might kick the faithful but failing old Senator John Sherman of Ohio in order to make room for Mark Hanna in the Senate. After all, Hanna had been largely instrumental in making McKinley president and he wanted to be a senator. When Mark Hanna wanted anything, he usually got it, and so poor old Sherman was "kicked upstairs" into the tremendously important job of heading our department of foreign affairs at a time when most important events were pending in our international relations. But such was America's attitude toward her foreign policy in those days.[29]

Upon such an unprepared Department of State there was suddenly dropped one of the biggest problems which had confronted America since she turned her back on Europe in 1815. Cuban and Spaniard were alike engaged in a ruthless destruction of property. Up to 1897 it had been the policy of the Spanish to try to protect all the sugar plantations, but in that year General Weyler changed his policy, under the impression that a total destruction of the agricultural resources of the island would starve

[28] S. Brooks, "The Significance of Mr. Hearst," *Fortnightly Review*, LXXXVIII, 919; and his "American Yellow Press," *Fortnightly Review*, LCVI, 1126.

[29] H. Croly, *Marcus Alonzo Hanna*, pp. 233ff.; J. B. Foraker, *Notes of a Busy Life*, I, 508-9.

out the insurgents and bring them to terms. This put a new aspect on the affair as the investments of the Americans began to suffer with those of the Cubans and Spaniards themselves. The new policy intensified the revolution to such an extent that President McKinley began to fear for the lives as well as the property of Americans in Cuba. He therefore sent the battleship *Maine* to Havana to protect the interests of the citizens of the United States and to be on the lookout for trouble. Trouble it found, for in February, 1898, it was blown up in Havana harbor with the loss of two hundred American lives.[30]

Meantime a Cuban junta had set itself in New York City, safely out of harm's way from the Spaniards, and was assuming to act as the government of Cuba. Its screaming dispatches could not be avoided by the American public nor by Congress, and the country was fairly seething with excitement and frequent demands were voiced that the United States do something to relieve the Cuban situation. Into this vortex one of the New York papers threw a bomb in the shape of a letter which the Spanish minister at Washington, De Lome, had written to a friend in Cuba. It was probably "surreptitiously, if not criminally obtained" said William R. Day, the Assistant Secretary of State, and its publication was the last thing in the world De Lome expected to see. In it the Spanish Minister said

"McKinley is weak and a bidder for the admiration of the crowd, besides being a would-be politician who tries to leave the door open behind himself while keeping on good terms with the jingoes of his party."

In the face of such an offense against the nation to which he was accredited, De Lome could do nothing but cable his resignation to Madrid, which was promptly accepted. Such is the power of the press in foreign affairs. Assistant Secretary Day put it mildly when he said that "the publication of this letter created a good deal of feeling among the Americans." [31]

Events pressed thick upon one another. Scarcely a week after

[30] Stephen Bonsall's testimony in *Affairs in Cuba*, supra, p. 397; F. E. Chadwick, supra, p. 524.
[31] *Foreign Relations of the United States, 1898*, pp. 680, 1007.

the De Lome episode the *Maine* was blown up in Havana harbor. The immediate cause of the destruction was admitted by everyone to be an explosion inside the forward magazine on the *Maine*. An investigation was made at once while the *Maine* lay on the bottom of the harbor. The Spanish made a very superficial report and returned a verdict that the whole thing was caused by an internal explosion for which of course the United States was to blame.[32] The United States Naval Board of Inquiry made a much more thorough investigation in 1898 and found a great deal of evidence from the condition of the keel and outer shell of the vessel to prove that a mine or torpedo had exploded outside the ship first and that this had set off the magazine. Such a verdict tended to imply that the Spanish or else the Cuban junta was responsible for the explosion.[33] Another investigation made in 1911, when the *Maine* was raised from the harbor of Havana, revealed to the satisfaction of the investigators that the *Maine* was sunk by an outside, and not by an inside explosion.[34] Certainly the condition of the hull when it was raised tended to support the American rather than the Spanish view. But the truth is, from the scientific standpoint, that we cannot be positive that the escaping gases as they proceeded upward did not "suck in" the sides and bottom of the ship and give it the effect of an exterior explosion.[35]

Under the circumstances, however, the Congress and the newspaper reading public in the United States were not willing to wait on academic and scientific argument. The time had come to strike and drive Spain out of Cuba forever, it was contended on all sides. Congressmen rushed to the White House and told McKinley that if he did not do something and do it quickly, Congress would take the matter out of the hands of the State Department. The "yellow journals" howled and Assistant Secretary of the Navy Roosevelt said "McKinley has no more

[32] *The Spanish Report, Sen. Rept. 885,* 54th Cong., 2d sess.
[23] *The U. S. Report in 1898, Sen. Doc. 207,* 55th Cong., 2d sess.
[34] *Rept. of the U. S. Naval Board in 1911, House Doc. 310,* 63d Cong., 2d sess.
[35] It is interesting to notice how little we still know, despite all our recent experience with submarine explosions.

backbone than a chocolate éclair." [31] Left alone, McKinley would probably have avoided a war, as he was a peaceful and gentle man who had imagination enough to count the frightful cost of war as few of his associates did. Congress nevertheless was bent on war and the populace clamored for war. The will of the masses overbore the judgment of the President and had its way. War came. The whole thing presents fascinatingly interesting evidence of the popular control of foreign policy. Is it a good thing? From the depths of lethargy about their foreign policy and from an appalling abyss of ignorance on the subject, the American people suddenly determined to control their own destinies in international relations.

But if America's leap into world politics was heralded by all these things of which we can hardly be very proud, still in its very declaration of war Congress did a thing which will forever mark the dawn of a new era in international relationships, a thing to which every American may point as an evidence of the fact that America had a mission in world politics which was not sordid, nor materialistic nor merely land-grabbing. In a burst of generous enthusiasm Congress not only declared that Cuba was free, but went on to announce to the world

"The United States hereby disclaims any intention or disposition to exercise sovereignty, jurisdiction or control, over said island, except for the pacification thereof, and asserts its determination when that is accomplished, to leave the government and control of the Island to its people." [37]

Naturally enough, European powers who were accustomed to proclaim solemnly their desire to preserve the "independence and territorial integrity" of a backward state as preparation for destroying both, regarded this declaration with a sneer.

The story of the war with Spain need not detain us long. The United States navy won the war in two of the most remarkable naval battles of the modern period, up to that time. It destroyed the naval power of Spain with the loss of but one American life. The army was wretchedly mismanaged. The United States

[36] J. F. Rhodes, *The McKinley and Roosevelt Administrations*, p. 57.
[37] *Foreign Relations, 1898*, liv.

entered this war, as it has entered all wars, unprepared and inefficient. The army captured Santiago in short order, but disease,
due partly to ignorance and partly to mismanagement, took a
frightful toll of human life. But if America was in a dream most
of the time the Spaniards, it has been well said, were in a trance.
Hence the United States won.

Within less than four months the French minister at Washington approached President McKinley for terms in behalf of Spain.
A protocol ended the war wherein Spain relinquished Cuba,
surrendered Porto Rico to the United States and left the status
of the Philippines to be decided at the conference. The Commissioners to sign a permanent peace met at Paris in October of
1898. It was just a hundred and fifteen years since Jay, Adams
and Franklin had met the British at Paris to establish a small new
Republic across the ocean. Now Secretary of State Day (he had
succeeded John Sherman), Chairman C. K. Davis of the Senate
Committee on Foreign Relations, Whitelaw Reid, Senator W. P.
Frye and Judge George Gray representing the Democratic minority met at Paris to dictate terms of peace to a nation which had
once been the haughtiest and mightiest in Europe. Here was a
great milestone in the progress of American foreign policy. The
little agricultural world in which Washington, Jefferson and the
other Virginia farmers, or the Adamses representing the small
New England tradesmen, had recommended that the United
States steer clear of European affairs, this little world was gone
beyond recovery. Conditions were changed because of steam-
ships and cables. Investments by Americans in foreign lands had
given her interests in foreign affairs which no political shibboleths
of a century ago could possibly destroy.[38]

At least three of the American commissioners were ardent
imperialists. The United States was caught in a vast tidal wave
of enthusiasm which swept it on to a frank avowal of its policy of
getting territory beyond the seas. Hence when the Spaniards met
with the American commissioners, they were dismayed to find

[38] J. F. Rhodes, supra, 101; F. E. Chadwick, *Relations of the United States and Spain*,
II, 436.

that the United States was going to keep the Philippines as well as Porto Rico. McKinley at first had an open mind in the matter. But he was one of those politicians who ever had his ear close to the ground, and he soon detected the fact that American public opinion, in so far as it was ascertainable at all, would back him up in taking the Philippines. Judge Gray was a lone voice in protest against what seemed to him denial of all our past policy and past idealism,

"[I] cannot agree that it is wise to take the Philippines in whole or in part. To do so would be to reverse the accepted continental policy of [our] country declared and acted upon throughout [our] history. . . . We should set an example in these respects, and not follow the selfish and vulgar greed for territory which Europe has inherited from medieval times." [39]

But the new Secretary of State, John Hay, telegraphed Commissioner Day that "the sentiment in the United States is almost universal" that we should take the Philippines, and take them we did. Probably the most honest reason why we took them can be found in the simple, sincere and naïve words of McKinley himself. We could not give them back to Spain in view of her four centuries of cruel misgovernment, that would be dishonorable. We could not give them to Germany (who stood ready to grab them the moment we let go) as that would be bad business for our oriental trade. We could not turn them over to themselves, as the Filipinos were in a vast majority illiterate savages, unfit for self-government. The only alternative was to assume our share of the white man's burden of civilizing these backward peoples and getting them ready to take care of themselves. [40]

It is easy enough for the Socialist or the "economic determinist" to sneer at McKinley's words and to say that "big business" forced him to take the Philippines and break our traditional policy. But there is a great deal more in it than that. In the first place this was not the first time that the United States had taken other

[39] *Foreign Relations, 1898*, p. 934; see R. Cortissoz, *Life of Whitelaw Reid* (N. Y., 1921), ch. xiii.
[40] J. F. Rhodes, supra, 105–6; *Foreign Relations, 1898*, 937.

people's property. If these pages show nothing else, they must show that American Foreign Policy from the time of John Jay to the time of John Hay was deeply concerned in getting all the land it could away from Spain. The story began when in 1778 John Jay went to Madrid to open the mouth of the Mississippi River, and the time has certainly come for American historians to admit that fact. Moreover one who studies McKinley's life finds it difficult to impugn his motives or question his sincerity of purpose. If McKinley was not anything else, he was a sincere Christian and he really believed what he said when he insisted

" . . . there is nothing left for us to do but take them all, and educate the Filipinos, and uplift and civilize them as our fellow men for whom Christ also died." [41]

That our Christian duty coincided with our economic interests is perfectly true, but that does not prove that the latter necessarily dictated our policy. Moreover what the United States has done for the Philippines is what few of the "realistic" powers of Europe have done for their colonies, for we have shouldered the responsibility and "done the very best we could by them." No wonder then that Mr. Kipling wrote his famous poem to McKinley:

> "Take up the White Man's Burden—
> And reap his old reward:
> The blame of those ye better,
> The Hate of those ye guard—

> "Take up the White Man's Burden—
> Ye dare not stoop to less—
> Nor call too loud on Freedom
> To cloak your weariness."

But one of the most creditable pages in American foreign policy was now to be written. Having promised not to take Cuba but to liberate her and give her back to herself, the United States now did an almost unprecedented thing in world politics,—she kept her promise. Cuba was given the chance to become a free and independent nation and she still has that chance. Yet

[41] C. S. Olcott, *Life of William McKinley*, II, 109.

somehow Cuba must be kept free of those devastating revolutions which had brought her to such an unhappy state, for American investments would grow, rather than diminish, with the return of peace. The Senate of the United States, therefore, passed
the so-called "Platt Amendment," which provided among other
things that Cuba should never make any agreements with other
powers which might tend to impair the independence of the island,
that the United States should have the right to maintain order
in Cuba when the Cubans were unable to do so themselves, and
that Cuba should not be permitted to borrow any more money
than she could reasonably expect to pay. The terms of this
"Platt Amendment" were then embodied in a formal treaty between Cuba and the United States and incorporated in the Constitution of Cuba.[42]

Cuba then started on her career as an independent nation.
Several times during her short existence as a republic it has been
necessary for the United States to intervene and stop violence
and bloodshed. After all, the habits of political incapacity bred
in four centuries of Spanish misrule cannot be overcome in a few
years. But every time the United States has sent troops to Cuba
to restore order and good government, she has withdrawn those
troops as soon as her aim was accomplished. The policy of the
United States has thus undergone a subtle change. At one time
we sympathized with people revolting against their masters.
Now we intervene to suppress revolutions. But this can best be
studied in the next chapter. The relationship between the United
States and Cuba has been called a "disguised protectorate" and
if we must have a name, that is as good as any.

The United States has a naval base on the coast of Cuba, by
the permission of the Cubans. But one might ask whether this
necessarily destroys the independence of Cuba any more than the
British hold on Gibraltar destroys the independence of Spain.
Perhaps when the world gets civilized enough to do without
navies, both properties will be returned to their owners. Cuba,
indeed, is not a real protectorate of the United States, for a pro-

42 W. Malloy, *Treaties and Conventions*, I, 362.

tectorate loses its right of conducting its own foreign relations. Cuba is so completely free in this respect that she had joined the League of Nations which the United States declined to enter in 1919. But the fact is that 75% of Cuba's trade is done with the United States and political safeguards have been arranged to recognize an economic intimacy, which makes the relationship peculiar.

Frankly and openly the United States embarked on her policy of imperialism, for which she had so often criticized European nations. Yet it was not without a fight. The election of 1900 was at hand and William J. Bryan, once more the Democratic candidate, deliberately chose "imperialism" as an issue and went up and down the country attacking it and the Republicans who had foisted it on the country. Did or did not the United States want to undertake the white man's burden of ruling the "silent sullen peoples, half-devil and half-child?" McKinley was again the Republican candidate and met the issue. The result was an election in which the American people, with their eyes open, and knowing what they were doing reëlected McKinley and started on the path to world power.

CHAPTER XIII

CREEPING DOWN THE CARIBBEAN

"Equity, which is required, and humanity, which is praised, toward individuals, are more requisite and praiseworthy toward nations, inasmuch as injury or kindness is greater with the number."—*Grotius*.

1. THE VENGEANCE OF VANDERBILT

The Caribbean policy of the United States has many explanations. But certainly one outstanding interpretation may be put upon it, and that is the desire for, and the building and the protection of a canal connecting the two oceans somewhere in Central America. We have seen how the rivalry of the United States and Britain for the Nicaragua route in the forties ended by both parties agreeing to get out and stay out, in the Clayton-Bulwer Treaty of 1850. But if that treaty forbade the United States to build a canal, it did not prevent private individuals from interesting themselves in the idea, and their interest in the fifties was very great. In the first place, there was manifest destiny still calling and yet unsatisfied, even if the United States had reached the Pacific Ocean. She had wheedled Britain out of all possible territory to the north in the Oregon Treaty of 1846 and she had almost bullied Mexico out of all possible territory to the south by the treaty of Guadaloupe Hidalgo in 1848. But the fixing of these limits to American expansion did not hinder that race of adventurers whose very existence was the second cause of American interests in the Caribbean.

It is a mistake to leave out of the story the influence and effect of the daring and audacious men whose motives are neither gain nor glory, but sheer excitement and who are never happier than when exhibiting cunning and physical prowess in overcoming danger. Such were the men who joined Sir Francis Drake, when

he scoured the seas to plunder the Spaniard. Such men explored
North and South America,—Cortez, Champlain, and John Smith.
Such men we have met in the story of Texas and the story of
Oregon. To-day we find the same breed fighting savage football
battles in the college coliseum, for the semi-professional, migra-
tory college athlete of today is of the stuff of which were made the
filibusters of the past. The sons of the men who had filibustered
into Texas now filibustered into Nicaragua.

But close on the heels of the filibuster come always the merchant and the trader whose aim it is to turn the acts of the adventurer into profits. When the jumping-jack despot of Central
America tempted the Yankee ne'er-do-well to come down and
drive him out of his palace, there was always somewhere in the
offing the Yankee trader, who was waiting around to supply
the adventurer with arms and ammunition and then to pick off
the profits which the carefree filibuster gambled away that he
might have the pleasure of starting all over again. The year 1850
marks two great events which turned the eyes of many Americans
toward Nicaragua, and which interested certain propertied men
of the United States in annexing that weak republic. The first
event was the Clayton-Bulwer Treaty which invited private
capital, and not governments, to build a canal. The continuous
stream of traveling humanity rushing to the gold fields of California was a standing invitation to any capitalist who wanted to
go into the transportation business. The second event was the
Compromise of 1850, where in his last great effort, John C. Calhoun warned the people of the Southern States that the equilibrium between slave states and free states was now hopelessly
upset. Unless the south could find more slave territory, it must
leave the Union. The slaveholders began to look toward the
stormy republic of Nicaragua whither their attention had been
directed by travelers going to and coming from the gold fields.

In 1849 Cornelius Vanderbilt of New York began to take his
money out of ocean transportation, for he saw that with the age
of iron ships, the United States merchant marine was going to
become a thing of the past. The United States could not com-

pete with the cheap labor and material in the British ship-yards. But Vanderbilt put his money into another form of transportation and got a monopoly from the Republic of Nicaragua for carrying passengers across the isthmus on their way to California. A glance at the map will show how on the surface he might have thought this was the best possible route for a canal, up the San Juan River, across Lake Nicaragua and then only a twelve-mile excavation through to the Pacific Ocean. So Vanderbilt in New York and some capitalists in San Francisco established the "Accessory Transit Company," to carry the hordes of emigrants while they made ready to build a canal.[1] (See Map, p. 230.)

Then came the filibusters. William Walker was a typical westerner of the kind which had founded Texas and plagued Santa Anna. When Texas was won he led an abortive filibustering expedition into lower California and at another time he was interested in annexing Cuba to the United States. In 1854 he gathered a band of buccaneers from the United States who descended on Nicaragua, then in the midst of one of its many revolutions. With incredible audacity and good luck, Walker overturned the government of that unhappy country and soon made himself master of its capital. He was not primarily actuated by a desire for slave territory, for New England Yankees joined Ohioans, and Cuban exiles joined ex-Prussian army officers to make up the motley army in a grand and exciting party around which "manifest destiny" threw something of halo.[2]

Toward this outrageous attack on a power with which the United States was at peace, the United States maintained at first a strictly correct attitude. True, the attack had been launched from the United States, and our authorities should not have permitted it to get away. But it was practically impossible to tell a group of filibusters from a group of adventurers who were really bound for the gold fields. The usual proclamations were made by President Pierce warning all good citizens against such scandalous conduct, and the United States attorneys in New York

[1] W. O. Scroggs, "William Walker and the Steamship Corporation of Nicaragua," *Amer. Historical Review*, X, 792ff.

[2] W. O. Scroggs, *Filibusters and Financiers* (N. Y., 1914), p. 7.

and New Orleans were ordered to stop any more such expeditions. These orders were carried out with the same lack of success which had been characteristic of the other wars of liberation in Latin America. Anyone who really wanted to could get away and join Walker's military empire in Central America. When Walker demanded recognition from the United States, Secretary of State Marcy at first refused, but subsequently recognition was allowed by President Pierce, who defended his action on the ground that Walker's government was the only one in Nicaragua and he had to recognize someone. At this, the southern Democrats rejoiced, because they saw more slave territory coming their way. And the northern Democrats rejoiced, because they were largely the Irish of New York, who were glad to see any direct slap at English interests.[3]

But in 1855 Vanderbilt made the mistake of going on a trip to Europe and leaving the Accessory Transit Company in the hands of his fellow-adventurer, Charles Morgan. Morgan determined to oust Vanderbilt in his absence and make all the money himself. Since William Walker was absolutely dependent on the good will of the Transit Company to supply him with men and munitions, he had to take orders from Morgan. Morgan made Walker annul the charter of the Accessory Transit Company and then create another company in which Morgan had the chief control and Vanderbilt was left out in the cold. Vanderbilt returned from Europe and when he found what had been done to him, he swore he would ruin Morgan, and incidentally William Walker.

Vanderbilt promptly went to work and was soon advancing money with which to pay for the armies of Walker's enemies in Honduras and Costa Rica, while Morgan backed Walker. Thus we have the spectacle of one American capitalist backing one set of Central American "patriots" while another American capitalist is egging on another set of "patriots." Needless to say Vanderbilt won out, as his armies from Costa Rica and Honduras defeated Walker, who was finally captured and shot. Meanwhile it seems to have been the policy of the United States to protest

[3] W. O. Scroggs, *Filibusters and Financiers*, pp. 172-6.

feebly against the activities of the filibusters while the American public applauded one or the other group of thugs, much as they applaud inter-collegiate football games to-day. If we understood the psychology back of the one, we understood what was back of the other.[4]

2. THE PUPPET PANAMA

Needless to say it was not by such antics that a canal was built. Moreover there is some ground for saying that all this turned the isthmian traffic away from Nicaragua and toward Panama. After all, the isthmus at Panama was the narrowest part of Central America. Here, too, the American interests had a railway which carried the gold diggers to California. This tempting bit of territory was owned by the Republic of New Granada (Colombia and Venezuela combined) and in 1848 the United States induced it to make a treaty which was to have momentous consequences. By this agreement the United States was granted a free right of way across the isthmus, in return for which

> "The United States guarantee . . . to New Granada . . . the perfect Neutrality of the before mentioned isthmus, with a view that the free transit from the one to the other sea, may not be interrupted or embarrassed at any future time while this treaty exists; and, in consequence, the United States also guarantee . . . the rights of sovereignty and property which New Granada has and possesses over the said territory." [5]

All of which clearly meant that the United States would protect the means of transit across the isthmus, railway or canal, and that New Granada gave her the right to protect this valuable means of communication, even though New Granada owned it. This amounted to giving the United States the permanent right to intervene for the protection of whatever railway or canal property she or her citizens built there.

But, as we have seen, the Clayton-Bulwer Treaty followed within two years and the canal was never built. Moreover, the Civil War in the United States soon distracted attention and by

[4] W. O. Scroggs, *Filibusters and Financiers*, 135-53; "William Walker and the Steamship Corporation of Nicaragua" in *Amer. Hist. Rev.*, X, 802-5; W. A. Croffut, *The Vanderbilts and the Story of their Fortune*, pp. 43ff.

[5] W. Malloy, *Treaties and Conventions*, I, 312.

the time that war was over the great transcontinental railways were being completed in North America, by which goods and emigrants could go directly overland to California. There was no longer any immediate need for worrying about a canal or railway at either Panama or Nicaragua.

Yet even if the United States lost interest in the canal, there were people who did not, and chief among these were the French. Her great engineer, De Lesseps, had just built the Suez Canal, why should he not repeat the feat at Panama? Moreover the war offices of the world were beginning to realize that there was something very valuable way down on the west coast of South America. More precious than the golden treasures which Pizarro had plundered from the Inca in 1535 were the nitrate beds of the desert of Atacama which neither Pizarro nor the Inca ever bothered to disturb. The age of chemistry had come. For centuries the chief constituent of gunpowder had been a nitrogenous compound. The English had had to go all the way to Bengal for their nitrates and the Germans counted themselves lucky when the discovery of their own great nitrate beds relieved them from the necessity of going far off. But the French stood in need of what Chile had to export. While it is not necessary to accept the idea that the French need for nitrates dictated her policy in Panama, still it is not surprising to find a French Company in 1878 getting a concession from the Republic of Colombia (which had superseded New Granada) to construct a waterway across the isthmus. In 1883 the French Company began to dig the canal, under the management of De Lesseps, with one Philippe Bunau-Varilla as chief engineer. We shall meet him again.[6]

All this aroused a great deal of discussion in the United States, whose hands had been tied to a certain extent by the Clayton-Bulwer Treaty. Secretary of State James G. Blaine and his successor F. T. Frelinghuysen tried to get rid of the incubus of the Clayton-Bulwer Treaty by insisting in the eighties that new conditions had arisen which changed the whole situation. In short,

---

[6] P. Bunau-Varilla, *Great Adventure in Panama* (N. Y., 1920), pp. 1–23, a book to be used with the utmost caution; E. C. Worden, *Nitro-cellulose Industry* (N. Y., 1911), II, 898ff.

the United States tried to break a contract without the consent of the other party, which is a dangerously Machiavellian doctrine whereby the State Department virtually announced it was going to break its promise because it was not to its interest to keep it. Fortunately for the credit of the United States, President Cleveland entered office at this juncture and withdrew from the Senate a treaty with Nicaragua which contemplated the building of a canal under American control in flagrant violation of our solemn promise to England. Although this saved the honor of the United States it did not build a canal, for the French Company soon failed signally on account of embezzlement and mismanagement of its funds, and because of the yet unconquered yellow fever.[7]

The Spanish American War, however, gave a dramatic illustration of the necessity for a canal. Not only did the battleship *Oregon* have to race all the way round Cape Horn in order to participate in the victory at Santiago,[8] but the new possessions of the United States in the Pacific were going to necessitate a quick passage of her fleet from ocean to ocean. The Clayton-Bulwer Treaty must in some way be ended. As has been seen, Secretary John Hay went about it as Blaine and Frelinghuysen ought to have gone at it in the first place. He negotiated the Hay-Pauncefote Treaty in 1900 whereby Britain at last released the United States from the galling burden of the Clayton-Bulwer Treaty and gave her a free hand to go ahead. There remained now only for the United States government to make up its mind where it would build a canal and get the consent of the owner of the territory. A Commission recommended that the canal be built at Nicaragua unless the French Company at Panama would sell its rights there for $40,000,000. Two lobbies in Congress were immediately formed, one backing the Nicaragua route and the other backing the Panama route.

Then came on the scene once more the picturesque figure of Philippe Bunau-Varilla. He had felt so keenly the failure of the

[7] M. W. Williams, *Anglo-American Isthmian Diplomacy*, p. 286.
[8] W. F. Johnson, *Four Centuries of the Panama Canal* (N. Y., 1906), pp. 99–108.

French to complete the canal that he had made his home in Panama, hoping against hope that some day the work would be completed. As a citizen of the isthmus and as a Frenchman he was interested in having the canal put at Panama and not at Nicaragua. How much further he was interested, it is impossible to say. But the activity he now displayed in going to Washington and dogging the footsteps of Mark Hanna, showed that he was very much interested indeed. Congress soon had before it the Hepburn Bill authorizing the construction of the canal at Nicaragua, but Bunau-Varilla and his lobby persuaded Senator Spooner to amend the bill so that if the French Company could be bought out and if Colombia could be induced to sell or rent a canal zone "within a reasonable length of time," the canal was to be built at Panama. Bunau-Varilla won over Mark Hanna, and Mark Hanna won over the Senate. But what was equally important, Bunau-Varilla now got his case before President Roosevelt and won him over, too.[9]

Secretary Hay promptly negotiated with Columbia the Hay-Herran Treaty of 1903, whereby the United States was to pay Colombia $10,000,000 and $250,000 per year and build the canal. Everything appeared to be going swimmingly when the Colombian Senate balked and refused to ratify the treaty. They seemed to think that strip of territory worth more than $10,000,000. President Roosevelt alleges that they wanted to delay matters until the French Company's franchise expired and then Colombia, instead of the French Company, would gather in the additional $40,000,000. At any rate the Colombians would not behave just as Roosevelt and Bunau-Varilla wanted them to. Bunau-Varilla was desperate. Something must be done or the canal might yet go to Nicaragua. Roosevelt with characteristic impatience became enraged at the procrastination of Colombia, and Bunau-Varilla danced around from Paris, to New York, to Panama.[10]

[9] H. Croly, *Marcus A. Hanna*, p. 379; S. M. Cullom, *Fifty Years of Public Service*, p. 281; P. Bunau-Varilla, *Panama, Its Creation, Destruction and Resurrection*, p. 247.

[10] T. Roosevelt, *Autobiography*, p. 565; J. F. Rhodes, supra, p. 267; *Foreign Relations for 1903*, 163.

Then the idea seems to have occurred to someone that if Panama could be induced to revolt against Colombia, it would be easier to deal with a new and tiny Republic which Bunau-Varilla could almost hold in his pocket, than with the recalcitrant Colombia. Revolutions were epidemic in Panama anyway. In fact in the previous fifty-three years there had been fifty-three revolutions or near revolutions. The United States, following the treaty of 1848 had usually interposed its force to protect its property and thus aided in putting down the disorder. Suppose instead of putting down the next one, the United States should simply let it go on and be successful? As Roosevelt says,

"I did not lift my finger to incite the revolutionists. I simply ceased to stamp out the different revolutionary fuses that were already burning." [11]

The result was soon apparent. A revolution broke out in Panama in 1902. This time the United States forces landed to protect the railway and refused to permit the Colombian troops to put down the revolt, on the ground that it would endanger American property rights, as most of the fighting would be bound to occur along the railway line. By this intervention, Colombia lost Panama in short order and forever. Roosevelt justified the intervention on the grounds that selfish nations like Colombia should not be allowed to hold up the progress of civilization by sitting like a dog in a manger across the most valuable transit route in the whole world. So Panama became an independent republic. Then the United States did one of the strangest things in the history of its foreign policy. We have seen many times in this volume that if there is one thing the United States has been careful about, it is the recognition of newly revolted countries before their independence was established beyond peradventure of a doubt. The Spanish American colonies had to wait years for recognition. But the United States recognized the new Republic of Panama within one week of its revolt! [12]

Moreover, the canal negotiations were now settled with M.

[11] T Roosevelt, *Autobiography*, p. 567; W. R. Thayer, *Life of John Hay*, II, 304–17.
[12] P. Bunau-Varilla, *Panama, Its Creation, Destruction and Resurrection*, p. 364; L. T. Chamberlain, "A Chapter of National Dishonor," *North American Review*, CXCV, 145.

Bunau-Varilla himself, at this time parading as "Envoy Extraordinary and Minister Plenipotentiary of the Republic of Panama." By the new "Hay-Bunau-Varilla" Treaty the Republic of Panama granted the United States a canal zone, ten miles wide, to be United States territory. For this, Panama now got the $10,000,000 and the rental of $250,000 per year which would otherwise have gone to Colombia. Moreover the United States guarantees the independence of Panama, and no subsequent action on the part of Panama may abridge this treaty. In fact Panama came under the sway of the United States as another "disguised protectorate." [13]

Thus was gained and built the Panama Canal. But one can scarcely read the story without some serious and embarrassing misgivings as to the conduct of the United States. Colombia felt that an outrageous injustice had been done to her. After all Panama was her territory, and if she chose to delay, or to refuse to sell it, it was her right. Roosevelt rode roughshod over her rights, for as he frankly says, "Colombia had forfeited every claim to consideration." This may or may not be true, but the fact will forever remain that the taking of Panama in the way it was done sent a shock through the whole of Latin America, and made every Latin American nation from Mexico to the Argentine feel that American foreign policy was now a thing which they had every reason to fear, instead of looking to it for protection, as they had in the past. The Monroe Doctrine had taken on a monstrous form to these Hispanic neighbors of the United States, and they have not hesitated to say that they do not like it in its new shape.[14]

After the excitement and enthusiasm of the affair had died down, the government of the United States began to realize that it had made a serious diplomatic blunder. The administration of President Taft tried to make amends by offering to pay Colombia some kind of an indemnity for what she had lost. Finally under Wilson's administration the United States agreed to pay $25,000,-

[13] P. Bunau-Varilla, supra, pp. 249, 364, 367, 372, 382; J. F. Rhodes, supra, p. 274.
[14] I. J. Cox, "The Colombia Treaty—Retrospect and Prospect," *Journal of International Relations*, XI, 549.

ooo to wipe out the blot caused by Roosevelt's Panama policy. This was practically an admission of the fact that what had been done was wrong and showed a desire to atone for it. This, at least, was creditable, for by the time the United States finally paid the sum in President Harding's administration she had become not only the most powerful nation in the western hemisphere, but the most powerful nation in the world. But to his death, Roosevelt opposed the treaty bitterly as blackmail, insisting that he had done what was right in Panama. In the midst of its world supremacy, the United States admitted its fault and paid for it. This, at least, was an example of international decency.[15]

Moreover, there is much to be said for what Roosevelt did. Latin American diplomacy seems to have inherited one of the worst qualities of Spanish diplomacy, and that is an inability to act quickly. The Latin American does not like to be hurried. But the building of a canal was a matter which demanded Yankee speed. That speed came into conflict with Latin leisureliness. Perhaps Roosevelt was right when he claimed that if he had not acted as he did, the canal would not have been built for several more years. Would this have made any difference? Well, M. Bunau-Varilla again gives a shrewd answer. The canal was finally opened in the same month which saw the opening of the European War. The nitrates for France did not begin to arrive one moment too soon. If Mr. Roosevelt had been more polite, perhaps they would still be coming by the long trip around Cape Horn.

3. Venezuela and the Drago Doctrine

While the United States continued its march down the Caribbean, Germany began to develop that policy of insisting that whenever anyone else got anything, she must have some "compensation" nearby. From the vantage point of years, it is now clear that German foreign policy was being shaped towards ends

[15] T. Roosevelt, *Fear God and take your own Part* (N. Y., 1916), pp. 305-42; *U. S. Treaty Series*, No. 661.

of which in 1902 the world was utterly ignorant. Having gotten her foothold in China and in Africa with the other powers of the world, Germany still lacked a naval base and coaling station in that American Mediterranean, the Caribbean Sea, where England and France held strategic points and where the United States had acquired Porto Rico. Moreover, Germany's political designs on Brazil, where German colonists were filling up the southern states, gave evidence of the power of the Pan-German movement.[16] She could hardly take any of the islands of the Caribbean as they were already owned by other European powers or were too close to the United States, so she selected that Caribbean nation most distant from the United States, where the merry-go-round of revolutions had given her a much desired opening to protect German interests.[17]

Venezuela, like so many of the Caribbean nations, had endured a century of despots since her independence, and each despot had borrowed money recklessly in Europe from English, French, or German bankers. Looking at England, the Germans believed that they, too, might build an empire on unpaid debts and assume their share of the white man's burden, with all its opportunities for the exploitation of backward races. After all, it was the fact that Egypt had borrowed money from England which she could not repay, that resulted in the British occupation of Egypt. Why should not Germany take Venezuela in the same way? Thereby she would acquire a coaling station within striking distance of the Panama Canal. Germany had not yet run afoul of the Monroe Doctrine and had on one occasion bullied Haiti under the threat of the bombardment of its capital, while the United States stood by and did nothing. To disguise her actions, Germany acted jointly with Britain and insisted that Venezuela at once pay those public debts which she owed bankers of the creditor states. There is no defense in either law or morals for Venezuela. Under the leadership of Cipriano Castro, a typical "caudillo" of the old school, Venezuela was steadily going

---

[16] L. Baum, "German Political Designs with Reference to Brazil," *Hispanic Amer. Hist. Review*, II, 586.

[17] J. Keim, *Forty Years of German-American Political Relations*, pp. 296–8.

from bad to worse and her action in refusing satisfaction certainly invited intervention and high-handed measures.[18]

Together Germany and England conducted a "pacific blockade" of Venezuela in 1901. The next logical step, when Castro was still obdurate, was forcible military occupation. But the result would have been to give Germany just that foothold she wanted in the Caribbean; for, following European precedent, it would have been a long time before she got out, once she had gotten in. Unless the Monroe Doctrine was to be forgotten, the United States must act. Secretary Hay notified both Germany and England that they must arbitrate. England showed her sincerity and her lack of ulterior motives by agreeing that an honest settlement of the public debts of Venezuela was just what she wanted, and if the United States could force Venezuela to arbitrate, that was exactly what England desired.

Germany showed her true colors by refusing to arbitrate. What she wanted was territory and she was so close to getting it from Venezuela that she had no intention of giving Venezuela time to recant. President Roosevelt was no man to avoid a direct challenge of this sort. He informed the German ambassador that unless Germany consented to arbitrate within a given length of time, the whole American Atlantic fleet under Admiral Dewey would be ordered to Venezuela to prevent the landing of the Germans. This was a notice to Germany that the American fleet would enforce the Monroe Doctrine against her. Still Germany did not take the matter seriously and on a second interview, Roosevelt told the German envoy that unless the Kaiser yielded to arbitration within forty-eight hours, Dewey would sail a day sooner than scheduled. Germany was suddenly and rudely awakened to the fact that this was an ultimatum and that further delay would mean war with the United States. That was the last thing Germany desired. She may have been planning a war at that time, but it was her aim to have England and the United States with her, and not against her when that war came. Within thirty-six hours the Kaiser offered to arbitrate and Roosevelt tactfully

[18] Keim, supra, 277, pp. 285-96.

praised him for his peaceful intentions. We have Dewey's own word for it that the Atlantic fleet was under orders to move with every battleship and every torpedo boat. It was this kind of an episode in which American foreign policy showed very definitely that the whole armed forces of the nation were now ready to back up the Monroe Doctrine, and that the British fleet, however much it had supported the Monroe Doctrine in the past, was now no longer necessary. The United States had her own "big stick," as Roosevelt phrased it.[19]

But the rebuff of Germany in Venezuela stirred up something else which was likely to have far greater import in the future. The United States interposed with the Monroe Doctrine at this point not so much because she was sorry for Venezuela as because she could not tolerate having a German naval base so close to the Canal. She intervened because it was to her interests to do so. The Argentine Republic now stepped on to the international stage and announced that there was something that vitally concerned it in all this. Acting as the spokesman for Latin America, the Argentine pointed out that the original cause of the trouble was the failure of Venezuela to pay her public debts. Luis Drago, the Argentinian minister for foreign affairs was unquestionably one of the ablest international lawyers in the world. He now addressed the United States and the world at large and announced that the Argentine would not admit that any nation, Germany or the United States, had the right to intervene in a South American Republic for the collection of a public debt. He pointed out the obvious fact that many nations in the past had suspended payment on their public debts, but that somehow intervention only seemed to follow in the case of those backward nations out of which the creditor nation thought that it could get some land. He pointed out with equal cogency that South American nations must be allowed to go through with the same period of international irresponsibility, though which each of the European nations had passed. If military intervention were allowed for

[19] W. R. Thayer, *Life of John Hay*, II, 286 and Appendix; N. Y. *Times*, May 27, 1916, for Dewey's testimony. J. H. Latané, *The United States and Latin America* (N. Y., 1921), p. 249ff.

the purpose of collecting debts due Englishmen, or Americans, or Germans, the whole of Latin America lately emerging from a backward condition would not be safe from the voracious great powers of the world.

Drago further insisted on the unquestioned fact that such intervention was a violation of the independence of the weaker state, which independence the United States had always boasted that it fostered and supported. A matter of purchasing government bonds from a notoriously revolutionary nation like Venezuela was a matter in which the foreign bankers ought to know that they were getting into trouble. The principle of "caveat emptor," or let the buyer beware of taking up such bonds, ought to be applied in cases of this sort. If, in spite of what he knew, a foreign banker persisted in buying the bonds of a stormy Caribbean republic, he had only himself to blame if he lost all his money. Certainly, contended Drago, he would have no right in international law to invoke military authority to help him out of the results of his own folly.[20]

This had in theory long been the policy of the United States, and the United States had tried not to interfere in behalf of its citizens who deliberately exposed themselves to the danger of losing their money in a foreign land. As President Roosevelt put it:

> "Our government has always refused to enforce such contractual obligations by an appeal to arms. It is to be wished that all foreign governments will take the same view."

It was only the backward debtor nation which actually committed violence that need fear the United States and her intervention, and Roosevelt drew a distinction between what the lawyers call a "tort" and what they call a "contract." In a case of "contract" the United States would not intervene to enforce the contract. But in the case of a "tort," which is a civil damage *not* arising from a contract, but from some other form of injury, the United States would not intervene to prevent the

[20] L. Drago, "State Loans in their Relation to International Policy," *Amer. Jour. of International Law*, I, 692ff,

LUIS M. DRAGO

offensive Caribbean Republic from getting exactly what it deserved.[21]

Drago wanted the United States to go on record as favoring a rule of international law which would prevent the forcible collection of public debts in the future. By this time the Argentine was big enough and strong enough and important enough to demand a hearing in the councils of the nations. Yet despite its lip loyalty to the Drago Doctrine at the Pan-American Conference at Rio in 1906 and at the Hague Conference in 1909, the United States soon became enmeshed in just the situation the keen-witted Drago had foreseen.

4. DOMINICAN DIFFICULTIES

When all is said and done, the United States has exercised some marvelous self-restraint in the Dominican Republic. A glance at the map is necessary here to understand that the Dominican Republic occupies the eastern end of that ancient Island of Hispaniola on which Columbus made his first settlement. It is practically a mulatto Republic, as the Spaniards killed off all the Indians centuries ago and hundreds of thousands of negro slaves took their place. (See Map, p. 310.)

Born amidst revolutions, this Republic has never given up the habit of rehearsing them at frequent intervals during its troubled existence. Its independence was due to a small group of really patriotic and enlightened men, whose aspirations were no sooner crowned with success than they fell out among themselves, and so began that series of tragical comedies best told by the continual repetition of the following formula: "A General rode into Santo-Domingo City; seized the customs-house; overthrew the government; had himself elected president and so remained until overthrown himself by a similar process." The customs-house was the crux of the situation, for the opposing army usually deserted to the side which had a paymaster, i. e., the side which held the customs-house.

From its independence in 1844 to its third annexation to

---

[21] *Foreign Relations of the United States 1906*, pt. I, p. xlix.

Spain in 1861, the story of the Dominican Republic revolves around the names of two "generals," Pedro Santana and Buenaventura Baez, who alternated in control of the Republic. Occasionally a puppet of one or the other of them gained the presidency, but in the main it is probably not far wrong to say that these two, by alternate revolutions, gained and lost the supreme power. With these revolutions went their usual accompaniments. There were practically no parties, save the personal following of the leaders. In Anglo-Saxon countries the attempt, at least, is made to designate parties by words which designate principles. In the more backward of the Latin American Caribbean Republics a party name is simply the name of the party leader with the letters "-ista" suffixed thereto. Politics is still a matter of personality rather than of principle.[22]

This period of swapping presidencies for exiles came to an end with each of the leaders trying to sell out his country to a foreign power. In 1861 Santana, actuated by various motives, not the least among which was a desire to make secure his own position and domination as a Spanish Captain-General, deliberately got Spain to reannex her lost colony. He chose a fortunate moment when the United States, busy with its war between the States, could not assert the Monroe Doctrine. But it did not last long, for another revolution caused Spain to get out which she was apparently glad to do to get rid of the troublesome Santo Domingo.[23]

Santana died in the midst of the last war for independence, and no sooner was the Spanish flag lowered for the last time on the customs-houses of Santo Domingo than the leaders revived the internecine strife which characterizes Dominican history. A protracted revolt, such as that which had driven out the Spaniard, always produced a crop of "generals," each with an equal claim to the presidency. Only one could be elected, and the others would stage a revolution and displace him. The displaced "general" would promptly take to the

[22] O. Schoenrich, *Santo Domingo, A Country with a Future* (N. Y., 1918).
[23] G. H. Stuart, *Latin America and the United States* (N. Y., 1922), pp. 209–10.

woods, join other disgruntled "generals," and make things hot for the newly "elected" president. Then, when the time was ripe, they would conduct another revolution, install another president, whose victim would take to the woods along with the late revolutionists who had not received fat rewards, or the "generals" who had not succeeded in becoming president. No comedy was ever penned which is, in one sense, more absurd than the political history of the Dominican Republic.

After the expulsion of the Spanish, Baez came back and began an administration which is marked by two important events. First of these was the Hartmont loan, the first of a series of almost childish financial transactions which ultimately led Santo Domingo into the position of semi-independence which it now occupies. To put this transaction briefly, President Baez induced the London bankers, Hartmont and Co., to float a loan for $3,788,000 for the Republic. Of this the Dominican Treasury was to receive about one-half ($1,600,000). Yet the Dominican Republic agreed to pay as interest and on the sinking fund in twenty-five years the amount of $7,362,500. Hartmont and Co. were to receive $500,000 as commission. In fact, the Dominican Republic received but $190,000 in this transaction, for which it was ultimately to repay $7,000,000! Approximately this represents borrowing money at 140% interest per annum; a very good investment from the standpoint of Hartmont and Co.[24]

The other important event of the last Baez administration was the attempt to get the United States to annex Santo Domingo. Approved by a plebiscite (conducted by the Baez administration) the project was taken up by President Grant, of the United States. One will scan the pages of the *Foreign Relations* in vain for any information about this business, and the reason is not far to seek. Grant never bothered to consult his Secretary of State! He simply sent one of his numerous idle army friends, General Babcock, to Santo Domingo to look the situation

[24] J. H. Hollander, "The Readjustment of San Domingo's Finances," *Quarterly Journal of Economics*, XXI, 405; "Financial Difficulties of San Domingo," *Annals of the Amer. Acad.*, XXX, 93.

over. The first thing official Washington knew, Babcock was back with a Treaty of Annexation all signed, sealed and delivered, and wanting only the consent of the United States Senate to make the Dominican Republic part of the United States. Secretary of State Hamilton Fish could but gasp at this high-handed dealing with matters which should have come under his care. The cabinet supported Fish in insisting that the thing had been improperly done. When the Senate got hold of the treaty Senator Sumner, who was then chairman of the Senate Committee on Foreign Relations, made a personal affair out of the thing and attacked Grant and all Grant's office-holding relatives with all the invective and sarcasm of which he was a master. The treaty was killed by Sumner's personal dislike for Grant. Then Grant had a regular treaty made in a regular way, after due investigation on the part of an American Commission properly sent out by the Department of State, but this second effort failed as the first one had. Suffice it to say that the United States twice had Santo Domingo within the hollow of its hand, *with the consent of the Dominicans*, and twice refused to take it in 1871.[24a]

But if the United States would not have her as a free gift the poor Dominican Republic was now condemned to more years of anarchy and dictatorship, with more of that wild financial mismanagement which has brought her to her present position. Since the original war of independence there had grown up in Santo Domingo a generation which could only look upon war and revolution as a normal state of affairs, and regard a successful revolution as a normal method of election. Baez gave way to a new dictator, General Ulises Heureaux, a full-blooded negro, a patriot, politician, bandit, and horse-thief. In 1887 he began that régime of enforced peace such as the Republic had not known for a long time. But it was a peace of terrorism, for Heureaux was probably the most ruthless, the most autocratic, the most tyrannical of all the Dominican despots. In his administration came another of those remarkable pieces of financial

[24a] J. B. Cox, "How Judge Hoar ceased to be Attorney-General," *Atlantic Monthly*, lxxvi, 164; *Report of the Secretary of State in Regard to San* [sic] *Domingo* (Wash., 1871); *Report of the Commission of Inquiry to Santo Domingo* (Wash., 1871).

manipulation which delivered the Republic into the hands of its creditors. The Dutch firm of Westendorp and Co. floated a loan for Heureaux and protected itself by organizing and taking over the management of the customs-houses. This was a good arrangement, but it was based on nothing stronger than the legal and moral rights of the Amsterdam bankers, rights which did not go very far in the land of revolutions. The result was a default in payments which charged up another account to be settled in the future. Meanwhile Heureaux was harried and harassed, like all Dominican presidents, by political conspiracies which had to be bought off or crushed—and either process required money. Yet at the same time he was dunned by insistent creditors, who were the very persons to whom he had to look for further advances. His methods were necessarily arbitrary, and he was fond of saying that he didn't care what history said about him, as he wouldn't be here to read it. Some New Yorkers organized the Santo Domingo Improvement Co., which attempted, after 1892, to handle the finances of the republic. This kept things going for a while, as the Improvement Company took charge of the collection of the customs duties and administered that branch of the civil service so as to get the most out of it. But the reckless waste, frightful inefficiency, and gross mismanagement, graft and corruption of the Dominican officials went on as before. The Santo Domingo Improvement Co. was in the position of a careful creditor who had no more to do than keep carefully his side of the accounts against a reckless debtor.

The debt was only partly funded and a large floating debt kept accumulating. It increased with every revolution, which entailed more veterans to pension, more enemies to buy off, more "generals" to whom blackmail must be paid, a greater destruction of foreign property to be paid for, more arms and munitions to be purchased, more "friends" to be mollified by graft. Heureaux' assassination in 1899 found the Republic in an almost inconceivable state, not only of bankruptcy, but of helplessness. It was in this situation that President Roosevelt finally decided that if the Monroe Doctrine forbade Belgium, France, Italy and

Germany from intervening, he would have to devise some other way of getting them paid. The Westendorp arrangement suggested the solution. Since the customs-houses were always the pawn in the game, the United States would take them over and supervise a few years of honest administration and stable government and clear off the debt.

But the Department of State then made a treaty with the Dominican Republic whereby that disorderly country, in order to escape the intervention which it richly deserved from Europe, agreed to let the United States act as its Receiver in Bankruptcy, to collect and spend its customs revenues and to stave off the European creditors. Under this arrangement, the Dominicans received only 45% of their revenues, and the other 55% went to satisfy their creditors. When this arrangement was finally put into operation, "on the forty-five per cent basis the Santo Domingan Government received from us a larger sum than it ever received before when nominally all the revenue went to it." [25]

When the Dominican Convention came before the Senate for its approval, there was strenuous protest. What constitutional warrant was there whereby the President should commit the United States to act as a receiver in bankruptcy for another nation? Senator Tillman, of South Carolina, denounced our new policy on the ground that the United States was saying to Santo Domingo, "Here we are, your big brother; you are not behaving right, you have got to settle and if you do not settle, we will whip you and make you settle." The opposition to the President's policy was so emphatic that the Senate adjourned without ratifying the treaty, and left the President in an awkward situation. But the resourceful Roosevelt promptly called the treaty an "executive agreement," proceeded to put it in force, and declared that he would keep on enforcing it that way until the Senate did ratify it. [26]

The effect in Santo Domingo was magical. The customs-houses,

[25] T. Roosevelt, *Autobiography*, ch. xiv.
[26] *Cong. Record*, Vol. 40, 798–9; 1174–5.

no longer being available for loot, the revolutions diminished, the debt was gradually paid off and the Senate even finally consented to ratify the treaty in a slightly amended form. But this very stability and prosperity made available other forms of public plunder and after some years of successful management, another revolution broke out and the old chaos came back. Something more severe was evidently required. In the Convention of 1907 there had been a section which provided that "the Government of the United States will give to the Receiver and his assistants such protection as it may find requisite for the performance of their duties." With another revolution imminent in 1916, the patience of the American Government was at last exhausted. The prospect presented two alternatives: either the United States could stand by and watch the Dominican Government enmesh itself further in domestic trouble with the consequent destruction of life and property, additional danger of foreign complication in the harm to foreign European interests, or else the United States could send its own troops into the country, quell the revolt and start the governmental machinery going again. So with the consent of the President of the Dominican Republic and under the clause in the treaty which gave the United States the right to protect the Receiver and his assistants, the United States marines in 1916 conducted a campaign in behalf of the *de jure* government against the revolutionist leader. There is no use of disguising this action under soft words. It was intervention of the plainest type. Strictly speaking, one may say that since the troops were invited to land, the interference was not contrary to the will of the Dominican Government. But one would want to know by whom the marines were invited to land and whether it was done by his own free will, for President Henriquez has insisted that neither the Treaty of 1907 nor any other treaty ever gave the United States any right of supervision over, or interference in, the political life of the Republic and his own abdication was in protest against the action of the United States Government.

A new treaty was then negotiated, the principal features of

which were the collection of the customs duties under American auspices, the appointment of an American financial adviser, and the establishment of a constabulary force officered by Americans. To this President Henriquez refused to accede on the ground that it destroyed Dominican independence, and thereupon Admiral Knapp of the United States Navy, acting under Article III of the Treaty of 1907, declared Santo Domingo under the military administration of the United States.

American occupation and administration dragged along until 1922, when Secretary of State Hughes induced the Dominicans to get together and start over again. Under this arrangement the United States troops could be withdrawn and the Dominican Republic started once more on her troubled and troublesome career. In reviewing the whole situation, a judicial observer cannot but see that while the Dominicans do not like very much what the United States has done, they dislike the way it has been done very much more. They seem to welcome American aid and advice, but they resent the lack of a definite policy. One minute they are independent and the next they certainly are not. Apparently the United States follows neither a fixed policy of assuming the responsibility which the Monroe Doctrine implies, nor will it permit any other nation to assume such a responsibility. But one cannot avoid the conclusion that if a Caribbean nation will not pay its debts, the United States will assume the position of being a receiver in bankruptcy and enforce her will with machine guns till that particular crisis is passed. The next crisis is handled as a separate problem, and the Dominicans cannot be sure just what the next solution will be. The policy of the United States seems to be to make the Dominican Republic pay her debts and then leave her until she gets into trouble again. During the period of American occupation the internal progress of the island, educational and social, is certainly marked. But people do not like to know that they are being civilized from the outside.[27]

---

[27] *Annual Report of the the Secretary of Navy for 1920*, pp. 193, 321–43; Carl Kelsey, "American Intervention in Haiti and Santo Domingo," in *Annals of the Amer. Acad.*, C, No. 189.

5. THE HANDLING OF HAITI

The rather lengthy story of the Dominican difficulties makes any extended consideration of Haiti unnecessary. The other end of the island of Hispaniola is occupied by one of the strangest Republics in the world. It can hardly be called even a mulatto republic, for it is really a black republic. Here during the French Revolution, we have seen how the slaves exterminated the whites and mulattoes. The blacks then spent about a hundred years trying to operate a responsible democratic government, with neither education nor experience and no inclination to acquire either. The result is a classic example of what happens when a backward people are left to their own devices and when the white man will not assume his burden. The frightful round of revolutionary orgies in Haiti make Dominican history seem very mild indeed. By 1915 it was perfectly evident that no civilized government could function there without outside assistance. There was the same story of money borrowed from European bankers, which the Haitians, to judge by their actions, did not intend to try to pay back. Indeed, Germany does not seem to have learned her lesson in Venezuela and on the very day the European War opened the German cruiser *Karlsrhue* unloaded an armed force of German troops who were headed off by the news that their presence was urgently needed against England. The United States had to act, not only to preserve the Monroe Doctrine again, but to terminate the perfectly appalling conditions of anarchy, savagery and oppression then prevalent in Haiti.[28]

When the armed forces of the United States landed in 1915 they reëstablished order by strong-arm methods. This was military intervention of the baldest kind. A treaty was forced on Haiti, whereby the United States practically established a protectorate. In creating this relationship, the United States marines used methods which practically amounted to war, and in the conflict which has been going on sporadically ever since, the conduct of the United States marines has been violently criticised

[28] R. Lansing, in *Cong. Record*, Vol. 62, pp. 6485–88.

and vigorously defended.[29] It has been alleged by the Haitians that American troops have committed all sorts of atrocities on the peaceful citizens of the Island. Considering the type of people with whom they had to deal, it is not difficult to understand that such men as make up the United States marines, might not have been exactly mild in their conduct. The problem is a fearfully complicated one and the educated Haitians are extremely sensitive and resentful of the virtual destruction of their independence, as evidenced by the following comments by a distinguished Haitian lawyer,

"We are a conquered and helpless people. The United States has abolished every real form of self-government. . . . Why do American interests want Haiti? For one thing, labor is cheaper there than almost any other place on earth. It can be obtained for the sum of 20 cents a day, a fact enthusiastically boasted of in a recent prospectus of the Haitian-American Sugar Co. . . . If the United States desires to annex Haiti, to make it an American colony, of which America's every single act affords convincing evidence—why not say so? Why continue the sham and hypocrisy of pretending, against the will of the entire Haitian people, that you are there for philanthropic reasons?"[30]

The policy of the United States seems to be to maintain an army of occupation in Haiti for an indefinite period under the treaty of 1915. Impartial Haitians must admit that the intervention has brought peace and political stability, but sincerely patriotic Haitians cannot but hope that the United States will live up to all its fine pretensions about the rights of small nations and get out. The lack of a consistent policy lays the United States open to a great deal of criticism from the various Latin American nations with whom she is trying hard to remain on good terms. It leaves her occupying strategic points in the Caribbean most of the time and dominating those republics in a way which hardly fits with the professions of political idealism which have so often been made at peace conferences and in the speech-making tours of the Presidents and Secretaries of State. The fact is that the Monroe Doctrine has reached a stage in its evolution where

[29] *Hearings of the Committee on Haiti and Santo Domingo* (Wash., 1922), pp. 336, 344, 348.
[30] Pierre Hudicourt, reprinted in *Cong. Record*, Vol. 62, 7222–4.

it no longer implies merely the right of the United States to protect those wayward children of the Caribbean, but it also implies
the responsibility for seeing to it that they do not make international nuisances of themselves. If the United States does not
see to it, some one else will. No wonder then, that an enlightened American observer calls upon his countrymen either
to get in or get out. At present it seems as if they were trying to do both.[31]

6. CENTRAL AMERICAN POLICY

If the American policy toward the islands of the Caribbean
has been opportunist the policy toward Central America has been
equally so. In that part of the world are some troublous states,
yet it seems once to have been the seat of a relatively high civilization, whose archælogical remains may be for the future what
the ruins of ancient Greece and Rome were to the nineteenth
century. But the descendants of that civilization have descended
so far that it now seems necessary to begin to civilize some of
them all over again. Time and again in the last hundred years
efforts have been made to get these five republics of Central
America together. But as often as treaties or constitutions have
been drawn up making a union of Guatemala, El Salvador, Honduras, Nicaragua and Costa Rica, so often have come revolutions
which broke them apart. If the United States has had any consistent policy in Central America, it has been to try to persuade
these nations to get together, and to help them in the establishment of a Central American Union. But apparently just now, it
cannot be done. In Guatemala alone there is an Indian population of 66%, which speaks 36 different dialects. There is no railway running the length of Central America and until some such
means of communication is built it seems useless to expect political union. Illiteracy averages 75%, and personality, not principle, is the rule in politics. Politics seem to mean revolutions.
Here, as in the island republics, is seen again the result of presum-

[31] Carl Kelsey, "American Intervention in Haiti and Santo Domingo," *Annals of Amer.
Acad.*, C, 163–5.

ing a people capable of self-government, when their political education has been sadly retarded.[32]

In 1906 an unusually severe round of wars and revolutions in Central America led the United States to conclude that President Zelaya of Nicaragua was a professional trouble-maker. In an effort to prevent continuous warfare in that region, the United States persuaded them all to sign a treaty creating a Central American Court of Justice, to which they were all to refer their differences and in which it was hoped they would compose those differences. President Zelaya participated in this matter with true Latin American courtesy, and a determination not to be bound by it. He continued his trouble-making and soon gave the United States an opening by executing two American citizens who were participating in a rebellion against him. The United States promptly severed diplomatic relations with Nicaragua, and that nation was in such a perilous financial condition that the action of the United States led to the downfall of Zelaya.[33]

But the revolutions in Nicaragua continued because Zelaya was, after all, the only type of a president who could maintain himself in Nicaragua. The United States had extensive property interests in Nicaragua, and there was always the idea that some day it would be necessary to build that long-delayed canal. Hence the United States intervened with an armed force in behalf of one of the groups of revolutionists. Having set up this group as a puppet government, a treaty was then arranged with it by which two sets of banking interests in New York were to lend their aid and the United States government was to supply the financial supervisor, with armed forces to back him up. It was hoped by this means to set Nicaragua on her feet as was being done in Santo Domingo. The New York banks began to do their part, when the United States Senate balked and naturally the bankers stopped advancing money. But they did hold the railway as security and naturally have demanded protection for

[32] E. Perry, "Central American Union," *Hispanic American Historical Review*, V, 30; W. E. Browning, "Central American Republics and their Problems," in *Mexico and the Caribbean* (Clark Univ., 1920), p. 277.
[33] D. C. Munro, *Five Republics of Central America* (Oxford, 1918), pp. 227ff.

that property whenever a revolution threatens. A permanent small army of occupation of United States marines is stationed at Managua, the capital of Nicaragua, and a warship is always on duty at Corinto, a Nicaraguan seaport.[34]

Having reëstablished order in Nicaragua with an iron hand in Taft's administration, the United States now proceeded to negotiate a treaty with the government which its forces were maintaining in power. By this agreement Nicaragua sold the United States for $3,000,000 the right to the San Juan River as a new canal route, and the right to have a naval base on the Gulf of Fonseca to protect the western end of the canal when built. This Bryan-Chamorro Treaty in 1916 looked like a step in the right direction and seemed to contemplate another canal, even though it was negotiated with a government which could not very well refuse us anything we asked. But the trouble was that Nicaragua was selling us something which she did not have the exclusive right to sell. Costa Rica claimed that she had some rights to the San Juan River and a glance at the map will show that it is a boundary river for part of its length and consequently could not be wholly disposed of by Nicaragua. El Salvador objected to the naval base on the Gulf of Fonseca, and another glance at the map will show that both Honduras and El Salvador front on that gulf as well as Nicaragua. They naturally took the case up in the Central American Court of Justice which handed down a decision in favor of Costa Rica and El Salvador and against the acts of Nicaragua and the United States. Having no jurisdiction over the United States, it could do no more. But the United States and Nicaragua serenely ignored the decision of the court, which thereafter speedily went out of existence, having been given its deathblow by the United States.[35] (See Map, p. 230.)

It is this kind of thing which makes it so hard to define our Central American policy. The Nicaraguan affair virtually left the United States in the position of establishing a court to keep peace in Central America, and then destroying it because it did

---

[34] Munro, supra, pp. 252–4.
[35] Ibid., pp. 254–7.

not decide her way. Since 1912 the Government of Nicaragua has been practically maintained by the support of the United States marines, and even though it has not necessarily represented the majority of the people of Nicaragua, it has at least kept order. Whether or not this is consistent with American political idealism, the reader can make up his own mind. But he ought not to forget that if he wants his bananas, his coffee and sugar on his cereal at breakfast and if he wants to eat them from a mahogany table, he has some responsibility for our Central American policy, from which those things come.[36]

A final abortive attempt to establish a Union of Central America was made by Secretary of State Hughes in 1921, but the non-adherence of Nicaragua and the revolution in Guatemala after the matter had been agreed upon, seem to prove this effort as futile as previous ones. There is indeed a big work for the formulation of the policy of the United States in Central America and the Caribbean.[37]

7. MODERN PAN-AMERICANISM

Having done all this, and many other things which seem equally illogical and hostile to the Latin American mind, the United States has also been struggling to advance a policy of coöperation with these nations to the south. For even if she were big and strong enough to lord it over these weaker brethren, it would be extremely shortsighted to do so. The fact that the United States was having her troubles with some of the backward republics of Central America had not prevented the growth and development of republics below the equator whose civilization and progress was quite the equal of her own. It was the policy of the United States to try to cultivate friendly relations with Argentine, Brazil, Chile, and Uruguay and the other advanced nations of Latin America. Now, as we have seen, Pan-Americanism was a thing which originated in South America itself, but in its early days it was a rather futile sentiment. Sev-

[36] S. G. Inman, "Present Situation in the Caribbean," in *Mexico and the Caribbean*, p. 260.
[37] S. de la Selva, "On the proposed Union of Central America," *Hispanic-American Historical Review*, III, 566.

eral efforts were made in South America to revive the idea after Bolivar passed from the stage, but these were aimed rather at creating a Latin American solidarity as against the United States and its filibusters, than at any scheme of coöperation between the Americas.

In 1879, when Chile, Peru and Bolivia were at war over the nitrate fields of the desert of Atacama, James G. Blaine, then Secretary of State for President Garfield, conceived the idea of resurrecting Pan-Americanism as a means of stopping that war. Blaine, whatever else may be said of him, was a man of large vision and when he was rebuffed in his efforts to get the warring Latin American powers to compose their differences, he turned his energies toward getting together a Conference representing all the independent nations of the Americas. President Garfield's untimely death cut short the plan and Blaine's successor, Frelinghuysen, did not seem to comprehend the possibilities of the movement. Moreover, the devasting War of the Pacific continued until Chile had thoroughly defeated both Bolivia and Peru, and taken from them the nitrate fields. This created a veritable Alsace-Lorraine in South America and for the time being any Conference whose keynote was coöperation was decidedly out of place.[38]

But by 1889 Mr. Blaine had again become Secretary of State under President Harrison and the idea of an inter-American meeting reached its fruition in the First Pan-American Conference, which met at Washington. Its principal accomplishment was the creation of the Bureau of American Republics, a kind of clearing house for information in matters inter-American. This organization is composed of the ministers at Washington from each of the American nations, under the presidency of the Secretary of State of the United States. It has since changed its name to the Pan-American Union and is housed in a magnificent marble building, the gift of Mr. Andrew Carnegie. It is the heart of the Pan-American Movement and was virtually "put on the

[38] A. C. Wilgus, "James G. Blaine and the Pan-American Movement," in *Hispanic American Historical Review*, V. 662; W. S. Robertson, *Hispanic-American Relations with the United States* (N. Y., 1923), pp. 151, 390.

map" by its Director John Barrett.   His work is at present being ably carried on by his successor, Dr. Leo S. Rowe.[39]

In the Pan-American Union, each nation retains its independence, of course, and all the recommendations are merely advisory. It has promoted the several Pan-American Conferences which have periodically tried to offer solutions for some of the most important inter-American problems.   The Second Pan-American

UNITED STATES PENETRATION IN THE CARIBBEAN SEA

Based on Bowman's "The New World" by permission of the author and the World Book Company, publishers.

Conference was held at Mexico City in 1901–2 and advanced the principle that pecuniary claims should be submitted to arbitration when other diplomatic means failed.   The Third Pan-American Conference met at Rio de Janeiro in 1906 and supported the Drago Doctrine, which it agreed to carry on to the Second Hague Conference which was to meet in 1909.   The Fourth Pan-American Conference met at Buenos Aires in 1910 and made a variety of recommendations, most of which were highly advisable but

[39] All readers interested in the Pan-American Movement should be familiar with the publications of the Pan-American Union.

which it will take a long time to work out. A Fifth Conference was planned for Santiago in Chile in 1914, but the European War postponed it. It finally met in 1923 and discovered a very much changed world. Most of the Latin American Nations had by this time joined the League of Nations, while the United States stayed out. The conference met under the chairmanship of Augustin Edwards of Chile, who was also President of the League of Nations. President Edwards made quite clear that he regarded Pan-Americanism as a useful factor in securing joint and coöperative action by the American nations in the League of Nations, and the whole conference left little doubt but that the Latin-Americans are now definitely committed to that League, despite the efforts of the United States to minimize it.[40] For the rest this conference, like its predecessors, had to confine itself to discussion, recommendations and the promotion of the coöperative spirit.

After all, that is about all there is to Pan-Americanism. It is a sentiment, or feeling, that there ought to be a better understanding and closer coöperation between the Americas. It is at least the avowed policy of all the members of the Pan-American Union to promote that feeling. In this world where it is beginning to be understood that a sentiment of friendship and a will to peace must underlie international coöperation, the usefulness of the Pan-American Movement must be admitted, even if it is somewhat nebulous in its purposes and accomplishments. That such a work of clearing up misunderstanding is badly needed is well evidenced by such remarks as the following from a Latin American author:

"South America detests the United States because of its fraudulent elections, its commercial deceit, its ridiculous Colonel Roosevelt, its shirt-sleeve diplomacy, . . . the secession of Panama, . . . its usurpation of the customs of Santo Domingo, the blood it has shed and the independence it has frustrated in Nicaragua, . . . the revolutions it has fomented in Mexico, its aggressive imperialism and its conduct towards Spanish America during the last half century." [41]

[40] Augustin Edwards, "Latin America and the League of Nations," Current History, XVIII, 181.
[41] Blanco Fombona, Los Grandes Escritores de América, p. 86.

Of course, this is not representative of Latin American opinion of the United States, but neither are the orations of fulsome praise which fill the pages of the reports of the Pan-American Conferences, and which are not always profound.[42]   There is no use for the people of the United States to blind themselves to the fact that there is a noisy and influential group of Latin Americans who make it their business to keep alive anti-United States propaganda.   Chief among these is one Manuel Ugarte who says, "The eagle of the North will bury its talons in the vitals of Latin America and devour it."   With dramatic gestures this group point to her creeping down the Caribbean as positive proof of the fact that the United States is bent on seizing republic after republic and nation after nation, dominating their politics, monopolizing their industries and acquiring their mines and oil wells, and enforcing the will of the Yankee "colossus" at the point of the bayonet.[43]

If the United States is misunderstood and reviled in Latin America because of all the land she has taken from Spanish America, from Florida and Louisiana to Nicaragua and Panama, it is not altogether the fault of Latin America.   It is this kind of misunderstanding that can only be cleared up by acts, not by professions, on the part of the United States.   But the popular misunderstandings due to racial antagonisms or business competitions or intellectual incompatibility can be to a large measure overcome by an intelligent Pan-Americanism.   The Pan-American Union is certainly doing its part, but there seems to be considerable doubt as to whether other agencies of the government always do their share.

[42] W. E. Dunn, "Post-War Attitude of Hispanic America toward the United States," *Hispanic American Historical Review*, III, 177.

[43] E. Perry, "Anti-American Propaganda in Hispanic America," *Hispanic American Historical Review*, III, 17ff; S. G. Inman, "Imperialistic America," *Atlantic Monthly*, CXXXIV, 107.

CHAPTER XIV

OPENING AND SHUTTING THE DOOR TO CHINA

"The patrimony of the people, the produce of which is destined
to support the burdens of the republic or the royal dignity, may not
be alienated by kings, neither in the whole nor in part."—*Grotius.*

1. THE PROBLEM OF CHINA

There have been two underlying principles in the policy of the
United States toward China. The first has been to keep the Chinese emigrants out of the United States. We have one race problem and we do not want another. The other policy has been to
insist that China be allowed to retain her political and economic
independence, because we wanted to sell to her and buy from her,
and we knew well that if she were partitioned among half a dozen
different nations, we could do neither.

China is possessed of an ancient civilization. The main trouble
with it is the fact that in modern times, it is still ancient. China
includes an area of the earth which is very rich, and despite centuries of unscientific agriculture, it continues to produce very
remarkable crops. Mineral wealth certainly lies beneath her
soil, in what quantities remains to be seen.[1] China has a population which numbers hundreds of millions. But it is extremely
doubtful whether China can be called a nation in any sense. She
is not even two nations; sometimes it seems as though she were
half a dozen nations.[2] Within those nations teems a population
which has been toiling for centuries to grub a bare subsistence
from the soil, and making a fearful failure of it. Famines periodically sweep away their millions. The greatest land empire of
history once included China. Mr. H. G. Wells does not have
much time for heroes, and particularly for military heroes. But

[1] P. S. Reinsch, *American Diplomat in China* (N. Y., 1922), p. 223. Early reports on
China's resources were probably exaggerated.

[2] John Dewey, "Divided China," *New Republic* XXV, 187; XXVII, 212, 235.

the rulers of the great Mongol Empires come in for a greater
share of glory than a Frederick the Great or Napoleon. China
was part of these great Mongol Empires.[3] China has in a sense
a glorious past, but that is part of her trouble. While she has
been contemplating that past, the nations of the west have
overtaken her in civilization and outstripped her in every line of
material progress. As to spiritual and intellectual progress,
both China and the United States can claim to be on a higher
plane than the other—there is no way of proving which is
right.

Indeed, it is this reverence of the Chinese for their ancestors
which has imbued them with characteristics which have made
western nations take a special attitude toward them. The Chinese seem to think that they owe it to their ancestors to breed
large families. They marry young and have many children. Old
maids are almost unknown and the childless woman is an object
of pitying contempt. While the United States is producing three
generations, the Chinese produce four. The result is their enormous population with its tremendous capacity for increase, held
in check only by the brutality of famines, the curse of ignorance
of hygiene and sanitation, and still, in many cases, the actual
killing of undesired female children. What would happen if the
benevolent medical missionaries could have their way and save
the hundreds of thousands of children who are dying? Where
would they live and who would feed them? The white nations
have evidently determined that they shall not overrun the lands
the white man has staked out for himself.[4]

Centuries of disease in China has enabled the survival of a race
which can exist on a far lower standard of living than is possible
among western nations. Hence in any competition with the
Chinese, it is by no means certain that the white man could ultimately hold his own. As a result, there has grown up among
western nations a set of half-fearful, half-naïve notions about
China. The idea is abroad that the slowly-multiplying, high-

[3] H. G. Wells, *Outline of History* (NR ed.), II, ch. xxxiv.
[4] E. A. Ross, *The Changing Chinese* (N. Y., 1914), ch. iv.

wage, white peoples will be swamped with the outward thrust of the overflowing Chinese. Another idea is current that the time will come when the white nations of the world, who have lately been so busy committing suicide, will be overmatched by the colossal armies of well-drilled and well-armed yellow men led by some second Jenghis Khan. Yet another fear has seized certain white men that China with her resources of coal, oil, and iron and her millions of cheap laborers, who know no hours of work nor labor laws, will finally produce an industrial civilization which will rapidly undersell the rest of the world. These fears taken collectively are known as the "yellow peril." It is the policy of most white nations, including the United States, to resist this possible expansion of China as threatening their own existence. But, at the same time, they want to do business with her. These two ideas explain much of the American diplomacy with China.[5]

2. THE BURLINGAME TREATY

The trade of the white nations with China and the orient explains some of the most important things in the history of the world. As we have seen, it underlay the very discovery of America itself. The urge to Oregon was, as was pointed out in the chapter on Anglo-American diplomacy, largely a question of fur and the fur found some of its best markets in China. But although the Chinese would allow fur to be sold to the merchants of Canton, they would open no other ports nor would they allow either trader or diplomat to get into the interior of China. Both British and Americans soon realized they had a great many things they could sell to the Chinese, but there was no getting by the door so politely but firmly shut in their faces by the rulers of the Empire. One of the by-products of Chinese civilization was that for centuries they felt themselves infinitely superior to all other nations. When the English first attempted to get into communication with the Chinese Emperor, that Celestial returned to George III a letter which, for withering sarcasm, pity-

[5] E. A. Ross, *Changing Chinese*, chs. ii, v.

ing contempt for the groveling foreigner and utter self-satisfied complacency, would be hard to beat.

"Swaying the wide world, I have but one aim in view" said the Emperor of China, "namely, to maintain a perfect governance and to fulfill the duties of the state. Strange and costly objects do not interest me. I . . . have no use for your country's manufactures. . . . It behooves you, O King, to respect my sentiments and to display even greater devotion and loyalty in the future, so that, by perpetual submission to our Throne, you may secure peace and prosperity for your country hereafter. . . . Our Celestial Empire possesses all things in prolific abundance and lacks no product within its own borders. There was therefore no need to import the manufactures of outside barbarians in exchange for our own produce. . . . I do not forget the lonely remoteness of your island, cut off from the world by intervening wastes of the sea, nor do I overlook your excusable ignorance of the usages of our Celestial Empire. . . . Tremblingly obey and show no negligence." [6]

However the English are not the kind of people who stand outside the door forever. If they think the people inside have something to exchange for British hardware and textiles, they are going to get in, and no government on earth has ever been able to keep them out. But the breaking in of the door to China came in a way which makes us pause and wonder whether, after all, we are conferring any particular benefit on these orientals by bringing to them the so-called "blessings" of our civilization. The British East India Company found it possible to realize a handsome profit from the sale of opium in China. The Chinese government very properly took steps to prevent the importation of opium into China and in the process destroyed a quantity of the drug in a Chinese port. But the opium belonged to the East India Company. This gave Britain her chance and she made war on China for destroying British property. China was decisively defeated and the British then insisted that as a price of peace the Chinese should allow the importation of opium and open five ports to trade with Britain. In addition China was forced to cede the city and island of Hong-Kong to Britain. From this treaty in 1842 down to the present time, all the great industrial

[6] Bertrand Russell, *The Problem of China*, pp. 46–7; E. T. Backhouse and J. O. P. Bland, *Annals and Memoirs of the Court of Peking*, London, 1914, pp. 322ff.

and capitalist nations of the world seem to have followed the British example to a greater or less extent—except the United States.[7]

Fortunately at this juncture there was an American naval officer on the spot, who immediately notified his government of the special advantages given the British merchants. Without waiting for instructions from Washington he secured from the Chinese an extension of all the trading privileges to the Americans, on the same basis on which they were given to the British. Commodore Kearney's urgent messages to the United States then brought to China the first American mission under Caleb Cushing, who, in 1844, made our first treaties with the Celestial Empire. Kearney's quickness to take advantage of the situation created by the British victory at once established the United States on the "most-favored-nation" basis in China. Cushing followed up this advantage and wrote the "most-favored-nation" clause into the treaty, and in addition obtained for the United States what is known as the privilege of "extraterritoriality." [8]

Chinese justice at this time was no worse, but no better, than the medieval legal procedure which survived in Europe down to the eighteenth century. Punishments were often extremely cruel and severe, involving torture and other atrocious measures. The prisons were filthy and unsanitary to the last degree, as might naturally be expected among a people who had not the slightest ideas of the principles of hygiene. The administration of justice was in the hands of Chinese officials who were many things besides being judges and who were still taught that "The barbarians [Americans were 'barbarians'] are like beasts and not to be ruled by the same principles as citizens of China." It was obvious that no American could trust himself to the tender mercies of a Chinese court of law. The standards of civilization were utterly different and the prejudice of the Chinese against foreigners was very great.[9] Yet the Chinese had the foreigners

[7] H. B. Morse, *International Relations of the Chinese Empire*, I, 230, 280–96.
[8] C. O. Paullin, *Diplomatic Negotiations of American Naval Officers*, 198–204.
[9] B. H. Williams, "Protection of American Citizens in China" in *Amer. Jour. of International Law*, XVI, 43.

absolutely at their mercy, for if an American ship captain refused to surrender a member of his crew for trial before a Chinese court, the Chinese held the whip hand and could cut off the trade or retaliate on other Americans resident in China. The accused man must take his chances in the doubtful justice of the Chinese law.[10]

So Cushing had incorporated into the treaty of 1844 what is known as the principle of extraterritoriality. By this principle, any American charged with an offense, either criminal or civil, against the laws of China, had the privilege of having his case tried before a court of his own country. This court was usually held before the local United States Consul, and appeal lay not to a higher Chinese court, but to the United States Federal Circuit Court for the District of California.[11] In Chinese theory, the American officials are enforcing Chinese law.[12] But in fact disputes between citizens of China and citizens of the United States are subject to the jurisdiction of the United States, even though they originate in China. No one pretends that this system is either perfect or permanent. All western nations have insisted on this privilege when dealing with eastern nations, but they freely admit they will be glad to dispense with it as soon as oriental justice and judicial organization reaches the level of the western judicial processes. This system deprives China of a certain amount of her independence. In addition to that, the foreigners' courts have on occasion done outrageous injustice to the Chinese, by giving a trifling punishment to heinous crimes like murder. Naturally the Chinese protest. But the standing reply to China still is that she must bring her own standards of justice up to western ideals before anything can be done about it. The Chinese are making remarkable progress in that direction, but the time has apparently not yet come when foreigners can trust Chinese justice.[13]

Cushing's treaty laid down several other cardinal principles of American policy toward China. He insisted that the United

[10] T. Dennett, *Americans in Eastern Asia*, p. 86.
[11] W. W. Willoughby, *Foreign Rights and Interests in China*, 25-33.
[12] V. Wellington Koo, *Status of Aliens in China*, p. 217.
[13] B. H. Williams, supra, p. 48; W. Malloy, *Treaties and Conventions*, I, 240.

States wanted no part of the territory of China, in contrast to the actions of the Europeans. Although the treaty fixed the customs duties to be levied on goods going in and out of China, the United States would not assume the job of collecting those duties, but insisted that China take the part of a real nation and collect her own duties. This was, however, not the policy of the European nations, who not only fixed China's tariff to suit themselves, but also put their own nationals into office in China to collect the money. The basis of the tariff was a five per cent *ad valorem* duty, fixed by the English, and the other nations adhered to that arrangement. By insisting on "most-favored-nation" treatment for the United States, Cushing fixed the American principle of the Open Door to China, which simply means that no nation shall have any more favorable treatment in the ports of China than any other nation receives. According to the position taken by the United States at the very outset, no nation should cause China to discriminate against any other nation, simply because the first nation had the physical power to force concessions from China.[14]

The next problem which confronted American diplomacy was to keep up with the concessions which France and England were wringing from the unwilling Chinese. This work was taken up in 1861 by Anson Burlingame, one of the really noted figures in our oriental diplomacy. It was evident that the countries of Europe wanted a great deal more than mere trading privileges in China. They wanted actual possession and sovereignty over large sections of Chinese territory, and ere long they were on the road to getting both. Burlingame let it be known in no uncertain language that the policy of the United States was to co-operate with the other powers in every possible way consistent with peace and the open door. He therefore warned the Chinese that they must not give land away to the foreigners, and to the foreigners he kept insisting on the preservation of the territorial integrity of the Chinese Empire.

[14] S. K. Hornbeck, *Contemporary Politics in the Far East* (N. Y., 1916), pp. 217-18; T. Dennett, *Americans in Eastern Asia* (N. Y., 1923), pp. 166-9.

Burlingame further made a treaty with China wherein both nations took the position that a man has an inalienable right to change his allegiance and emigrate whither he wants to go, in contradiction to the old English doctrine of indelible allegiance which had played such a part in our troubles with England before the War of 1812. All this and Burlingame's generally sympathetic attitude toward China so endeared him to those people that when his useful mission was at an end, the Chinese employed him to be their envoy in a general mission to the countries of Europe. This was a rare tribute to the way in which he had captivated the Chinese and convinced them of the real desire of the United States for a square deal to China above all else.

3. THE CHINESE EXCLUSION ACT

But generous as were Burlingame and his treaty, the policy of the United States was destined for a speedy change. The settlement of California and the building of the transcontinental railways filled up the west with cheap, Chinese coolie laborers. This was all right when times were good. But in 1876 came a drought in the west. Crops were bad and labor was laid off. Mining machinery operated by hydraulic power was idle and the miners went to swell the ranks of the unemployed. Naturally the high-paid laborers were laid off if cheaper labor could be found and the Chinese soon had jobs where the white men were out of work, because they would accept lower wages. This immediately provoked riots and violence against the yellow men in which all sorts of outrages were perpetrated against the peaceful Chinese. California demanded that the Chinese be excluded from the United States. They were coming in droves to the land of plenty and their propensity for multiplying rapidly threatened all the terrors of the "yellow peril." Congress passed an act excluding the Chinese laborers, but President Hayes promptly and properly vetoed it as a violation of the promise we had made to China in the Burlingame Treaty when we both recognized the rights of men to emigrate. So it was necessary to patch up another treaty with China, whereby that nation generously agreed

ANSON BURLINGAME

to release us from our promise. Congress was then at liberty to pass an exclusion act which it did in 1882 and since that time the Chinese emigrants have not been allowed to enter the United States. In addition to this the Chinese are by law rendered ineligible to citizenship in the United States. Race problems are frequently caused by unchecked emigration and the United States by this act wrote into its foreign policy the fact that it was going to shut out such immigration lest it overwhelm the white civilization on our west coast.[15]

4. The Open Door Policy

But the main current of our Chinese policy had to do, not with the Chinese in America, but with the United States' interests in China. This was due to a great change which came over the whole world as a result of the Industrial Revolution. The change of western Europe and the United States from a state of agriculture to that of industry, produced fabulous wealth which was utterly impossible before the invention of machinery and the harnessing of steam and electricity. These manufacturing nations, with England at their head, had now more and ever more reasons for getting into the innermost recesses of China to sell their goods. Quantity production which came with the standardization of products, resulted in enormous surpluses of manufactured goods, and every year this surplus must find a market somewhere or England would starve. What better market than China which showed no signs of industrialization? It was not longer a question of trade following the flag. Capital, surplus wealth, penetrated the uttermost nations of the world and dragged both the flag and trade along with it. The British traders carried their goods to all ports of China, sold them, established business relationships, and got into trouble. Trouble demanded the immediate intervention of the British government to protect its merchants.

The whole world of western nations had by this time been caught in the current of what has been aptly called "economic

[15] J. F. Rhodes, *History of the United States, 1877–1896*, pp. 180–97.

imperialism." The diplomats were not only feverishly at work
protecting the merchants who wanted to sell goods in China,

THE FAR EAST

but they were even more concerned with the protection of their
capitalists who wanted to invest money in Chinese enterprise.
Somehow China must be staked out and sections of her territory
allocated so that the merchants and the investors of each capi-

talist nation would have its share apart from each other nation. This tentative partitioning of China was easy enough under the old régime of the Emperor, when China blandly and supinely allowed nation after nation to take her land as England did at Hong-Kong, or to lease territory for ninety-nine years, as Germany did at Kiau-Chow, or to mark off huge sections of China which were to be separated from China in the future, as they were all doing. The first process was frank land-grabbing, but the latter paraded under the respectable name of declaring "spheres of influence." A sphere of influence was an arrangement not between China and a western power for the selling or renting of Chinese territory, but an arrangement between two western powers whereby they agreed that when the time came to grab a particular section of China, they would partition it between themselves on whatever basis the agreement provided. China, unfortunately, was not a party to these agreements at all. But she had certainly no one but herself to blame for getting into such a muddle, because of the careless way she had signed away her freedom and her territory to a half dozen different nations. No wonder the nations licked their chops in anticipation of the next dismemberment.[16]

By 1898 France had acquired large sections of southern China; England had Hong-Kong, Russia had secured the valley of the Amur, Germany had her grip on Shantung and Japan had wrested Formosa from China by force of arms in the Chino-Japanese War. Russia and Japan both had an eye on Port Arthur and soon came to blows about it. In that same year of 1898 the United States, as we have seen, also entered upon a new phase of her history and joined in the ranks of the so-called "imperialistic nations." We have already observed how the United States became an industrial and exporting nation, and how she had acquired possessions in the Pacific Ocean and the Caribbean Sea on which she was tightening her grip with all the remorseless disregard of the rights of backward nations for which

[16] A. Viallate, *Economic Imperialism and International Relations during the last Fifty Years* (N. Y., 1923), introduction.

she had always criticised Great Britain. Yet, as we have seen, it was economically inevitable, for she must sell her goods and she must get raw materials. Even so the United States was loath to abandon her traditional policy of keeping her hands off China.

One of the most remarkable facts about modern history is the expansion of Europe. Europe had peopled and partitioned and dominated the Americas and Africa. She was on a fair way to do the same with Asia. China was the one great nation which remained to be divided up. If the United States merely contented herself with saying that China's territorial integrity must be respected she would not help China nor would she get her share of Chinese markets. The United States must do one of three things. She could oppose all the powers of Europe and tell them to stay out of Asia. But this was manifestly foolhardy, as Europe was already there and heroics of this kind would not save China. Second, the United States could have stepped out of the whole situation and stood aloof in a kind of isolated self-righteousness. But her own rapidly growing trade would not permit any such act, nor would this kind of theatrical pharisaism have protected China from the hungry powers of Europe. The only remaining alternative was to coöperate with the Europeans and try to restrain them and their selfish ambitions as far as was possible, at the same time refusing to have any part in the land-grabbing or to demand any special concessions for American merchants and investors. Certainly this was the only consistent thing to do.[17]

By 1899 the United States was confronted with a situation in which it had to act, or be eliminated from the whole business. So Secretary John Hay reaffirmed the policy which the United States had maintained from the days of Caleb Cushing and addressed notes to the great powers, England, Russia, Germany, Japan, France and Italy in which he proposed three things for their consideration. *First*, that the powers having "spheres of influence" in China would not interfere with any treaty port which happened to be within that sphere, so that all nations

[17] T. Dennett, *Americans in Eastern Asia*, pp. 644-9.

might trade equally and freely in that port. *Second*, that the duties collected within any "sphere of influence" should be fixed by the regular Chinese tariff, and not by the European who held the "sphere." This was to prevent the powers from discriminating in favor of their own merchants and against the United States. *Third*, that European nations in their "spheres of influence," would levy no higher harbor dues on vessels of another nationality frequenting such sphere than they levied on their own vessels, and no higher charges on railways within the sphere.[18]

To these proposals the European powers and Japan gave lip service, protesting that these had always been their own ideals. Yet it has been very properly said,

> "No assumption is more ridiculous than the one so often made that John Hay was the author of the open-door doctrine. One cannot point to a time when the United States government did not assert its demand for commercial equality. It was applied in the East in the first commercial treaties, those with Siam and Muscat, and was repeated in the first treaties with China, Japan, Hawaii and Korea. It is quite clear that this element in American policy is not changing, nor is it likely to change." [19]

However, no sooner had the imperialistic powers given their smiling assent to the doctrine of the "Open Door" than the Chinese woke up to what had been happening to them and broke out with a fearful and thoughtless insurrection. The aim of this "Boxer Uprising" (so called from the Chinese secret society which engineered it) was apparently the extermination of all the "foreign devils" in China and their exclusion in the future. More unfortunately for China, the Empress herself was mixed up in the affair. The Boxers were at first successful, they killed the German minister and drove all the foreign residents into the British legation at Peking where they besieged the foreigners. Foreign property was destroyed, foreign lives lost and China gave every evidence of being intent on wreaking a terrible vengeance on the powers for their "economic imperialism."

---

[18] This is best told by the documents themselves in W. Malloy, *Treaties and Conventions*, I, 244–60.

[19] T. Dennett, "American Policy in the Far East," in *Current History*, XVIII, 598.

But the powers, including the United States, at once sent a joint military expedition to Peking, which rescued the victims huddled in the British legation, and then proceeded to retaliate on the Chinese with all the frightful efficiency of modern warfare.

Having thoroughly and cruelly chastised the Chinese, the European powers now saw a splendid opportunity for extending their control over their prostrate victim. They not only insisted in the right to maintain a permanent military force to guard the legations at Peking (a regular army of occupation) but they saddled China with an indemnity which they knew well she could not pay. China would have to borrow the money from the European powers with which to pay for the damage she had wrought, and that would put her into the hands of her creditors, which was just what they wanted. It is not quite fair to say that China did not have the money with which to pay this debt. She has tremendous wealth within her own country, but she has never been able to get at it. Her own wealthy citizens apparently have never had enough confidence in their own government to lend money to it, and taxation is really absurdly low, although the Chinese people get very little from their government in return for their taxes.[20]

5. CHINA AND HER CREDITORS

So China had to borrow in Europe again, and this gave the European lending powers just the grip they wanted, for they could insist that money which they lent be spent as they directed. This began a practice of lending money to China on condition that she would spend it in the country which lent it, thereby flooding China with ever more and more European goods. For the money never left the creditor country but was simply exchanged for goods which the Chinese needed. All the powers exaggerated their demands for indemnity, except the United States. At the very moment when the Chinese were attacking the legations in Peking, Secretary Hay launched another effort to save China for and from herself. American policy was not to

[20] W. W. Willoughby, *Foreign Rights and Interests in China*, pp. 483–4.

be vengeful, but compassionate, taking for granted that the action of the Boxers was not the will of China herself. Of course, in international law, China was bound to make herself responsible for her failure to protect foreigners, and to pay damages. But further punishment for the sake of aggrandizing the imperialistic powers was utterly contrary to the American policy.[21]

Secretary Hay insisted:

"We adhere to the policy initiated by us in 1857 of peace with the Chinese nation, of furtherance of lawful commerce, of the protection of the lives and property of our citizens by all means guaranteed under the extraterritorial treaty rights and by the law of nations"; *but*, in addition to this, "The policy of the Government of the United States is to seek a solution which may bring about permanent safety and peace in China, preserve Chinese territorial and administrative entity, protect all the rights of friendly powers by treaty and international law, and safeguard for the world the principle of equal and impartial trade with all parts of China." [22]

But it was of little avail, for the European powers continued their encroachments and extended their tentacles ever further and further into China. The Germans found the mines of Shantung most interesting fields for investment by German capital. The British laid claim to the valley of the Yangstze River. Russia continued to get more and more power in Mongolia and Manchuria, while the Japanese laid their plans for getting Korea into their own hands. The victors soon fell out and Japan and Russia had to fight a war to decide which should get the much desired Port Arthur, despite the fact that it was Chinese. This war was fought on Chinese territory in the main, although China protested her neutrality. Japan won the war and enlarged her holding on all sides. It seemed to be only a question of time when the Chinese Empire would be entirely extinct, despite the best efforts of the United States.

But in 1910–11 the Chinese at last realized that it was their own

---

[21] T. Dennett, *Americans in Eastern Asia*, pp. 656–7.

[22] *Foreign Relations of the U. S., 1901*, Appendix, *The Rockhill Correspondence*, pp. 12, 363ff. The happy phrase, "administrative entity" is said to have been the contribution of the Second Assistant Secretary of State, Alvey A. Adee. It is fitting to pause here and recognize the fifty-four years service of this faithful officer. See E. G. Lowery's "The Remarkable Mr. Adee" in his *Washington Close-ups* (N. Y., 1921), p. 143. Mr. Adee died July 5, 1924.

corrupt government which was principally to blame for their plight. A revolution occurred wherein the Emperor was deposed and China became a Republic. She let it be known that she was going to take her place among the nations of the world as a great self-respecting state, willing to assume her international obligations and demand her international rights. At last it seemed as though China was willing to set her own house in order. This was very much to the liking of the United States, and the Chinese invited American political advisers to aid in the task of regenerating the Chinese political machine. But China was and is in a condition which will require years of enlightened statesmanship and wise leadership. Education is the key to the situation, but a country such as China has shown herself to be presents a fearful problem to educators. Since the amount of the indemnity which the United States had extracted from China for the "Boxer Uprising" proved more than enough to satisfy the claims, the United States set an example of international decency by returning the unused portion with instructions to spend it on education. Young Chinese students promptly came to the United States to study and many of them have done excellent work in the great American universities, particularly in international and public law. It is in these subjects in which the new China will first of all have to be informed in order to secure her rights in international society.

But the old Chinese government had allowed itself to be so tied hand and foot by the foreigners, that the problems of new China were appalling even for an highly advanced nation. Of course the contracts made by the old imperial government were binding on the new government. Moreover it must be understood that all these foreign loans to China for whatever purpose somehow involve the Chinese government. Invariably the matter of loans, private as well as public, for the building of railways as well as for paying indemnities, somehow seem to get mixed up with politics and become an international matter.[23]

[23] Ching-Chun Wang, "The Hankow-Szechuan Railway Loan," *Amer. Jour. International Law*, V, 653.

In the course of events, China has utterly lost her financial independence. For the European bankers who loaned the money insisted on supervising not only the spending of the money, but also the collection of the revenue which went to pay back the loans. This was the situation of semi-independence in which the new rulers of China found themselves placed. They could neither fix nor collect their own import duties.

Even before the actual establishment of the Republic in China, plans for governmental reorganization and for the building of railways were under way. This meant the opening up of even greater fields for activity by the western powers. But it also involved spending and borrowing more money. When President Taft undertook to direct American foreign policy, he decided to depart somewhat from the American policy of strict non-intervention in China and non-participation in these loans which always became political issues. In so far as lending money to China destroyed her independence, he would not undertake to force American money on China. But he saw clearly that China needed railroads and he knew that America, above all other nations, had the genius and the capital for building them. The State Department had always taken the position that it would not go beyond ordinary diplomatic protests to protect Americans who risked their capital by investing it in China. The United States government would not assume responsibility for, nor would it guarantee, any American commercial or industrial enterprise in China. This had been an avowed policy which both Republican and Democratic administrations had upheld. The United States would not invest in China for the sake of getting that unfortunate nation into her hands. It was contrary to her policy of no foreign entanglements, but more than that it was a violation of the political ideals which entitled China to the same independence that the United States demanded for herself.[24]

But was not the altruistic policy of the United States a little too much like leaving China to the tender mercies of European

[24] *Foreign Relations of the U. S., 1897*, p. 56; J. B. Moore, *Digest of International Law*, VI, 288.

powers who had already shown little consideration for her? There is such a thing as minding your own business, but there is also such a thing as leaving the traveler to Jericho bleeding in the ditch while you pass by on the other side. Taft and his Secretary of State, P. C. Knox, came to the conclusion that by refusing to support American bankers in their Chinese investments, the United States were doing China no good and were merely excluding herself and them from the benefits of American investments there. Then President Taft announced to Congress:

> "In China the policy of encouraging financial investment to enable that country to help itself has had the result of giving new life and practical application to the open door policy. The consistent purpose of the present administration has been to encourage the use of American capital in the development of China by the promotion of those essential reforms to which China is pledged by treaties with the United States and other powers. The hypothecation to foreign bankers in connexion with certain industrial enterprises, such as the Hukuang railways, of the national revenues on which these reforms depended, led the Department of State, early in the administration, to demand for American citizens participation in such enterprises, in order that the United States might have equal rights and an equal voice in all questions pertaining to the disposition of the public revenues concerned." [25]

In other words, Taft thought that the doctrine of isolation was in conflict with the doctrine of the open door and he was going to follow the open door idea. American bankers were requested by the United States government to share in the loan to China, in which the other participants were to be Great Britain, France, Germany, Russia and Japan. The conclusion was unavoidable that the United States was not only going out of its way to get American bankers to invest in China, it would also protect them there as had been done before by Europe but never by the United States. This might involve the use of military force.[26]

However before the deal could be consummated the Democratic administration of President Woodrow Wilson took over the

---

[25] *Cong. Rec.*, Dec. 3, 1912, Vol. 49, Pt. I, p. 9.
[26] G. A. Finch, "American Diplomacy and the Financing of China," *Amer. Jour. of International Law*, XVI, 25.

Department of State, and forced the American bankers to withdraw. President Wilson on looking over the situation decided that the proposed Six-Power Consortium was frankly going to deprive China still further of her independence and he did not want to have the United States share in any such scheme which he believed so contrary to her old policy of keeping out of the scramble for the control of China. He explained

> "The conditions of the loan seem to us to touch very nearly the administrative independence of China itself; and this administration does not feel that it ought, even by implication, to be a party to those conditions. The conditions include not only the pledging of particular taxes, some of them antiquated and burdensome, to secure a loan, but also the administration of those taxes by foreign agents."

If Taft thought the open-door policy more important than the isolation policy, Wilson believed that we should not secure the open door at the expense of an even older principle of American foreign policy, that of refusing to do anything to injure the independence of other countries. To Wilson such a plan was "obnoxious to the principles upon which the government of our people rests." Denied the support of their government, the American bankers withdrew.[27]

6. Fencing with Japan

But the great European War turned the principles and policies of all nations upside down. The Japanese rushed into the war ostensibly to comply with the promise she had made England in the Anglo-Japanese Alliance, but actually to shove Germany out of Kiau-Chow and Shantung and get them for herself. Again a war was fought on Chinese territory, for control of Chinese lands, when China was neutral. Then while Europe was distracted with her life and death struggle, the Japanese pushed their advantage in China. After capturing the German leaseholds in China in 1914, the Japanese in 1915 presented the Chinese government with certain demands which, if accepted, would virtually have made China the vassal state of Japan. The world was thinking

[27] W. W. Willoughby, *Foreign Rights and Interests in China*, pp. 501–11; also *Amer. Jour. of International Law*, VII, 355–41.

of something else. Europe was in the agony of her own troubles, and the United States had deliberately elected to keep its hands off China. The celebrated "Twenty-one Demands" which Japan made upon China in 1915 and which China agreed to for the most part gave Japanese economic concessions in China, gave her control over the administration of Chinese affairs, and practically put Japan in a position where if China was going to borrow any more money, she would have to get Japan's permission and then borrow it—from Japan. Moreover Japan extracted from China the promise that she (China) would agree in advance to whatever the Peace Conference which ended the war did in disposing of Shantung. Then Japan sewed up the European powers with promises to give Shantung to her (Japan) when the war was over. China sold herself to Japan more effectively than she has ever surrendered her freedom to any European powers. News of these events was carefully concealed by the Japanese and China was not yet well enough organized to get the ear of the other powers of the world, even if they had been in a position to hear.[27]

The United States was the one nation whose hands were free and who might have come to the aid of China in her sad plight. It is impossible to read the story of these days in China as written by the American Ambassador, Paul S. Reinsch, without coming to the conclusion that Secretary W. J. Bryan's policy of peaceful persuasion was as out of place here as elsewhere. Moreover, Mr. Reinsch seems to have been left to guess at the State Department's views as much as was Ambassador Page in London, and was even more helpless because at a greater distance. Ambassador Page's comment on Bryan's management of the Department of State is a classic:

"Now the Department of State seeems to be utterly chaotic—silent when it ought to respond, loquacious when it ought to be silent. . . . I see nothing to do but to suggest to the president to put somebody in the Department who will stay there and give intelligent attention to diplomatic telegrams and letters—some assistant or clerk. . . . The whole thing is disorganizing and demoralizing beyond description." [28]

[27] S. K. Hornbeck, *Contemporary Politics in the Far East*, pp. 301-43.
[28] B. J. Hendrick, *Life and Letters of Walter H. Page*, II, 225-6.

Page's outspoken condemnation of the conduct of affairs in the State Department under Bryan throws a flood of light on Ambassador Reinsch's gentle remark:

> "I had to be particularly careful not to express my own judgment as to what our course of action should be, in order not to arouse any hopes among the Chinese as to what my government would do. *Instructions had been slow in coming.*" [29]

Mr. Reinsch had to guard the open door and he did it remarkably well. But the United States government would take no other action than to recommend that Japan and China go slow, which as Mr. Reinsch well says was "like whispering a gentle admonition through the keyhole after the door had been slammed to." [30] After Japan was entirely through and had by threats of military force bullied the Chinese Government into agreeing to the outrageous demands, the United States notified China that it would not recognize any agreement which impaired the treaty rights of the United States, or violated the open door. The only hope for China was the fact that she had been sold out by an unrepresentative government, and the people of China had neither been consulted nor had they consented to Japan's demands.

The Chinese apparently saw that their salvation now lay in getting the whole story exposed at the peace table at the end of the war. In 1917 the United States entered the European War and invited China among other neutrals to break off diplomatic relations with Germany. With infinite skill Mr. Reinsch led them up to that point. At first the Japanese were not enthusiastic about China's getting into the war, as they did not want their sins exhibited at a Peace Conference. But as they had England and France committed to giving them Shantung, the Japanese finally agreed to get enthusiastic about welcoming China into the war. The Japanese in fact tried to dicker with Russia to get concessions as the price of their being able to persuade China to enter the war when they found the United States had already accomplished that task. Then came quickly the

---

[29] P. S. Reinsch, *An American Diplomat in China,* p. 144 (italics are not in original).
[30] Reinsch, supra, pp. 148–49.

question of who would finance China to take her part in the war. European powers were now in the third year of the war and utterly incapable of lending money to outsiders. Japan was willing to lend some of her war-swollen millions, on the usual terms which would have put China under deeper obligations to her.[31]

At this point President Wilson realized that a vast change had come over the world since he pulled the American bankers out of the consortium in 1913. Two nations in the world had gotten vastly rich as a result of the war because they had sold quantities of goods to Europe and Europe would pay almost any price. The United States and Japan had virtually passed from the stage of being debtor nations to the stage of being great creditor nations. Especially had the United States assumed the leadership in world finance and New York was now the mecca to which the powers of the earth sent suppliants begging more and more money to help them fight the war. So following the lead of President Taft, Wilson revived the idea of the consortium and in June of 1918 invited the American bankers to participate in a loan to China. Step by step the United States was forced to abandon her classic position of being unwilling to support her investors in China. Now she was fairly beseeching her bankers to place some of their tremendous war profits at the disposal of China lest Japan become the only creditor of China and thereby get China completely in her power. The American bankers consented to lend to China, but the United States was thereby virtually placed in a position where she must give her investors in China more than mere diplomatic support. What this means, the future alone can tell.[32]

But this much at least can be said for American policy. She has not forced her loans on China. The Chinese have taken the position that if the United States will not help them, they will be forced to rely upon Japan, which would mean subservience to Japan. Japan, instead of following the lead of the United States, seems to have chosen rather to follow the very worst

[31] P. S. Reinsch, *American Diplomat in China*, p. 253.
[32] G. A. Finch, "American Diplomacy and Financing China," *Amer. Jour. of International Law*, XVI, 25–41.

precedents in European practice, coercing an unwilling China into sacrifices beyond her strength and creating an abundance of distrust. It is hardly likely that China will much longer endure the international obligations which have been forced upon her. When the time comes for China to throw off those obligations, the United States will have cause to congratulate her that she has always stood for equal commercial opportunity in China, for Chinese independence and for coöperation with the European powers only in so far as that coöperation was for the mutual benefit of China and the powers.

CHAPTER XV

THE RIVALRY WITH JAPAN FOR THE PACIFIC

"If the two parties reckon themselves equal, then, as Caesar holds, is the best time for treating of peace, since each trusts himself."—*Grotius*.

1. THE TRANSFORMATION OF JAPAN

It was once the custom among European nations to regard shipwrecked sailors as prisoners of war, even in times of peace. The story is told of how William the Conqueror once got Earl Harold into his power, because Harold was shipwrecked on the coast of Normandy. William is said to have made Harold swear to help him become King of England, and Harold, being in William's power, agreed. Harold broke his oath, so William said, and William invaded England in the Norman Conquest. Such were the earliest relations between Japan and the United States, and we are not far wrong in saying that in the beginning of the nineteenth century, the Japanese were in many respects about the same stage of civilization as England in the eleventh century. If this is correct, Japan has jumped eight centuries since 1850. There are few episodes in history more dramatic than the transformation of Japan in the last seventy years. At first, only the Dutch had the right to trade with Japan, for the Japanese government maintained that same air-tight policy of excluding all foreigners from interference and intercourse with her that was characteristic of China. The first American vessels to trade with China had to camouflage themselves under a Dutch flag and even the Dutch were confined to the single port of Nagasaki. In 1846 Commodore Biddle attempted to open up trade with Japan and was politely told to go his way and never return.[1]

But the world was getting too small to allow any nation to treat

[1] C. O. Paullin, *Diplomatic Negotiations of American Naval Officers, 1778–1883*, pp. 222–31.

another in such a fashion.. Despite the fact that an early American vessel visiting the shores of Japan had returned some shipwrecked Japanese sailors, the Japanese did not treat the shipwrecked American whalers with equal courtesy. Indeed the Yankees who were getting whale oil in the Pacific and who had the misfortune to be cast away on the shores of Japan, were imprisoned with the same lack of ceremony which characterized the Norman treatment of Earl Harold in the eleventh century.[2]

By 1850, however, three events had coincided to bring Japan and the United States face to face across the Pacific. The Mexican War and the Oregon Treaty gave the title to the Pacific coast to the United States. The discovery of gold in California peopled the Pacific coast. In fact, there is some reason for saying that the enthusiasm for westward expansion to the Pacific was a part of that same ceaseless urge which led the Columbian navigators to seek China and the orient.[3] Steamship lines from the west coast to China needed a stopping point and Japan's ports provided such points. Contacts could no longer be avoided and the stage was set for the opening up of Japan. That opening was consummated by the historic expedition of Commodore M. C. Perry in 1854, when, with a naval expedition sent out by the United States government he landed in Japan and demanded an audience with the ruling powers.

The social and political organization of Japan at that time was akin to a feudalism, which bore allegiance to a cloistered Mikado, or Emperor, who was shut up in his palace by an hereditary prime minister called the Shogun, who was the real ruler. The Shogun was loath to grant any audiences or concessions, but under Perry's combination of tactful persistence and veiled threats he gave way and allowed an audience. It seems clear now that Perry's policy would have led him to more forceful measures if the Shogun has not finally yielded. A treaty was made between Japan and the United States which provided for the opening up of certain ports

[2] I. Nitobe, "American-Japanese Intercourse prior to the Advent of Perry," in *Amer. Hist. Assoc. Rept.*, 1911, I, 131.
[3] R. G. Cleland, "Asiatic Trade and the American Occupation of the Pacific Coast," *Amer. Hist. Assoc. Rept.*, 1914, I, 283.

to trade with the United States, for a crude form of extraterritoriality and for the sending of an American consul if either party
deemed it necessary.[4]

It now remained to send a regular envoy and the selection made
by President Pierce was a most fortunate one. Although individuals probably count for a little history, still Townsend Harris as
American consul to Japan for several years did a remarkable
work in smoothing out differences between Japan and the United
States and enabling the former to bridge the gap of centuries.
His treaties in 1857–8 confirmed the opening up of the ports, and
defined more clearly the rights of extraterritoriality which the
Japanese were forced to concede the United States while they
prepared to bring their own laws into harmony with western
ideas of justice. It is evident, however, that all the eloquence and
tact of Townsend Harris would not have availed to secure the
confirmation of these treaties by the Shogun, had there not existed within Japan a very definite group who favored opening up
relations with the outer world. The Shogun who first let Perry
get into Japan met with strenuous opposition for his act, but he
also found support. The Japanese rulers and leaders were apparently split. But other powers now appeared on the scene,
Great Britain and France, and they were fresh from bloody wars
in which they had forced such treaties on China at the point of
the bayonet. Realizing that Japan might meet a similar fate,
the Shogun signed the treaties and Japan embarked on her career
of diplomacy.[5]

Even so the battle was not over. The Japanese anti-foreign
party were mollified with the promise that the treaties were only
temporary and that if intercourse with the foreigners proved unsuccessful or unwholesome from the Japanese point of view,
they could withdraw their promises within a certain length of
time. Then an interesting constitutional struggle took place
within the country. Perry's visit took place about the same time
that a movement got under way to destroy the power of the Sho-

[4] T. Dennett, *Americans in Eastern Asia*, pp. 265–77.
[5] P. J. Treat, *Japan and the United States, 1853–1921* (Boston, 1922), pp. 26–41.

TOWNSEND HARRIS

gun and put the Mikado back in power as the supreme ruler of
the nation. All who hated the Shogun for giving way to the foreigners identified themselves with the party of the Mikado and
the conflict became a struggle between the Shogun and his foreign policy and the Mikado and an anti-foreign policy. The
Shogun was in an embarrassing position, trying to keep his promises to the foreigners, and at the same time to save his waning
power within the empire. In the struggle that followed, foreign
politics became inextricably mixed with domestic concerns. The
Japanese feudal lords who opposed the Shogun gave notice that
having had a taste of foreign intercourse, they did not like it.
This meant that as the Harris treaties were about to expire the
Japanese might not be willing to renew them, in which case all
the work of Perry and Harris would be undone and Japan would
relapse into her seclusion once more.[6]

However the belligerent feudal lords overplayed their hand.
An American vessel trying to get through the Straits at Shimonoseki in 1863 was fired on by the local feudal potentate who was
one of the anti-foreign party. This was notice to the foreign
powers that they could not any longer ply their accustomed
routes of trade. Great Britain was as much concerned as the
United States and so the powers, including the United States,
organized a joint naval expedition against the refractory lord at
Shimonoseki. That gentleman was speedily brought to terms by
the smashing up of his forts and the burning of his town. Indeed, he was required to pay the bill of the expedition. The other
powers joined with the United States in demanding an indemnity
from the Shogun for his inability to control the feudal noble and
his failure to protect foreign interests. They gave the Shogun
the alternative of opening more ports, but he refused and chose
to pay the damages. The Shimonoseki expedition broke the back
of foreign opposition and the Mikado, now rising in power, decided wisely to yield to the foreigners and confirm their treaties.
So instead of Japan's withdrawing into her shell again at the end
of the time limit, she agreed that her lands had been opened up

[6] P. J. Treat, *Japan and the United States, 1853-1921*, pp. 43-60.

permanently. The Mikado evidently did not wish to risk any such wars as Britain had inflicted on the defenseless Chinese.[7]

For the time being this was a victory for the Shogun and his foreign policy. But his power was rapidly diminishing and he was badly beaten in an effort to punish the anti-foreign noble at Shimonoseki. In this fight which occurred in 1865 the Shogun soldiers fought as the soldiers of William of Normandy had fought at Senlac in 1066, with spears and shields and medieval armor. In 1915, only sixty years later the Japanese troops were fighting the Germans with all the modern equipment of aëroplanes and machine guns. The prestige of the Shogun was at an end and very soon he resigned leaving the Mikado to rule his own lands. The Emperor signalized his return to power by assuring the foreign minister that Japan would keep her contracts. Governmental reorganization went on rapidly. A Japanese administrator of foreign affairs was appointed and a representative government was planned. The Mikado notified the feudal nobles that "knowledge shall be sought for all over the world." It was to be Japan's policy to find out everything the western nations could teach her. She learned quickly with the intense desire to be equal in the councils of the world with those foreign nations who had humiliated her. Unlike the Chinese who chose to spend another half century in complacent self-satisfaction, the Japanese elected to be westernized and lost no time getting about it.[8]

2. THE EMANCIPATION OF JAPAN

But Japan still suffered from treaties which allowed the foreigners to fix her tariffs, and which gave them the right of extraterritoriality. Both these were marks of a nation which is not entirely free and independent. The Japanese now bent every effort to get rid of these disabilities. The rise of New Japan is, as we have pointed out, a truly astonishing tale of how a man can add a cubit to his height by taking thought. Verily, Japan has done

[7] T. Dennett, *Americans in Eastern Asia*, p. 401.
[8] P. J. Treat, *Japan and the United States, 1853–1921*, p. 91.

just that. Without losing the vital elements in her own culture and civilization she speedily became industrialized and modernized. Christianity was tolerated in Japan (it had existed there for centuries under cover) and the sound common sense which characterized the American missionaries to Japan did much to keep them and their activities out of trouble. Indeed, the American missionary to Japan has always been primarily an educator, and what the Japanese desired above all else was education.[9]

The good will of the United States was made constantly manifest throughout this period. After his term of office, President Grant went on his trip around the world and did much to cement cordial relations between the two countries. But more important than this was the lesson in international decency taught the powers of the world by the United States when, in 1883, it returned to Japan nearly three-quarters of a million dollars which the latter had been forced to pay as the Shimonoseki indemnity. The United States really had no use for this money and its act in returning the fine to Japan only served to create better feeling between the two nations. The Japanese naturally wanted their tariff autonomy restored at the earliest possible moment and the United States consistently advocated this course. But the United States was alone in her position, for the European powers wished to retain as long as possible those favorable trading privileges which they had extracted from Japan in the days of her weakness. In these matters it is not far from wrong to say that Japan had signed away her sovereignty without knowing just what she was doing. Moreover, as long as foreigners could be tried in their own courts in Japan and not in Japanese courts, Japan could not be said to have administrative independence.[10]

By 1894, however, the English, whose trade interests in Japan were greater than those of any other nation, were finally induced to agree to a revision of the old treaties, whereby Japan again became mistress of her own tariffs and resumed jurisdiction over

---

[9] A. J. Brown, *The Mastery of the Far East* (N. Y., 1921), p. 624.
[10] P. J. Treat, *Japan and the United States, 1853–1921*, pp. 116–32.

foreigners in her own courts. The tariff freedom was not quite complete, but it was as free as England would grant at the time, and it was not long before Japan was a full-fledged member of the family of nations without having to apologize to anyone for her conduct of her own affairs. The emancipation of Japan had been accomplished by the will of the Japanese themselves, and their determination to show foreign nations that they were not a backward people. Japan not only learned what western nations wanted to teach her, but she now proceeded to learn from them some things they were not so anxious to have her understand.

For Japan now began to feel the effects of westernization and industrialization. As we have seen so often, an industrial nation requires more territory into which to expand with her surplus population, more lands from which to get raw material, more markets into which to put her manufactured products. At first glance it does not seem as though it were necessary actually to annex more lands by conquest for these purposes. But such has been the history of European nations. They have begun by trading, and have usually ended by annexing the lands of backward and defenseless people. Japan now needed such lands and right across the Sea of Japan lay one of the most backward nations the world has ever seen. Korea had existed as a nation for centuries. It claimed to be four thousand years old, but it was a tempting morsel for the now land-hungry Japanese. It owed a vague allegiance to China. So Japan soon got herself into a war with China for the "liberation" of Korea, which was to be but a preliminary step to taking Korea herself. Japan with her western military and naval forces proceeded to defeat China with a deftness and completeness which amazed even the Europeans. When China was entirely defeated, the United States offered to mediate between the two, but Japan declined the offer and forced Li Hung-Chang to come and sue for peace in behalf of China. In the peace negotiations each side employed an American international lawyer to help in the conference. Hon. John W. Foster was attached to the Chinese Mission and Mr.

H. W. Dennison who had been in the Japanese foreign office for many years was a member of the Japanese delegation.

The Treaty of Shimonoseki which ended the Chino-Japanese War in 1895 put Japan on the map as a world power with imperialistic ambitions. She took Formosa from China and staked out her claim to Korea and Port Arthur. Only the intervention of the powers prevented her from actually taking Port Arthur. But Russia had her eye on that ice-free port, and Japan had to fight another war to get it. There can be no doubt but that the powers of Europe robbed Japan of the fruits of her victory over China and Japan clearly resented that interference. She had to fight another war in order to show her teeth to Europe. This came about when Russia and Japan came to blows about Port Arthur. Russia's ceaseless urge to find her ice-free port made her fasten her attention at last on Port Arthur in the Far East as once that same impulse had gotten her into trouble over Constantinople and the Persian Gulf. The public sympathy of the United States, in so far as there was any such thing, was clearly on the side of Japan. In 1904–5 Japan treated the great colossus of Europe to one of the worst military and naval defeats in her history. The Russian fleets were annihilated, and the Russian armies were driven back out of Korea up into the northern part of Manchuria. Europe was at last forced to take Japan seriously and "that jumpy creature," Kaiser Wilhelm II of Germany, made the wires to Washington hum with requests to President Roosevelt to intervene and stop Japan before she overthrew the whole white race and destroyed the principle of autocracy in European nations. The nations of central Europe sympathized with Russia, but England veered around now to the side of the United States.

In 1902 the British admiralty had decided that they must concentrate the British fleet in the North Sea against the time when they would have to fight Germany. Hence they had to withdraw some units from the Orient. England shrewdly made a deal with Japan whereby the two nations got into a defensive alliance, in which Japan undertook to police the Far East for

England and England had her hands free to deal with Germany. This Anglo-Japanese Alliance committed England to coming to the defense of Japan under certain circumstances and was going to make trouble in the future. But for the present, the English congratulated themselves that they had bet on the right horse for once.

3. JAPANESE IMMIGRATION

But despite her victories, Japan could not continue the war indefinitely. Within four days of Admiral Togo's great victory over the Russian fleet in the Sea of Japan, the Japanese intimated to President Roosevelt that if he would please invite them to a peace conference, they would be glad to accept. The President promptly did so and soon had both the Russians and Japanese at Portsmouth discussing terms. The coming of the Japanese envoys marks the beginning of some of our most difficult diplomatic problems with that nation. Japan had succeeded well. In fact she had done too well. Her envoys at Portsmouth were determined to get what territory they had conquered and a great indemnity from the defeated Russians. The Muscovites came led by the greatest statesman of the Empire, Count Witte, who began by winning over the American newspaper correspondents. He went out of his way to cultivate friendly relations with the all-powerful press of the United States, while Baron Komura, the Japanese envoy, exhibited a reserve characteristic of his nation and misunderstood by the typical cub reporter in the United States.[13]

Witte agreed to give up the Russian pretensions to Port Arthur and Korea, and the lower half of Sakhalian Island. But he absolutely refused an indemnity. The negotiations were deadlocked, for the Japanese government had led its people to believe that Russia would be saddled with the cost of the war. But the Japanese could not afford to continue the war and the Russians were apparently ready to quit and go home. At this point President Roosevelt stepped into the situation and persuaded the Japanese to give up the indemnity. This made peace,

[13] S. Witte, *Memoirs of Count Witte* (N. Y., 1921), pp. 140–1.

but the peace was bitterly resented by the Japanese people. Japan could not have gone on with the war, and her government knew it and accepted the terms which Witte and Komura agreed upon. Rioting and disorder broke out in the various Japanese cities in protest against the terms of peace, but the government put down the disturbances. Naturally Roosevelt came in for his share of the blame in which the Japanese roundly condemned their own envoys. But the fact remains unquestioned that Japan's resources were badly strained. Witte admitted later that Russia, too, was on the verge of a debacle which was postponed to 1917 by the timely peace.[12]

But the thoughtlessness of the Japanese press toward America was as nothing compared with the trouble which now began to be stirred up by the American press against Japan. Certain disreputable, but widely read, journals in the United States now began to harp on the "yellow peril" theme. Since Japan had defeated the greatest power of Europe, would she not try now to measure her strength against the United States? Japan became a problem for American diplomacy and the United States was forced to reconsider its foreign policy in relation to that nation.

First among these problems was that of Japanese emigration to the United States. The difficulty from the Japanese standpoint is readily understood. Japan consists of a few small islands. Within those islands she has cooped up a population of some 55,000,000 people, with a yearly increase of 700,000. She has half the population of the United States crowded into an area barely the size of the State of California. Japan has 380 inhabitants per square mile, while the United States has but 31 inhabitants in the same space. In Japan only 16% of the land can be used for raising food, while in Great Britain 77% of the land can be so used. Japan has been industrialized, just as England has been, but it is evident that she is far less able than England to feed her own population.[13]

[12] J. B. Bishop, *Theodore Roosevelt and His Times*, I, 410–12; T. Roosevelt, *Autobiography* p. 583; W. W. McLaren, *Political History of Japan during the Meiji Era* (N. Y., 1916), pp. 299–301.

[13] T. Iyenaga and K. Sato, *Japan and the California Problem* (N. Y., 1921), pp. 45–57.

What have European nations done when confronted with this situation of surplus population? America herself is the answer to the question. Back in the fifteenth and sixteenth centuries the nations of Europe began to feel the pressure of a population which could not be supported or given employment at home. The result was that great movement of peoples which we know as "the Expansion of Europe." By it the Europeans have poured their surplus millions into every corner of the earth. In some cases they have sent emigrants to other countries, but in many other cases they have simply expropriated the lands of other peoples and other races, and made those lands subject to the domination and colonization of the white man from Europe and his American descendants. The white or Caucasian peoples (an admittedly vague term) constitute roughly 35% of the peoples of the earth. They occupy or control 90% of the land surface of the earth. The remaining 65% of races of other colors have a beggarly 10% in which to live, or they must live in a country which the white man dominates. The world is all divided up now. North America is a transplanted northern Europe. South America is a transplanted southern Europe. Africa is carved up among half a dozen different European nations and only the small nation of Abyssinia and the pitiful speck of Liberia remain independent. Yet there remains the Japanese nation of 55,000,-000 restricted to its small rocky island empire and no place to go because the white man has staked out his claims to all the rest of the world. That is a problem.[14]

Such a problem not only involves where Japan shall send her people, but where she shall sell her manufactures that those who remain at home may live. England's very life blood, as we have pointed out so many times, depends on her having great fields in which to get her raw material and great markets in which to sell what she makes. Her colonies have always helped to supply this need. Her spheres of influence, such as she has carved from China, supply more. To live, Japan must also have lands into

[14] The 1920 Census reports give the U. S. a population of 105,710,620 and Japan, 56,-961,140; R. L. Buell, *Japanese Immigration* (World Peace Foundation, 1924).

which she can dump her people, lands from which she can get coal and iron and oil, lands in which she can sell what she makes to support those 55,000,000 people. But where are those lands? What could Japan do? Europe had taught her what to do. Right at her own doorstep lay the one remaining country where Europeans were staking out their claims, namely, China. The Japanese are not responsible for the international arrangement in vogue in China, whereby the so-called advanced nations have marked out the land they want. But Japan followed the example of her preceptors and marked out Manchuria and Korea for herself. She had to fight first China and then Russia before she finally got her foothold in China and then just about the time she was getting somewhere the newspaper world began to raise a hue and cry against Japan for following *her* "manifest destiny." There is no occasion for defending Japan, but it is hard to see why her designs on China should be wrong if the like designs of England, France and Russia were right.

Nevertheless newspaper opinion in America did begin to manifest hostility. Then came the question of surplus population and Japan began dumping her laborer into the garden spot of America, the state of California. That was the nearest to Japan in both geography and climate. Could the people of California show enough tolerance of an alien race to adjust human relationships and live and let live? The United States has had one race problem for two hundred years and no one pretends that it is solved yet. The United States is not enlightened enough to settle the negro problem, how then can she take on another like it? The same California which had demanded and secured the exclusion of the Chinese now demanded the exclusion of the Japanese. The question came to an issue over the segregation of Japanese children into separate schools in the city of San Francisco. Every southern city had segregated its negroes since the Civil War. But the Japanese government resented this discrimination against its people. Whereupon the alarmist writers began to drag in questions of race amalgamation, race degeneration, intermarriage of the races and all the undefinable but highly inflammable discussion which is so familiar to students of our negro history.[15]

President Roosevelt took hold of the matter and soon discovered that the root of the evil was Japanese emigration to the United States. Our treaty of 1894 had specifically provided that

> "The citizens of each of the two High Contracting Parties shall have the full liberty to enter, travel or reside in any part of the territories of the other contracting Party, and shall enjoy full and perfect protection of their persons and property." [16]

It would seem as though a treaty should override a state law, but the Californians were not technically violating the treaty. The question was one of extreme delicacy and the United States government could not interfere in a matter of exclusive state concern such as the administration of its school laws. The real question at issue was unfortunately one which seriously endangered good feeling between the two nations. But California was panic-stricken lest it be overrun by Japanese emigrants. Secretary of State Root solved the problem by an agreement made with the Japanese whereby that government generously consented not to grant passports to the horde of coolies who were getting ready to descend on the United States. The flood of aliens was stopped at the source by a friendly agreement which did not even become a treaty. This "Gentleman's Agreement" kept the Japanese at home and the Japanese government seems to have faithfully and sincerely upheld its side of the bargain.[17]

This, however, has not yet satisfied the residents on the Pacific Coast. There were 10,000 Japanese in California in 1900. The "Gentleman's Agreement" was made in 1906. By 1910 there were 40,000 Japanese in California. The census of 1920 showed a further increase to 70,000. This alarmed the Californians tremendously. The Japanese already in the United States apparently multiply much faster than the native-born whites. The fecundity of the Japanese women is in fact three times that of the

---

[15] V. S. McClatchy, "The Japanese in the Melting Pot," in *Annals of Amer. Acad.*, XCIII, 29.

[16] W. Malloy,*Treaties and Conventions*, I, 1029.

[17] P. J. Treat, *Japan and the United States, 1853–1921*, pp. 255–6.

white women. In the decade 1910–20 the Japanese did increase
much faster than the whites. But these figures become much less
alarming when we consider that the Japanese are still barely 2%
of the whole population of California and that the birthrate of
the Japanese has steadily decreased since 1917, as every sociolo-
gist predicted it would. The second generation of emigrants always has fewer children than the first. If the Japanese increased
400% in the decade 1900–1910, they apparently increased less
than 100% in the next ten years. There is no very substantial
ground for fearing that California will be swamped in a yellow
flood.[18]

But another side of the question has been raised by the fact
that the Japanese are said to be able to underbid the American
workman and take his job away from him. The Japanese are
able to live on less than the white man. The Japanese laborer
will eat rice; the white laborer eats beef. A pound of rice costs
half as much and goes twice as far as a pound of beef. Yet,
even admitting this, there is reason for believing that as the Japanese workman gets more efficient in his work he is coming to
demand and to receive equal if not higher wages. This is hardly
a matter which diplomacy can settle, but it does serve to keep
up racial antagonism. The well known skill of the Japanese
farmers in California has given them control of certain agricultural lands and crops so that by 1920 90% of the celery, 88% of
the berries, 86% of the asparagus and 80% of the tomatoes raised
in California were produced by the Japanese. When one con-
siders what a tremendous part the California canned fruits and
vegetables play in the life of the nation, this is rather a significant matter. The Japanese have bought up and control certain
choice lands to the exclusion of the whites, and this raises more
troubles. The fact that the Japanese hold but half a million of
the eleven million improved acres in California, does not seem to
render it any less serious to the native whites. Neither does the
fact that the Japanese have very largely reclaimed their lands

---

[18] *California and the Oriental* (Cal. State Bd. of Control; Revised edition, 1922), pp. 25–6,
40–41, and comment thereon by K. K. Kawakami *Real Japanese Question* (N. Y., 1921),
p. 42; R. L. Buell, *Japanese Immigration*, pp. 284–5.

from the sixteen million acres of unimproved lands seem to relieve the fears of the white population. The Californians have tried to keep the orientals off the land by forbidding aliens not eligible to citizenship to hold land.[19]

This presents another phase of the whole situation which complicates the diplomatic problems. The yellow peoples are not elegible to citizenship by naturalization in the United States. Congress has by law forbidden the naturalization of the Chinese, and the Supreme Court has decided that Japanese are not eligible to naturalization, either. This, the Japanese hold, is unjust discrimination against them. There is no doubt about its being discrimination. The Californians have therefore by legislation forbidden the purchase or leasing of lands by aliens not eligible to citizens, thus trying to prevent the Japanese from acquiring any more farm lands. But this law has been evaded by reason of the fact that the children of Japanese emigrants who are born in the United States are citizens by the Constitution itself. They can own lands, and their parents can get lands in their name. The only remaining alternative for the Californians is to secure an amendment to the Constitution of the United States forbidding the naturalization of children of aliens ineligible to citizenship, even if they are born in the United States. But the passage of such an amendment is still doubtful as the rest of the United States has not been roused by the sense of impending danger as has California, and besides that such tampering with citizenship will lead the Southern States to demand some similar treatment of the negro.[20]

Another vexing question which further diplomacy has had to solve is the practice of the Japanese of regarding every child born of Japanese parents as a Japanese citizen, and liable to military service in the Japanese army. We have seen how much trouble this made between England and the United States leading up to the War of 1812. Although a Japanese born in California was an American citizen under the constitution, he was also a Japanese

[19] *California and the Oriental*, pp. 47, 66ff.; K. K. Kawakami, *Real Japanese Question*, p. 43.
[20] R. Malcolm, "American Citizenship and the Japanese," *Ann. Amer. Acad.*, XCIII, 77.

subject. For a long time the Japanese have been unwilling to recognize the right of expatriation which we had such difficulty in making England understand. Finally in 1916 a law passed the Japanese Parliament making this possible, but the permission to Japanese to expatriate themselves was still hedged around with restrictions.

In 1924 the Japanese passed a law abolishing this "dual nationality," and providing that Japanese born abroad should hereafter lose their Japanese nationality, unless they took formal action to preserve it. This act will go far to solve a critical problem, and is all the more generous on Japan's part since it came shortly after the sensibilities of Japan had been seriously wounded by the formal exclusion of Japanese immigrants to the United States.[21]

4. THE COMMERCE OF THE PACIFIC

But the greatest of all our problems with Japan lies rather in our rivalry for the control of the Pacific Ocean and our conflicting interests in China. The sensible man might think that the Pacific Ocean was big enough for both and certainly China can absorb all the goods either Japan or the United States can send to her. Nevertheless the history of the world is one long series of demonstrations of the fact that the world is not always big enough for two such nations. Were nations rational in their feelings toward one another, and in their dealings with each other, or had nations as yet emerged from the stone age of international politics, such a rivalry, with threats of conflict, would be unnecessary. But as we have had occasion to see so many times in these pages, nations are neither sensible nor rational when "honor" and "rights" are involved, nor has international law yet reached that stage of actual enforcement, which our municipal law reached centuries ago. We have to reckon with this rivalry, senseless as it may seem to thinking people.

After the Russo-Japanese War, Japan, as we have seen, con-

[21] R. L. Buell, "Some Legal Aspects of the Japanese Question," *Amer. Jour. of International Law*, XVII, pp. 33–5, 151; N. Y. *Times*, July 15, 1924.

sidered herself free to go ahead and exploit her spheres of influence in China after the example of European nations. It soon became evident that she was going to run afoul of American interests. The United States gently but firmly kept reasserting the open door principle, but the complaints kept coming into the Department of State that American business men in China were being unfairly treated by the Japanese officials in the Japanese spheres of influence. In 1908, therefore, Secretary Root and Ambassador Takahira at Washington, exchanged notes and made another informal "agreement" which restated and redefined the "open door." Each nation promised not to interfere with the equal rights of the other to trade in China and they mutually promised that if any misunderstanding did arise they would at once communicate with one another and take steps to allay the trouble.[22]

But somehow the idea got abroad that by this agreement the United States sanctioned the Japanese aggressions in China. Then came the European War. Japan got a tremendous lead over the other nations trading in China, not only because European trade fell off, but because Japanese goods supplanted those European goods. Japan soon gained a commanding position in the Orient, both political and economic, and naturally she wanted a recognition of that position. It would not have been consistent with the traditional American policy to admit any such supremacy of Japan, but there was no denying the fact that the war gave Japan an era of prosperity, the like of which she could never have known otherwise. With the tremendous increase in demand for Japanese goods, and with no competitors to restrain her, Japan went ruthlessly ahead to bring China under her domination.[23]

And so it came about that the next exchange of notes between Japan and the United States put Japan in an even more favorable position. When America entered the World War in 1917, the Japanese sent Viscount Ishii to Washington to arrange for co-

[22] P. J. Treat, *Japan and the United States, 1853–1921*, pp. 194–5.
[23] A. J. Brown, *Mastery of the Far East* (N. Y., 1921), pp. 416–29.

operation between the two countries in defeating Germany. In the course of the negotiations the following agreement was made supplementary to the Root-Takahira Agreement:

> "The governments of the United States and Japan recognize that territorial propinquity creates special relations between countries, and consequently the government of the United States recognizes that Japan has special interests in China, particularly in parts to which her possessions are contiguous." [24]

Aside from this, the two powers again agreed upon the "open door" policy.

But what did the United States mean by this new departure in which she recognized that Japan had special interests in certain parts of China? Certainly it was true in fact. Moreover the United States has never hesitated to assert and maintain that she had special interests in certain Latin American nations because of their proximity. Whether Ishii was trying to announce a Monroe Doctrine for the Far East, with himself in the rôle of Monroe or whether he was not, the fact is that the impression soon got abroad that the United States had radically departed from its traditional policy in the Far East. The Japanese did not hesitate to notify the Chinese of the agreement and translate the words "special interests" into Chinese words which unmistakably meant "predominant interests." Secretary Lansing had in fact made no such concession and had indeed expressly refused to admit that Japan had any "predominant interests" in China. His principal purpose was to reassert the "open door." But the United States now joined the other powers of the world in being principally occupied with defeating the German Kaiser and his hordes. [25]

Japan went quietly ahead, lending money to China, because no one else had very much money to lend, and making those loans the excuse for further control over the administration of China. Japan further laid herself open to criticism in the matter of a

[24] P. J. Treat, *Japan and the United States, 1853–1921,* pp. 224–5.
[25] B. "Situation in the Far East," in *Foreign Relations,* I, pp. 21–2; Secretary Lansing before the Senate Committee on Foreign Affairs in *Sen. Doc. 106,* 66th Cong., 1st sess., p. 226 passim.

joint military expedition to Siberia with the United States. The Japanese sent an expeditionary force out of all proportion to her agreement, and ten times the size of the United States forces. This raised the suspicion that she had designs on Siberia as well as China and the length of time her troops remained after the Americans had left lent further color to this idea. Moreover the treatment which Japan had meted out to hapless Korea was now dragged out to prove Japan an autocratic militaristic nation bristling with all the faults of the Prussian Junker. In 1910 Japan had annexed Korea to her empire without any diplomatic protest from the United States. In 1919 under the spell of a world set on fire by the idea of the freedom of small oppressed nationalities, the Koreans revolted against their Japanese masters and were put down with a good deal of cruelty. This raised further bad feeling in the United States against Japan, particularly as the Koreans advertised that the Japanese actions were really for the purpose of stamping out Christianity in Korea.[26]

It was apparent that the relationship between Japan and the United States badly needed adjustment and clarification by 1919. The accumulated woes of Japan in the California matter were not helped by a modification of the Monroe Doctrine in 1912 to include Japan, among those nations who could not acquire territory on the American continents. At that time it was rumored that the Japanese were trying to acquire Magdelena Bay, on the coast of Lower California, as a naval base for future operations against the United States. Although Secretary Knox assured the Senate that there was no truth in the report, still that body adopted a resolution which forbade any foreign government, European or otherwise, to acquire land for a naval base in the Americas. So the Asiatic powers were added to the European powers in the list of those who might not interfere with our special interests in Latin America.[27]

The Peace Conference at Versailles did little to clear up the problems of the Pacific Ocean, for it was too busy re-drawing the

---

[26] A. J. Brown, *Mastery of the Far East*, pp. 195–207, 524–38.
[27] A. B. Hart, *The Monroe Doctrine*, p. 235.

Map of Europe to pay much attention to China. The result was that it played right into the hands of Japan and thereby created a whole host of other problems which meant that America would have to call a conference of her own to settle the outstanding troubles with Japan. This occurred in the Washington Conference in 1921.

The problem of Japanese emigration to the United States remains one of extreme delicacy. In 1924, Congress had under consideration a new immigration bill, designed to check further the tremendous influx into the United States of foreigners fleeing from the burdens of a devastated and tax ridden old world. In this bill was a provision for the exclusion of all Asiatics ineligible to citizenship, which meant that Japanese were hereafter to be excluded as were the Chinese at an earlier date. The Japanese government felt this was an unnecessary affront to a proud nation, and that the same practical effect was being secured by the "Gentleman's Agreement." Secretary of State Hughes cautiously and tactfully advised Congress not to take such a step, but to rely on diplomacy and not cause unnecessary friction with Japan. Ambassador Hanihara, apparently feeling that Congress was on the verge of passing the bill, transmitted to the Department of State a vigorous note stating the Japanese position and warning the United States that the exclusion bill would bring "grave consequences" on Japanese-American relations. Instead of having the effect intended of making Congress pause, it had exactly the opposite effect, as the legislators at Washington saw in Hanihara's letter a veiled threat and an attempt to dictate to them. Consequently they bridled at once, and passed the bill by a huge majority effectively cutting off Japanese emigration on the same terms on which the Chinese had been excluded.[28]

[28] N. Y. *Times*, April 12, April 15, 1924; R. L. Buell, *Japanese Immigration*, pp. 307–319.

CHAPTER XVI

FORSAKING THE NEUTRAL TRADITION

"For the state which has reduced others to slavery does not in a more real fashion enslave them than the state which has the power to prevent it, yet looks carelessly on, although claiming as its pre-eminent distinction that it is the liberator of Hellas."

—*Thucydides.*

1. The Peace Movements

The dawn of the twentieth century revealed a world headed for international disaster. Nationalism, that curious and undefinable mixture of emotion, an egotistical sense of national honor, and a similarity of ways of thinking, had been erected into an idol. National patriotism the world over had been awakened and developed, as the extension of popular education aroused an ever greater and greater number of people to a sense of their unity with their neighbors in the next town, but not, alas, with their neighbors across the river. Whatever nationalism may be, the world had a bad attack of it.[1] Nationalism was accompanied by a rapid extension of univeral military service, based on the Prussian and Napoleonic models. This resulted in the maintenance of huge armies in time of peace for the possible defense of national boundaries and national honor. Science and invention had perfected instruments of destruction which made the preparation for war ever more and more costly. The wars of the nineteenth century overturned all old-fashioned notions of warfare. The new systems of organized destruction required an expenditure of money and time which would have staggered the imagination of our great-grandfathers.

Each nation of Europe was bent on outbuilding her neighbors, in the piling of up huge armaments and armies. England had the greatest navy and Germany the most efficient army. Europe

[1] W. T. Laprade, "Nationalism," *Amer. Hist. Assoc. Rept. 1915*, pp. 223–9.

was a veritable barrel of dynamite that the smallest spark might set off. At the same time that property-holders gave reluctant consent to the tremendous taxes necessary to support these armaments, there began to surge up from beneath the indignation of the unpropertied classes, who, after all, made up the rank and file of armies. The masses had begun to think for the first time in history. It was a very elementary and confused kind of thinking, but the increase in popular education and the industrial revolution with its growth of city life could only result in cogitation by the man who would be called upon to give up his life. Socialist doctrinaires were busy spreading their gospel that all war is a rich man's conspiracy, wherein the laborers of one country kill the laborers of another country while rich men of both countries wax fat on war profits. With the increase in armies came the increased protest against all war, as such.

Now it had often occurred to American statesmen, that war was a bad thing. The European has suffered more, but apparently the suffering has not always resulted in making him despise war. Compare the American cantonments in the late war with a French "caserne." The American barracks were hastily constructed wooden structures which were as hastily pulled down. War is a temporary and highly regrettable episode in American history. French barracks, on the contrary, are huge stone structures, often the most imposing buildings in the town. The "caserne" has always been there and it always will be there, swallowing up its annual quota of young men. War seems to be a permanent institution in Europe.

American diplomacy has, as we have seen, been characterized by a stern determination to avoid wars, particularly European wars. Whether in fact we have avoided them is another question. A whole philosophy of opposition to war grew up in America as a part of that national idealism, in which America at least tried to state the case, even if she did not practice what she preached.

There are two principal reasons why war has been opposed as wrong. The first is that it is unchristian. It is hard to conceive of Christ in a uniform serving a machine-gun. But another argument has had even more weight in a world which apparently is not yet ready to follow spiritual leadership. That argument is simply that war does not pay. Victor and vanquished are alike unhappy, impoverished, and distressed. This is one of the oldest arguments against war, for Plutarch records that Cineas endeavored to dissuade Pyrrhus from his conquests on the ground that, after he had defeated the Roman legions, he would be no better off than before as far as the real things of life are concerned.[2]

Yet the founder of the peace movement in America, like the father of international law, grounded his opposition to war squarely on the fact that war is contrary to the teachings of the New Testament. David Low Dodge, a New York merchant, in 1809 began his agitation against war in the face of the impending struggle with England. His work was carried on during the next half century by William Ladd whose essay on the subject will ever remain a great classic in American peace literature.[3] It contains the best expression of the American idea that the proper way to settle international disputes is not war, but a Congress of Nations for the adjustment of irritations and an International Court for the settlement of justiciable cases.[4] But Americans were not the first in this field. Many a European statesman and philosopher has suggested a plan to stop wars. The trouble, however, with most of the previous plans was that they failed to take into consideration the fact mentioned at the opening of this chapter, that nations were coming to be more and more jealous of their independence and less willing to surrender one iota of their so-called sovereignty in the interests of international peace. William Ladd's *Essay* was one of the first to treat human nature as it actually is. Instead of presenting a Utopian scheme based on the idea that the people of the world really wanted peace and would be charitable and self-sacrificing about it, he acted the part of a political engineer and tried to

---

[2] Plutarch, *Lives* (Clough tr.), II, 73-4.

[3] William Ladd, *An Essay on the Congress of Nations* (Boston, 1840).

[4] J. B. Scott, *Introduction* to 1916 edition of Ladd's *Essay*, p. vii.

devise a Congress of Nations which should be a political machine. In it each nation was to have one vote, thus guarding against the possibility of the small nations being swallowed up by their larger neighbors. This was to be a diplomatic body which considered and adjusted quarrels, that could not be settled by law, since frequently there was no international law on the point at issue. All questions which were "justiciable," or could be settled by fairly well known canons of international law, were to be referred to the second part of his plan, a "Court of Nations," or world court.[5]

Our evidence of the importance of Ladd's propositions is the fact that when the First Hague Conference met in 1899, it followed out the American's suggestions with remarkable fidelity. The war-machine had, by the end of the nineteenth century, become too expensive; and naturally that nation with the biggest army, Russia, felt it most. Moreover, in Russia were the rumblings of socialism the most ominous, as evidenced by what has happened there since 1917. In Russia (Poland) was written that remarkable book *The Future of War*, by Jean de Bloch. De Bloch's work took up the thoroughly practical argument that war was futile. His plea was that of a Polish business man who insisted that war simply does not pay. Moreover the progress of invention had made necessary about this time the overhauling of the Russian military equipment; therefore economy as well as economic considerations inside of Russia combined with the influence of this book to lead the Tsar of Russia to call the First Congress of Nations at the Hague in 1899.[6]

Twenty-six nations were represented at this first organized international effort to rid the world of the curse of war and the burden of armaments. These included most of the Europeans, China, Japan, Persia, and Siam, while the United States and Mexico were the sole representatives of the American continents. The American delegation was headed by Andrew D. White and it was instructed on all the points which the Russians proposed

[5] J. B. Scott, *Introduction* to Ladd's *Essay*, xl, 8ff., 34ff.
[6] J. de Bloch, *The Future of War* (Boston, 1914).

for discussion. But an additional instruction was given covering a matter which the Russians had not proposed to discuss in terms. Secretary John Hay called the attention of the delegates to the fact that America had always contended for a world court for the settlement of international disputes, and he directed them to bend their efforts toward getting such a court set up.[7]

Faithful to her program Russia placed before the Conference a plan for the limitation of armies and navies, and made a very earnest and sincere plea for its adoption. As was expected, opposition developed at once, and, as was further to be expected, the Germans were most vehement in refusing to tolerate any plan which would limit the size of their army. The matter could get no further than the recommendation that the powers study the case and take it up again at some future date. The Germans even went to some pains to deny that their people felt the burden of armaments, and insinuated that German people were proud to pay the taxes for the support of their military machine. This attitude showed how far behind the civilized opinion of the world the Germans were at the time, and how impossible it was to get anything definite done while the German spirit prevailed.[8]

But if the Conference could do nothing about the biggest thing it had to do, at least it worked up a whole group of treaties aimed at the amelioration of the conditions and results of warfare, and a code of rules for the conduct of a more humane type of war. Moreover, Americans, true to their traditional policy, brought the American notion of a world court to the attention of the assembled delegates. From the moment of their arrival at The Hague the Americans began to talk about this project. Opposition came from the Germans again, who at length consented to it only after further consultation with Wilhelmstrasse. The Conference finally adopted both the plans forecast by William Ladd sixty years before. The Conference itself was his "Congress of Nations," and the provision for a Permanent Court of Inter-

[7] *Instructions to the American Delegates to the Hague Conferences*, etc., edited by J. B. Scott (Wash., 1916), p. 8.

[8] F. W. Holls, *The Peace Conference at The Hague* (N. Y., 1900), p. 77.

national Arbitration followed out his idea of a "Court of Nations." In this court the parties to the suit were to select their own judges from a panel composed of distinguished jurists offered as candidates by all the nations.[9]

The First Hague Conference did not stop wars. Hardly was the ink dry on the treaties than Great Britain and the Boer Republics were at death grips in South Africa and in a few years Russia herself began her bloody struggle with Japan. Yet the practical politicians of the world seem somehow to have been impressed with the possibilities of the idea and in 1907 another Hague Conference met to take up the work anew. When the roll of the nations was called this time, the number had risen from twenty-six to forty-four. The increase was explained when the delegates from the nations of Latin America were found seated with all those from the old world. Secretary of State Root's insistence on the inclusion of the South Americans had made the second meeting a truly world conference.

There is no need here to go into the details of the second conference. It took up the business where the first meeting had left off and doubtless the representatives of all the nations worked sincerely and earnestly for international concord. This must not, however, allow one to conclude that the nations these gentlemen represented were in any way disposed to be either sincere or earnest in the matter. Cynics and conservatives without number scoffed at the whole proceeding. Yet the instructions given the American delegates by Secretary Root contained much sound common sense:

> "In the discussion upon every question, it is important to remember that the object of the Conference is agreement, and not compulsion. . . . It is important also, that the agreements reached shall be genuine and not reluctant. . . . The immediate results of such a conference must always be limited to a small part of the field which the more sanguine have hoped to see covered; but each successive conference will make the positions reached in the preceding conference its point of departure and . . . as each conference will inevitably make further progress by successive steps, results may be accomplished which have formerly seemed impossible." [10]

9 F. W. Holls, *Peace Conference at The Hague*, pp. 231, 246.
10 *Instructions to the American Delegates*, etc., pp. 71-2.

In other words, Rome was not to be built in a day, and the world must not be disappointed if the matter of getting rid of war proceeded very slowly.   Joseph H. Choate, the chairman of the American delegation to the Second Conference, was particularly and justly indignant at the London *Times*, which denounced the whole thing as a sham.[11]   Said Mr. Choate with some feeling, "Because we did not do everything, the London *Times* said we did nothing."

Having asserted the American idea of a world court at the first conference, the second American delegation brought before the second conference another great principle of American foreign policy, the freedom of the seas to neutrals.   It must now be apparent that much of our diplomacy with England has been colored by the controversy over the rights of the innocent bystander in the time of war.   Secretary Root instructed the Americans to get the conference to take some action in the whole matter of the crystallization of the laws of contraband and all the multifarious problems of neutrality connected therewith. The whole question of the War of 1812 was up again, still as unsettled as ever.   No wonder Mr. Root gave the representatives of this country directions to have the matter brought to an issue. But here, as in the case of disarmament at the first meeting, little could be done save to have the whole thing referred to a special Naval Conference which was ordered to meet in London the next year.   The matter of another Hague Conference was discussed and generally approved, and it should have met in 1915.   But a year before that date an international catastrophe (hinted at in the opening of this chapter) overtook civilization.[12]

The American delegations at both Hague Conferences went on record in the following language:

"Nothing contained in this convention shall be so construed as to require the United States to depart from its traditional policy of not entering upon, interfering with, or entangling itself in the political questions or internal administration of any foreign State, nor shall anything contained

11 J. H. Choate, *The Two Hague Conferences* (Princeton, 1913), pp. 55–6.
12 *Instructions to the American Delegates*, etc., pp. 83, 123–8.

in the said convention be so construed as to require the relinquishment by
the United States of America, of its traditional attitude toward purely
American questions."

In other words, the United States still wanted the privilege of
falling back on the doctrines of isolation and Monroe, if it seemed
convenient to do so.[13]

Following the second meeting at The Hague came the London
Naval Conference of 1908, which took up the work of trying to
define contraband and to reach some intelligible conclusions out
of the confusions which make up our practice on belligerent treatment of neutral vessels and commerce. The Conference issued the
so-called "Declaration of London of 1909" which laid down certain
fairly definite rules for the conduct of naval warfare and for the
classification of contraband. Now, at last, it was thought, every
one can agree on what is actually absolute contraband and what
is conditional contraband. Without such a code of maritime law
the rules of naval warfare as regards neutrals were chaotic. But
the only fact that concerns us is the fact that by 1914 the Declaration of London was still not properly ratified by all the parties
to it, and so it was not international law, and not binding on anyone who did not wish to be bound by it.[14]

The Second Hague Conference was followed by another burst
of peace propaganda in both the United States and England.
Mr. Norman Angell came out with his "Great Illusion," pointing out, as had De Bloch, that victory was as ruinous to the victor
as it was destructive to the vanquished. Mr. Angell's work was
well reasoned and his main thesis was, not that war was impossible, but that it was useless. Although an Englishman, he lectured
extensively in the United States in an effort to arouse the interest
of Americans in their foreign policy. Yet hot on the heels of the
Second Hague Conference came the destructive Italo-Turkish
War of 1911 and the terrible Balkan Wars of 1912–13. The whole
question of Turkey and the Near East was aflame once more and
the powers of Europe watched anxiously and piled up more arma-

[13] *Instructions to the American Delegates*, etc., pp. 74, 98.
[14] J. W. Garner, *International Law and the European War*, I, 27ff.

ments. It was the old, old question of who should fall heir to the fast shrinking dominions of the Sultan of Turkey. Russia and Austria both wanted the same thing and both were angry and disappointed to see the renascent nationalism of the Balkan States deprive them of their chance to take Turkish lands. The German Kaiser rattled his sabre at every opportunity to display petty dignity, and all Europe was in momentary danger of disaster.[15]

Meantime Woodrow Wilson had become President of the United States with the peace-loving William J. Bryan as Secretary of State. Both men hated war with an almost religious fervor, reminiscent of the days of Thomas Jefferson. Bryan at once set about getting the United States committed by a set of arbitration treaties not to go to war with anyone, except after a year's delay for investigation and adjustment. He succeeded in negotiating a large number of such treaties and advanced greatly the cause of the peaceful settlement of international disputes where the United States might be a party. His one conspicuous failure was his inability to convince Germany that she ought to enter into such an agreement with us. For better or for worse, this left the United States and Germany in a position where any cause of war would not be put in "cold-storage" for a year.

While Bryan was trying to arrange the foreign affairs of the United States in accordance with this policy, the President and two other men saw with unusual vision the abyss toward which Europe was heading. His personal adviser, Colonel E. M. House, and the brilliant Walter H. Page whom Wilson had dispatched to London as the American Ambassador urged on the President the importance of forestalling the inevitable catastrophe by getting England, France and Germany together. Page was insistent that this must be done on a large scale, and he called upon the President to "work on a world plan. Nothing but blue chips, you know," in one last desperate effort to prevent the deluge of blood which any student of European politics could see coming. Such a plan involved a closer coöperation between Great Britain

[15] Norman Angell, *The Great Illusion* (N. Y., 1910).

and the United States, for if the two great English-speaking nations cannot live peaceably in the same world, how can they expect anyone else to do so? The anti-English hyphenates in America railed at Page for his outspoken advocacy of Anglo-American coöperation, but he went courageously ahead and soon Colonel House was dispatched to Germany, France and England to get them all together on a disarmament plan such as the Hague Conferences had utterly failed to evolve. It was a forlorn hope. The Kaiser, obsessed with the idea that European civilization was about to be engulfed by a "yellow peril" from Asia, would not hold up his military or naval program for an instant. When House visited Paris, he found it agog with a political murder trial, which necessitated his going on to England. But London, too, was in a wild state of excitement, for the Irish question was reaching a state which threatened civil war, not only in Ireland, but in England herself, and officers were daily resigning from the army rather than carry out the government's instructions. President Wilson's plans of world peace were hopeless from the start. Germany did not want peace and neither England nor France could, for the time being, get her attention off of domestic politics.[16]

2. NAGGING THE BRITISH LION

So the peace movements were all to no purpose. In June of 1914 came the flash that set off the dynamite when a Serbian assassinated the Austrian Archduke at Serajevo. An obscure person in a corner of Europe which most Americans never heard of shot a man that few Americans cared anything about. Perhaps a few Americans looked up Serajevo on the map, but it is doubtful. To American students of European politics and old ladies who read memoirs of the European courts, it was merely another tragedy in the Hapsburg family. Then, late in July, Germany gave Austria a blank check and told her to go ahead. Germany cannot be accused of starting the war, but she can be justly accused of having blindly promised to support anything Austria did.

[16] B. J. Hendrick, *Life and Letters of Walter H. Page* (N. Y., 1922), I, 270-300.

Having been promised this backing if she went to the limit, Austria promptly did so and made a series of bullying demands on Serbia which meant only that Austria purposed to have war and nothing would stop her. War was the immediate result of Austria's act and Germany must bear her heavy responsibility of having been the nation who could have prevented it. Russia joined Serbia at once, whereupon Germany declared war on Russia and attacked France. Into the maze of European alliances which necessitated Germany's action, we need not enter. They were all part of a general system of European militarism against which the Hague Conferences had been aimed. Realizing the futility of trying to get into France through the Verdun-Belfort line of forts, the Germans put themselves everlastingly in the wrong by again attacking a neighbor they had promised to defend, as had Frederick the Great in Silesia nearly two hundred years before. Germany violated the neutrality of Belgium, when she herself had been a party to the treaty guaranteeing Belgium's neutrality. This brought England into the conflict at once, inasmuch as England could not see the Kaiser sitting in Antwerp any more than she could tolerate Napoleon's doing it. In a few days Europe was smoking with battlefields from end to end.[17]

President Wilson at once issued a proclamation of neutrality and hastened to ask the belligerents what they proposed to do about the Declaration of London. America, again the great neutral, would soon be shipping supplies and munitions to both sets of fighting nations. The questions of contraband, continuous voyage and the like were in as unsatisfactory a condition in 1914 as they had been in 1814. Replies from the warring powers made it clear that the Declaration of London was a dead letter. Great Britain said she would observe it, subject to so many qualifications that it amounted to a refusal to be bound by the Declaration. Secretary Bryan then notified the powers at war that the United States would conduct herself under the rules of interna-

17 S. B. Fay, "New Light on the Origins of the World War," *Amer. Hist. Rev.*, XXV, 616, XXVI, 37, 225; B. Schmitt, "Triple Alliance and Triple Entente," *Amer. Hist. Rev.*, XXIX, 449; G. P. Gooch, in *Cam. Hist. of British Foreign Policy*, III, 385-486.

tional law as they were before the Declaration of London, which simply meant that we would cling to our traditional position. This, as has been made abundantly clear, was not England's interpretation of the same rules.[18]

Now in this matter of shipping contraband goods to a belligerent, the offense consists in getting caught. A neutral merchant had a right to send any goods at all to a belligerent. If he sent arms and munitions, he did not violate the neutrality of his country; the shipment was legal and the trade was lawful. But if he got caught he was penalized by the loss of his goods. A belligerent has a right to prevent certain goods from reaching his enemy for his military use; yet those very goods the neutral has a right to send. It is just here that a confusion of terms arises. The trade in contraband articles has been termed "illegal," "illicit" and "unlawful," by certain jurists who do not thereby mean to imply that the trade was forbidden by international law. Judge Story had used the expression "illicit or contraband trade," [19] and Chief Justice Chase remarked that the "conveyance by neutrals to belligerents of contraband articles is always unlawful." [20] Strange as it may seem, neither of these gentlemen meant what they said. The true law has been put by another American judge, Chancellor Kent, who has said "A trade by a neutral in articles contraband of war, is a lawful trade, though a trade of necessity subject to inconvenience and loss." [21] So perhaps the best way to put it is to say that the shipment of contraband is legal unless the neutral shipper gets caught. The belligerent must be his own policeman and the neutral is under no obligations to stop her citizens from shipping contraband. Thus was the confusion of the law when the world was confronted by a situation which demanded immediate action and could not wait on legal formulæ.[22]

[18] *Diplomatic Corr. with Belligerent Governments Relating to Neutral Rights and Commerce*, *Sp. Supp. Amer. Jour. Internat. Law*, IX, 7. J. W. Garner, *International Law and the World War*, I, 29ff.

[19] Carrington *v.* Insurance Co., 8 Peters, 495 (1834).

[20] "Peterhoff," 5 Wallace, 28 (1866).

[21] Seton *v.* Low, 1 Johnson (N. Y.), 1, 1799.

[22] R. G. Adams, "Growth of Belligerent Rights over Neutral Trade," *Univ. of Penna. Law Review*, LXVIII, 20ff.

Grotius' classic tripartite division of contraband into "absolute," "conditional" and "non-contraband," fell to pieces like a house of cards. How could any distinction be made between goods intended for the civilian population and goods intended for the fighting forces, when nations drafted every available man into the army and every available woman into a munition factory? The expressions "a nation in arms," "the mobilization of industry," or "pooling of national resources" meant exactly what they said. The distinction between combatants and noncombatants might be all right for academic discussion, but for a practical situation was it of any consequence? Then again, in this age of chemistry, how could there be any distinction between warlike and unwarlike goods? Gunpowder might be "absolute contraband" and lip-sticks and manicuring sets might look like non-contraband. But in this day of science, the lip-sticks might be converted into glycerine and thence into explosives and cargoes of nail-files certainly were used to fill shrapnel-cases. Shipments of condensed milk might be sent ostensibly to feed German babies, but it was too easy to reduce the fats in the milk to explosives and the cans were easily adaptable for the celebrated German "potato-masher" hand grenade." [23]

Observe the operation of the celebrated "Rathenau Plan," under which Germany plundered her own as well as conquered territory. The army requisitioned "individual and firm name-plates, door knobs and knockers," "velvet, plush and silk textiles," "curtain rods, stein covers, stair rods, clothes hangers," and the like. [24] Could there any longer be a distinction between absolute and conditional contraband? Indeed, was there any such thing as non-contraband? One English writer hazarded the guess that "with the exception of human hair, there is not a single element or substance which could not in some way be made to serve a military purpose." Yet at that very time "hair"

---

[23] A. M. Low, *Law of Blockade* (London, 1916), p. 18; for a thoughtful plea against the destruction of the distinction between combatants and non-conbatants, see J. B. Moore, *International Law and Some Current Illusions*, pp. 5ff.

[24] "German Treatment of Conquered Territory," edited by D. G. Munro and others (Wash., 1918), Red, White and Blue Ser. No. 8.

was already in the Manual of the Quartermaster Corps of the United States Army as an article which might be properly requisitioned, along with "school-books, corkscrews, cuspidors, pencil-sharpeners, rat-traps, whistles, clothespins," etc., etc. Again, it is fair to put the question, is there any object in trying to classify contraband? [25]

No wonder then, England began again her system of Orders in Council which had so enraged the Americans before the War of 1812. No wonder Britain, again the mistress of the seas, was holding up every imaginable kind of shipment from the United States to Germany. England did not at once declare a blockade, but she did publish a series of contraband lists, which included ever more and more kinds of goods with each successive Order in Council. At first England made a great concession to the southern cotton grower in the United States by not considering cotton contraband. But this was only an act of charity on the part of Great Britain toward the United States, because cotton was the basis of gun cotton, a form of high explosive. Ultimately England and her allies absorbed all the cotton the United States could send them and that problem solved itself. Moreover Germany's notorious violations of almost every known rule of the laws of war soon put England in a mood where the Premier informed the House of Commons:

"In dealing with opponents who have openly repudiated all restraints of both law and humanity, we are not going to allow ourselves to be strangled by a network of judicial niceties," for "there is no form of economic pressure to which we do not consider ourselves entitled to resort." [26]

Finally the distinction between absolute and conditional contraband having become manifestly untenable, the British did the only sensible thing by abandoning it altogether. [27]

A blockade of Germany was really unnecessary, for the German merchant marine was swept from the seas and the German

---

[25] *Manual of the Quartermaster Corps, U. S. A.*, par. 2207; *War Trade Board Journal*, May, 1918, pp. 4–5.

[26] *Hansard*, 5th ser., LXX, 600; J. W. Garner, *International Law and the World War* II, 287.

[27] The "Kim," 113 Law Times Reports, 1002 (1915).

fleet never but once dared come out of port. The British fleet policed the whole of the North Sea and no neutrals could get to Hamburg or Bremen. But what did happen was the shipment of vast supplies from the United States and from South America to those neutral nations, Denmark and Holland, which bordered on Germany. Thousands of head of pork went via Copenhagen and thousands of barrels of petroleum put in at Rotterdam. Could Britain allow this? It was shipment from a neutral to a neutral and surely, argued the Germans, no belligerent would have a right to hold up such a traffic. So Germany was being supplied with goods which went right by England's front door, and which, so neutrals contended, could not be stopped because ostensibly they were going to Dutch and Danish merchants.

However, we have met this situation before and England dragged from its resting place the old "Rule of 1756" with its corollary "Doctrine of Continuous Voyage." In reply to the complaints of the United States that our shipments to neutrals were being held up by unlawful British action, Sir Edward Grey, the British Minister of Foreign Affairs, pointed out that England was grounding her claims solely on the old English policy of continuous voyage. The neutral shippers thought to get around this by addressing their packages to a neutral merchant. But the British met this by another Order in Council of October 29th, 1915, whereby if the ultimate destination of the goods was not clearly proved in the ship's papers, the burden of proof was put on the neutral to prove that the destination was not Germany. If the Doctrine of Continuous Voyage aroused the anger of American shippers, this shifting of the burden of proof made them even more indignant, for, they contended, it was like presuming a man guilty until he had proved himself innocent. But the English Judge, Sir Samuel Evans, sitting in the seat of Lord Stowell, insisted:

"As to the modifications regarding presumption and the burden of proof . . . these are matters really affecting the rules of evidence and methods of proof in this court. . . . I fail to see how it is possible that they are violations of international law." [27]

[27] See "Kim," supra.

If the Americans had examined their own great authority on the law of evidence they would have found out that the British were quite right.[28]

The case of Denmark was particularly instructive. Normally an exporter of meat and meat products, the Danes suddenly began to import immense quantities of these goods, especially animal fats. It was perfectly obvious that these goods were going to Germany by the same old ruse which had appeared in every war since the beginning of the seventeenth century. England had always refused to tolerate it, and the European practice had come to agree with her. In the American Civil War, it will be recalled, even the United States went completely over to the British point of view. During the conflict with the Confederate States, the American Supreme Court under Chief Justice Chase had ruled as the British were now ruling and had stopped the flood of so-called neutral goods going to Nassau and Matamoras. We have seen how during the Civil War the Americans were irritated at Palmerston because he, refusing to understand that the North was fighting for freedom, merely growled "We want cotton." In 1915 an American critic unconsciously imitated Palmerston and wailed "What directly concerns us is that our trade with the Central Empires is cut off and our trade with the neutral neighbors of those empires is limited by measures of at least doubtful legality." [29] But their legality did not remain doubtful very long after the United States entered the war. The Germans accused the English of being all sorts of criminals for the holding up of neutral trade through the neutral ports, and the United States kept sending notes to Ambassador Page asking him to protest against this or that trifling act of the British navy which impeded the free course of contraband goods to Germany. Granting that the English were "criminals," when the United

[28] J. W. Garner, "Contraband, Right of Search and Conditional Voyage," *Amer. Jour. Internat. Law*, 372, 383; *Measures Adopted to Intercept the Sea-borne Commerce of Germany*, British *Accounts and Papers*, Misc. No. 2, Cd. 8145; J. B. Thayer, *Treatise on the Law of Evidence*, 314ff., 357ff.; R. G. Adams, "Growth of Belligerent Rights," supra, pp. 42–3; on the whole subject see H. R. Pyke, *The Law of Contraband of War* (Oxford, 1915).

[29] Monroe Smith, "American Diplomacy in the European War," *Pol. Sci. Quar.*, XXXI, 49.

States got into the war the age-long struggle for neutral rights went into the waste-basket and America took her place beside England as tolerating and practicing exactly the things we had previously protested against. Mr. F. L. Polk, the Counselor of the State Department, put the thing very well to Mr. Balfour when he said:

> "It took Great Britain three years to reach a point where it was pre-pared to violate all the laws of blockade. You will find it will take us only two months to become as great criminals as you are." [30]

Pro-German and Irish-Americans and other Americans who carried a perpetual chip on their shoulders as far as England was concerned, accused England of blocking our neutral trade in the interests of their own manufacturers. The State Department was hounded by these people into nagging Great Britain with petty matters, as irritating as Palmerston ever was, quite inno-cently oblivious of Ambassador Page's lucid observation:

> "The truth is, in their (the British) present depressed mood, the United States is forgotten—everything is forgotten, but the one great matter in hand. For the moment, at least, the English do not care what we do, or what we think or whether we exist. . . . I pick up an American news-paper eight days old and read solemn evidence to show that the British Government is interrupting our trade in order to advance its own at our expense, whereas the truth is that the British Government hasn't given six seconds' thought in six months to anybody's trade—not even its own. . . . I try to picture to myself the British Minister in Washington making inquiry on the day after Bull Run, why the sailing boat loaded with per-simmon blocks to make golf clubs is delayed in Hampton Roads." [31]

The historian of the future is likely to agree with Page that the rôle played by the United States in her diplomacy with England in the years 1914–1917 is not one of which we have any reason to be proud. America was still slowly waking up to what it was all about. The policy of isolation with its ostrich philosophy, the hundred years of provincial history teaching and still more pro-vincial Fourth-of-July orations, the spread-eagled speech-making of four generations of American politicians who thought they

[30] B. J. Hendricks, *Life and Letters of Walter H. Page*, II, 265.
[31] Ibid., 64.

Portrait by Philip Lazlo, Courtesy of Doubleday, Page and Company.

WALTER HINES PAGE

were patriotic when in the depths of their ignorance they attacked England on very debateable grounds, were all bearing fruit in America's tardy recognition of her obligations in world politics. This is a chapter of American history which we would rather omit, but it has had far too great an influence on the history of our foreign policy for us to pass on without recognizing it.

It is difficult to avoid the conclusion that when the events of the war drove the United States into the struggle, we abandoned our traditional position on neutral rights. The "blacklisting" of certain American firms which were known to be sympathetic to Germany, had aroused much feeling against Britain, because "blacklisting" meant that these pro-German firms in New York could not have English coal. We contended this was an unwarranted interference with neutral rights. Yet when we got into the war it has been well said that the United States

"Became more inexorable than Great Britain ever had been in keeping foodstuffs out of the neutral countries that were contiguous to Germany." [32]

3. GERMANY DRIVES THE UNITED STATES INTO WAR

With Germany and her allies, our relations were infinitely more serious and complicated. From the outset, both sets of belligerents kept complaining to the United States of their enemies' violations of international law. In this case President Wilson was put in the position of having to listen to all the complaints of each side against the other. The Germans began a heavy campaign of propaganda in the United States, which was as clumsy as it was ineffective. When it became apparent that the British fleet was going to keep Germany from getting munitions and supplies from the United States, the Germans began to cry that America was unneutral in her conduct. Senator Stone, of the Senate Committee on Foreign Affairs brought the matter to an issue in a correspondence with the Department of State. Stone represented Missouri, where there is a large German population. Bryan's reply to Stone demonstrated conclusively that what

[32] W. L. Rodgers, "Suggestions as to Changes in International Law for Maritime War," *Amer. Jour. of Internat. Law*, XVII, 1, 14.

Germany really wanted was to have the United States violate her neutrality in favor of Germany. Not one of Germany's allegations against the United States has ever been proven.[33]

Failing in this effort Germany got her ally Austria to enter a similar protest, based on the fact that supplies without number were going from the United States to England and France, but none were getting to Germany and Austria. This, Austria maintained, was a violation of the neutrality of the United States. Secretary Lansing made short work of this rather absurd argument by pointing out that these shipments were the commerce of private firms in the United States, which, under international law, they had a perfect right to send. Indeed, Lansing cleverly quoted German authorities and German practice to prove that the United States was not in any sense violating its neutral obligations.[34] As a matter of fact, Austrian diplomacy during the war was very stupid indeed, for soon the Austrian Ambassador, Count Dumba, was caught red-handed in an effort to instigate and promote strikes in the American steel works which were shipping supplies to Europe. His recall was demanded and he went home.[35]

But our real quarrel with Germany came over the old question of the freedom of the seas. Immediately after the outbreak of the war, Germany notified the world that she was sowing mines in the open seas, and floating mines, at that. This Germany had promised at the Hague in 1907 not to do. Naturally, thereafter no one else could observe the Hague promises, either. The British retaliated by putting mines in the North Sea, at the same time warning neutrals to keep away. This was in no way a threat, but merely a "Danger" sign to neutral ships. In January, 1915, when the German food administration took over the rationing of that country, it thereby destroyed all distinction between the combatant and non-combatant population. This naturally led Britain to stop all food going to Germany and Germany promptly

---

[33] J. B. Scott, *Survey of the International Relations between the U. S. and Germany, 1914 - 1917* (N. Y,, 1917), pp. 54ff.

[34] *Dipl. Corr. of the U. S. with Belligerent Govts.*, Spec. Suppl. to *Amer. Jour. of Internat. Law*, Oct., 1916, pp. 166–71.

[35] J. B. McMaster, *The United States in the World War*, I, 173–9.

retaliated by declaring in February, 1915, a "war-zone" around the British Isles, threatening deliberately to sink by using her submarines, any vessel of the enemy found on the seas designated, without bothering to give crew and passengers time to get away. This at once involved the United States. Americans were accustomed to travel to Europe in foreign vessels, as the merchant marine of the United States had not been adequate to its needs for fifty years. What would happen if an American citizen, traveling on an unarmed British merchant vessel, was killed? Long before any overt act occurred, the State Department warned Germany that the United States would not tolerate such conduct, so Germany went ahead in the full knowledge that her conduct would involve the gravest consequences even to war with the United States.[36]

In international law, it should be repeated, a belligerent war-vessel may capture her enemy's trading vessels wherever she can take them on the high seas, but she must take her prize into port and have it condemned in a prize court, thus saving the lives of the crew and passengers. In such extreme cases as that of the *Alabama*, captains who could not get to their home ports occasionally had sunk their prizes to avoid recapture. But even Admiral Semmes had always been scrupulously careful to preserve the passengers and crew of the captured vessel.[37] At this point, however, a new factor entered the situation, the submarine. A German U-boat could not take her prizes into the ports of Bremen or Hamburg and so, like Semmes, might be forced to sink what English vessels they captured. But, unlike Semmes, the U-boat carried a small crew of about fifty and had no room for the thousands of passengers who might be on the vessel they were about to sink. Moreover they could not put a prize crew on board, because they could not spare the men. Further, the submarine could not stop and search its intended prize as one blow from the bow of the merchant would crack the submarine in two like an egg shell. Therefore, reasoned the Germans, the subma-

---

[36] *Dept. of State, Corr. with European Govts., 1918*, IV, 21.

[37] J. A. Bolles, "Why Semmes of the Alabama was not tried," *Atlantic Monthly*, XXX, 95ff.

rine must act without giving warning. The Germans are a thoroughly logical people, and they drew the logical conclusion that they must sink all English vessels without warning, and let the crews, English, Americans and everyone else, go to a watery grave without ever knowing what hit them.[38]

After due consideration this is exactly what they did, and in May of 1915 the civilized world was horrified by the news that a German submarine had sunk the British steamship *Lusitania*, without warning, and thereby killing seven hundred passengers, including many prominent Americans. That the *Lusitania* was not an armed vessel is now established beyond a shadow of doubt. As far as international law was concerned, the crime was inexcusable. What made it worse was the fact that the German Government, ignoring all the courtesy of diplomatic practice, addressed the people of the United States, over the heads of the Government of the United States, and publicly warned them exactly what was going to happen. Such a piece of diplomatic impertinence had not occurred since President Washington sent Citizen Genet packing for his disregard of international courtesy.[39]

A vast wave of indignation swept over the United States, and converted many pro-Germans to the cause of the Allies, as well it might. Many wished the United States to enter the war at once and help whip Germany, but these enthusiasts were mainly confined to the eastern seaboard of the United States. President Wilson diagnosed the state of public opinion in the United States and concluded that America would not follow him into a war with Germany, even if he were himself inclined to go, and very evidently he was not so inclined. He still hoped that the United States might act as the mediator between the two sets of warring powers. Consequently, instead of sending the German ambassador home, he inquired of Germany what she meant by such conduct. The Germans replied that the *Lusitania* was an armed vessel, thus practically admitting that they had no right to sink her if she was not armed. Wilson promptly informed them that

[38] J. B. Scott's *Survey*, etc., pp. 36, 136ff.

[39] N. Y. *Times*, May 1, 1915, p. 19; *Amer. Jour. of Internat. Law, Spec. Suppl.*, July, 1915, p. 132.

they had been misinformed and that they had better think up a better excuse quickly, or trouble would follow. This was too much for Secretary of State Bryan, who was apparently afraid that Wilson would go to war, whereupon he very properly resigned. Germany then weakened and alleged that the mere presence of American passengers on board the *Lusitania* could not protect her. Another message from Wilson set them right on this score and the Germans admitted that they were completely in the wrong, promising to warn vessels in the future before sinking them. While some historians of the future may say that Wilson did right in trying to keep his country out of war, his mistake was placing any confidence in any promises Germany made at this juncture. It was from this point on not possible to keep out of the war. Yet the United States abounded still with enthusiasts of a dozen sorts who were bent on avoiding participation in the war and it would be difficult to prove that the country would have stood behind the President in war at this juncture. It would be equally difficult to prove the opposite.[40]

Yet, though Germany backed down and promised not to do it again, still three months later came evidence of her faithlessness in the sinking of the *Arabic*, another English vessel, with the loss of more American lives. Without waiting for a message from Wilson, the German Ambassador, Count Bernstorff hastened to request a delay and finally explained that the submarine captain who sank the *Arabic* was acting contrary to orders. Germany apologized and offered to pay an indemnity. Again a wave of anger swept more and more Americans from the pro-German into the pro-Ally camp. Louder grew the protests of these who claimed that Germany was only playing with the United States, and that apologies would never bring the drowned men and women back to life. Again Wilson was urged to go to war, but again he accepted the German promises at their face value, believing the German Government was honorable.

Germany's next trick was soon played when the news came in that the Italian liner *Ancona* had been sunk in the Mediterranean

[40] *Amer. Jour. of Internat. Law, Spec. Suppl.*, Oct., 1916, pp. 129–41, 149, 155.

Sea, under rather atrocious circumstances, since the submarines not content with sinking the vessel also shelled the women and children trying to get away in lifeboats. Before any protest was possible, Austria at once avowed the act as hers, and the whole situation had to be gone over with again before this belligerent was induced to promise to be decent and agree with the American interpretation of the law of the sea. This might have been regarded as a diplomatic victory on the part of the United States had Germany and her allies been capable of good faith. But the Allies, at least, had long since lost faith in Germany's ability to keep her word and were now arming their merchantmen with guns. This gave Germany a chance to allege that the merchant vessels thereby became war vessels, and hence entitled her to attack them. Foreseeing the trouble this would inevitably provoke, the United States endeavored to dissuade the Allies from such a step, but Britain's reply well expressed the sentiments of all the Allies on the subject:

> "Great Britain is unable to agree that upon any non-guaranteed German promise, human life may be surrendered defenseless to the mercy of an enemy who, in circumstances of this kind, as in many others, has shown himself to be both faithless and lawless." [41]

Within a short time Germany amply justified Britain's answer by attacking the *Sussex*,[42] an unarmed channel steamer, killing or wounding eighty passengers, including Americans. This was certainly a flat violation of the promises given in the case of the *Arabic*. On being taxed with the act, the Germans tried to shuffle and evade. First they said they did not do it. Then they argued they had a right to do it, and then, as opinion in America was swinging steadily toward war with Germany, Secretary Lansing notified the Germans that the whole use of submarines was evidently incompatible with the principles of humanity and that unless Germany forthwith abandoned the undersea warfare against passenger vessels, the United States would sever diplomatic relations, which meant ultimate war. In alarm, Germany at once

[41] *Dept. of State, Dipl. Corr. with Belligerent Govts.*, 1918, IV, 147–78.
[42] Ibid., Oct., 1916, 336–7.

yielded and pledged herself that hereafter no merchant vessels should be sunk without due warning and without giving the passengers and crew a chance to get away, unless the vessel tried to escape or attack the submarine. Then in a characteristically German way, she proceeded to tack on to these pledges the proviso that this would be done only if the United States forced England to give up the blockade and the doctrine of continuous voyage. Germany was trying Napoleon's old game of making promises conditional on the United States compelling England to do something. But Wilson refused to be caught as was Jefferson. He sent back word to Germany immediately that the United States would discuss English relations with England and German relations with Germany, and that it was none of Germany's business what we said or did with regard to England,

" . . . the United States notifies the Imperial Government that it cannot for a moment entertain, much less discuss, a suggestion that respect by the German naval authorities for the rights of citizens of the United States upon the high seas should in any way or the slightest degree be made contingent upon the conduct of any other government affecting the rights of neutrals or non-combatants. Responsibility in such matters is single, not joint; absolute, not relative." [43]

Perhaps there may be some reason for saying that Germany really tried to live up to this promise, but as the fighting wore on it became increasingly obvious that Germany could not win. At least it became obvious to the German war lords. Despite their spectacular victories in Russia, Serbia, Rumania and France, the Germans at home began to starve. Unless Germany could resume her unrestricted submarine warfare, the rulers of Germany felt that their successes were but Pyrrhic victories. In October of 1916, the Kaiser practically notified President Wilson that if he could not very shortly induce England to come to terms, Germany would resume her submarine warfare without limit.[44] Wilson had in mind a last effort at peace at this time and was unfortunately forestalled by one of the Kaiser's periodic "peace offensives" in December of 1916. Giving this a chance to be re-

---

[43] *Amer. Jour. of Internat. Law, Spec. Suppl.*, Oct., 1916, 190–200.
[44] Ibid., Oct., 1917, p. 323.

fused, as it inevitably was, Wilson then asked all the belligerents to state their war aims. The Allies replied quite frankly they would not quit until the menace of German militarism had been removed from the world, and until they had delivered the territory which Germany was occupying. Germany was content to reply to Wilson by generalizing about her victories and making bumptious remarks about what she expected other people to do.

On January 22d, therefore, President Wilson went before the Senate and informed them of what he had done and laid before that body an idea which had been in his mind for some time, that however the war might end, there must be formed some kind of League of Peace to prevent future wars. He pointed out that America could not stay out of world politics, even if she would. He explained his proposal by calling it a Monroe doctrine applied to the whole world.

> "That no nation should seek to extend its polity over any other nation or people . . . that all nations henceforth avoid entangling alliances which drew them into competitions of powers."

In general he wanted the nations of the world to get together on the basic political ideals of free government, free seas and disarmament. His speech met a wide variety of responses. Europeans were in the main frankly cynical. Because he had allowed himself to say that these plans depended on a "peace without victory," he was understood in many quarters to mean that he favored leaving the war as it stood, which would have meant an unquestioned German victory. The ever-swelling ranks of allied sympathizers in the United States resented the suggestion. Many people looked upon his suggestion of a League of Peace, a world political organization, as a bit of dreamy idealism. Yet by many others he was regarded as the herald of a new spirit in international relationships.[45]

A week later the whole thing was dashed to pieces when Germany, desperate at her inability to break the iron ring of the allied armies, announced that she would no longer observe the *Sussex* pledges and would reopen the unrestricted submarine

[45] J. B. McMaster, *The United States in the World War*, I, 310–314.

warfare. At last convinced of Germany's insincerity, the President shipped Ambassador Bernstoff home at once and summoned the American Ambassador Gerard home from Berlin. In telling the United States that she was going to break her pledges, the Germans directed America to keep all its vessels and citizens off the high seas in the neighborhood of Europe; save that one vessel a week, elaborately painted to assure her identity, might go to and from Southampton. If the United States had bowed to Germany's will in this matter she would have had to admit that she was no longer an independent nation. If America had submitted to this dictation from a foreign nation, President Wilson would have meekly had to tell the American people hereafter to take their orders from Berlin and not from Washington. The issue could not be more clear-cut. The United States had no choice. Either she must now fight, or admit that her career as an independent nation was over.[46]

By this time the outrages and insults which Germany had heaped upon the United States had solidified the articulate public of the country into backing any steps the President might be inclined to take. The people were tired of having their friends and relatives drowned, business men were very tired of having the German embassy engineer strikes in their industrial works, American shippers were weary of having the paid agents of Germany attach time-bombs to vessels leaving New York harbor, the traveling public was on edge with the consciousness that the bridge over which they were passing might be blown up by a paid hireling from the German embassy at Washington, and above all the thinking men and women of the country had come to realize that the swashbuckling political philosophy of the ruling caste in Germany was intent upon the destruction of the democratic institutions on which our government was founded.

In contemplating the foreign policy of the United States toward Germany in those three years from 1914 to 1917 certain things must stand out in the mind of the historian who will ultimately depict the period more thoroughly than is possible in such a vol-

[46] *Amer. Jour. Internat. Law, Spec. Suppl.*, Oct., 1917, pp. 330 ff.

ume as this. In the first place it is impossible to deny that the United States tried desperately to stay out of the war, in the face of the clamors of a body of citizens centering around such men as Roosevelt, who from the start felt that we should be in the war on the side of the Allies. In the second place the future historian will, in all probability, conclude that if President Wilson had entered the war any sooner than he did, he would have lacked the united support which had rallied behind the war idea by 1917. This is a thing which it is difficult for eager partisans of the Allies to understand, yet the middle and far west were not a unit in their sympathy with England and France, and, as we have pointed out, more than half the people in the United States live west of the Appalachian Mountains. Moreover, even in the East, the population of Boston is notoriously Irish, and hence unsympathetic with England. In New York, another great seaboard city, there were millions more of Irish and millions of pro-German, or perhaps it would be better to say anti-Russian, Jews, Socialists and others who were not anxious to go to war with Germany or anyone else. Now it is not at all profitable to call these people hard names, and abuse them as cowards and renegades. They were for the most part honest and sincere people, who had quite as much right to their opinions as had men like Theodore Roosevelt or Walter Page who had absolutely no patience with them. Yet the historian is going to have to reckon with these people.

In the third place, the future historian is going to be very apt to come to the conclusion that never in the whole history of our country was a more wholehearted effort made to steer clear of a European quarrel, never was greater patience exhibited in the face of a foreign nation gone mad with lust of power and desperate fear of defeat. If the United States were drawn into the war, it was probably because the United States could not stay out of this European War any more than America had stayed out of any of general European conflicts since the days of the Spanish Armada. As has been pointed out a number of times in this volume, a close study of the history of the last two hundred and fifty years must convince us that America's policy has been in fact to get into every general European war and the years 1914–1918 were not the breaking with a traditional policy, but a frank following out of what our economic and political interests had always led us to do. Moreover with the increasing political and economic interdependence of nations, it would be very difficult to prophesy that America would stay out of general European conflicts in the future. She seldom has in the past. She may indeed remain aloof from local conflicts such as were the Crimean and Balkan wars, but anything that can be dignified by the name of a general European war has usually found American soldiers and sailors on one side or the other.

Accordingly the United States was forced to make her choice and decide which set of belligerents deserved her support. In the midst of the excitement caused by the German action, the Associated Press circulated a dispatch which had been intercepted by the British going from the German Minister of Foreign Affairs, Zimmermann, to the German Ambassador in Mexico. It pointed out that as the submarine warfare was likely to bring the United States into the conflict, Mexico was cordially invited to join with Germany in making war on the United States, it being "understood that Mexico is to reconquer the lost territory of New Mexico, Texas and Arizona." It was further proposed that Mexico induce Japan to change sides and attack the United States. Americans can afford to laugh at the notion that Texas might rejoin Mexico, or even that Mexico wanted back the unruly Yankees that they were well rid of in 1849, but the whole episode illustrated how utterly ignorant of the real nature of the Americans was the German Foreign Office.[47]

The story of the last minute efforts to stay out of the war with Germany by means of a resurrection of the old "Armed Neutrality," and by various groups of pacifists, need not detain us here. President Wilson announced to Congress on February 3, 1917, that the German Ambassador had received his passports. On the 2d of April he formally advised Congress to declare war,

[47] J. B. McMaster, *United States in the World War*, I, 343; *Congressional Record*, LV, No. 4, p. 194.

making clear that it was the intent of the United States to protect itself and its citizens in the undoubted rights they had on the high seas in international law. Great Britain and Germany had both adopted measures in the war which we believed had infringed our rights as neutrals, but the great difference between the two was that whatever damage Great Britain had done she could pay for when the war was over, but what Germany was doing in the slaughter of innocent women and children could never be paid for by any sum of money. American foreign policy was able to distinguish between the offenses of the English and those of the Germans, although many Germans did not seem to be able to see any difference. America was going into the war primarily to preserve law, the right to live peacefully in the family of nations, and this Germany had made impossible.[48]

Germany's surprise and chagrin at finding that the United States would fight was very great. It was heightened into a feeling of desperation when she found that the United States proposed to send an army to Europe. The Teutonic powers therefore gathered themselves for their mightiest offensive of the war, but it was too late. The troops of Britain, France and Italy were driven back, but their lines were not broken. Germany could not get through. Early in 1918 the olive-drab soldiers from across the seas began to arrive in the ports of England and France by the tens of thousands. French ports which heretofore could entertain but three or four vessels were transformed by American engineers until they could unload a dozen vessels at once. Huge American locomotives and box cars were placed assembled in the holds of vessels and picked out at the other end of the voyage by mighty cranes made in America. Within a few hours after landing a locomotive thus put on shore would be steaming off under its own power to carry supplies to the front. The allied armies were for the first time put under the unified command of the French General Ferdinand Foch, whose philosophy of war was attack, not defense, and who, like Napoleon, always believed in being stronger than the enemy at the point of

[48] Lindsay Rogers, *America's Case Against Germany* (N. Y., 1919), pp. 5, 49.

contact. Rotten and discontented within, her defenses shattered by the tremendous blows of the Allies who were heartened by the prospect of American aid, Germany's morale began to weaken. The German army was driven from land it had held for four years, while riots and disorders broke out the inside of the Central Empires. Unable to recover from the sledge hammer blows of Foch's armies, and utterly unable to support the troops now fast falling back into Germany herself, the German Government at last sent word to President Wilson that it was ready to negotiate.

In January of 1918, President Wilson had addressed Congress on the aims of the United States and had laid down fourteen points which he hoped would be the basis of America's war aims. These were practically the conditions on which America would undertake to make peace. They certainly involved the defeat of Germany, the restoration of Alsace and Lorraine to France, the utter break up of Austria and Turkey, the re-drawing of the map of the world on the basis of the wishes of the populations involved and the creation of a League or Association of Nations.[49] Germany now notified him that she would talk peace on the basis of the fourteen points. Wilson immediately replied that the Germans could discuss that matter with Marshal Foch. The French commander dictated terms of an armistice which amounted to an abject surrender on the part of Germany, and the disintegration of Austria into a half a dozen different nations. Foch's terms were agreed to by Germany on November 11, 1918, and they left the German powers impotent to renew the war, even if internal conditions had permitted any such thing.

The task which now faced the treaty-making powers in the United States was not only to frame a peace, but to decide whether or not President Wilson's idea of a League of Nations could be adopted for all the world. Great Britain, France and their allies were enraged beyond measure at the four years of atrocious fighting and bestial warfare which they attributed to Germany. They were out to make Germany pay the last penny

[49] N. Y. *Times*, Jan. 9, 1918.

and the last drop of blood. Mr. Lloyd-George, the British premier, heretofore a radical liberal, had his party reëlect him immediately after the armistice on a platform which called for the hanging of the Kaiser and making Germany pay the whole costs of the war. France, under her tiger, Clemenceau, was in no mood to be forgiving or charitable. She had suffered too much. Other nations felt a bitterness toward Germany which was the measure of the cruelty Germany had meted out to them. The one voice crying for a peace of moderation was that of President Wilson, and he had been repudiated by his people in an election which took place but a few days before the signing of the armistice. Thus did the United States enter upon the task of making peace, with just exactly the situation which Wilson, in his doctoral dissertation thirty-five years earlier, had pointed out was the curse of the American government. The President represented one political party and the coördinate body for the conduct of foreign relations, the Senate, represented the opposite political party.[50]

[50] W. Wilson, *Congressional Government* (Boston, 1884).

CHAPTER XVII

THE PEACE, THE LEAGUE AND THE SENATE

"Moreover—and this is an excuse which must not be lightly brushed aside—the task before them was one of unprecedented difficulty. New States had to be created, territories redistributed, indemnities secured and all upon a scale incomparably greater than any international conference or congress had ever before attempted to deal with. A task so great needed not politicians of the usual type, but persons of the qualities which it is the fashion to call those of the Superman. . . . Such men did not appear. Why should they have appeared? Why should they have been expected? There is no saying more false than that which declares that the Hour brings the Man."—*James Bryce.*

1. The Impossible Task

"The position occupied by President Wilson in the world's imagination at the close of the World War, and at the beginning of the peace conference was terrible in its greatness. Probably to no other human being in all history did the hopes, the prayers, the aspirations of so many of his fellows turn with such poignant intensity as to him at the close of the war." [1] There can be no doubt but that during the trying period of neutrality it had been Wilson's ambition to have the United States occupy at the end of the war some such position as he personally held when he went to Paris.[2] The difficulty lay in the fact that the United States as such was incapable of taking its place at the peace table as the impersonal arbiter of the nations, voicing the ideals of a new world order. Woodrow Wilson could, and did; but he failed to realize those ideals because such ideals must be national, not personal, and the United States was no more ready than any other nation to make those ideals its own. Given the undivided support of the people of the United States, he might conceivably

---

[1] J. C. Smuts, in the N. Y. *Times*, Mar. 3, 1921.
[2] J. Tumulty, *Woodrow Wilson as I know Him*, p. 234.

have succeeded in asserting what he believed to be the culmina-
tion of American political theory; but even this is doubtful,
as he had the rest of the world's statesmen against him.[3] But
in fact he started out already repudiated by his own people in
the November election of 1918, accompanied by commissioners
who, though of his own choosing, yet neither fully understood
nor fully sympathized with what he purposed to do.[4]

During the war, President Wilson had attempted to state the
war aims of the allied nations by laying down his famous fourteen
points, upon which the world was to be remade.   Embodying
the highest principles of international morality, these ideas had
captured the imagination of oppressed peoples everywhere,
at home as well as abroad.[5] As Wilson understood them, they
simply expressed American political ideas such as government
by the consent of the governed, the "open door" in international
trade, the abolition of old-fashioned secret diplomacy, and the
formation of a kind of universal Monroe Doctrine in a League
of Nations for the protection of nations and the maintenance
of international order.[6] This naturally involved the break-up
of nations like Austria-Hungary, which were held together against
the will of the people. It likewise involved applying to the whole
world the principles which the United States had tried to apply
to the liberation and opening up of China and its relief from selfish commercial monopolies But above all it involved the abolition of war among nations by the application of the same
principles which had abolished war among private individuals.

On the basis of these principles, Germany agreed to surrender.
But it is at once apparent that generalizations such as the fourteen points must be susceptible to so many and such varied interpretations, that the acceptance of them by Germany and the
allies meant nothing at all. Possibly for that reason, President
Wilson determined to go to Europe himself in order to make
sure that the principles were not violated. By doing so he broke

[3] Wilson to the Senate in N. Y. *Times*, Jan. 23, 1917.
[4] R. Lansing, *Peace Negotiations*, pp. 38, 97, 137.
[5] N. Y. *Times*, Jan. 9, 1918, for the "Fourteen Points" speech.
[6] Ibid., Jan. 23, 1917, for the "League of Nations" speech.

a time-honored tradition which had dictated that the President
should not leave the country during his term of office. This
created considerable excitement and opposition in the United
States, not only among the Republicans but in his own party.[7]

Moreover, as delegates to the Conference, he did not select any
member of the Senate which had to ratify whatever he did. In
this he was perfectly within his rights, and followed the time-
honored practice in which the President negotiates treaties before
sending them to the Senate. But the selection of the commissioners opened Wilson to criticism. Although the election of 1918
had been a victory for the Republicans, yet he chose as the American representatives, Secretary Lansing, Colonel House, both
Democrats, General Bliss as the military adviser, and Mr. Henry
White, a veteran diplomat, as a sop to the Republicans. In view
of the fact that the Republican party held such able diplomats as
Elihu Root, and William H. Taft, the selection of White was
somewhat offensive to the Republicans, as was the choice of Colonel House who had never held public office and was looked upon
simply as the personal friend of President Wilson. Yet one may
question this resentment against White, as Mr. Roosevelt himself
has said "The most useful man in the entire diplomatic service,
during my presidency, and for many years before, was Henry
White." Root and Taft were both considered by Wilson but
were passed over.[8] There need be no proper criticism of Wilson
for going himself. The corresponding executive official of every
other country was in Paris, and it would have been decidedly inappropriate as well as disadvantageous if the chief executive of the
United States had absented himself, while the chief executives of
other nations were present.[9]

The atmosphere in which Wilson arrived in Europe must be
understood. A world of autocracy had just crashed to the ground

[7] J. B. McMaster, *U. S. and the World War*, II, 242; R. Lansing, *Peace Negotiations*,
p. 23.

[8] J. Tumulty, *Woodrow Wilson as I know Him*, p. 337; N. Y. *Times*, Nov. 25, 28, 30, 1918,
Mar. 2, 1919; T. Roosevelt, *Autobiography*, p. 388.

[9] It is frequently overlooked that the prime minister in a parliamentary government exer-
cises functions similar to those intrusted to the President in the United States, while our
Secretary of State is really but a Minister of Foreign Affairs.

before the assaults of democracy. From the ruins came rushing to Paris the leaders of between twenty and thirty submerged nationalities, notably Poles, Bohemians, and Slavs of many kinds who had been oppressed for centuries. From the closets of the victors emerged the family skeletons of oppression and mis-government, like the Irish, the Chinese, the Egyptians, the Per-sians, and Albanians. All were crying the magic words "self-determination of peoples," without considering whether they were sufficiently civilized to govern themselves. All took the fourteen points literally and besieged Wilson with prayers to give them land, liberty, property, and everything else down to Rubens paintings and coin collections.

From the vanquished millions in Austria and Germany came cries for mercy and for food. From Soviet Russia came dire threats of world revolution, the end of capitalist society, the utter annihilation of autocracy and democracy alike before the red conflagration of bolshevism.[10]

Wilson's name was on the lips of everyone as he went on his triumphal tours to Paris, to London, and to Rome. He was re-garded as a savior by an intoxicated world. Yet no one knew better than did Wilson himself that most of these poor people were doomed to disappointment.[11] Autocracy might be crushed in Central Europe, but its influence still remained in France, Italy, England, and the United States. To imagine that the world could now be made over, that hereafter everyone was going to be good and happy was a dream of folly. But the only point which the historian need notice is that the world was composed of foolish men, that it was a world drunk and insane, not only with a sense of victory, but also with a sense of relief that the most terrible tragedy of the ages had ended. To expect such a world to act rationally was absurd. This must never be forgotten.

When President Wilson arrived in Paris he found awaiting him an array of statesmen, the like of which the world has seldom seen gathered together at any one time. He found himself pitted

[10] R. S. Baker, *Woodrow Wilson and the World Settlement* (N. Y., 1922), I, 6–10.
[11] G. Creel, *The War, the World and Wilson* (N. Y., 1920), p. 163.

against the keenest minds of Europe in the persons of the chief executives of the principal allied nations. There was Premier Clemenceau of France in the chair. At his left was clever Premier Lloyd-George of England and the astute Mr. Balfour, and supporting them were the premiers of the four principal British Dominions, now no longer colonies, but co-equal nations with Great Britain in the Britannic Commonwealth. There was the huge Premier Massey of New Zealand, the ever alert Premier Hughes of Australia leaning forward with his ear phone to catch every word. With them the impressive Canadian Premier, Sir Robert Borden and the ex-Boer General, Premier Botha of South Africa with his brilliant partner General Smuts. These men were not going to be lightly subordinated to the desires of Britain as had happened to colonial statesmen in a dozen previous Peace Congresses. They had stipulated in advance that "the consent of the kings to the various treaties should in respect to the Dominions be signified by the signature of the Dominion representatives," for they were no longer the dependencies or colonies or subject states of Britain, but equal partners with her in the management of the great Britannic Commonwealth.[12]

Besides these was Premier Orlando of Italy; Premier Venizelos of Greece, the brains of the Balkans; the canny Premier Bratiano of Rumania, one of the ablest political manipulators in the world, and the veteran Premier Pachitch of Serbia (now Jugo-Slavia). During the sobering awfulness of war these men had subscribed to the Wilsonian idealism and they had come to Paris to remake the world and to remake it right. Yet no sooner was the stress of the war over, than they all sank back into being very human individuals, with all the passions and selfishness of human beings.[13] To twist and garble the fourteen points into doing the duty of selfishness was as easy as it is for the devil to quote scripture. So the fourteen points upon which the vanquished had relied to save them from utter dismemberment and annihilation, were seized upon by the victors to serve their selfish ends. If Wilson

12 Sir Robert Borden in the N. Y. *Sun*, Oct. 7, 1919.
13 Baker, I, 82.

had any misgivings about the necessity for his presence in Paris, they must have been dispelled when he saw Mr. Lloyd George appear backed up by the mandate of the "khaki election" of 1918 in which he had promised to give England about everything possible including the privilege of hanging the Kaiser. Clemenceau could not and would not forget what France had suffered, and France was determined to make Germany pay for that suffering.[14]

The Italians and the Japanese appeared smilingly confident, their sleeves stuffed with aces and marked cards in the shape of treaties which they had in secret extorted from the Entente as their price of joining in the war. Those treaties were taken too lightly by Wilson and the Americans, some of whom appear not even to have appreciated the existence of such treaties. Yet they committed the allies in advance to parceling out the peoples of Europe and Asia to a new set of masters after the fashion of the cattle fair at Vienna in 1815.[15] President Wilson's ideals were all right as a cry to deceive the mob, as a sop to socialism and labor, and as high-sounding eloquence with which to whip up war spirit; but the diplomats had little intention of taking them seriously.[16]

The inevitable disagreements among the victors began to appear as soon as it was evident that President Wilson was a strong-willed person who had no idea of surrendering his principles to a lot of old world land-grabbers. His friends and his critics alike agreed that Wilson was a perfect tower of strength in support of the right as he saw it. Frequently his opponents agreed that he was morally right, but they apparently argued that this wicked world was no place for the application of Principle.[17] Expediency, not right, was to be the rule of the Conference and the marvelous thing to the historian is not that Wilson failed to secure the fourteen points in every case, but that he ever got them applied in any case. The world after all, was being run by men who

[14] A. Tardieu's *Truth About the Treaty* is proof of this.

[15] *Hearings before the Senate Committee on Foreign Relations*, 66th Cong., 1st Sess., *Senate Document No. 106*, hereafter cited as "*Sen. Doc. 106*," p. 518. These treaties were in fact matters of common knowledge before Wilson went to Paris, and had been commented upon by enlightened writers in America during the two previous years. See, for example, the articles of Dr. H. A. Gibbons in the *Century* during the years 1917 and 1918.

[16] Baker, I, 52, 61.   [17] Ibid., II, 35.

had been born and brought up in the period before 1914 and that world had quite as much difficulty in understanding what Wilson was driving at as the Jews of two thousand years ago had in comprehending the Sermon on the Mount.

Indeed on many occasions it seems that the only weapon held by the American was the fact that fundamentally he was right. The ignorance of the envoys from the United States handicapped them from the outset. This ignorance does not refer to the corps of trained historians, ethnologists, geographers, economists, and legal experts which Wilson took to Paris. These men apparently did their work well. But the ordinary facts about the diplomacy of Old Europe which ought to have been furnished by the Department of State and the Diplomatic Service were sadly lacking. This was not the fault of the Department of State so much as it was the fault of the American system of appointing executive officials and diplomats. For a hundred years Congress had been "economizing" in the running of the department of foreign affairs. The Department of State had never had sufficient appropriation to find out the things all European diplomats knew anyway. For a century it had been the practice of incoming presidents to appoint rich men with social ambitions or "Main Street" bankers to the diplomatic service, as rewards for service rendered in the presidential campaign. For decades the United States had been following an isolation policy which had discouraged interest in foreign affairs, and for generations the history books and popular orators had been telling the public that America was good and virtuous while Europe was a contaminated thing to be left strictly alone. For years there had persisted a foreign policy the principal tenet of which had been the Monroe Doctrine, which the man in the street understood to mean that Americans were the "best people on earth." [18] Republican presidents and Democratic presidents alike had regarded the position of Secretary of State as a political plum, and not as a position of responsibility to be filled by a great international lawyer. Even Lincoln had given the job to his most astute political rival, Sew-

[18] A. B. Hart, *The Monroe Doctrine, An Interpretation*, p. 387.

ard, while Wilson himself had summoned the orator Bryan to the position, and both were unequipped for it. No wonder that lesser lights like McKinley had regarded the secretaryship of state as a convenient shelf upon which to place an old friend to make room for a new one in the Senate. No wonder the American delegation was unfit to handle the problems that confronted it at Paris, but this was not primarily the fault of President Wilson, nor of his experts, but the fault of fifty years of Democratic presidents before 1860 and half a century of Republican rule since.[19]

So it was that President Wilson faced the Conference and learned that the cards had been stacked against him in advance. Italy and Japan appeared with their secret agreements by which they had been paid to come into the war, and those agreements were dead against the self-determination of peoples, Germans, Slavs and Chinese. Possibly Wilson should have taken these secret treaties more seriously, for the Bolsheviki had discovered them in the foreign office archives of the old Czarist régime and published them broadcast in 1918, but at that time a wildly excited world regarded them only as more soviet propaganda.[20] At any rate Wilson came to Paris determined to ignore all such old-fashioned star-chamber diplomacy, only to find that the rest of the people at the peace table were intent on asserting it.[21]

As has been so often pointed out, it was not primarily the diplomats with which he had to contend, but the strong vested property interests, vague, and in most cases undiscoverable, which have been making diplomats dance since diplomacy began. The Italians and the French demanded their pound of flesh in the carving up of Turkey, and pipe lines were being laid to drain the oil from the Ottomans while yet the conference was in session.[22] In vain Wilson asked that the facts of the wishes of the people

[19] W. Lippmann, "For a Department of State," *New Republic*, XX, 194; Baker, I, 36–7; *Sen. Doc. No. 106*, 518. For amelioration of this condition see the discussion of the Rogers Bill in 1924, ch. XVIII, infra. A little reading of some of the speeches in opposition to this bill will be apt to suggest that the many Democrats are still of the ante-bellum frame of mind—the bellum being the Civil War.

[20] F. S. Cocks, ed., *Secret Treaties* (Lond., 1918, U. D. C.).

[21] Baker, I, 52, 61.

[22] Baker, I, 64.

be ascertained. There is probably no more erroneous supersti-
tion abroad than the idea that Wilson would not find the facts
from his experts.[23] He was one of the few men at the Conference who really and courageously were willing to face the facts.
In this very question of the carving up of Turkey he insisted on
sending out a special mission to get the facts, and it found out
what he wanted to know, but other nations would not coöperate
with similar fact-finding commissions and the American report
was not published till four years after the Conference.[24]

At the outset of the Conference the very first of the fourteen
points went on the rocks. "Open covenants, openly arrived at"
was not the Old World Order's idea of doing things, and the
newspaper men were enraged to find they had to be contented
with a colorless daily summary of events. True it is that the
correspondents got more from this Conference than they ever had
from any previous Conference, and true it is that Wilson explained
that irresponsible newspaper men should not interpret him to
mean that they might witness "the birth pains of the peace."
These things could never be understood by the people at large,
nor by journalists. Wilson tried to explain that "the essence
of democratic method is not that the deliberations of government
should be conducted in public, but that its conclusions should
be subject to a popular chamber and to free and open discussion on platform and in press." But this was of no avail, for the
newspapermen had been led to expect too much and were disappointed.[25]

As soon as the Conference opened there also occurred a conflict between the group headed by Wilson who desired a negotiated peace and the group best represented by Foch who wanted
to dictate a peace of force. Wilson had constantly to deprecate
the use of force and this made him unpopular with those who had
suffered so much from German frightfulness. While it can prob-

---

[23] Baker, I, 113–14; Tumulty, 354–8; C. H. Haskins and R. Lord, *Some Problems of the
Peace Conference* (Harvard Press, 1920), p. 31; E. House and C. Seymour, *What Really
Happened at Paris* (N. Y., 1920), pp. 447–9, 459, 273.

[24] The King-Crane Report, in *Editor and Publisher*, LV, 1–28; Baker, I, 77.

[25] Baker, I, 116–35, 137, 150–1, 193.

ably be said that Wilson did repeatedly save the Conference from committing outrageous injustice by his firm stand against parceling out undisputed German territory to French or Poles, yet in the end it did not profit him greatly. Indeed he was so often calling for fair play that upon one occasion Clemenceau called him pro-German, which did not help matters very much.[26]

All President Wilson's efforts to interpret the higher international morality were based on the certain fact that every unjust settlement would simply breed more wars. But the dead hand of the past was heavy on the Conference, "it was the dead ages speaking and they did not all speak the same language."[27] The more evident this became, the more determined was Wilson to secure from the wreckage of his ideals at least the League of Nations to right the numerous wrongs it was apparent the Conference was going to commit. The dead ages and the Old Order in Europe insisted on a brutal peace, with an eye for an eye and a tooth for a tooth. When Wilson insisted that they be fair to the Germans who had so despitefully used them Clemenceau was reported to have remarked scornfully that the President was talking like Jesus Christ.[28]

At any rate the Conference did not listen to all the language spoken. The equality of nations before the law in international practice had been a cardinal principle of American diplomacy. But in these later years the United States had certainly departed from it, principally in its relations with the states of Central and Caribbean America. The Conference frankly went on record as making the reconstruction of the world the business of the great powers, in spite of the evident misgivings of the lawyerlike Lansing.[29] Again one must understand the setting. Madmen were screaming at the keyhole, said Mr. Lloyd George, and newspapermen the world over were howling with disgust at the slowness, the dilatory tactics, the protraction of the negotiations. The world, they said, was falling to pieces like a house of cards while Wilson and his colleagues were dallying over

[26] Baker, I, 173.   [27] Tardieu, p. 95.
[28] H. W. Harris, in his *Peace in the Making*, p. 48, is eager to authenticate this.
[29] Baker, I, 179–83; Lansing, p. 219.

petty territorial adjustments. The necessity for speed became so evident that a Council of Ten was formed, representing United States, Great Britain, Japan, Italy and France. This expedited matters somewhat, while the experts busied themselves with details. But even this did not make matters move quickly enough. The Japanese were bored with endless discussion of European affairs and so they dropped out and there was formed the Council of Four, Wilson, Clemenceau, Lloyd-George and Orlando. By this action it seems frankly admitted for the first time by the United States that although nations may have equal rights and an equal status in a court of international justice, still in international administration, the doctrine of equality had to give way to the primacy of the great states. After all, Clemenceau was quite right in his insistence that France had a great deal more at stake in this business than had Cuba.[30]

The language of diplomacy for centuries had been French, but the Versailles Conference put English on a parity with it. This was but natural, as certainly English was spoken by more peoples represented at Paris than any other language except Chinese, and no one proposed to make that a medium of international intercourse. The negotiations were conducted in both languages and the treaty was written in both.[31]

2. MIXING THE LEAGUE AND TREATY

The preliminaries out of the way, Wilson went straight as an arrow to his big idea, the League of Nations. To his way of thinking, nothing permanent could be done until he had that established. He was determined to make it an integral part of the treaty, so that any injustices done in the treaty could carry their own cure.[32] The idea of a League of Nations was certainly not a new one, nor was it Wilson's own, but it had never been undertaken before on a world-wide scale.[33] Disregarding Lan-

---

[30] S. W. Armstrong, "Doctrine of Equality of Nations in International Law and the Relation of the Doctrine to the Treaty of Versailles," *Amer. Jour. of Internat. Law*, XIV, 540.

[31] Baker, I, 203–9; official text will be found in 66th Cong., 1st sess., *Sen. Doc. No. 51.*

[32] Haskins and Lord, chs. v–viii.

[33] P. B. Potter, *International Organization* (N. Y., 1922), p. 23.

sing's protest that the United States could not enter any agreement which would involve getting it into war, because the Constitution had given Congress the power over war and peace, he whipped the Conference into drawing up a constitution for such a league.[34] There was to be an Assembly in which each nation had one vote. There was to be a Council composed of the great powers with certain changing representatives of the smaller powers. There was to be a permanent secretariat located at the seat of the League. Meetings were to be occasional. But Article X of the draft obligated the members "to respect and preserve as against external aggression the territorial integrity and existing political independence of the members." Further machinery was provided for settling international disputes without recourse to war through the mediumship of the League.

Immediately Wilson had a fight on his hands to get the League accepted as an integral part of the treaty. Mr. Lloyd-George tried to sidetrack the whole matter, in order to get Wilson's mind off the theoretical idealism of a new world order and down to the sordid business of dividing up the spoils. For this purpose the British premier marshaled in the galaxy of Dominion premiers, all of whom wanted to know what they were going to get in the way of plunder. But Wilson met them with the cold statement that the world was not going to be chopped up and parceled out as at the Congress of Vienna. In reply to the question of what was going to be done with the German colonies, he proceeded to develop General Smuts' idea of an international Trusteeship. The German colonies were not going to be given to anyone outright. They were to be assigned to various trustees as "mandatories" who were to hold the land in trust for the League of Nations and were to report to and to be responsible to the League. Thus adroitly he led Lloyd-George and his brother premiers straight back to the main issue, the League of Nations.[35]

As soon as this preliminary draft was completed, Wilson took it on a special trip back to the United States to get the "advice and consent of the Senate," and to consult with various American

34 Lansing, p. 49.   35 Baker, I, 255, 260–75.

statesmen. On his arrival he immediately invited the entire membership of the House and Senate Committees on Foreign Relations to dinner at the White House and gave them every opportunity to quiz him and to say what they had on their minds about what he had been doing. But this did not satisfy the Republicans who felt disgruntled over the whole performance. Many old-fashioned Republicans and Democrats alike felt that any such proposition as a League of Nations was wholly inacceptable because it infringed the sovereignty of the United States. They had the old idea that there really was such a thing as sovereignty, and they failed to grasp the fact that the whole trend of international relations was gradually destroying the sovereignty of every nation in the old sense of national independence.[36] There were others who felt that such a League would deprive Congress of its constitutional right to declare war and make peace, and give that power to the Executive. They were men who failed to understand that the executive had long since possessed the power anyway of putting the United States into a war in a perfectly constitutional manner.[37] Another group felt that the Monroe Doctrine was not properly safe-guarded and that the United States could enter no League of Nations unless it was so preserved. Various changes were made in the constitution of the League after consultation with the Republican leaders, in and out of Congress, but it was obvious that they were not satisfactory.[38] The very nature of the objections themselves show how deep-rooted were the misunderstandings, and no mere dinner conference could eradicate these, nor could any such social gathering obliterate the intense personal hostility of certain Republican senators toward anything done by a Democratic President.

At this point the United States Senate was reconstituted in accordance with the vote of the people in the November election of 1918. As the result of the form of government which persists

[36] *New Republic*, XVII, 232, has an excellent analysis of the positions of Senators Borah and Reed on this point.

[37] W. Lippmann, *The Stakes of Diplomacy*, ch. I.

[38] N. Y. *Times*, Feb. 29, 1919; Creel, 320.

in the United States it is possible for the President to be of one political party and Congress of another. Such a situation is of course impossible in most European countries where they have the parliamentary form of government. But the conflict is still possible in the United States, to the great detriment of public business. This anomalous situation had been the object of searching attacks by many writers in the United States for many years. But no one had ever attacked it more brilliantly or with more closely reasoned thought than had Wilson himself, thirty years before he ever thought of becoming President. But the clumsy constitutional mechanism which had been the point of attack of his doctoral dissertation at Johns Hopkins University in 1884 was still clumsy and inefficient in 1919 and rendered his efforts at Paris nugatory.[39] The United States had been unable to follow Wilson in his flights of idealistic diplomacy. They frankly said so in the election of 1918. Not only did Clemenceau have his doubts about the fourteen points, but the people of the United States, in so far as they were articulate at all, were suspicious about them. Theodore Roosevelt in a speech in November, 1918, frankly invited the European powers to disregard these fundamental principles.[40]

Moreover, the attitude of the older Republicans, who had been educated in the period of the aftermath of the Civil War, must be understood. These men could see little good in a Democrat. For seven years that party which had ruled the country since 1860 had been forced to sit by and see a Southerner and a Democrat, a hated descendant of the "rebels," sitting in the presidential chair. These Republicans of the old school had been brought up in the tradition that Democrats were rascals and traitors. Yet during the most spectacular and tempestuous years of the country's history, a Democrat had been sitting in the place of Washington and Lincoln. For the first time since 1912, the Republicans managed to get control of Congress and they were bent on humiliating Wilson before the world. The hatred of Wilson which

[39] Wilson, *Congressional Government* (Boston, 1885), pp. 50–52, and his *Constitutional Government in the United States* (N. Y., 1908), 139–40.
[40] Tumulty, p. 314.

characterized the Roosevelt group was intense and personal and they did their best to second the efforts of the Old Order diplomats in Europe to defeat Wilson's program.[41]

The Senate which was organized in March of 1919 to defeat the treaty, gave ample evidence of the desperate measures which the Republicans were willing to adopt to secure the defeat of the President and his plans. The Republican party could claim a bare majority in the Senate, only by claiming the vote of the insurgent Senator LaFollette, and the newly elected Senator Newberry of Michigan. Newberry had been elected in the famous November election of 1918, in a spectacular political campaign against Henry Ford, the Democratic candidate. Unusually large sums of money were expended in behalf of Newberry under such circumstances as to raise serious questions of propriety of his being admitted to the Senate. In fact, after a trial which was denounced by his friends as unfair, Newberry was sentenced to two years in the penitentiary under the Federal Corrupt Practices Act, from which he was only saved by the Supreme Court's act in declaring that law unconstitutional. Yet Newberry's vote was necessary to secure a Republican control in the Senate. On such a shaky majority the Republicans were able to organize the upper chamber, make Lodge of Massachusetts chairman of the Senate Committee on Foreign Relations and pack the Committee with enemies of the President.

While Wilson was securing from the Peace Conference the acknowledgment that the League "was the key of the whole settlement," and should be made an integral part of the treaty, Senator Lodge and the Republican majority were insisting that the League ought not to be taken up until after the treaty was signed. Wilson had a terrific fight to get the Old Order diplomats interested in a League at all. Then, when he took it back to the United States the Republican majority served notice that it was not satisfactory and insisted on several changes, putting in the kindergarten language about the Monroe Doctrine, which gave the

[41] W. E. Dodd, *Woodrow Wilson and His Work* (N. Y., 1921), gives an excellent analysis of this anti-southern feeling, pp. 259, 276, 354, 379, 384.

Old Order diplomats just the chance they wanted to say that the United States must give as well as ask, and that if they gave Wilson his League, he must give them the privilege of land-grabbing.[42] Just before the President sailed back to Europe on his second trip, Senator Lodge announced in the Senate that 37 senators had pledged themselves to oppose the League as drafted and directed the Peace Conference to separate the treaty and the League. Taft and Root behaved in a more sportsmanlike manner and suggested changes, but Lodge declined to make any statement other than that the peace ought to be made first and the League afterward. Lodge was going to be chairman of the new Senate Committee on Foreign Relations and was biding his time.[43]

On his way back to Paris, Wilson learned that contrary to the agreement not to take up any but routine matters in his absence, the Old Order had gotten possession of the Conference and had deliberately tried to sidetrack the League. As Sonnino of Italy put it, they wanted to know "exactly what they were going to get."[44] Wilson learned by wireless that the all-important question of the indemnities was to be taken up and that Germany was to be saddled not only with damages for the havoc she had wrought, but with punitive war costs, that is to reimburse the allies for what they had been forced to spend in defeating her. This would have been a huge sum which she could not have paid in centuries of hard work. Wilson met both issues in a characteristic manner. He sent a radio to his colleagues "to dissent and to dissent publicly if necessary from a procedure so clearly inconsistent with what we had deliberately led the enemy to expect," as imposing on Germany the whole cost of the war.[45] Immediately on his reappearance in Paris he coolly announced that he was going to take up matters exactly where he had left them and led the whole Conference back to a consideration of the League of Nations. The revisions insisted on by the United States were

[42] Baker, I, 292.
[43] Cong. Rec., 66th Cong., 1st Sess., Mar. 4, 1919, Creel, p. 202; New Republic, XVIII, 160.
[44] Baker, I, 273, 290, 300-12.
[45] B. Baruch, Making of the Reparation and Economic Sections of the Treaty (N. Y., 1920), p. 25.

incorporated into the League Covenant, as it was now called, thereby making the Monroe Doctrine international law for the first time, since now all the world gave assent to it in a formal way. It also specifically excluded from the jurisdiction of the League domestic questions like the tariff and emigration, thereby leaving the United States free to deal with Japan on that score.[46]

Wilson then proceeded to put into definite form his theory that the League of Nations was a Monroe Doctrine for the whole world. The doctrine has had two sides. The one in which the United States offers service, interested Wilson and appealed to him as a great ideal. The other side, in which the United States simply warns "hands off," did not seem to him to offer any curative qualities to a very sick world. Wilson wanted to apply the positive and helpful side of the doctrine and to ignore its negative and forbidding side. This would have broken up the "isolation policy" which had characterized American diplomacy for so long. But after all these had been the very essence of Wilsonian diplomacy from the start. So the draft of the League was finally worded to include these ideas by the combined efforts of Wilson, House, Lansing and D. H. Miller for the United States, and Lord Robert Cecil, Baron Phillimore and General Smuts for the Britannic Commonwealth. But this was flying in the face of the old-time Republican majority in the Senate.[47]

In a last effort to head off Wilson and get the Conference down to land-grabbing before the League was adopted, Clemenceau introduced Foch into the discussion once more, and the Marshal made an eloquent plea for impossible military conditions and boundaries which would have handed millions of Germans to France.[48] Wilson frankly took up the cudgels for Germany under the fourteen points. This entailed a serious breach between the Allies and Wilson sent a message to his steamer, the *George Washington*, and let it be known that he was going home rather than participate any further in such a disgraceful affair. The bluff worked and the French withdrew their claims. They got

[46] Baker, I, 323–5.   [47] Ibid., I, 228.
[48] D. Johnson, in House and Seymour, p. 465.

Alsace-Lorraine and the coal from the Saar Valley and that was all.[49]

No sooner had he staved off a French crisis at the cost of earning the enmity of the French than the Italians appeared with their extravagant demands based on the Treaty of London of 1915. It was now apparent that the Italians were going to exact every penny of the bribe that had brought them into the war in that year. This involved giving a large part of the Dalmatian coast to Italy. They insisted on thus choking off Jugo-Slavia from the sea. Wilson could not but have remembered that it was this very policy of keeping Jugo-Slavia (then Serbia) from the sea that had caused the murder of the Archduke of Austria in 1914, and set the whole world on fire. He borrowed a leaf from the notebook of James Madison and played a bit of shirtsleeve diplomacy by publishing to the world a statement denouncing the Italians for their selfish imperialistic aims. This so enraged the Italians that they withdrew from the Conference for a time. Wilson had saved Jugo-Slavia but again at the cost of offending an ally.[50]

No sooner was this obstacle surmounted than there appeared the Japanese with another secret treaty by which they had been induced to come to the support of the Entente by the promise of getting the German rights in Shantung, in China. This land had been leased by China to Germany for 99 years in the days when China was selling herself off piecemeal. Since that time China had awakened and had had an internal revolution which established a new government on a more democratic basis and had finally joined in the war against Germany. This act, she claimed, had voided the treaty leasing Shantung to Germany and she insisted that Shantung revert to her. But the Japanese coolly produced Old Order secret treaties. One was the treaty by which the Entente had bought Japan's services. Another was a treaty apparently extorted by force from China, wherein China agreed to any disposition that the Peace Conference was to make of Shantung. Japan had an iron-clad case. China was pledged to

[49] Baker, II, 35, 52, 57, 75; Haskins and Lord, 143.
[50] Baker, II, 166; J. B. McMaster, *United States and the World War*, II, 337–42.

whatever the Peace Conference did and the Peace Conference was pledged in advance to give Shantung to Japan. Wilson tried to break the combination but it was too strong for him. He would either have to let Japan have her plunder or else make England and France break faith with Japan. If he followed principle and refused to let Japan have Shantung, he could hardly expect her to follow him into the League of Nations, for the Japanese had instructions to quit if they did not get Shantung. It was a question of saving the League and as Italy was already sulking in her tent Wilson gave way and let Japan have the Chinese province. This saved the day, but again at the expense of a friend, for this provision made the Chinese refuse to sign the treaty.[51]

Having disposed of the land-hungry powers, the Conference turned to the question of what Germany should pay. Wilson had already headed off a determined effort to get Germany to pay not only tremendous damages but the appallingly incalculable war costs. The allies owed the United States billions of dollars for moneys advanced during 1917 and 1918. Unless they could collect from Germany, they said they could not pay the United States. Keynes, the brilliant representative of the British Treasury, suggested that since Germany owed money to all the allies and the allies owed money to the United States, there should be a general set-off all around, which would let the allies out and leave the United States to hold the bag and get what she could out of Germany.[52] Wilson wanted to fix the indemnity, but France would not hear of it.[53] She knew that Germany could not pay for the war. If the indemnity were left undetermined, France could keep the whip hand over Germany indefinitely by claiming that the latter had not fulfilled the terms of the treaty. France succeeded in getting the matter left to a Reparations Commission, with tremendous powers to deprive Germany of every cent she could make for years to come. The attitude of Wilson was consistent with his position all along; peoples ought not to be

[51] Baker, II, 204–58, also I, xxxiv; Tumulty, p. 384; *Sen. Doc. 106*, 182, 528.
[52] Baruch, p. 25; Baker, II, 289.
[53] *Sen. Doc. No. 106*, p. 527; Baruch, pp. 66–70.

punished for the mistaken crimes of their discredited leaders. Germany ought to be fed to prevent her from slipping into Bolshevism.[54] Indeed, Wilson insisted on a unanimous vote on the Reparations Commission, so that the American members of the Commission could veto every estimate that was too high.

About all the American economic experts got from the tangle was the assurance that the property of German citizens which the United States had taken under its control should not be returned to them but should be left at the mercy of the United States government. It has always been customary thus to confiscate the property of an enemy government, but this confiscation of the private property of citizens established a dangerous precedent not in keeping with American policy in the past. It did, of course, enable the United States to seize those valuable German patents and copyrights on scientific discoveries which were now enriching American citizens instead of their original German owners. The economic clauses of the treaty (about one-half the text) were largely contrary to the fourteen points and in general were opposed by the Americans. As the British expert, J. M. Keynes, pointed out, the thing simply was not enforceable, and events have justified his warning. About all that concerns American foreign policy is that the Americans in general protested against the punitive policy, yet felt its necessity to support the finished treaty or see Europe descend into chaos.[55]

The use of experts by all sides was a characteristic of the meeting which deserves more than passing notice. As time went on Wilson came more and more to rely upon his experts and to shape his policies by the facts they presented. But the Old Order did not want facts. It wanted land, oil wells or German colonies, and facts did not help get them. During the heat of the Republican indignation at Wilson's conduct of foreign affairs,

[54] Baruch, p. 69.
[55] Baruch, pp. 103ff. See also J. M. Keynes, *Economic Consequences of the Peace* (1920), pp. 113–298; pp. 27–56 constitute a clever and somewhat unreliable picture of the Conference. Unfortunately it is this part of the book, which has attracted most attention. It is not serious history but only a kind of sugar-coating to make the rest of the book acceptable for popular consumption.

there was considerable criticism of him for playing a lone hand and refusing to avail himself of the advice of his colleagues. There seems to be some ground for the assertion that the other four members of the Commissions did not figure as largely as did Wilson, but this use of a single representative from each state was necessary for speed.

Moreover even in Paris there was an evident lack of sympathy between Wilson and Lansing. It is very much to the credit of Secretary Lansing that he did not resign at the time, as such an act would have given great comfort to the Germans, and to all enemies of the League. Lansing's position was most embarrassing, but on the whole he acted the patriotic part in standing by Wilson and not making the open break which his detractors assert he should have made at the time.[56] The weight of opinion among the peacemakers is that Wilson was always open to suggestions from his experts, and that he displayed an almost uncanny ability for mastering details of an intricate problem in a short time. That he insisted on being the sole spokesman most of the time is probably true. Mr. Lloyd George on frequent occasions made use of one or another of the Dominion statesmen as his mouthpiece, but this was an easier matter, since most of them wanted something more tangible than general principles, whereas it seems as though Wilson was practically alone in his insistence on international idealism.[57] If he ignored his commissioners, he certainly did not ignore his experts.

3. THE LEAGUE BEFORE THE SENATE

When the President brought the treaty back to the United States, it was apparent that he had been true to his principles "we desire no conquest, we seek no material compensation."[58] No other nation could say that. The one thing which might have meant the most to the United States was the League and after nearly a year's fight before the Senate, the whole thing,

---

[56] Lansing, p. 276; *Letters of Franklin K. Lane*, p. 463.
[57] Tumulty, pp. 354–8; "A Lone Hand," *New Republic*, XVII, p. 264; Haskins and Lamont in House and Seymour, pp. 272, 449.
[58] N. Y. *Times*, Apr. 3, 1917.

League and treaty were lost. The proposed guarantee treaty with France was lost in the shuffle. It had been framed as a temporary measure to protect France during the organization of the League. The treaty was of course referred to the Senate Committee on Foreign Relations, of which Wilson's avowed enemy, Senator Lodge, was now chairman. As to the attitude of the country as a whole on the subject of the treaty and the League, probably nothing better has been said than the following:

> "Some of the Republican Senators would have none of it on any terms, some wanted amendments, while others were willing to ratify it with moderate reservations. The result is an illustration of the way the presenting, or failure to present, alternatives operates in popular government. Probably a majority of the American people desired then some method of preventing the recurrence of war. Probably a majority of the Republican Senators would have favored heartily a league of nations for this purpose if presented by their leaders; but while there were serious objections raised to the Covenant, the Republican Senators could not agree upon an alternative to the document as it stood, and therefore Republican opinion in the senate drifted toward a mere negative." [59]

It was the combined effect of many senators opposed to the treaty for different and often contradictory reasons that defeated it. The members of the Commissions and the experts were called to give testimony and the questions of the senators was frequently couched in such a way as to make it plain that they were more anxious to discredit Wilson than to get the facts. It was useless to explain as Haskins did, that strategy, ethnology, history, nationalism and economics frequently each pulled in a different direction.[60] It was equally useless to explain the perfectly evident fact that in the statistics of language areas the figures were hopelessly garbled in favor of the compiler.[61] It was hopeless to try to make clear to the Senate that many of the territorial adjustments were like trying to unscramble the proverbial scrambled egg. The Irish, the Albanians, the Egyptians, the Hungarians and the Persians who had been denied a hearing at Paris were all called to air their views before the United States

[59] A. L. Lowell, *Public Opinion in War and Peace* (Boston, 1923), p. 247.
[60] Haskins and Lord, pp. 19-20.
[61] Ibid., pp. 173ff.

Senate. The net result was to arouse more antagonism to the treaty.[62]

Gradually, however, the attack centered on a few main points. In the first place the surrender of Shantung was regarded as an inexcusable piece of highway robbery. In the second place Article X in the Covenant of the League seemed to guarantee the *status quo* even though it be unjust, and obligate the United States to defend these unjust territorial arrangements by the use of American troops. Would the United States thus be called on to send troops to far-away Hungary or Rumania? The President insisted that the obligations of the United States to enforce the decisions of the League were moral and not legal obligations, but the members of the Senate seemed unable to make such a distinction.[63] Borah, Knox and Reed still harped on sovereignty. The League, they said, destroyed the sovereignty of the United States and it was useless to point out to them that all progress toward international decency is based on the limitation of sovereignty.[64] Prominent Republicans like Root, Taft and Lowell wanted the League. Lodge reported the treaty to the Senate with a series of reservations. The aim of these was to make the United States a limited partner in the League, with limited obligations, and the right to get out at any time for her own reasons. Several other senators offered reservations the general tenor of which was that the United States was not going to accept all the burdens of international duty which the League imposed. The "isolation policy" of the past suddenly took a new lease of life. Jefferson and Washington were quoted, requoted and misquoted to prove points for and against the idea of the United States moving from a position of isolation to a position of world leadership.[65] Before Wilson had started to Paris the Knox resolutions had warned him that the Republican majority was about to revert to type. As time went on the opposition to the treaty grew, not so much because the Senate wanted no League,

[62] *Sen. Doc. No. 106*, pp. 757, 947, 971, 1011.
[63] Ibid., pp. 515ff.
[64] *New Republic*, XVIII, 232; P. C. Knox in N. Y. *Times*, Mar. 2, 1919.
[65] 66th Cong., 1st Sess., *Sen. Doc. No. 150*, for the reservations.

as because a majority wanted at least some reservations and with these ideas the President refused to compromise. In the Senate were Democrats who favored League and treaty, Republicans who favored the League with reservations and the 'bitter enders' who wanted no League. Because they could not get a League with reservations, the moderate Republicans found themselves practically in the position of voting against the League.[66]

In desperation President Wilson started on a speech-making tour to sell his idea to the country. It was his last card, an appeal to the people over heads of Congress. But in the midst of the trip he was stricken with a severe illness and was forced to give up the fight.[67]   Col. House was ill, and Lansing was conscientiously unable to support the treaty, and the whole great dream collapsed as far as American foreign policy was concerned. Without wasting any explanations on the personal hatred of Wilson felt by men like Lodge, or on the rather provincial and parochial outlook of men like Johnson of California, there is considerable ground for explaining the failure of the treaty in the homely words attributed to Senator Norris of Nebraska:—

"I started this thing in good faith. No man had more honest and beautiful intentions than I had when the peace conference met at Versailles. No man in the world was more anxious than I to have permanent peace. I believed that our allies were honest and honorable. I thought they were square; I thought they were fair; and when the league of nations part of the treaty was first given to the world, while I disliked some of it, I was on the point of swallowing it. But when I discovered that these same men who had talked eloquently here to us had in their pockets secret treaties when they did it; when I discovered that they pulled out those secret treaties at the peace table in contravention of and in contradiction to every agreement they had made when we entered the peace conference, when I saw that they were demanding that those secret treaties be legalized, and more than all, when I saw our President lie down and give in and submit to the disgrace, the dishonor, the crime and the sin of that treaty, then I said 'Great God! I don't believe I want to have any dealing with you people. You are dishonest! You have concluded to act here just the same as you were acting in barbarous days, after proclaiming to

[66] *New Republic*, XVII, 178, analyzes this.
[67] 66th Cong., 1st Sess., *Sen. Doc. No. 120*, contains the collected addresses of Pres. Wilson on the last western trip.

us, and after we believed that you were in earnest and fighting for democracy to build a peace, and a world peace, a league of nations that would bring peace and happiness forever to a suffering people.'" [68]

Such a statement goes far to explain the final fate of the League and the treaty. Yet the failure does not mean that the people of the United States were utterly incapable of following Wilson's leadership once they understood the mighty battle he had fought to avoid the very things of which Norris accused him. The issue of the League was kept alive until the election of 1920 when the Republicans nominated an old-fashioned standpatter, Harding, from the Foreign Relations Committee to carry the issue to the country. The Democratic candidate, Cox, took up the cudgels for the League. But unfortunately the League was not really the issue in the election at all. Millions of Democrats voted for Cox, not because they wanted a League but because they wanted to maintain the social system in the south. The Republican vote was quite as meaningless.

"The Republican majority was composed of men and women who thought a Republican victory would kill the League, plus those who thought it would be the most practical way to secure the League, plus those who thought it the surest way to obtain an amended League. All these voters were inextricably entangled with their own desire, or with the desire of other voters to improve business, or to put labor in its place, or to punish the Democrats for going to war, or to punish them for not having gone sooner, or to get rid of Mr. Burleson, or to improve the price of wheat, or to lower taxes, or to stop Mr. Daniels from out-building the world, or to help Mr. Harding do the same thing." [69]

Root, Taft, Hughes, Hoover, Lowell and other prominent Republicans got together and signed a manifesto announcing that they were voting for Harding because they thought he would get them into a League of Nations.[70] Johnson voted the same ticket for the opposite reason. Millions voted the Republican ticket for reasons that had nothing to do with the League of Nations, because when all is said and done, the bulk of the American people had scant interest in foreign affairs. The elec-

[68] E. G. Lowry, *Washington Close-ups* (Boston, 1921), p. 112.
[69] Walter Lippmann, *Public Opinion* (N. Y., 1922), pp. 194ff.
[70] N. Y. *Times*, Oct. 15, 1920.

tion of Harding was a foregone conclusion, for he promised to take the country back to "normalcy," which in foreign affairs simply meant an atavistic reversal to the type of isolation and the negative side of the Monroe Doctrine, which had been intelligent before the days of aëroplanes and radio-communication. The newly elected vice-president, Calvin Coolidge, was not given to much talk without thought, so his comment on the election of 1920 is of deep significance:

> "I doubt if any particular mandate was given at the last election on the question of the League of Nations and if that was the preponderant issue. In the south where there was decided opposition to the League, they voted the Democratic ticket. And, as far as the League of Nations was concerned in the north, the vote was with equal and even greater preponderance in favor of the Republican ticket. Of course many men voted thus who were in favor of the League. With them it became simply a question of supporting the Republican or Democratic party. So you can't say there was a preponderance of votes against the League of Nations." [71]

Although Hughes became the new Secretary of State, he could not make good his implied promise to get the United States into the League with reservations. A separate peace was made with Germany, whereby the United States coolly reserved for herself all her privileges under the Treaty of Versailles, but assumed none of the obligations.[72] Wilson's ideal that America, because of her great power was destined to be the servant and not the master of mankind, was rejected, not because America was unwilling, but partly because Wilson would not compromise his league and partly because of the lack of any machinery in the United States for obtaining any other public opinion than yes or no on any given set of questions.

[71] N. Y. *Times*, Nov. 24, 1920.
[72] Text in *Treaties, Conventions, &c. between the U. S. A. and Other Powers*, III, 2596.

CHAPTER XVIII

AN UNFINISHED STORY

"Then to side with Truth is noble when we share her wretched
      crust,
   Ere her cause bring fame a profit, and 'tis prosperous to be just;
Then it is the brave man chooses, while the coward stands aside,
   Doubting in his abject spirit, till his Lord is crucified,
And the multitude make virtue of the faith they had denied."

*　　　*　　　*　　　*　　　*　　　*

"For Humanity sweeps onward: where today the martyr stands,
   On the morrow crouches Judas with the silver in his hands:
Far in front the cross stands ready and the crackling faggots burn,
   While the hooting mob of yesterday in silent awe returns
To glean up the scattered ashes into History's golden urn."
                        —James Russell Lowell.

1. THE QUESTION OF RUSSIAN RECOGNITION

While the battle over the treaty was at its height, another question of foreign policy caused an equally acrimonious dispute in
the United States, and that was the question of Russia. Russian-
American relations had been fairly cordial for a hundred years
after the proclamation of the Monroe Doctrine. Russia could
feel only gratitude toward the United States for her mediation
in the Russo-Japanese War; for, as a consequence of Roosevelt's
good offices, the Tsar got a good deal more than he might otherwise have recovered from the disasters of that conflict. In 1912,
however, there occurred an incident which illustrated how utterly
at variance in fact were the political systems of the two nations.
Perhaps it is due rather to a lack of contacts than to any virtue
on either side that our diplomacy with Russia has been so free
from vexatious problems. The Russians had long discriminated
against the Jews in the empire of the Tsar, particularly by forbidding the entry into Russia of alien Jews. The United States
had a treaty of Commerce and Friendship with Russia, concluded

in 1832, which gave Americans the right to come and go in the dominions of the Little Father Nicholas. The United States had become a refuge for Russian Jews and many of them had become naturalized citizens of the United States, without having been given authority to divest themselves of their allegiance to the Tsar. Members of the persecuted race then frequently returned to Russia, claiming that being now American citizens, they could not be excluded as Jews. The treaty, of course, was inadequate, in failing to cover exactly this point. The Russians therefore interpreted it to mean that no Jews could come in, while the Americans protested this was a violation of their promised rights. Finally the matter could be endured no longer by the United States, and Congress denounced the treaty in 1912.[1]

When the European War broke out the democratic nations of England and France were found fighting for the liberty of nations on the side of autocratic Russia. There was a great pother made in attempting to gloss this over by propaganda which glorified the Russian "soul," and which interpreted the dense and superstitious ignorance of the Russian peasant as deep spirituality. But first and last it was perfectly apparent that Russia was a nation in which 75% of the population was illiterate, ruled as best it might be by a corrupt oligarchy. The Revolution of 1905 in Russia had started her along the path to free government, but nothing could be expected speedily from a nation with such a terrific educational problem on its hands. The war bore much harder on Russia than any other nation, for the corrupt military administration, the absence of railways, and the general inefficiency of the Russian system caused the death of millions of Russian soldiers who were sent into battle inadequately supported. It was abundantly evident that the time had come to get rid of the old régime and in 1917 Russia delighted the democratic nations of the world by throwing off the rule of the Romanoffs and setting up a parliamentary government. But a democratic government cannot be imposed on an ignorant electorate. Russia

---

[1] "Passport Question between the United States and Russia," *Amer. Jour. of Internat. Law*, VI, 186.

had been ruled for centuries by little coteries of despots because that was probably the best way to control her mass of illiterates. Therefore the democratic régime soon fell and was succeeded by a Communist group which attempted to put into practice the theories of Marxian Socialism. This simply meant that the Russian government busied itself in destroying the institution of private property, wrecking the industries of the nation by putting their control into inept hands and exiling or killing off the so-called middle class which really contained the brains of the nation. Not content with this, the Communist leaders, who called themselves Bolshevists, were so confident that they were inaugurating a new political and economic system for the whole world that they undertook to revolutionize the other nations of the earth and to stop all wars by destroying the capitalist system everywhere for, according to their theory, capitalism was the cause of all war.

Russian envoys were sent to other countries with instructions not only to act as diplomats, but apparently also with instructions to help overthrow the governments to which they were accredited. No nation can tolerate an ambassador from another country who is secretly plotting the destruction of the government which is entertaining him. Indeed, under such circumstances, it is very doubtful whether an envoy is entitled to his diplomatic immunity.[2] Hence Russia soon found herself a pariah among the nations. Yet in America there was a body of opinion which felt that the new Russian régime should be recognized and its diplomatic representative received, in spite of all this. Some Americans were socialists themselves, or perhaps even Communists. Others felt that it was none of our business what government the Russians had, and that to refuse recognition was practically trying to dictate to Russia what kind of a government she should have. It is altogether possible that American foreign policy of the days of Thomas Jefferson might have pointed toward the recognition of the new Russian Government just because it was a revolutionary government, for as we have seen, Jefferson had some rather pro-

[2] *Gyllenborg's Case* in C. De Martens, *Causes Célebrès*, I, 75–173.

nounced ideas on the innate virtues of revolutions. But our American policy of recognition has undergone a distinct change since Jefferson's day. Our first Secretary of State was inclined to accept the surface evidence that a revolution was the people's will. Gradually, however, the idea has crept into American foreign policy, that before recognition is granted, the United States should ascertain whether or not the revolutionary government actually does represent popular wishes. This has been particularly noticeable in our relations with the republics of Central and Caribbean America. Finally Wilson introduced the moral criterion as well when he refused to recognize the government of Huerta in Mexico in 1914.[3]

In dealing with Russia, Wilson realized that the Bolshevist government could not represent the will of the people, simply because a population with a majority of illiterates cannot have any articulate will. Moreover the Bolshevist's government announced publicly and frequently that it aimed at the destruction of such forms of government as we have in the United States. The natural consequence was that Secretary of State Colby phrased American foreign policy as to Russia thus,

"There can be no mutual confidence or trust, no respect even, if pledges are to be given and agreements made with a cynical repudiation of their obligations already in the mind of one of the parties. We cannot recognize, hold official relations with, or give friendly reception to a government which is determined and bound to conspire against our institutions; whose diplomats will be agitators of dangerous revolt, whose spokesmen say that they sign agreements with no intention of keeping them." [4]

This stinging indictment of the Bolshevist régime formulated American foreign policy toward a nation which was attempting a new experiment in government, based on ideas somewhat at variance with our own. However, it was not because of their new political philosophy, that the United States refused to deal with Bolshevist Russia, but because the Bolshevists themselves warned us that we were dealing with another faithless nation and we had

---

[3] V. A. Belaunde, "Latin-America's New Rulers and the United States," *Current History*, XVIII, 98.

[4] N. Y. *Times*, Aug. 11, 1920.

only too recently experienced great tragedies at the hands of a nation whose rulers could not keep their word.

When President Harding came into office the Russians made another attempt to open up negotiations by proposing the resumption of trade relations. By this time the economic disorganization of Russia was completed by the war and the destruction of capital in the Bolshevist régime. She wanted to trade with the United States, yet because of that same destruction and disorganization she had nothing to offer in exchange for what she desired from America. Secretary of Commerce Herbert Hoover's position in the cabinet enabled him to state with some degree of authority that Russia was not producing anything and therefore it was idle talk of resuming trade relations. This, some Russians felt, was cruel, since they were starving and needed American goods. But the Secretary of Commerce was the same Herbert Hoover, who, as head of the American Relief Administration, had for years been feeding starving Europeans in the greatest charity the world had ever known. This fact constituted a rather effective answer to the complaints of the Bolshevists. No one could help Russia until she herself removed the cause of her own distress, and this is exactly the position which Secretary of State Hughes then took in again refusing recognition. No amount of trading could relieve starving Russia as long as Russia continued to harbor those ideas which had destroyed trade.[5]

Moreover, when groups of citizens inside the United States continued to press for the recognition of Russia, Secretary Hughes raised the question of whether Russia was ready to resume her place as an honorable member of the family of nations by considering the payment of her old debts. The Bolshevists had at first announced that they would never pay the loans contracted under the old Tsarist régime. After a while, they began to see that they utterly destroyed their credit in the world, and they began to suggest that they might pay, but as they hedged their promises around with impossible conditions nothing could be done. This was a situation the United States had met with many

[5] N. Y. *Times*, Mar. 21–26, 1921.

times in her history, and there was nothing to be done except to wait patiently until the recalcitrant debtor got into the hands of some people who had some sense of international obligations. It was not necessary that Russia should pay, for indeed she could not, but it was necessary for her to cease boasting she would never pay.[6]

There has been every indication recently that Russia has begun to understand the hints of Hughes and Hoover that she must first clean house herself before she could expect her neighbors to visit her. The Bolshevist government, frankly an oligarchy as small and in many respects as tyrannical as the old Tsarist régime, has tried out the Marxian doctrines and has found them wanting in several important respects. The peasants, when denied the fruits of their toil, folded their hands and Russia starved. Lack of the brains of the capitalist class, lack of technically trained experts, has led the Bolshevist leaders to shift their ground and to make concessions to the old capitalist system in order to attract back to Russia the resources and ability which will once more make her a producing nation.[7]

2. THE WASHINGTON CONFERENCE

One principle of foreign policy for which the United States had struggled during many years was the principle of disarmament. The European War was a ghastly lesson in the results of competitive armaments. The United States herself was not likely to enroll a big army, but, at the close of the war, she was in a fair way to engage in a naval competition with both Great Britain and Japan, which was just the kind of thing she had fought the war to avoid. Like other nations of the world, more than half her national income was still going to pay for wars, past, present, and future. In 1912, a year of peace, France spent two hundred million dollars on preparation for war. In the year of peace 1920 she spent over a billion, and this while she owed the United States billions of dollars she could not pay. The European War had

[6] J. B. Scott, "Recognition of Soviet Russia," *Amer. Jour. of Internat. Law*, XVII, 296.
[7] J. P. Goodrich, "Evolution of Soviet Russia," *International Conciliation*, No. 185, pp. 233-5.

killed fifteen million men, not to mention the millions maimed and the other millions starved to death. Since 1870 military and naval expenditures had increased more than one thousand per cent, and the European War, instead of discouraging this kind of thing, rather induced rulers to strain every nerve to perpetuate the system. The proverbial battleship which cost twenty-five millions of dollars and five years to build, could be sunk in five minutes.[8]

If the European War could have been foretold from competitive armaments then it was evident that very shortly there might be another war on the Pacific Ocean, as the imperialistic ambitions of England, Japan, and the United States were already clashing in that area. The nature of the conflict of American and Japanese aims in the Pacific has already been discussed: Japan had to have room for her expanding population and she alleged that the United States and the Britannic Dominions had slammed the door in her face in California, the Philippines, Australia, and New Zealand.[9] American goods needed a Chinese market and Japan was tempted to retaliate by trying to slam the Chinese door against those goods. It was this kind of thing which had produced wars in the past and there is no reason why it should not go on producing wars in the future. Borah demanded that the Republicans take some action on disarmament, so President Harding was led to call the Washington Conference of 1921.

Fortunately for the moment, the government was not hamstrung by a conflict between the Senate and the Executive. Moreover, President Harding, in choosing the American delegates, wisely forestalled trouble by selecting Senator Lodge, chairman of the always captious Senate Committee on Foreign Relations, as one of the American representatives. Secretary of State Hughes headed the American delegation, and America's great international lawyer, Mr. Elihu Root, was induced to return to semi-political life to serve the cause. The Democrats were represented by Senator Underwood of Alabama, following the usual

---

[8] *Hearings before House Committee on Naval Affairs*, 66th Cong., 3d sess., and *Annual Report of the Secretary of the Treasury, 1920*, as analyzed in *League of Nations*, IV, 301ff.

[9] James Bryce, *Modern Democracies*, II, 311.

practice of giving the minority party representation in such gatherings. The other nations who were invited to the Conference were the British Empire, France, Italy, Belgium, Portugal, Holland, China, and Japan; for these were the nations of the world whose conflicting colonial and imperialist pretensions might well produce another war.

Secretary Hughes was selected as the presiding officer of the Conference which met at Washington, on Armistice Day, 1921. With characteristic American speed, he got down to an actual program in his opening address, with a plan that fairly staggered the Conference. He coolly proposed just how many and what naval vessels each nation should scrap. He destroyed more British vessels in five minutes than the Germany navy had done in any battle of the war. The British navy lords were naturally taken aback with these suggestions to destroy the precious units which made Britannia the mistress of the waves. But the important thing is that they did not resent the suggestions. They had been sobered into a knowledge of the fact that something had to be done and done quickly to forestall bankruptcy. Hughes went on to propose that England, Japan, and the United States, as the three great naval powers, should take a ten-year naval holiday, and dismantle millions of dollars worth of battleships already under construction. The ratio of naval power on which the nations were to begin any replacement was to be as 5-5-3, that is, England and the United States were to be equal in power and Japan was to be as 3 to 5 in proportion.[10]

Committees at once got to work on these ideas and the nations finally agreed on the Hughes' plan. Each power promised to make no replacements for ten years and to destroy "capital ships" in order to comply with the terms of the agreement. "Capital ships" signified, in the main, battleships. The Japanese made a long and strenuous objection to being placed in a position thus inferior to Britain and the United States and held out for a ratio of 7 to 10. But they finally gave way when the United States made definite promises not to continue the fortification

[10] *Senate Document No. 126*, 67th Cong., 2d sess., pp. 46ff.

of the American possessions in the Orient. By agreeing not to build any further defenses for the Philippines, Guam, and the Aleutian Islands, the United States practically laid themselves open to Japan in case of a war with that nation, but it showed Japan that we were sincere and bought Japan's adherence to the naval treaty. This kind of self-sacrificing honesty goes a long way toward establishing genuinely cordial international relationships, which are our only true defenses against war.[11]

But this only involved capital ships. The menace of the submarine was discussed, but France prevented any agreement on the limitation of the building of that terrible weapon. The submarine was left as an object for further competitive armaments and to be a future trouble-maker. The whole thing amounted in the end simply to this: there was a saving of money for those who no longer had to squander millions on battleships of whose value in future wars there was considerable doubt. It did not prevent a possible dangerous race in submarine armaments, which in the end might prove as fatal as had the race in battleship-building. It did not assure the world against a future war in the Pacific, but it did show that the participants in that war were sincere in their desire to avoid such a tragedy.

Better insurance against a future war in the Pacific Ocean was the "Four Power Pact," whereby the British Empire, France, the United States, and Japan agreed mutually to respect one another's territories in the Pacific Ocean for the next ten years. If any disagreement should arise, the four powers agreed to get together and deliberate further on the subject before going to war. This is the principal guarantee the United States has for her possessions in the Far East and it must be apparent that everything depends on the willingness of the powers to be honorable and keep their word. As an instrument of protection, this treaty is worth no more than the treaty which was supposed to insure the neutrality of Belgium in 1914, but it is exceedingly doubtful whether at the present time the world can expect anything more. The "Four Power Pact" was a thing which mani-

[11] *Senate Document No. 126*, 67th Cong,. 2d sess., p. 875.

fested a good feeling in official circles at least, and a willingness to coöperate which in themselves were happy auguries, when we bear in mind the conduct of Germany at the Hague Conferences.[12]

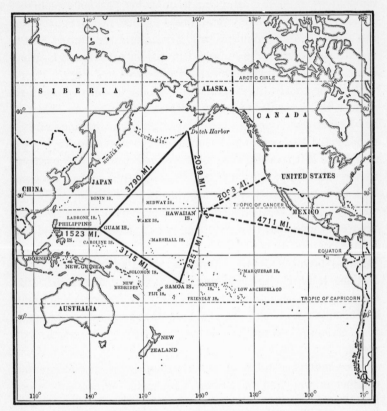

UNITED STATES NAVAL DEFENSE IN THE PACIFIC
Based on Bowman's "The New World" by permission of the author and the World Book Company, publishers.

As the United States had suggested the Naval Compromise, and as Britain had undertaken the suggestion of the Pacific Ocean adjustments, so France, the greatest military power in the world, was expected to suggest the possibility of land disarmaments. M. Briand, the head of the French delegation, arose

[12] *Senate Document No. 126*, 67th Cong., 2d sess., pp. 77–88; N. Y. *Times*, Nov. 25, 1921.

and delivered an address which is a classic as a defense of French military policy. Germany, he argued, was still armed and still unrepentant. France would be delighted to be relieved from the tremendous drain her army made upon her national resources, if she could be adequately guaranteed against future aggression. But before France would disarm, Britain and the United States would be expected to promise aid in case of future attacks from Germany or Bolshevist Russia. Paper promises were all very well for the United States with three thousand miles of ocean to protect her, or for Great Britain with the North Sea as a barrier, but France had suffered too many times from invasions on her unprotected frontier to put too much confidence in anybody's good will. With consummate skill, Briand brought the Americans to a realization of the fact that President Wilson had brought back with him from Paris a treaty for the protection of France and that if this treaty had been ratified by the United States, Senate, France might be more convinced of the sincerity of the United States. But as the United States had failed to back up Wilson's promises about a protective treaty and a League of Nations, the French were forced to look out for themselves. To these implied charges, it was difficult for the Americans to make any adequate reply and the whole question of limiting armies had to be given up. Nothing could be done while France was in that mood.[13]

The Conference did go on record as approving a more humane conduct of war, and the powers represented agreed not to use poison gases and not to sink merchant vessels without first placing the passengers and crew in a place of safety. This only amounted to a set of pious aspirations, as the old Hague Conventions had done much the same kind of thing and had been flagrantly disregarded when war actually came. Moreover the nation which had the dishonor of introducing the world to poison gas and the drowning of innocent passengers was not represented at the Washington conference nor were other nations who might

[13] N. Y. *Times*, N. Y. *World* (editorial), November 25th, 1921; S. Katsuizumi, *Index to Newspaper Articles on the Armament Conference at Washington* (n. p. n. d.).

be expected to do that kind of thing. Without their agreement, the treaty was of even less value than the old Hague promises, except in so far as the world had learned a lesson of just how frightful war could be by the use of such atrocious methods of fighting. International law was still without any real sanction, or means of enforcement, and the Washington Conference did practically nothing to provide an international police force which might make international law really effective in critical cases.[14]

At one stage of the Conference President Harding addressed the meeting and suggested that the Conference meet annually, looking toward the formation of an "Association of Nations." But the grim humor of the situation was too much for the Europeans. One "Association of Nations" insisted on by the Americans was already in existence and functioning, but the United States had failed conspicuously in giving its support to that body. Another such suggestion from the United States could not but provoke a smile, and the American delegation quietly dropped overboard President Harding's somewhat naïve suggestion. One League of Nations made in America was already at work on these problems of international law, and it was asking a little too much to expect the Europeans to follow our uncertain lead again in such a matter.[15]

But from the standpoint of world politics, probably the greatest accomplishment of the Washington Conference was the Nine-Power Treaty as to China. It marked the end, it was hoped, of the land-grabbing in the Celestial Empire. Indeed, many of the Europeans agreed to give up claims and holdings that they had already staked out for themselves. England surrendered Wei-Hai-Wei and, most important of all, Japan agreed to give up Shantung, if China would compensate her for the moneys she had expended there in railway building. The "Open Door" was reasserted at the behest of America and the powers agreed not to support their citizens who might try to secure special

[14] *Conference on the Limitation of Armaments* (Wash., 1922), pp. 1605ff.

[15] A. J. Balfour in N. Y. *Times*, Jan. 8, 1922, and N. Y. *Tribune, Herald* and *Sun* (ed.) Jan. 22, 1922.

privileges or monopolies in China. The value of this agreement
has yet to be demonstrated as there is a good deal of difference
between keeping the spirit and the letter of such a law. Nevertheless, the Nine-Power Treaty did supplant the old Lansing-
Ishii Agreement which was now formally abrogated. The United
States no longer recognized that Japan's interests in China were
superior to those of anyone else.[16]

In giving this Washington Conference its place in the history
of American foreign policy, we must recognize that it was a splendid effort. If the Republican Party had turned down Mr. Wilson's League of Nations, it at least showed that its leaders were
keenly aware of the actual responsibility of the United States
in international politics. The Conference must be judged in the
light of Secretary Root's instructions to the delegates to the
Second Hague Conference. It was not right to expect that the
Conference would do very much and any little it did would be a
step in the right direction. Secretary Hughes knew what he
wanted and he practically got a large part of it. Great Britain
deserves the greatest praise for having coöperated in a move
which practically took away from her the supremacy of the seas
which she had held for so many centuries. This does not mean
that any other nation replaced Great Britain in that supremacy;
it means rather that the supremacy of the seas passed into the
hands of a board of trustees of which Britain was a member. Had
Germany displayed a similar spirit at The Hague, many things
might not have happened. The Conference showed the two great
branches of the English-speaking peoples working together in a
harmony which could only inspire optimism for the future of
world politics. The conference, among other things, ended the
Anglo-Japanese Alliance, for the Britannic Dominions had practically given notice that they would not support Britain in a war
which meant fighting on the side of Japan against the United
States. The Four-Power Pact was designed to terminate the
now dangerous Anglo-Japanese Treaty, in order to satisfy the
United States and the Britannic Dominions, without at the same

[16] *Senate Document, No. 126*, 67th Cong., 2d sess., p. 893; *U. S. Treaty Series*, No. 667.

time giving offense to Japan. If it did this, it did a great deal. Moreover the Conference put the future of China squarely up to the Chinese themselves, by relieving that nation of many embarrassing spheres of influence.

That the Conference did not do more is to be attributed less to the members themselves than to the state of mind of the nations they represented. If nations would be more trustful and have a greater understanding of one another, their diplomats could do a great deal more in preventing wars.

3. CANADIAN RELATIONS

One of the most striking developments in international politics in the last few decades has been the transformation of the British Empire into a Britannic Commonwealth of Nations. As the Parliament at Westminster has surrendered its power to control the destinies of the one-time colonies, the question has naturally arisen as to whether and how far the Britannic Dominions might conduct their own foreign relations. For some time past there has been no doubt that a Dominion Government is constitutionally competent to negotiate an agreement with a foreign government in matters of commerce. This naturally affects the question of the foreign policy of the United States toward the Dominion of Canada, with whom she is bound by so many ties—cultural, racial, and economic.

In 1911 a proposal was made of commercial reciprocity between the United States and the Dominion of Canada. The British Ambassador, James Bryce, instructed Secretary of State Knox to negotiate directly with the Dominion representatives at Ottawa. This was done, and in an exchange of notes an agreement was reached. At this stage it was submitted to both the Senate of the United States and the Canadian Parliament. From the standpoint of the United States the proposed arrangement seemed desirable enough, but in advocating it certain public men in the United States displayed an imprudent candor in allowing the impression to get abroad that such a policy suggested an ultimate political union between the Dominion

and the republic to the south of her. This was too much for
the Canadians, and in a general election the Canadian Liberal
Government which had been responsible for the proposed agreement was defeated. Canada wanted it distinctly understood
that her nascent nationalism did not presage union with the
United States.[17]

The insistence of the Dominions on their separate representation at the Versailles Conference in 1919 has been noticed. The
natural consequence of that action, and England's acquiescence
in it, was apparent in 1923 when the United States and Canada
had occasion to negotiate the Halibut Fisheries convention. The
Britannic Dominions had agitated for a recognition of their
international status at the Washington Conference in 1921, but
the United States did not yet fully understand the constitutional
changes taking place within the Britannic Commonwealth and
refused to recognize them. However by Convention of 1923,
the Canadians seem to have brought the matter up again.[18]
Sir Auckland Geddes, the British Ambassador at Washington,
conducted some of the negotiations, but when it came time to
sign the agreement, the Governor-General of Canada, Lord
Byng, notified Geddes that Mr. Lapointe, the Canadian Minister
of Marine and Fisheries, would sign the document on behalf of
Canada. Not only this, but Mr. Lapointe signed to the exclusion
of Geddes. Canada contended that this was a matter between
the Dominion and the United States, and that hence the signature of the British ambassador was unnecessary. However, when
the treaty came before the Senate for ratification, that body
stipulated that the treaty should be binding on other members of
the Britannic Commonwealth. Members of the House of Commons in England instantly wanted to know whether a Canadian
minister could bind the whole Britannic Commonwealth.
Premier Bonar Law of Great Britain took the attitude that Mr.
Lapointe was acting as the King's plenipotentiary in the matter—
and that Canada was quite within her rights. This is obviously

---

[17] A. B. Keith, *Imperial Unity in the Dominions*, p. 273; *Canadian Annual Review*, 1911,
p. 23; 66 Cong. 1st sess. H. Doc. No. 2.

[18] A. L. Lowell, "Canada's Treaty Making Power," *Foreign Affairs*, XIX, 963.

going to raise a whole host of questions, constitutional and diplomatic.[19]

In any event the United States must now recognize that Canada is not bound by any trade agreement to which that Dominion has not expressly given her consent. Moreover whatever the ultimate status of Canada and the other Dominions may be in the rapidly changing constitutional evolution of the Britannic Commonwealth, it is certain that if Canada ever achieves complete independence, it will not be for the purpose of joining the United States. In the meantime it is possible that Canada will be before long represented at Washington by her own diplomatic envoy. Canada's prominence among the nations of the world, her separate membership in the League of Nations, and her increasing community of interests with the United States would give such an envoy plenty to do. Moreover Canadians have not hesitated to claim that by the Halibut Fisheries convention the United States has in fact recognized the international status of Canada and helped thereby to admit her into the family of nations.[20]

4. ENEMY PROPERTY IN WAR TIME

It has, in the main, been a cardinal principle of American foreign policy to involve private property as little as possible in warfare. The insistence with which America's representatives have stressed the immunity of private property at sea in time of war is some evidence of this. In cases of war in which the United States has participated, it has usually been the declared policy of the United States not to confiscate the property of enemy citizens who happened to have their property in the United States when the war broke out. As early as 1796 the Supreme Court remarked that the "practice of confiscation has long been considered disreputable" while Chief Justice John Marshall though asserting that "war gives the sovereign full right to take the persons and

[19] J. A. R. Marriott, "Empire Foreign Policy," *Fortnightly Review*, CXIX, 788.
[20] A. L. Lowell, supra; W. P. M. Kennedy, *Constitution of Canada* (Oxford, 1922), p. 344. In 1924 the new Irish Free-State proposed to send a separate envoy to the United States.

confiscate the property of the enemy," yet insisted that no nation could exercise such a right without "obloquy." [21]

When Germany and the United States went to war a half a billion dollars worth of the property of alien enemies of the United States was in America, earning money for her enemy. According to practice, all of this was put under the control of an Alien Property Custodian, with the understanding that it should not be used to benefit Germany and her allies during the war, but should he held in trust by the United States government and returned to the enemy alien citizens at the close of the war. [22]

The European War was, however, exceptional in more than one way. Before the United States actually joined in, Germany and her allies had committed numerous depredations against the lives and property of citizens of the United States, for which she was bound to pay. By refusing to ratify the treaty of Versailles, America had put herself beyond any participation in reparations, so in the separate treaty made between the United States and Germany, there was a clause inserted which expressly provided that the United States had not given up these claims and that it was going to hold on to the enemy property then in the hands of the Alien Property Custodian, until Germany and her allies paid the damages due.

The question then came up in Congress and aroused a good deal of feeling. One group insisted that the only honorable thing to do, now that the war was over, was to follow the practice of international decency and return the property to its German owners. Another group pointed out with considerable cogency that in view of the utter economic prostration of Germany, this property ought to be held as a pledge until Germany paid. The matter was finally decided by the passage of the Winslow Bill (became a law March 4, 1923), by which the property of most of the small German owners was returned, amounting to about $45,000,000, but that a few of the big German property interests, amounting to hundreds of millions should be held as security until such time

[21] Justice James Wilson in *Ware* v. *Hylton* (3 Dall. 199, 1796); *Brown* v. *U. S.* (8 Cranch, 122, 1814).

[22] *Alien Property Custodian Report, 1918–19* (Wash., 1919), pp. 7–23.

as Germany should show how she intended to satisfy the claims of the United States against her. This was attacked by a minority committee report as amounting to confiscation and being utterly at variance with the age-long policy of the United States in this matter of private property in time of war. The distinctions between public and private property, were, however, not so clear now as once they had been, and the majority felt that the German property kept as a pledge was something of a bird in the hand.[23]

Yet it would seem that it had been a cardinal principle of the foreign policy of the United States to distinguish as far as possible between combatants and non-combatants and not to inflict the rigors of war upon the latter. There are, therefore, those who regret to see this fundamental distinction attacked, and to see the United States "depart from the principle of trusteeship" in the matter of alien property in time of war.[24]

5. Recrudescent Isolation

But if the United States invited other powers to come to Washington and help settle some of the ills of humanity, it was not so ready to take a hand in settling difficulties which many Americans thought were strictly European. Chief among these were the manifold problems which grew out of the question of the settlement of the debts due the United States from European Powers. The facts were briefly these: When the United States entered the war in 1917, one of the most insistent problems the Allies had to face was how they might continue to pay for the war. They wanted to go on buying great quantities of supplies in America, but could not pay for them unless credits were so extended that they could pay the American manufacturer with money borrowed from the United States. The United States Treasury arranged to advance this money to France, England and other nations.[25] It amounted simply to this, that the United States loaned money to the allies with which to hold back the Germans until our own

[23] A. G. Hays, *Enemy Property in America* (Albany, 1923), pp. 47ff., 329ff.
[24] J. B. Moore, *International Law and Some Current Illusions*, pp. 21-22.
[25] *Senate Document No. 86*, 67th Cong., 2d sess., pp. 10, 27ff.

tardy preparations enabled us to take up our share of the fighting. It was the old, old story:

> "Since the birth of the nation, we have been engaged in a series of identical cycles, which find us at the outbreak of every war in a disgraceful state of unpreparedness, resulting in untold waste of money and human lives." [26]

We were, as usual, unready and some one had to carry on for us until we were ready. When the war was over, the truth of Norman Angell's prophecies was apparent, for even the victors were on the verge of bankruptcy, except the United States. She was the principal creditor nation of the world, there being due her about eleven billion dollars from her late allies.

This debt the allies were in no position to pay, and not even the interest was forthcoming. But in 1922, four years after the conclusion of the fighting, the United States approached Great Britain and asked her what she proposed to do about it. Earl Balfour, the British minister of foreign affairs, then put the matter up to the other allies. If the continental countries would only pay England what they owed her, she would be able to pay the United States her share of the debt, for she owed the United States about five billion dollars and had over nine billion due her from her European allies. [27] To this Poincaré of France responded that France could pay nobody, until she had paid for rebuilding the areas which Germany had devastated. According to the terms of the Treaty of Versailles, Germany should have paid for this, but she had failed to do so and France had to look out for her own people. Hence she was in no position to repay either England or the United States what she owed. [28] It amounted then, to this: Germany would not pay France; France could not pay England or the United States and England was hard put to it to find any sources of income with which to satisfy America.

Then came up the whole question of the desirability of having the allies repay America at all. We had more than half the world's gold supply anyway. It was rather desirable to sell some

[26] J. J. Pershing, in *Amer. Hist. Rev.*, XXVIII, 704.
[27] *Accounts and Papers*, Cmd. 1737 (1922).
[28] N. Y. *Times*, Sept. 2, 1922.

American goods in Europe, but the Europeans had little with which to pay for those goods, and would certainly have nothing at all, if we insisted on a repayment of the debt. The classic, but tragic manifestation of this was the fact that the farmers in Iowa were burning their surplus corn while the farmers in Russia were starving to death for lack of it. This, some Americans believed, was our concern. Others believed it was none of our business. Some Americans thought we should cancel a large part of the debt and call it our contribution to the war. Certainly we had never done anywhere near as much fighting as had our late allies, and they had fought our battles for a year, if not more.

Such a situation amply illustrates the complex character of modern diplomacy. Should or should not the United States demand repayment? This involved a great deal more than the mere question of international credit; it involved questions of moral responsibility in connection with paying for the war and the welfare of other people in other lands; it involved questions of foreign trade, for obviously we could not afford to bankrupt or starve our customers, lest in the future we have no customers. The New York banker Thomas Lamont paid a visit to France and raised this point:

> "In our discussions of reparations over here, the American attitude has, on the whole, been critical of the French for apparently not realizing more quickly the facts of the situation and thus drastically scaling down the reparation payments. In fact, many critics over here have been advising France to forgive a good part of the German debt. To these critics Frenchmen have not unnaturally replied: 'It is easy for Americans to advise us to forgive the German debts due us in repair of the frightful havoc caused by Germany upon our homes and industries; but what about America, in turn, doing a little of the debt-forgiving business, especially as the debts that were contracted with the American government were made in order to enable us, in large measure, to do America's fighting before her own soldiers got into the firing line.' " [29]

Mr. Hoover frankly expressed the opinion that the allies should repay the United States on the ground that the United States derived no benefit from the war either in reparations or in terri-

[29] N. Y. *Times*, Oct. 4, 1922.

tory.[30] Dr. E. R. A. Seligman pointedly inquired whether America wanted the reputation of a Shylock among the nations.[31]

The British finally sent their Chancellor of the Exchequer, Mr. Stanley Baldwin, over to negotiate about the matter. But by that time, Congress had rather tied the hands of the Executive Department by laying down just what terms were to be exacted from Great Britain. Baldwin felt that the United States drove an unnecessarily hard bargain, and he laid this to the provincialism and general ignorance of foreign affairs of the United States Senate. Said he,

> "In the early days, the Secretary of Treasury could undoubtedly have arranged terms with the British Government. But the situation is now complicated because the matter is in the hands of Congress. . . . We have got men of our way of thinking in the Eastern States, but that does not cut any ice at all with regard to other parts of America. If you will look at the Senate, you will see that the majority come from agricultural and pastoral communities and they do not realize the meaning of an international debt." [32]

Naturally Congress resented such language and there was talk of demanding an apology from Great Britain. But in view of the first sentence quoted above it is a fair question to ask whether Mr. Baldwin did not get that conception of the United States Congress from some Americans themselves. In that case, it is not the complaint of a disappointed Briton with which we have to deal, but once more an illustration of the results of intrusting our foreign policy to the inept hands of men who have no real interest in, or knowledge of foreign affairs.[33]

[30] N. Y. *Times*, Oct. 16, 1922.   [31] Ibid., Nov. 5, 1922.
[32] Ibid., Jan. 28, 29 and 30, 1923.

[33] Lest the reader feel that undue space has been devoted to the indifference of public officers in matters of foreign policy, the following anecdote may be pertinent. Attention has many times been directed in these pages to a publication called *Foreign Relations*. It is a volume published annually by the United States Government, containing the publishable diplomatic correspondence for the year. The exigencies of public service have dictated that these volumes appear from five to ten years after the year to which they refer, but they may always be expected with each recurring year, and are of first rate importance to the students of foreign affairs, and are well known to him. An historian some time since wrote a Congressman, requesting a copy of the current issue of *Foreign Relations*. The particular Congressman selected happened to be a member of the Committee of Foreign Affairs. The historian received a courteous reply informing him that there was no such publication as *Foreign Relations*. Somewhat taken aback, the historian wrote again and explained that there must be some mistake. The Congressman, after some delay, replied

Great debts could not be paid by exporting gold from England to America—especially since America already had most of the gold in the world. Moreover, what was principally needed to restore order and equilibrium in Europe was to stop, not to increase, the flow of gold from Europe to America. Only thus could Europe get on her feet and become our good customers once more. It was this, apparently, that the United States Congress failed to comprehend, for besides insisting that England pay, Congress busied itself in raising the tariff so as to discourage imports from Europe to the United States, when the import of these European goods was the only way Europe could pay us. The whole episode shows once more the results of the divided control of American foreign relations. But although England settled terms and began to pay her debts, billions of dollars due the United States from the other nations of Europe had to wait for more stable political conditions inside of Europe itself. It was useless to press for repayment of those billions when Europe had no money with which to pay. American taxes had to be maintained at a higher level to meet our own obligations to our citizens because Europe would not pay and in general many Americans began to realize that their lives was not so isolated from Europe after all.[34]

President Harding became convinced of this, and he felt that the Washington Conference had not done enough to assure American participation in world politics. Although he could hardly consistently push membership in the League of Nations, yet he did go before the Senate in February of 1923 and advocate that the United States participate in the Permanent Court of International Justice provided for by the League. He stipulated that in so doing the United States ought to remain free

apologizing for his ignorance, and saying that on further investigation he had discovered that there really was such a publication, but that it had been suspended many years ago and would never be issued again. The historian wrote a third time, explaining once more that the volume always appeared late and that in fact a volume had just been issued. He finally received what he wanted through a friendly Senator who was a little bit better informed.

[34] J. F. Bass and H. G. Moulton, *America and the Balance Sheet of Europe* (N. Y., 1922), pp. 344–8; G. A. Finch, "Settlement of the British Debt," *American Journal of International Law*, XVII, 319ff.

from any legal relationship with the League itself, or from any obligations in connection with that organization. Inasmuch as the members of the League had decided that the Judges on the Permanent Court of International Justice were to be elected by the Council and the Assembly of the League, it was difficult to see how the United States could participate in the Court without being permitted a voice in the selection of judges. Incidentally, Mr. John Bassett Moore, America's most distinguished international lawyer, was at the time serving on the Court, elected not by his own countrymen, but by the members of the League themselves. Mr. Hughes then had to work out some way whereby the United States could vote as a member of the League in electing judges but not in any other case. This, he believed, was not impossible, because the Court had been formed by an international agreement which was totally separate from the Covenant of the League of Nations. In accepting the protocol on which the Court rested, we would not necessarily be accepting the Covenant of the League, which was a separate and distinct treaty. The only connection between the Court and the League lay in the method of selecting the judges, as noted above. Hughes argued therefore that in designating representatives to vote with the Council and Assembly of the League in this matter the United States did not assume any legal relationship or obligation to the League itself.[35] The League of Nations itself voted to admit to participation in the Court nations which were not members of the League in order to facilitate the working out of Hughes' plan,[36] so that the United States could join the Court without joining the League.

The Senate did not act promptly on the President's recommendation and he took occasion to plead for the membership in the Court on his western trip in the summer of 1923. From this trip President Harding never returned alive. But in his first message in December of 1923, President Coolidge took up the cudgels once more for participation in the Court, with the stipulation

---

[35] Senate Document No. 309, 67th Cong., 4th sess.
[36] N. Y. *Times*, Apr. 25, 28, 1923.

against participation in the League. The leaders of the Republican party who sympathized with the Court idea, and even in many cases, with the League itself, pointed out that as a result of the Hague Conference of 1899, and largely because of the wishes of the United States, there had been established a Permanent Court of Arbitration at the Hague, which had been generally approved by both political parties. Moreover it was pointed out that the whole history of our foreign policy showed we had been always favorable to such a Court. The old Hague Permanent Court of Arbitration had not been adequate to all cases, and the present proposition for an additional Permanent Court of International Justice was just the thing for which the United States had always striven, an agency for the judicial settlement of international disputes.

Care must be taken to distinguish the permanent Court of Arbitration, which had been established at The Hague as a result of the Conference of 1899, from the new Permanent Court of International Justice, which was the outcome of the Versailles Conference. The older body is ably characterized by John Bassett Moore in these words:

"The Permanent Court of Arbitration has heard and determined a number of cases, and has performed in fact a very useful part. Only the other evening some one made to me the remark that the reputation of the Permanent Court of Arbitration had been very much injured by reason of the fact that it did not prevent the war of 1914. My reply was simply this: That, if we are to apply that test, we must begin by abolishing the Supreme Court of the United States, because the Supreme Court of the United States not only did not prevent the Civil War in the United States but by the decision it rendered, or the opinion it gave in the Dred Scott case, materially contributed to the bringing on of the conflict. In other words, we cannot test the value of an institution, by its capacity to re-create human nature overnight." [37]

An effort to establish a more competent court at the Hague in 1907 had failed, and the present scheme was simply another such effort to make more effective the old idea. But there was a strong reaction toward the old isolation policy after the European War,

[37] J. B. Moore, "The Permanent Court of International Justice," *Columbia Alumni News*, Feb. 29, 1924.

and this traditionally American project provoked a good deal of opposition inside the United States. The war, like all wars, had artificially stimulated a type of nationalistic patriotism, which is distinctly hostile to the development of a spirit of international coöperation. Although the scientific student of politics might agree with the reflective man in other fields that some kind of world organization was necessary, still this idea had not penetrated very deeply into the minds of voters and Congressmen generally. Mr. H. G. Wells might say that the problem of international organization was the supreme problem of politics, and that pending its solution, the world was engaged in a race between education and catastrophe. Well-informed and judicial writers might point out in technical journals that the political engineers of the world were centuries behind every other kind of scientist in having failed to work out some scheme of world organization. But to get the people of the United States to act on these facts was quite another matter. There is much food for thought in Mr. Van Loon's remark:

"A Zulu in a frock coat is still a Zulu. A dog trained to ride a bicycle and smoke a pipe is still a dog. And a human being with the mind of a sixteenth century tradesman driving a 1921 Rolls-Royce is still a human being with the mind of a sixteenth century tradesman."

He might well have added that an American frontiersman, with the firm conviction that everything American is all right and that every European is pitiable and contemptible, is still the same kind of a person, even if you transplant him into the age of aëroplanes, radio-communication, and moving pictures. The pioneer in western Pennsylvania who engaged in the Whiskey Rebellion a century and a quarter ago saw no real reason for coöperating with the national government in the establishment of internal law and order. Take that same kind of a mind and expose it to the thin veneer of education, you are likely in 1924 to have the same kind of a mind underneath. The possessor of that mind might find it just as difficult to understand the necessity for American coöperation in world politics as his ancestor found it to see the advisability of working with his fellow Americans in intra-national politics. Had the Whiskey insurrectionists been able to see the matter from other than the narrow and particularist point of view their environment dictated, they might have been able to trace the history of their country and see how it was leading up to the establishment of a firm national government, which it was to their interest to support.[38]

Realizing that one of the first essentials of an intelligent foreign policy was intelligence in the conduct of foreign affairs, the Harding-Coolidge administration secured the passage in 1924 of the Rogers Bill for the reorganization of the United States diplomatic corps and correlated departments. As has been pointed out many times in this volume, Americans have for decades been apologizing for the inadequacy of their foreign service. In urging the bill Secretary of State Hughes pointed out

" Since the war all the principal countries of the world have reorganized their foreign services to meet the requirements of post war conditions and yet the position of none of these in international affairs has altered so appreciably as that of the United States."

When the people of the United States come to understand the profound truth in Mr. Hughes' statement that there has been an appreciable change in the international status of the United States, we may hope for better things. But it is disheartening to read some of the speeches made in Congress in opposition to the Rogers Bill and to realize how inactive are the imaginations of some of the representatives of what Mr. Stanley Baldwin so unkindly called our "pastoral communities." [39]

6. THE ISSUE

All history is an unfinished story, and it is not possible to carry this tale further at the present time. Two paths lie before the people of the United States. One is indicated by such men as William Randolph Hearst who attacked President Coolidge's

[38] H. G. Wells, *Outline of History* (N. Y., 1921), p. 461; P. B. Potter, "Politics in the International Field," *Amer. Pol. Sci. Rev.*, XVII, 381; H. W. Van Loon, *Story of Mankind* (N. Y., 1921), p. 461.
[39] *Congressional Digest*, III, 115.

mild recommendation on the World Court by saying "that the people of the United States are most determined . . . to keep entirely free from any further European complications." [40] The other path is pointed by such men as Walter H. Page who drily commented "I see little hope of doing anything so long as we choose to be ruled by an obsolete remark made by George Washington." [41] In either case there is no partisan appeal in the statement of the winner of the Bok Peace Prize in 1924:

"Only as we are faithful to our ideals of justice, which is the purest patriotism, and only as we embody these ideals with common sense in our national administration and our international relations, can we remain in a position to exert our influence and our strength in the councils of nations for a world organization in the interest of permanent peace." [42]

[40] See a Hearst paper for Dec. 7, 1923.
[41] B. J. Hendrick, *Life and Letters of Walter H. Page*, I, 283.
[42] C. H. Levermore. This remark was made in 1915 in his *Preparedness—For what?*

APPENDIX A

BIBLIOGRAPHICAL ESSAY ON THE HISTORY OF THE FOREIGN POLICY OF THE UNITED STATES

For general bibliographical work in connection with the subject of this volume, we will consider here only the printed material. The manuscript sources to be found in the great libraries of Europe and the United States, and the contemporary material lying in the great newspaper repositories, suggest themselves as obvious places for original research and investigation. But as this volume is designed primarily to sum up the results of research, the bibliographical information of most value is that published in a form fairly well accessible to all who have an ordinarily good library at their command. Therefore in listing works, I have had in mind more the needs of the librarian in building up a collection on American Foreign Policy, or American Diplomacy. Every good library should contain as its principal bibliographical work in this field, D. P. Myers' *Manual of Collections of Treaties and Collections Relating to Treaties* (Harvard Press, 1922). The five great series representing the diplomatic correspondence between the United States and foreign countries should also be found in such libraries. The period from 1775 to 1783 is best covered by F. Wharton's *Revolutionary Diplomatic Correspondence* (5 vols., Washington, 1889). From 1783 to 1798 we have *The Diplomatic Correspondence of the United States of America from the signing of the Definitive Treaty of Peace of 1783 to the Adoption of the Constitution in 1789* (3 vols., Washington, 1837). Next follows the *American State Papers, Foreign Relations* (6 vols., Washington, 1832–59), which cover the period from 1789 to 1833. There are various other editions of the foregoing collections. From 1833 to 1861 there is no collected set of Diplomatic Correspondence, as the material is scattered through hundreds of volumes of Congressional Reports. The key to this maze will be found in A. R. Hasse's *Index to United States Documents Relating to Foreign Affairs* (3 vols., Washington, 1914). Beginning in 1861 and continuing to the present the published diplomatic correspondence will be found in *Papers Relating to Foreign Affairs*, issued annually at Washington. No volume was issued in 1869. The binder's title was *Diplomatic Correspondence* from 1861 to 1868. Since then both the title page and

441

back title are *Foreign Relations of the United States*. There is an index covering the years 1861–1899.

The printed collection of treaties relating to America are best discovered through Myers' volume. But every good library should contain sets which will cover the whole period. Those most readily available are as follows: For the period up to 1648, F. G. Davenport's *European Treaties Bearing on the History of the United States and its Dependencies to 1648* (Washington, 1917). From the year 1648 to the end of the period during which the United States was part of the British Empire we have Charles Jenkinson's *Collection of All the Treaties of Peace, Alliance and Commerce between Great Britain and Other Powers, 1648–1783* (3 vols., London, 1785). Covering the history of the United States as such, W. M. Malloy's *Treaties and Conventions between the United States of America and Other Powers* (2 vols., Washington, 1909) best presents the treaties from 1778 to 1909. A third volume covering the years 1910 to 1923 has been issued as Senate Document No. 348. 67th Cong., 4th sess.

The general secondary works devoted to the history of American diplomacy are not numerous, and the history of our foreign policy has usually been treated as a side issue in the greater histories such as McMaster, Channing, Henry Adams and Rhodes, four sets which should be in every library. One of the earliest efforts at a separate treatment of our foreign policy was Theodore Lyman's *Diplomacy of the United States* (Boston, 1826; 2 vol. ed., 1828). A quarter century elapsed before there appeared the next works, W. H. Trescot's *Diplomacy of the Revolution* (Boston, 1852) and his *Diplomatic History of the Administrations of Washington and Adams* (Boston, 1857). More than twenty-five years again passed by before the next work appeared, Eugene Schuyler's *American Diplomacy and the Furtherance of Commerce* (N. Y., 1886). After the Spanish War came John W. Foster's *Century of American Diplomacy, 1776–1876* (Boston, 1900) and his *American Diplomacy in the Orient* (Boston, 1903). J. B. Moore then skimmed the cream off his encyclopædic knowledge and presented his single volume work, *Principles of American Diplomacy*, (N. Y., 1905, 1918), a book necessarily brief but arranged topically rather than chronologically. C. R. Fish's *American Diplomacy* (N. Y., 1915, 1924) is the best general text and very useful for reference. W. F. Johnson's *America's Foreign Relations* (N. Y., 1916) quotes extensively from original documents and is useful for that purpose. But we still lack anything like a comprehensive or monumental work on the subject and probably we will be without it for many years to come. The difficulties are obvious, and the last twenty-five years are still too full of feeling and prejudice for the cautious historian to rush into them. Moreover one can hardly blame the historian who feels hesitant about setting pen to paper until material stops piling up too fast for one human mind to digest it all.

For bibliographical information on the various phases of the history of American foreign policy, the reader is referred to the footnotes of the different chapters. I have endeavored to render these more serviceable for general reference by including in the index of the present volume notation of all the authors cited in the footnotes.

In addition to those cited in the footnote references, there are certain other works, which I would not have the reader think any the less important because I have made no direct reference to them. The Monroe Doctrine, for example, has a whole literature of its own, which it did not seem fitting to enter upon in a survey of this character. Nevertheless one should not forget that one of the best books on the subject is in German (Herbert Kraus, *Die Monroedoktrin*, Berlin, 1913) and another is in French (Hector Petain, *Les Etats Unis et la Doctrine de Monroe*, Paris, 1901). Add to this the great wealth of material to be gleaned from biographical studies from Fitzmaurice's *Shelburne* (Lord E. Fitzmaurice, *Life of William, Earl of Shelburne*, 2 vols., London, 1912) to the *Life and Letters of Walter H. Page*, and the reader can see that it is hardly possible that a brief survey such as this volume should have attached to it an exhaustive bibliography.

The principal periodicals to be followed in this field are *The American Journal of International Law*, a technical journal, and *Foreign Relations*, a more popular, but exceedingly well edited quarterly. Besides these the *American Historical Review*, *American Political Science Review*, the *Annals of the American Academy*, and the *Political Science Quarterly* often contain excellent studies in diplomacy.

On the general subject of International Relations so much has been written in recent years that an entire volume could be filled with bibliographical references on the subject. Among those most worthy of mention is James Bryce, *International Relations* (N. Y., Macmillan, 1922). These are his lectures before the Institute of Politics at Williamstown, almost the last book he prepared, and constitute the essence of his thought upon a subject to which he devoted most of his life. Much older but still stimulating is Charles Seignobos' chapter "Les Relations Internationales" in his *Histoire de la Civilization au Moyen Age et dans les Temps Moderns* (Paris, Masson, 9th ed.). It had been translated. Andrew D. White's chapters on Grotius in his *Seven Great Statesmen* (N. Y. Century, 1912) are exceedingly suggestive. For a short historical sketch, W. Allison Philips' article on "Diplomacy" in the *Encyclopædia Britannica* (11th edition) is concise and informative. Attention should be drawn to R. G. Gray's article

"International Tribunals in the Light of the History of Law," *Harvard Law Review*, XXXII, 825. The necessity for the historical perspective on all discussions of international relations is more ably and more cogently stated in this article than in many volumes devoted to the subject.

APPENDIX B

THE SECRETARIES OF STATE OF THE UNITED STATES 1789-1924

Presidents.	Secretaries of State	Date of commission.
George Washington	Thomas Jefferson, of Virginia	Sept. 26, 1789.

Entered upon duties March 22, 1790. Retired December 31, 1793.

Do	Edmund Randolph, of Virginia	Jan. 2, 1794.

Entered upon duties January 2, 1794. Retired August 19, 1795.

Do......Timothy Pickering, of Pennsylvania (Secretary of War).

Ad interim August 20, 1795, to December 9, 1795.

Do..........{ Timothy Pickering, of Pennsylvania..Dec. 10, 1795.
John Adams....... { Entered upon duties December 10, 1795. Retired May 12, 1800.

Do............Charles Lee, of Virginia (Attorney General).

Ad interim May 13, 1800, to June 5, 1800.

Do.............John Marshall, of Virginia.........May 13, 1800.

Entered upon duties June 6, 1800. Retired February 4, 1801.

Do............John Marshall, of Virginia (Chief Justice of the United States).

Ad interim February 4, 1801, to March 4, 1801.

Thomas Jefferson.....Levi Lincoln, of Massachusetts (Attorney General).

Ad interim March 4, 1801, to May 1, 1801.

Do............James Madison, of Virginia.........Mar. 5, 1801.

Entered upon duties May 2, 1801. Retired March 3, 1809.

James Madison.......Robert Smith, of Maryland.........Mar. 6, 1809.

Entered upon duties March 6, 1809. Retired April 1, 1811.

Presidents.	Secretaries of State.	Date of commission.

James Madison ......James Monroe, of Virginia.......... Apr. 2, 1811.
Entered upon duties April 6, 1811.
Retired September 30, 1814.

Do.............James Monroe, of Virginia (Secretary of War).
Ad interim October 1, 1814, to February 28, 1815.

Do.............James Monroe, of Virginia.......... Feb. 28, 1815.
Entered upon duties March 1, 1815.
Retired March 3, 1817.

James Monroe.......John Graham (Chief Clerk).
Ad interim March 4, 1817, to March 9, 1817.

Do.............Richard Rush, of Pennsylvania (Attorney General).
Ad interim March 10, 1817, to September 22, 1817.

Do............John Quincy Adams, of Massachusetts........................ ....Mar. 5, 1817.
Entered upon duties September 22, 1817. Retired March 3, 1825.

John Quincy Adams...Daniel Brent (Chief Clerk).
Ad interim March 4, 1825, to March 8, 1825.

Do.............Henry Clay, of Kentucky..........Mar. 7, 1825.
Entered upon duties March 9, 1825.
Retired March 3, 1829.

Andrew Jackson......James A. Hamilton, of New York....Mar. 4, 1829.
Ad interim March 4, 1829, to March 27, 1829.

Do.............Martin Van Buren, of New York.....Mar. 6, 1829.
Entered upon duties March 28, 1829.
Retired May 23, 1831.

Do.............Edward Livingston, of Louisiana....May 24, 1831.
Entered upon duties May 24, 1831.
Retired May 29, 1833.

Do.............Louis McLane, of Delaware........May 29, 1833.
Entered upon duties May 29, 1833.
Retired June 30, 1834.

Do........... ⎧ John Forsyth, of Georgia..........June 27, 1834.
Martin Van Buren.. ⎨ Entered upon duties July 1, 1834.
          ⎩ Retired March 3, 1841

William H. Harrison..J. L. Martin (chief clerk).
Ad interim March 4, 1841, to March 5, 1841.

Presidents.	Secretaries of State.	Date of commission.

William H. Harrison
John Tyler........ { Daniel Webster, of Massachusetts....Mar. 5, 1841.
Entered upon duties March 6, 1841.
Retired May 8, 1843.

Do............Hugh S. Legaré, of South Carolina (Attorney General).
Ad interim May 9, 1843, to June 20, 1843. Died June 20, 1843.

Do............William S. Derrick (chief clerk).
Ad interim June 21, 1843, to June 23, 1843.

Do............Abel P. Upshur, of Virginia (Secretary of the Navy).
Ad interim June 24, 1843, to July 23, 1843.

Do............Abel P. Upshur, of Virginia........July 24, 1843.
Entered upon duties July 24, 1843.
Died February 28, 1844.

Do............John Nelson, of Maryland (Attorney General).
Ad interim February 29, 1844, to March 31, 1844.

Do............John C. Calhoun, of South Carolina..Mar. 6, 1844.
Entered upon duties April 1, 1844.
Retired March 10, 1845.

James K. Polk.......James Buchanan, of Pennsylvania....Mar. 6, 1845.
Entered upon duties March 10, 1845.
Retired March 7, 1849.

Zachary Taylor.....
Millard Fillmore.... { John M. Clayton, of Delaware......Mar. 7, 1849.
Entered upon duties March 8, 1849.
Retired July 22, 1850.

Do............Daniel Webster, of Massachusetts...July 22, 1850.
Entered upon duties July 23, 1850.
Died October 24, 1852.

Do............Charles M. Conrad, of Louisiana (Secretary of War).
Ad interim October 25, 1852, to November 5, 1852.

Do............Edward Everett, of Massachusetts...Nov. 6, 1852.
Entered upon duties November 6, 1852. Retired March 3, 1853.

Franklin Pierce.......William Hunter, jr. (chief clerk).
Ad interim March 4, 1853, to March 7, 1853.

Do............William L. Marcy, of New York......Mar. 7, 1853.
Entered upon duties March 8, 1853.
Retired March 6, 1857.

Presidents.	Secretaries of State.	Dates of commission.

James Buchanan.....Lewis Cass, of Michigan ....Mar. 6, 1857.
Entered upon duties March 6, 1857.
Retired December 14, 1860.

Do............William Hunter, Jr. (chief clerk).
Ad interim December 15, 1860, to
December 16, 1860.

Do............Jeremiah S. Black, of Pennsylvania...Dec. 17, 1860.
Entered upon duties December 17,
1860. Retired March 5, 1861.

Abraham Lincoln... ⌠ William H. Seward, of New York.....Mar. 5, 1861.
Andrew Johnson.... ⟨ Entered upon duties March 6, 1861.
⌡ Retired March 4, 1869.

Ulysses S. Grant......Elihu B. Washburne, of Illinois......Mar. 5, 1869.
Entered upon duties March 5, 1869.
Retired March 16, 1869.

Do............Hamilton Fish, of New York........Mar. 11, 1869.
Entered upon duties March 17, 1869.
Recommissioned................Mar. 17, 1873.
Retired March 12, 1877.

Rutherford B. Hayes..William M. Evarts, of New York....Mar. 12, 1877.
Entered upon duties March 12,
1877. Retired March 7, 1881.

James A. Garfield... ⌠ James G. Blaine, of Maine.........Mar. 5, 1881.
Chester A. Arthur... ⟨ Entered upon duties March 7, 1881.
⌡ Retired December 19, 1881.

Do............Frederick T. Frelinghuysen, of New
Jersey......................Dec. 12, 1881.
Entered upon duties December 19,
1881. Retired March 6, 1885.

Grover Cleveland.....Thomas F. Bayard, of Delaware.....Mar. 6, 1885.
Entered upon duties March 7,
1885. Retired March 6, 1889.

Benjamin Harrison...James G. Blaine, of Maine.........Mar. 5, 1889.
Entered upon duties March 7, 1889.
Retired June 4, 1892.

Do............William F. Wharton, of Massachusetts
(Assistant Secretary).
Ad interim June 4, 1892, to June 29,
1892.

Do............John W. Foster, of Indiana........June 29, 1892.
Entered upon duties June 29, 1892.
Retired February 23, 1893.

Do............William F. Wharton, of Massachusetts
(Assistant Secretary).
Ad interim February 24, 1893, to
March 6, 1893.

Presidents.	Secretaries of State.	Date of commission.

Grover Cleveland.....Walter Q. Gresham, of Illinois........Mar. 6, 1893.
Entered upon duties March 7, 1893.
Died May 28, 1895.

Do............Edwin F. Uhl, of Michigan (Assistant
Secretary).
Ad interim May 28, 1895, to June 9,
1895.

Do............Richard Olney, of Massachusetts....June 8, 1895.
Entered upon duties June 10, 1895.
Retired March 5, 1897.

William McKinley....John Sherman, of Ohio............Mar. 5, 1897.
Entered upon duties March 6, 1897.
Retired April 27, 1898.

Do............William R. Day, of Ohio..........April 26, 1898.
Entered upon duties April 28, 1898.
Retired September 16, 1898.

Do............Alvey A. Adee, of the District of Columbia (Second Assistant Secre-
tary). Ad interim September 17,
1898, to September 29, 1898.

Do............ ⎰ John Hay, of the District of Columbia. Sept. 20, 1898.
Theodore Roosevelt. ⎱ Entered upon duties September 30,
1898.
Recommissioned...............Mar. 5, 1901.
Recommissioned...............Mar. 6, 1905.
Died July 1, 1905.

Do............Francis B. Loomis, of Ohio (Assistant
Secretary).
Ad interim July 1, 1905, to July 18,
1905.

Do............Elihu Root, of New York.........July 7, 1905.
Entered upon duties July 19, 1905.
Retired January 27, 1909.

Do............Robert Bacon, of New York........Jan. 27, 1909.
Entered upon duties January 27,
1909. Retired March 5, 1909.

William H. Taft......Philander C. Knox, of Pennsylvania..Mar. 5, 1909.
Entered upon duties March 6, 1909.
Retired March 5, 1913.

Woodrow Wilson.....William Jennings Bryan, of Nebraska.Mar. 5, 1913.
Entered upon duties March 5, 1913.
Retired June 9, 1915.

Do............Robert Lansing, of New York (Counselor for the Department of State).
Ad interim June 9, 1915, to June 23,
1915.

Presidents.	Secretaries of State.	Date of commissioner.
Woodrow Wilson	Robert Lansing, of New York	June 23, 1915.
	Entered upon duties June 24, 1915.	
	Retired February 13, 1920.	
Do	Frank Lyon Polk, of New York (Under Secretary).	
	Acting February 14, 1920, to March 13, 1920.	
Do	Bainbridge Colby, of New York	Mar. 22, 1920.
	Entered upon duties March 23, 1920.	
	Retired March 4, 1921.	
Warren G. Harding	Charles Evans Hughes, of New York	Mar. 4, 1921.
Calvin Coolidge	Entered upon duties March 5, 1921.	

INDEX

many's violation of her neutrality, 366.

Belgrano, Manuel, and the liberation of the Argentine, 167.

Belize, 231.

Belligerency, recognition of as distinguished from recognition of independence, 236.

Bemis, S. F., *The Jay Treaty*, 102.

Bengal, nitrate deposits used by English, 285.

Benton, T. H., *Thirty Years View*, 147, quoted on the lure of Mexico, 185; and the Oregon boundary, 229.

Bering Sea, Russian efforts to make it a closed Sea, 179; U. S. efforts to same end, 248.

Berlin Decree, 115, 123, 125.

"Bermuda," The, 239.

Bernstorff, Johan, German Ambassador at Washington, and the "Lusitania" and "Arabic" affairs, 376–377.

Berthier, Louis Alexandre, negotiates for Louisiana with Spain, 138.

Biddle, James, Commodore, and the effort to open up trade with Japan in 1846, 336.

Bishop, J. B., *Theodore Roosevelt and his Times*, 345.

Bismarck, and Schleswig-Holstein, influence on Maximilian's Empire in Mexico, 198; and the Samoan affair, 262.

Black, Jeremiah S., Secretary of State, his term as, 448.

Black Sea, Russian search for port, 245.

"Black Warrior," The, 265.

Blacklist, the, of pro-German firms in the U. S., by Great Britain, 372.

Blaine, James G., Secretary of State, tries to void the Clayton-Bulwer Treaty, 285; his error remedied by Hay, 286; his resurrection of Pan-Americanism, 309–310; his term as Secretary of State, 448.

Blenheim, Battle of, 23.

Bliss, Tasker M., U. S. Peace Commissioner in 1919, 389.

Blockade, rule of in Armed Neutrality of 1780, 45; as practiced during Napoleonic Wars, 114 ff.; Fox's, 114; and Declaration of Paris, 234; and

the U. S. Civil War, 236, 238; in the European War, 368–380.

Boer Republics and war with England in 1900, 361.

Bogota, delegate of U. S. directed to go from to Panama Congress in 1826, 182.

Bok Peace Prize in 1924, 439.

Bolivar, Simon, victor at Carabobo, 172; his reaction to Monroe Doctrine, 180; the calling of the Panama Conference of 1826, 181.

Bolivia, and the War of the Pacific, 309.

Bolles, J. A., "Why Semmes of the Alabama was not tried," 374.

Bolshevism and the question of Russian recognition, 415–417.

Bolton, H. E., "Location of La Salle's Colony," 27; "Spanish Occupation of Texas," 150.

Bonar Law, A., British Premier and the foreign relations of Canada, 427.

Bond, B. W., *Monroe Mission to France*, 106.

Bond, Phineas, Letters of, 101.

Bonsall, Stephen, testimony on affairs in Cuba, 272.

Boone, Daniel, 49.

Borah, William B., Senator, and the Treaty of Versailles, 399, 408; and the calling of the Washington Conference, 419.

Borchard, E. M., trans. of Fiore, 4; *Diplomatic Protection of Citizens Abroad*, 209.

Bordeaux, merchants of, protest against Napoleon's Continental System, 125.

Borden, Sir Robert, Premier of Canada at Versailles Conference, 29, 391; statement on the constitution of the Britannic Commonwealth, 391.

Borgne, Lake, and the Florida boundary question, 31.

Bosphorus, Russian desire for, 245.

Boston *Transcript*, 271.

Botha, Gen. Louis, Premier of South Africa at Versailles Conference in 1919, 29, 391.

Bourne, E. G., "Proposed Absorption of Mexico in 1847–48," 195; "Aspects of Oregon History prior to 1840," 225.

Hart, A. B., *The Monroe Doctrine*, 177.
"Postulates of the Mexican Situation," 205.
Hartley, David, and Treaty of 1783, 67.
Hartmont Loan to Dominican Republic, 297.
Haskins, C. H., and Lord, R., *Some Problems of the Peace Conference*, 395; Haskins on conflicting forces at Versailles Conference, 408.
Hasse, A. R., *Index to Documents relating to Foreign Affairs*, 441.
Hats, beaver and silk, significance in diplomacy, 179.
Havana, loss of the "Maine" at, 272.
Hawaii, the annexation of, 257–260.
Hawkins, John, English sea captain, 26.
Haworth, P. L., "Frederick the Great and the American Revolution," 51.
Hay, John, Secretary of State, and the treaty with Pauncefote, 249–253, 286; and the annexation of Samoa, 263; becomes Secretary of State and instructs U. S. Commissioners to take Philippines and Porto Rico, 276; analogy of his policy with that of John Jay, 277; negotiates Hay-Herran Treaty, 287; notifies Germany and England to arbitrate Venezuelan affair in 1901, 292; his reaffirmation of the Open Door to China, 324–325; not the author of the Open Door Doctrine, 325; tries to protect China from European aggression, 327; instructions to American delegates at First Hague Conference on a World Court, 360; his term as Secretary of State, 448.
Hay-Pauncefote Treaty, 249–253, 286.
Hayden, J. R., *The Senate and Treaties, 1780–1817*, 90.
Hayes, R. B., President of the U. S., deals with Mexico, 200; vetoes first Chinese Exclusion Bill, 320.
Hays, A. G., *Enemy Property in America*, 430.
Hazard, B. E., *Beaumarchais and the American Revolution*, 38.
Hearst, W. R., and the Spanish War, 270; quoted, 438.
Heinz, G., *Die Beziehungen zwischen*

Russland, England und Nord Amerika im Jahr 1823, 180.
Hendrick, B. J., *Life and Letters of Page*, 250; *Age of Big Business*, 255.
Henriquez Carvaial, President of Dominican Republic, and his protests against U. S. policy, 301.
Henry VIII, of England, 13.
Hepburn Bill, and the Panama Canal, 287.
Heureaux, U., Dominican dictator, 298; his assassination, 299.
Hill, D. J., "Shall We Standardize Our Diplomatic Service?" 60.
Hispanic-America, the revolt of from Spain, 146, 152, 164–174; recognition by the U. S., 175–6; asks for Monroe Doctrine, 176.
Hispaniola, Spanish colony on, 295.
Hoar, Geo. F., quoted, 254.
Holland, see Netherlands.
Hollander, J. H., "Readjustment of San Domingo's Finances," 297; "Financial Difficulties of San Domingo," 297.
Holls, F. W., *Peace Conference at the Hague*, 360.
Holmes, O. W., on law and logic, 253.
Holy Alliance, Castlereagh on the, 172; nature of, 172; and independence of Hispanic-America, 175; Metternich and the, 174; and Treaty of Verona, 175; and its relation to the Monroe Doctrine, 178.
Honduras, British lumber interests in, in 18th Century, 40; in 19th Century, 231 ff.; Vanderbilt backs H. against William Walker, 283; and Central American Union, 305–308.
Hong-Kong, ceded to England, 316, 323.
Honolulu, port of, and annexation of Hawaii, 257.
Hoover, H., and the election of 1920, 410; his attitude on Russian recognition, 417; his part in the American Relief Administration, 417.
Hornbeck, S. K., *Contemporary Politics in the Far East*, 319.
"Hortalez and Co.," 38.
House, E. M., and his European trip of 1914, 364; U. S. peace Commis-

Lowell, A. L., *Public Opinion in War and Peace*, 408; attitude on the amended League of Nations, 409; and the election of 1920, 411; "Canada's Treaty-Making Powers," 426.

Lowell, F. C., "American Diplomacy," 60.

Lowell, James Russell, quoted, 413.

Lower California, U. S. attempts to buy, 196.

Lowry, E. G., *Washington Close-ups*, 411.

Lovejoy, E. P., abolitionist, murder of, 159.

Loyalists, under Treaty of 1783 with Great Britain, 63.

Lumber Interests, British, in Central America, 230.

Lundy, Benjamin, influences J. Q. Adams in matter of Texas, 157.

"Lusitania," The, sinking of, 376; proven not an armed vessel, 376; notes consequent thereon, 376–377.

Lybyer, A. H., "Ottoman Turks and Routes of Oriental Trade," 13.

Lyman, T., *Diplomacy of the U. S.*, 442.

Macaulay, T. B., quoted, 24.

McClatchy, V. S., "Japanese in the Melting Pot," 348.

MacCorkle, W. A., *James Monroe*.

MacDonald, Wm., *A New Constitution for a New America*, 3; *Select Documents in U. S. Hist.*, 55.

MacHugh, R. J., *Modern Mexico*, 188.

McKinley Tariff of 1890, and Cuban Sugar industry, 268.

McKinley, William, quoted, 254; and the annexation of Hawaii, 259, and the annexation of Samoa, 263; becomes Pres. of U. S., 271; makes Sherman Secretary of State, 271; sends "Maine" to Havana, 272; is insulted by DeLome, 272; urged to declare war, but hesitates, 273–274; France asks terms for Spain, 275; decides to keep Philippines and Porto Rico, 276–277; his reasons, 277.

McLane, Louis, Secretary of State, his term, 446.

MacLaren, W. W., *Political History of Japan*, 345.

McLaughlin, A. C., *Confederation and Constitution*, 58; "Western Posts and British Debts," 72.

Maclay, William, Journal of, 90.

McLeod, Alexander, the affair of, 219, 220–1.

McLoughlin, John, and the Oregon settlers, 225.

McMaster, J. B., *History of the People of the U. S.*, 86; U. S. in the World War, 374.

Madero, Francisco, President of Mexico, 198.

Madison, James, authorship of the *Federalist*, 77; writes "Helvidius," 87; becomes President, 124; efforts to secure American rights against France and England, 125; and the W. Florida affair, 145; message to Congress on recognition of Hispanic-America, 168; advice on Canning's proposal in 1823, 175; and the disarmament of the Great Lakes, 213; his term as Secretary of State, 445.

Magdelena Bay incident and the extension of the Monroe Doctrine to Asiatics, 354.

Mahan, A. T., *Influence of Sea Power in History*, 54; *Influence of Sea Power upon the French Revolution and Empire*, 96.

Maine, as part of Province of Massachusetts, 30; boundary with Canada, 30, 62, 160, 218–222.

"Maine," The, and its loss, 272; the investigations of, 273.

Maitland, F. W., quoted, 254.

Malcolm, R., "American Citizenship and the Japanese," 350.

Malloy, W. M., *Treaties and Conventions*, 47, 442.

Managua, U. S. marines stationed at, 307.

Manchuria, Russian advance in, 327.

Mandatory, the idea of attributed to General Smuts, 398; its adoption at Conference of Versailles in 1919, 398.

Manifest Destiny, 134 ff.

Manning, W. R., "Nootka Sound Affair," 83; *Early Diplomatic Relations between the U. S. and Mexico*, 193.

Muscat, Open Door principle asserted in first commercial treaty with, 325.

Musser, J., *Foundation of Maximilian's Empire in Mexico*, 196.

Munster, Treaty of, 14.

Myers, D. P., *Manual of Collections of Treaties*, 441.

Nagasaki, Dutch allowed to visit, 336.

Napoleon Bonaparte, and the wars of, 96; and the treaty of 1800, 109; his Continental System, 116; Berlin Decree, 116, 123, 125; Milan Decree, 116, 123, 125; his Navigation System, 123; Bayonne Decree, 124; Rambouillet Decree, 124; the Bordeaux merchants, 125; the Cadore Letter, 125; starts on the Russian campaign, 126; and the cession of Louisiana, 139–142; on the Louisiana boundary, 143; and Spain in matter of Florida, 145; influence on the liberation of Hispanic-America, 165;

Napoleon III and the Mexican Expedition, 197.

Nassau, port of, and the contraband trade in the Civil War, 238–239.

Natchitoches, French settlement at, 27.

Nation, differentiated from State, 3.

Nationalism, its doubtful value, 217; its influence, 356–358.

Naval disarmament, on the Great Lakes, 212–214; the problem of, 418–419; the Washington Conference of 1919, 419–426.

Negro-slavery, importation under Treaty of Utrecht, 23.

Nelson, Horatio, in command of W. Indian Station, 71.

Nelson, J. L., Secretary of State, his term, 447.

Netherlands, revolt from Spain, 14; rise in world politics, 18; loses New York, 20; early practice Rule of 1756, 33; William Lee makes treaty with, 51; John Adams makes treaty with, 53; her merchants the first to trade with Japan, 336; contraband shipments in European War, 370.

Neutrality, laws, of, in 16th and 17th Centuries, 15 ff.; provisions of treaty of 1778 with France in relation to,

44; Armed Neutrality of 1780, 45; discussed as policy for U. S. in Nootka Sound Affair, 83–84; proclamation of in 1793, 87; Armed Neutrality of 1800, 110; of U. S. in Mexican Texan War, 155; weakening of U. S. policy of during Civil War, 239; discussed at Second Hague Conference, 362–363; U. S. proclamation of in 1914, 366; U. S. forsakes traditional positions on, 373.

Nevada, part of Mexican cession of 1848, 194.

New Brunswick, boundary controversy with Maine, 218–222.

New England, United Colonies of, first American Treaty, 15; conduct of during war of 1812, 132.

New Granada, Republic of, U. S. treaty with in 1848, 284.

New Hampshire, Province of in 1763, 29.

New Jersey, Province of in 1763, 29.

New Mexico, part of Mexican cession of 1848, 194; and the Gila River boundary, 195; and the Zimmerman dispatch, 383.

New Orleans, 31; importance of the right of deposit at, as affecting U. S. diplomacy, 42; the "Island of New Orleans," 49–50; as a port of deposit under Treaty of San Lorenzo, 92; Riots and the Italian murders, 81; and aquisition of Louisiana, 137–42; filibusters from to help Hispanic-American independence, 147; filibusters from to Cuba, 264–265; filibusters from to Nicaragua, 283.

New Spain, Vice-royalty of, 25; lost to Spain, 175.

New York, Province of in 1763, 29; filibustering from N. Y. city, 146; and the "Caroline" affair, 219; Russian fleet sent to, 245; filibusters from to Cuba 264–265; the Cuban junta in, 272; and the Accessory Transit Co., 282; filibusters from to Nicaragua, 283.

New Zealand, and her separate participation in the Versailles Conference, 391; and her policy of excluding

Trescot, W. H., *Diplomacy of the Revolution*, 442; *Diplomatic History of the Administrations of Washington and Adams*, 442.

Tripoli, the Ambassador from and John Adams, 75; see also Barbary Pirates.

Trist, Nicholas, troubles with Scott, 194; negotiates Treaty of Guadeloupe Hidalgo, 194–195; is recalled, 194; his treaty accepted, 194–195.

Trollope, Mrs. Frances, *Domestic Manners of the Americans*, 217.

Troppau, Congress at, 175.

Trowbridge, E. D., *Mexico Today and Tomorrow*, 188.

Tumulty J. P., *Woodrow Wilson as I know Him*, 206.

Tunis, see Barbary Pirates.

Turgot, French minister of Finance, opposes Vergennes foreign policy, 36.

Turkey, Ambassador of outranks U. S. minister, 81; and Napoleonic Wars, 115; and the near Eastern Question in 1912, 363; disintegration of, 385; the question of at Versailles Conference in 1919, 394–395.

Turner, F. J., "Frontier in American History," 2; "Policy of France toward Mississippi Valley," 59; "Correspondence of Clark and Genet," 87, "Mangourit Correspondence," 87; "Origin of Genet's Projected Attack on Louisiana," 87; "Significance of the Mississippi Valley," 134; "Ohio Valley in Am. Hist.," 135.

Tuscany, Duchy of, and the Louisiana cession, 139.

"Twen Gebrodre," The, 114.

Twenty-One Demands of Japan on China in 1915, 331.

Tyler, John, succeeds to presidency, 160–1.

Ugarte, Manuel, and anti-American Propaganda in Hispanic America, 312.

Uhl, Edwin F., Secretary of State, 449.

Ultimate Destination, Doctrine of, 238–239.

Underwood, Senator Oscar, U. S.

delegate at Washington Conference of 1921, 419.

U. S. *vs.* Hutchins, 168.

U. S. *vs.* Palmer, 168.

Updyke, F. A., *Diplomacy of the War of 1812*, 121.

Upshur, Abel P., becomes Secretary of State, 161; and the annexation of Texas, 161; his term as Secretary of State, 447.

Uruguay, U. S. efforts to secure cooperation of in Pan-Americanism, 308.

Utah, part of Mexican cession of 1848, 194.

Uti possedetis, principle of at Ghent in 1815, 129.

Utrecht, Peace of, 23.

Van Buren, Martin, becomes president of the U. S., 157, his term as Secretary of State, 446.

Vancouver, Fort, Hudson Bay Company withdraws from, 228.

Vancouver, G., exploration of the northwest, 223.

Vancouver Island, 82, 223.

Vanderbilt, Cornelius, and the Accessory Transit Co. in Nicaragua, 281–284.

Van der Linden, H., see DeLannoy, 12.

Van Loon, H., quoted, 437.

Van Tyne, C. H., "Influences which determined French Government to make Treaty with U. S. in 1776," 39; "Sovereignty in the American Revolution," 55; *Loyalists in the American Revolution*, 64.

Vattel Jean, *Droit de Gens*, 25; quoted 25, 95.

Venezuela, independence declared and recognition sought, 168; and boundary dispute with England, 243–245; orgy under Cipriano Castro leads to intervention by Germany, 291; U. S. asserts Monroe Doctrine for benefit of, 292–294.

Venice, and Medieval Trade Routes, 12; ships seized under Rule of 1756, 33.

Venizelos, E., Premier of Greece at Versailles Conference in 1919, 391.